Future Days

by the same author

FEAR OF MUSIC: WHY PEOPLE GET ROTHKO BUT DON'T GET STOCKHAUSEN
JIMI HENDRIX: THE STORIES BEHIND EVERY SONG
EMINEM: THE STORIES BEHIND EVERY SONG

Future Days

Krautrock and the Birth of a Revolutionary New Music

David Stubbs

MELVILLE HOUSE
BROOKLYN • LONDON

Future Days

First published in Great Britain in 2014 by Faber and Faber Ltd

First Melville House Printing: July 2015

Melville House Publishing
145 Plymouth Street
Brooklyn, NY 11201

and

8 Blackstock Mews
Islington,
London N4 2BT

mhpbooks.com facebook.com/mhpbooks @melvillehouse

ISBN: 978-1-61219-474-5

Printed in the United States of America
10 9 8 7 6 5 4 3 2 1

A catalog record for this book is available from
the Library of Congress

Contents

Unna, West Germany, 1970

Can

This footage has lain dormant since it was first broadcast well over forty years ago, one among a pile of cylinders in the archive rooms of the German WDR TV station. It's scarcely been seen since – only through connections to connections am I able to sit in a darkened room and experience it again on a screen.

We've crash-landed back in the monochrome mists of time, back in late 1970, in the small town of Unna, in North Rhine-Westphalia, in what is then West Germany. Even the youngest person present in this makeshift concert hall, a giant, improvised tent, would be of pensionable age now, though strangely they'd probably not look at all out of place if they mingled with today's generation of postmodern hipsters. The hair, the clothes, the cool rimmed specs, trimmed beards, polo-necked jumpers – they'd all pass. Was that you, Grandma? Grandad?

It's a televised gig, three hours in duration. Black and white. By today's standards, it would be considered dreadful television. There's no compèring, no way of knowing who's coming on next, no order, no chaos, no way of knowing who's running things. Raw, grey footage, broadcast as it happened. Two stages, neither of them elevated, at either side of a large screen, onto which are projected a series of bizarre, short films, inexpertly loaded into the machine. In the first of them, a severe-looking, middle-aged local arts director crops up, staring out with an inadvertent Big Brotherly air from the screen through the thick-rimmed spectacles of his blighted generation. He barks out a few stern words, general reflections on art and culture in West Germany.

The camera scans jerkily, almost nervously about the crowd, who are as inattentive to the improving words of the overbearing arts director as kids before the headmaster in a school assembly. Hardly anybody is drinking, but drifting curlicues of smoke gently thicken the air. A few young men have struck up a chant of '*Fertig, los!*' ('C'mon, let's go!'). The rest, either cross-legged on the floor, standing or gently canoodling with their partners, represent a gamut of passive emotions, their pale faces bathed in the reflected light from the stage set-up – bored, intrigued, bemused, patient, rapt, amused, checking out their images on the monitors, reflecting on the fact that they're here for a good reason, even if they're not sure what it is. This, after all, is 1970 and everything is new.

Without the slightest of fanfares, a dimming of the lights or even an introduction, four young men take up their instruments on the left of the stage. The drummer discreetly establishes a repetitive, percussive pattern. The moustached, intent bassist bobs busily as he maintains a metronomic pulse. A cigar hangs louche off the bottom lip of the young guitarist, who at least faintly looks the swaggering, Jaggerish part of a rock star, as he chops out regular licks. A bespectacled man, slightly senior, is positioned behind the keyboards, both monitoring and maintaining the musical flow. A frail young Japanese singer, hair hanging about him, stands almost shivering at the centre of all this. To call him a frontman would be a misnomer. He's caught in the middle, in the maelstrom. It's as if he is channelling the sound, as if it is inflicting some sort of compulsory catharsis on him. His fey vocals swirl in the mix. Where is the leader? Who is directing what's happening onstage? Something's happening, but what? None of the musicians seems to be doing anything in particular, yet the music seems almost to elevate the giant tent from its moorings. It's going everywhere, nowhere and somewhere at the same time.

Just one song, a wave of polite applause and then back to another intermission – a film of student types lounging around on sofas in a room with a prominent Che Guevara poster, engaged in mumbling political conversation. The room, briefly shaken, settles back down again. Music, then political discussion – how do these things connect with each other? Who was that group? That was 'The Can', right? Will we hear any more from them?

Now, a strange, buzzing drone begins to emanate from stage right. It's reminiscent of warplanes, circling, swooping and strafing, and might well make one or two of the older cameramen wince with its reminders. As eyes, and the camera, swing to the right-hand corner of the stage, we see a mullet-headed twenty-something, his leather jacket not quite offsetting the nerdiness of his glasses. A *Spiesser*, the Germans might say – a square. A *Spiesser* in leather clothing. He's working an upright, tubular instrument, a hybrid of guitar and synthesizer. Nobody recognises him. The strafing carries on for several minutes. The crowd look on patiently, maybe hoping the plane will come in to land. Is this music? Are we allowed to leave the tent? Impossible. It's packed solid. Gradually, however, a rhythmic underpinning emerges. There's a drummer, a Viking-like, crooked-nosed presence whose tank top accentuates his muscular frame. The crowd, thrown a bone, begin to clap and stomp along. Someone starts keening furiously away on a whistle. The drums intensify, the *Spiesser* tussles with his electric instrument, which emits clipped, farting noises. Maybe these are the birth pangs of something. Who was that group? And why was their set decorated with a traffic cone? Was the cone supposed to make it art?

But then, another intermission. This time, a resounding clip of a tune by the almost supernaturally awful Heino rings round the tent rafters. He's a superstar of Schlager, the ultra-kitsch German MOR to which the new German music is utterly antithetical. The audience begin to clap along, jeering and sardonic and yet, you feel, secretly a little grateful for the tonal respite and the familiarity of the tune. This segues abruptly into a clip of B. B. King. The blues is loved in West Germany – then, and later, blues artists will get more work in West Germany and Japan than back in the USA. However, in the context of tonight's strange, novel proceedings, the blues feel as out of kilter as Heino.

The group on the left slide up and strap on their guitars again. 'Oh Yeah.' It's from an album called *Tago Mago* but there's no apparent flicker of recognition from the crowd. The four musicians strike up by rote – this is no sloppy, inferior live version of a studio construct; this is effortless replication of the technical, levitating brilliance of the track as presented on the album, with added live extensions. We're going to hear something now. Lift-off. The Japanese guy is dissolving before our eyes, a dervish, dashing and thrashing the air with his yelping, wordless, Pollock-like sprays of paint onto an invisible canvas. A blonde girl starts blowing bubbles. Idiot dancing breaks out. Others nod furiously, affirmatively. Nothing else is happening in Unna tonight. Nothing better is happening in Unna tonight. We don't know what this is, but this is it. Such tantric restraint, the way the group lock in their potential energy. No release, so liberating. They could go on forever.

Once again, however, in the didactic, democratic spirit of the evening, Can are cut short. More films, this time a discussion on the arts–politics interface. 'These are complex questions . . .' proffers a young girl nervously, before being harangued with undue aggression by a forthright man in a beard. There's a John Heartfield-esque satire on commodity, with an unsubtle *Ker-CHING!* soundtrack, as a film presents an old white German male on whose forehead is superimposed a cash register. There are other stiffly instructive political messages, including one depicting a black South African reduced to the indignity of acting as a human guide dog to a blind white man. The camera picks out a single black person in the crowd tonight.

Enter from stage right *Spiesser* and the Cone Group once more.

In the crowd, a young man with muttonchop whiskers visibly groans. These guys again? This time, they're accompanied by a gangly fellow in a paisley shirt wielding a flute. They strike up – a regular pulse, caustic organ strokes, in which the muscular drummer and the mulleted man in glasses work together to create a synergy of man and machine. The crowd are engrossed, intrigued, if not exactly moshing with euphoria. The *Spiesser* guy seems to be wrangling frustratedly with his keyboards, trying to wring something out of them that's not in there. But they're building something. The drummer is workmanlike in the sublime, not the dull, sense of that word, lips pursed, physically dedicated to art and industry. The man in the paisley shirt spits frantic flute phrases into the head of an antique microphone. This is something. It's as if this group have evolved since last time they were onstage. Now we've hit the road, we're on a trip. Maybe the seventies start here. But not everybody's ready. As the group wend to a conclusion, the crowd are a little confused by the experimental digressions of the *Spiesser* guy towards the end, which disrupt the strangely pleasurable, hypnotic rhythm-reverie. The playing stops. There is only a smattering of applause. If this is the end, what and where were the beginning and the middle? The drummer feels obliged to land a final, emphatic thump with his right stick as if to indicate the set is finished, to remind the crowd that something just happened. It did. The drummer: Klaus Dinger, who would go on to co-found Neu!. The group: Kraftwerk, led by a barely recognisable Ralf Hütter, years before they were reborn as paradigms of a new, Bauhaus-inspired synthpop. Neu! before they were born, Kraftwerk in the process of being born, and Can, fully alive – all three under the same canvas on the same night. This happened. Foundations, giant lengths of cable were laid. In Berlin, Hamburg, Munich, Cologne and Düsseldorf, and now stretching to Unna. Were you really there that night, Grandma? Grandad? Nothing better happened in the world that night.

Introduction

Popol Vuh

Krautrock has taken its fixed place in the firmament. From tiny groups in Stoke Newington basements ploughing endless grooves on analogue synthesizers and raging guitars, to the lofty likes of U2, Coldplay and Dave Stewart, it is revered. Whenever a new group wish to show their experimental credentials, they will reach up and pick out the word 'Krautrock' like a condiment to add a radical dash to their press release.

Yet it is well over three decades since Krautrock petered out, its demise practically unnoticed as the media were sent into paroxysms by punk, or confounded by the supersonic sequencers of Donna Summer's 'I Feel Love' and the emergence of disco, which threatened to reset the global pulse. It died away unmourned in that era of strobes and spittle.

How did Krautrock, so lightly regarded in its own day both at home and abroad, become one of the cornerstones for modern pop and rock music? Its influence has been long reaching and wide ranging. Without Krautrock, hip hop, techno, electropop, ambient and post-rock might never have evolved. In the 1970s, however, Krautrock was considered marginal, indeed, barely considered at all. Germanophobia still held sway, though it now took the shape of condescending amusement, rather than outright hostility. Krautrock, to many ears, sounded like the unfortunate music of a country too incorrigibly Prussian to really let its hair down that was nonetheless trying, with risible results, to master both the English language and the metre of rock music, in which, of course, the English and Americans were dominant. Kraftwerk were, as all synthesizer-based acts were considered to be, a novelty act, a curio featured on *Tomorrow's World*. Can? Faust? Popol Vuh? Who were they? Only late-night denizens of the John Peel show or particularly dedicated *NME* readers would even know their names.

Krautrock's birth as a phenomenon, as a reference point, came practically at the moment of its demise. Its existence has been largely posthumous. From early punk champions like Pete Shelley and John Lydon to more recent, informed aficionados like the Horrors, it is a music that has been revived, time and again, in wave after wave. It's treasured and revisited far more than prog rock, which was considered by many to be far and away the most structurally advanced rock music of its day, an attempt to have rock graduate to classical status. However, the 'sonic cathedrals' constructed by the likes of Yes, ELP and Genesis across double and triple albums, all those topographical excursions and faux-mediaeval fantasias are relatively disregarded follies in our own time compared with Can's *Tago Mago*, Kraftwerk's *Trans-Europe Express* or the first album by Neu!.

Krautrock has become common currency in modern music criticism but it is a rather vague and contested term. For my purposes, I'm thinking of something a bit more specific than the nebulous idea of longhaired 1970s German rockers who played a prolonged, stiffly rhythmic version of rock with added Teutonic knobs on. I'm thinking of a select few, acting simultaneously yet quite separately from one another, in cities as far apart as Berlin, Hamburg, Munich, Cologne and Düsseldorf, who sought to reinvent music, to build a new legacy in sound that reconnected with older German traditions, who refused to replicate the internationally dominant blues-rock of the era, and in so doing created new templates that have been referred back to time and again, years after they were first laid down.

Krautrock has its share of archaeological obsessives, with some crate-diggers and vinyl bloodhounds willing to pay hundreds of pounds, dollars or euros to secure original LP releases from online stores and canny dealers. Dedicated websites unearth new discoveries, obscure acts who wailed away unnoticed in their own time, disappearing after a single album, but who are now regarded as being as precious as ingots. These websites, these curators, are an invaluable resource, but it's not my intention in this book to provide an exhaustive Krautrock directory, in which equal billing is given to all artists who fall within the remit of the broad genre. While fresh finds are always a welcome and gratifying pleasure, artists and albums very often lapse into obscurity for a reason. I don't believe there is any lost Atlantis on the Krautrock map, a yet-to-be-unearthed group of vast, seismic importance. We basically know who was who and what was what. There were major and minor players, and I've sought to give each their due prominence, to explain the broad history from which they arose and the broader culture to which they contributed, rather than treat them as distantly obscure, esoteric objects. Conversely, there are those who would clearly love to know more about Krautrock but whose knowledge of the subject is stuck at around mid-period Kraftwerk. There are also those whose knowledge of what the term might represent is rather less than sketchy, such as the radio DJ who, when her interviewee mentioned Krautrock, said, 'Oh, you mean like Rammstein?'

And then there are those who object to the absurdly catch-all and offensive term of 'Krautrock' itself. 'The Germans have every right to be critical of the word "Krautrock",' says Wire's Colin Newman, and it's hard to disagree. It would be one thing if the word had been coined by the Germans themselves, the way African Americans reclaimed the word 'nigger' or gay people the word 'queer'. But they did not. No one is absolutely certain who first came up with the term – the finger often points at the late Ian MacDonald of the *NME.* When I speak to Richard Williams, who worked at *Melody Maker* in the 1970s, however, he guiltily wonders aloud if he might have invented it. 'I've a funny feeling I did!' he laughs. 'I'm not sure. If I did it was inadvertent, and I'd never have used it twice.'

Whether Williams originated the phrase or not, 'inadvertent' would be the word. It seems to have been a product of enthusiasm, but an unfortunate one. Imagine the appalled offence if some journalist, in a fit of unreconstructed excitement at the arrival of Jimi Hendrix, had dubbed his music 'Spaderock'.

John Weinzierl of Amon Düül has always despised the term. He describes whoever coined the word as a 'criminal' and Julian Cope as on the 'blacklist' for having incorporated it into the title of his *Krautrocksampler*. He doesn't accept my assurance that it was meant positively. 'Aah, it wasn't!' he cries. 'My definition of Krautrock was always "German musicians trying to sound like American or English musicians". That, for me, is Krautrock. I always recommended Scorpions as being one of them. I don't think they like that.'

Achim Reichel, in his sleevenotes for the Harmonia album *Musik von Harmonia*, is similarly contemptuous. 'People often mistakenly believed that *Musik von Harmonia* belongs to the category of so-called "Krautrock". Careless critics and reviewers tried to hide their lack of knowledge and expertise by pressing this ghastly label even on the few artists that wouldn't behave like those stoned dancing bears.'

No German musician of that generation accepts the word 'Krautrock', or the word as it is understood by English writers. In approaching any of them for interview it was necessary to use tactful phrasing along the lines of 'experimental German music of the sixties and seventies'. And fair enough. None of the Krautrock groups actually are Krautrock. Indeed, in the very unlikely event that any of them were to nod in assent and agree of themselves, 'Yes, Krautrock. That's us in a nutshell,' your respect for them would fall away. How are Kraftwerk, who ruthlessly stripped away both guitars and hair from their sound and appearance, Krautrock? Can's Jaki Liebezeit is equally bemused that such a phrase should apply to Can, who were . . . well, Can. Faust composed a track by the title of 'Krautrock' for their album *Faust IV*, but as an act of deep sarcasm at the English-imported tag, which they found both insulting and injurious. Conrad Schnitzler, who detested hippie culture, also titled a piece of his 'Krautrock', as if to say, 'Listen. It patently isn't.'

How could a single word encapsulate both the spacey, ambient extremes of Ash Ra Tempel and the heavy industrial collage of Faust? The faux-bourgeois placidity of Kraftwerk and the angry, messy agitation of Amon Düül? The ecclesiastical heights of Popol Vuh and the sacrilegious depths of Can? The extreme, maximal, suffocating noise of Kluster and the spare, horticultural, ambient beauty of Cluster?

A defence, then, of this word that has appalled so many in its time. I'm reminded of Roger Armstrong, who was vilified for helping inaugurate the tag 'world music' in the mid-eighties. For him, however, it was 'just a rack in a record shop', a helpful marketing device which directed customers to music from the far-flung reaches of South America, Africa, Asia which would hitherto have been similarly far-flung across the alphabetical ranks of the Megastore, if indeed it had been stocked at all. 'Krautrock' performs a similar, pragmatic function. Some, though not all, of the musicians of the sixties and seventies philosophically accept the fact that the popularisation of the word 'Krautrock' by Julian Cope and others has boosted retrospective interest in their own work. Others note with philosophical amusement that the word '*Kraut*' means 'herb' in German – 'Herb rock' is really not so bad, as spurious categories go. What's more, over the years the word 'Krautrock' has lost the accidentally pejorative connotation it once had. It's become semantically cleansed with the wash of time. It's used unselfconsciously by a generation who would no more dream of calling Germans 'Krauts' than they would call them 'Jerries', 'Fritz' or 'the Boche'. There is, quite simply, something jaggedly appealing about the very way in which the word sits on the page or rolls off the tongue. It's certainly preferable to other options that never really stuck, such as 'Teutonic Railroad Rock 'n' Roll'.

Strangely, however, when the word 'Krautrock' is invoked, it is either used to imply something too broad or too narrow. There are many who subscribe to something similar to Weinzierl's definition – Germans who play rock music. In which case the Scorpions or Jane or Ton Steine Scherben all count. Except that they don't. Few nowadays, I'd venture to suggest, are thinking of Michael Schenker when they think of Krautrock. Conversely, when the word 'Krautrock' is invoked today by groups, quite often they are thinking of little more than the *motorik*, the Dingerbeat you can slip into in order to impress the critics, yourselves and the more thoughtful of your fans.

'I wasn't aware of Krautrock until the early eighties. It was after the moniker was given and adopted when I became a fan,' says Sonic Youth drummer Steve Shelley. 'Because we loved the music so much the term never had negative connotations to us – these days when I hear the term I tend to think of it as describing Neu!-like music or using Klaus Dinger's rhythms, but maybe that's just me.'

None of the groups banded together under the 'Krautrock' heading fit the cap. However, they do intersect – there are common values and properties to Krautrock; Krautrock was a cultural and historical phenomenon, rather than a mode of playing. What's more, 'Krautrock', and all the inadvertent, clumsy contempt the word carries with it, you could say to be a retrospective badge of honour – this is a music that has survived, despite the scorn and indifference it suffered in its own time. The very term carries the marks of that neglect.

And so, at the risk of offending and of packing together groups who don't deserve to be crammed into a two-syllable compound noun of dubious origin, I'll be using the word repeatedly and in the hope that the breadth of meaning with which I've tried to invest it is understood. For Krautrock, despite its dissonant elements, was a rainbow coalition of tempers and colours, styles and tones that represented a hankering for a lost unity, an idealism that was both futuristic and as old as the very forests and hills. Krautrock ranges. It drew on the gamut of styles – twentieth-century classical, musique concrète, jazz, rock, blues, psychedelia, funk, electronic, as well as its own, hand-wrought originality. A similarly lengthy host of styles would descend from it – ambient, hip hop, post-rock, electropop, psych-rock, trance, rave, post-punk and others still unborn. In his genuinely magisterial, compendious *The German Genius: Europe's Third Renaissance, the Second Scientific Revolution and the Twentieth Century*, Peter Watson pays the following tribute to Krautrock. Well, actually, consulting the index, he doesn't. He manages a few perfunctory lines about Stockhausen ('He famously pioneered electronic music . . . becoming a cult figure in the 1970s, not least among certain rock musicians'), but about those 'certain rock musicians', not a word. This lofty oversight only helps bolster the sense that Krautrock's practitioners are, to borrow Percy Bysshe Shelley's phrase, the 'unacknowledged legislators' of our time. For all its hipness, it is still disregarded or only dimly understood. All the more reason to tell Krautrock's story, not just its role in shaping modern music but how it was born out of the trauma and upheavals of postwar history and the rebirth of a nation.

*

My relationship to Germany and the Germans was conventional enough as a very small boy. Like many others in the late sixties and very early seventies I was reared on Second World War movies and comics like *Warlord*. At the very moment students were rising up in campuses across West Germany, or Can were assembling in a rehearsal room with a view to playing rock music as if they were the first group of musicians ever to do so, I was doubtless in a back room in a small village outside Leeds blackening a piece of paper with a pencil worn to the nub, depicting British Spitfires blasting oncoming Luftwaffe planes into plumes of smoke, sending them in a descending spiral into the English Channel, their pilots screaming '*Hilfe!*' in that high-pitched, fretful manner I understood from TV's Corporal Jones to be common to all German servicemen in distress.

To grow up at that time was to be assailed in everyday popular culture with stereotypes served up as if they were as harmless as mashed potatoes for lunch. The vanquished and risible 'Krauts' were especially fair game. I did know one German fellow, as it happened – he had been a paratrooper, captured and sent to work on one of the local farms, who settled in the village after the war and become one of its little cast of characters. He never spoke about Mr Hitler or the Nazis, merely complained that he had been denied his war pension, his case lost in the postwar transition. He was too genial to be a 'real' German, however. Real Germans spat the word '*Achtung*' at regular intervals, or spoke in the clipped tones of Philip Madoc in *Dad's Army* adding Private Pike's name to his list, or like Dennis Waterman's visiting German 'Franz Wasserman' in a *Man About the House* episode entitled 'Did You Ever Meet Rommel?'. When asked if he enjoyed the TV series *The World at War*, he replies, 'I enjoyed zer beginning but not so much zer ending,' to gales of studio laughter.

Concurrent with all of this, however, was a burgeoning fascination with West Germany. It probably began with football, the first great passion of my young life. Michael Rother of Neu! has suggested that one of the inspirations for the regular, functional *motorik* beat was the experience of playing football with members of Kraftwerk (who despite their prim, anti-manly image were in fact a very physical, sporty bunch).

Watching European Cup games on midweek school nights was an extra-special treat. Satellite link-ups had only been introduced a few years earlier but there was still a certain graininess, a glow and fuzz around the edges of the players as images were transmitted onto our black-and-white televisions from the continent. British fans liked to bask in the long-discredited idea that our football teams were the best in the world, but watching teams like Ajax of Amsterdam and Bayern Munich win the European Cup in successive years was a chastening, albeit infrequent reminder of superior forces abroad. The wonderful sense of distance between the living-room TV set and the events on screen was enhanced by the fact that the commentaries back then sounded like they were being conveyed over a special transcontinental telephone line.

The biggest difference of all, however, was in the crowd noise. In the UK, this was a collective boorish roar, punctuated by handclaps, chants based on pop songs and an underlying nastiness of the sort that you wouldn't want to hear coming in your direction if you were alone in a railway station. It didn't stop me from loving the game but it seemed also to speak about English maleness, about bonding, frustration and violence. Watch a game involving Bayern Munich, however, crowned European Cup winners three times between 1974 and 1976, or West Germany, European Champions in 1972 and World Cup winners in 1974, and the noise was very different. It was a sea of air horns, an abstract wall of klaxons, an incessant, aerosol-fuelled drone, occasionally receding before crescendoing at particularly exciting moments in the game. It was a constant reminder that this was foreign football you were watching and, frankly, an experience of a different and more advanced order.

I'm convinced that it was a love of those drones, as well as their association with Europe, which associated in my mind the ideas of Europe, alternative music and noise – and superiority. It would be nice to record that it was a precocious perusal of the novels of

Günter Grass which proved formative, but that would come later. The air horns of German football fans blasted a neural pathway in my mind. Retrospectively, I believe it was a pathway that cut through the dismal churlishness of England in the 1970s, though I didn't think of it in those terms at the time, or make those connections. It was a pathway down which would later proceed Stockhausen, a TV documentary about whom I recorded onto a mono cassette machine and listened to over and over. I acquired records of his from Leeds Record Library, borrowing three or four at a time and recording them onto blank C90 cassettes, whose covers I would decorate with little abstract collages cut out from old magazines and travel brochures, à la Kurt Schwitters. It was from Leeds City Library that I acquired my first Krautrock record – a battered vinyl edition whose very scratches I learned to love along with the rest of the album after I taped it.

Before that, I'd taken up German as an O-level option. To assist us with the rudiments of the language, the class was issued with standard textbooks in which we followed the adventures of Herr Körner, a middle-aged journalist who lived in Westphalia and could generally be found hunched over his *Schreibsmaschine*, or chatting with his landlady, a rather fetching widow by the name of Frau Schütze. I don't know why the educational authorities had imagined that these characters were best suited to introduce the delights of the German language to British third-form pupils, but I for one was very taken with what seemed to be the idyllic life of Herr Körner, in his smartly appointed study, his domestic needs attended to by the widow Schütze. I decided I, too, would become a writer.

I read the *NME* passionately but was aware that even then, at the height of its powers, with writers like Paul Morley, Danny Baker, Ian Penman, Charles Shaar Murray, Andy Gill and Nick Kent holding sway, it wasn't always absolutely to be trusted on more extreme music. They did an A–Z round-up of post-punk in which they cursorily disparaged This Heat as a group who 'pushed sounds together to make noise' – or was it 'pushed noises together to make sounds'? Either way, they said it like it was a bad thing, and having saved up and acquired This Heat's debut album, I knew that they were a very good thing.

And so I began buying records from Recommended Records, whose channels ran deeper than those of the *NME*, which was still a bit overloaded with Jam and Costello to fulfil all my needs. They extended my consciousness of European rock in general – Czechoslovakia's dissident group Plastic People of the Universe, Italy's Stormy Six, Sweden's Samla Mammas Manna, France's ZNR and Albert Marcœur, and from Belgium, Aqsak Maboul, and the Rock In Opposition axis. Recommended Records was run by Chris Cutler (it continues to this day as ReR), who had no time for punk or post-punk and for whom Recommended Records was a lonely, idiosyncratic furrow that led back to his days as drummer for the English avant-prog group Henry Cow. Only one Krautrock group intersected with his tastes – Faust, whose first two albums, their self-titled debut and the follow-up *So Far*, Recommended were reissuing in 1980. From his description of the group, one thing was clear – I had to have Faust. I extended my career as Yorkshire's oldest paperboy in order to raise the funds for these releases, a limited run of six hundred (I would be number 58), and sent off my cheque. Due to a variety of complications at the supply end, however, the reissues didn't emerge for many months. There were occasional postal updates assuring purchasers that these epochal albums, one of which would be issued on clear vinyl, were coming down the pipeline.

There being no YouTube or Spotify available, I began to dream about these albums, of which copies had apparently changed hands for hundreds of pounds among collectors since they were first released in 1971 and 1972. In several years of listening to John Peel, collecting music and reading avidly about music, I had never heard a single mention of Faust – and neither had many of my friends (of whom more later). Only rarely did I entertain the idea that I was the victim of a massive hoax, but given the established bona fides of Recommended, it seemed unlikely that their string of releases and catalogues hitherto were all the elaborate front for a scam in order to bilk an ageing paperboy out of three weeks of his wages.

I dreamed about these albums. I dreamed of faceless, über-radical hippies who, like the Residents, were systematically at odds with rock's cult of personality, sublimating all their ego and energies into a collective beatnik rock noise, itself rocked by exploding, humanity-destroying Hindenbergs of inflated electronics, of music that was defiantly ugly and magnificently beautiful by turns, that was powered by the engines of West Germany and elevated by the greater European modern art movements stretching back to Futurism. A sustained, electric shock of noise that spanned all that was beautiful and tragic about the twentieth century.

Finally, the albums arrived. Of course, they couldn't possibly live up to the fevered hyperbole of my imagination. And yet they did. Oh, my stars and worn-down styluses, they did. It was as if my ridiculous expectations had somehow enhanced these albums, as if they had colluded with my visions of them, as opposed to being a let-down. These were, and would remain in my estimation for a long while to come, the greatest recordings ever made by anybody. Prior to listening to them I'd been on a Frank Zappa/Mothers of Invention binge, but suddenly albums like *Uncle Meat* and *Burnt Weeny Sandwich* sounded like snide, sterile exercises in instrumental virtuosity, lacking the gigantic, electric, emotional whoomph! of Faust.

It would have been cruel to keep these records to myself. The only other feedback I had had was from my immediate family, specifically my father. Hearing the monotonous, thudding bass drum of 'It's a Rainy Day, Sunshine Girl' from *So Far* reverberating from my bedroom, he had thundered up the stairs, spanner in hand, and headed straight for the airing cupboard, assuming the boiler to be malfunctioning. I needed to cast more widely among my peers. And so, fired up with missionary zeal, I took advantage of a 'show and tell'-type section in the General Studies A-level course I was doing to play these albums to my schoolmates. It was a harsh and lifelong lesson in the chortling, turn-this-shit-off resistance which is the lot of avant-garde music, and the obdurate conservatism that's characteristic of most music fans who consider themselves to be pretty cutting-edge, with their love of David Bowie and R.E.M. and what have you.

I began with side one of Faust's debut album, and 'Why Don't You Eat Carrots?'. My announcement of the title alone set off a ripple of mirth among the assembled sixth-form lads, and raised my first suspicion that they weren't disposed to take my educative efforts altogether seriously. This was pretty much confirmed within minutes as the track proceeded, with its swooping collage of faux-brass bands, spoken-word sections, Beethovenesque descents and giddying eruptions of oily geyser-like electronic noise. Some of my classmates were sitting quite close to the record player and decided it would be a good idea to introduce a Dadaist element of chance of their own, by stomping their feet hard at key points, causing the needle to jump across the record. At which point, I gave up.

Even at the time a part of me could see how I deserved to be the butt of the joke. However, it went slightly beyond that. When the snickering had died down, it was replaced by a growing anger among some of my friends at what they'd been subjected to, that such music existed and that one of their own kind was listening to it and finding something in what just seemed like a random series of strange noises to them. These were grammar-school lads who were at an age where they were beginning to measure their self-esteem on the basis of their record collections. In 1980, for many, this still meant Led Zeppelin, Deep Purple, Genesis and Pink

Floyd, advanced appreciation of which was a rite of passage into the sixth form and maturity. Another wing found a similar sense of self-importance in their ostentatious grasp of David Bowie and his acolytes. And now here was this 'Faust' thrown into the equation. At the end of the lesson the music teacher drily remarked on his surprise at the level of hostility my choice of record had managed to generate. Three years earlier, I had laughed along with everyone else when he had gamely but vainly attempted to introduce us to new music by putting on Frank Zappa's 'Help, I'm a Rock'.

An altercation in the common room along these lines, with a friend who considered Gary Numan to be the last word in extreme listening, was charged with indignation and, perhaps on his part, the suspicion that something was happening on this Faust album that he didn't quite get. His protest that it was a fraud of some sort rang hollow even to himself. Now, I felt better – this was the sort of anger deliberately provoked by the Futurists in their theatrical events, which generally ended in rioting by the paying public. In the redness of a sixth-former's face and the spittle in mine as he argued with me, I realised, with a spasm of quiet, insufferable smugness – gotcha. I was right. And some day . . .

Later years would bring myriad Krautrock adventures, as I returned again and again to the music that itself returned again and again to the vanguard of relevance, as, wave by wave, era by era, it seemed that more and more people were beginning to get it. My friend the late Neil Jones supplied me with cassette recordings of Neu!, Harmonia and early Kraftwerk in the years when these recordings were generally unavailable. There was Kraftwerk at Brixton Academy in 1991 and the 'Robots' encore, proof to me that humour and the sublime in music weren't, as I sometimes argued, as incompatible as ice cream and gravy – that they could mix. Then there were the Can members, who appeared at a Barbican concert in 1999 under the banner Can-Solo-Projects, with Irmin Schmidt hinting at vast reserves of virtuosity as he went to work in the innards of a grand piano. There was the closest music has brought me to a moment of pure terror, on first hearing Popol Vuh. There was the beatific Hans-Joachim Roedelius live, Michael Rother and his pacific, oceanic guitar wowing a hallful of disciples, a Faust concert in which they took to the stage with cement mixers, another in which, in a strange reprise of the anger they had wrought when I first played them in the sixth form, an audience member was stabbed during an argument. Like Ralf Hütter, calling me on the phone just as I'd settled into a bath to clarify a point he'd made about musique concrète, the music itself kept calling you back. It's everywhere and everywhen. Its day has come again and again since the day it died, and it will carry on coming, carry on surprising and revealing itself in its many lights, dark and light.

Prologue

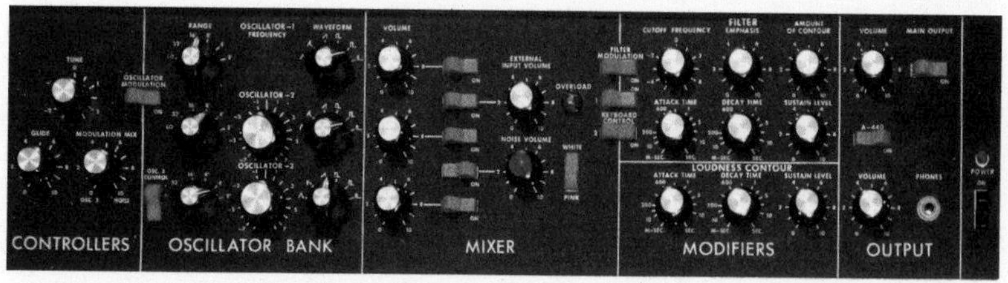

Front panel, Minimoog synthesizer

Musicians are often loath to subscribe to the broader cultural explanations imposed on their work by journalists or writers, disliking the idea that what they do is to any extent governed by external factors, rather than purely driven by their own innate creativity. However, it is freely admitted by all of the major players that in the sixties and early seventies, German music, in common with the arts, cinema and literature, went through a rebirth that was connected with the aftermath of the Second World War. As the titanic free-jazz saxophonist Peter Brötzmann put it, 'What has happened to us in Germany is a kind of trauma of our generation . . . as a German, I come back to my own history. Of course we are not guilty for what happened in Germany in the war, but there is a very special German fate, there is a great shame here and a terrible kind of trauma. And that's why maybe the German way of playing this kind of music sounds always a bit different from the other parts of Europe, at least. It's always more kind of a scream. More brutal, more aggressive. When we started, we thought, "Okay, enough of Art Blakey, enough Horace Silver, enough of form and notation and measures and all kinds of ways. We don't need that."'

Brötzmann's father had served in the German army before being captured by the Russians, but after the war he never spoke about his experiences and refused, until on his deathbed, to acknowledge the 'scream' of his son's music. That terrible, beyond-awkward silence, and the scream that proceeds from it, is one of Krautrock's vital birth pangs.

Not that Krautrock was always a scream – it varied in its tones, from the chaotic and brutal to the serene and pastoral. It was post-rock, before rock had even run its course, but post-jazz, too. For musicians like Jaki Liebezeit, even the 'free' jazz movement had its own limitations, and, albeit extreme and modernistic, was still jazz, an imported, transatlantic voice. It did not satisfy his own need to begin again, utterly anew, start from scratch. This was the common impulse that drove Can, Faust, Neu!, Kraftwerk, Cluster and the rest.

Krautrock was paradoxical. It loathed the prevailing German pop culture of Schlager, banal drinking-to-forget songs dripping with nostalgia but in which the horrors of the Third Reich were conveniently airbrushed away. Yet it wanted to create something German in origin that was not beholden to the Anglo-American beat music or jazz traditions, so strong in West Germany after the Marshall Plan, thanks to the number of British and American troops still stationed in the country and the unrivalled potency and attraction of the Beatles, the Who, Dylan, Hendrix. These groups were adored and initially imitated by most of the Krautrock musicians themselves, as they earned their spurs in clubs and concert halls in Hamburg, Düsseldorf, Cologne. However, a broader disaffection with America's imperial misadventures in Vietnam, which prompted a wave of student demonstrations in the late sixties, making many think again about what amounted to an Anglo-American cultural occupying force. What had once been the soundtrack of young rebellion now itself needed to be rebelled against.

'I think that ambivalence started in 1968,' says filmmaker and German music documentarian Stefan Morawietz. 'That was the first time anyone in Germany started criticising anything American. Before that, anything American was brilliant – the Marshall Plan, the food packages, but also the best cars and cigarettes, the coolest music, they were the heroes of the new time. All we had were the old things of the past. Only the old people wanted that. Most of the rock 'n' roll records weren't available over here, you never heard them on the radio – things really started with the Beatles. And when they came over, people were horrified. They were everything the older generation hated – long hair, unwashed – and what they called over here negro music. Up to 1963, all you would hear in this country was German Schlager. Nothing else. You wouldn't hear it. Not even Frank Sinatra. Not in German pubs or fairs or anything like that – in American or British military clubs, maybe. So the Beatles were a revelation, the starting point of a new time. All that Schlager was a dream world, nothing to do with the real world, and young people didn't want that any more.'

The Beatles had been so beloved that they inspired flagrant imitators, in particular the Rattles (not to be confused with the Rutles), who formed in Hamburg, where the original Fab Four had germinated unnoticed at the turn of the sixties. A sense of shame at being straitjacketed as a moptop doppelgänger would eventually overcome their leader, singer Achim Reichel, and in the seventies he went solo to release a series of albums under the title of Achim Reichel & Machines, whose fried, echo-drenched and mutated guitars occupied a similar *kosmische* orbit to the likes of Ash Ra Tempel. (In a still further, perverse twist he later returned to the mainstream as an actor and curator of folk shanties.) Reichel's need to break away from the initially liberating imposition of beat-music norms was widely shared by ambitious young musicians fired up by the general revolutionary, countercultural spirit in towns and cities across West Germany.

Irmin Schmidt, co-founder of Can, was older than most of the Krautrock generation – older than Ringo Starr. 'That's one of the reasons why our music lasts, because we were older, we were not teenagers. We had the consciousness of this experience. That made the difference. I really have talked a lot about it; Jaki [Liebezeit] mentions very little about it. I fought my father like mad when I was fifteen or sixteen. But still, that makes the difference in the consciousness with which we made music.' Schmidt did not come via the beat route to the music. He was a highly gifted composer and conductor who could have settled down quite nicely in the upper seats of *Hoch* music culture but who, having studied under Stockhausen and with eyes open to such manifestations as the Fluxus art movement of the 1950s and 1960s, shared a need to return to a point zero, to begin again. Despite the restored prosperity of postwar Germany following the 'economic miracle', he was haunted by a sense of ruin, of that which remained unreconstructed.

'Until the late sixties, everything came from outside. Everything was imitation, especially of the English. But that was normal, especially after the devastation suffered by German culture. It wasn't just the towns that were in ruins, it was the culture that was in ruins. Minds were in ruins. Everything was ruined.'

So, another paradox. In order to invent anew, it would be necessary for people like Schmidt to reject Anglo-American dominance by drawing from it.

'It was quite natural to take from the outside, where things had gone on. So, Stockhausen had to study in Paris because there was nothing in Germany. In the late forties and the beginning of the 1950s when I was twelve, I saw hundreds of Westerns. It opened another world. I was living in Dortmund in a real ruined, bombed town. The cinema represented something quite outside all that. It was quite normal, to reconstruct German culture by first going outside of it.'

Schmidt travelled to America and absorbed the Velvet Underground, Terry Riley and the minimalists. For others, Pink Floyd's new burst of Technicolor psychedelia was a jumping-off point. Floyd played the Essener festival, a gateway experience for many young or would-be musicians, as did Frank Zappa's Mothers of Invention, whose mixture of highly disciplined arrangements and scathing countercultural anti-American dissent struck multiple chords. It would not be long before a mood of disaffection, even humiliation grew among young German musicians at the prospect of forever functioning as covers musicians in covers bands in a covers nation. This would converge with a general dissatisfaction among young people over the place they were expected to take in society as a whole.

The major Krautrock players varied from those trained to classical standards to self-taught musicians who started out with a strong aesthetic sense but whose abilities didn't stretch much further than bashing pieces of metal. Some came from very well-heeled backgrounds, while others like Klaus Dinger were, as he said of himself, 'working-class heroes'. As a result of the non-commercial decisions they had made, some Krautrock musicians descended into conditions of abject poverty. What drove them all, however, was an imperative to invent, by whatever means – fusion, modification, electronics. To reject something as fundamental as the blues tradition and its dominant tonality, not out of repulsion but because it did not speak fundamentally to their identity as young Germans, involved radical reworking at a basic level. In this respect they were futurists, of course, but they were also deeply conscious of Germany's longstanding traditions of invention, stretching back to the late eighteenth century, to the sheer spate of innovations of Haydn, Mozart and Beethoven to sate the highly educated appetites of the Viennese nobles who provided their patronage. It had continued into the twentieth century in the arts, with the Berlin and Cologne branches of Dada, musicians like Paul Hindemith and the Bauhaus movement. One of Hitler's peculiarities as a dictator was his fixation with art movements. He pinpointed them, quite accurately, as inimical to the values of the Third Reich. Hence the Degenerate Art and later Degenerate Music exhibitions, and his remarkably specific referencing of the 'Cubists, Futurists and Dadaists' in a 1934 speech as 'spoilers of art'. It was hard not to regard the avant-garde as inherently anti-Nazi.

The rearrangement of rhythm in Krautrock, its novel textures and colouring, the relationship between instruments, song structures and spontaneous improvisation, are all metaphors for a necessary postwar reconstruction, the re-establishment of cultural identity. But it was innate. Invention, quite simply, was what Germans did. Industry and manufacture are key to the functioning of the German state, even today when economies such as the UK have all but abandoned their manufacturing base for less tangible 'service industries'. When Kraftwerk named themselves thus, the German word for 'power plant', they did so ironically but not scornfully. *Mensch, Natur, Technik* – here were man and machine, function and aesthetics, operating together in harmony, in tandem, as Bauhaus had decreed before them.

'It's something embedded in German culture, that sense of building something collective, building a new society,' says the writer and musician David Toop. 'Germany had these incredibly well developed traditions – making things, inventing things. I remember going to Essen with my parents in the 1950s, to this kind of museum with all of these inventions made by Krupps – even my father, who'd been in the war and was infected by that experience, was very impressed. Similarly in music-making, why not take advantage of the latest inventions, the latest devices? It's very much in the culture.'

The Krautrock generation were born into a mostly prosperous, highly industrialised society, which, thanks to both the Marshall Plan and its own, heads-down efforts, had managed to achieve material stability long before it attended to any great process of moral self-examination. West Germans weren't alone in taking tremendous solace, after the horrors and privations of the Second World War, in material goods, with American imports not only making life more fun and comfortable but amounting to a new culture in their own right. Despite its rebelliousness, rock 'n' roll was essentially a celebration of this new economic prosperity, which extended all the way down to young people, giving them an autonomy and spending power they'd never had before. The sugar tasted so good that it would be some years before anyone other than the killjoys raised the question as to whether all those boons weren't merely capitalism's sweeteners.

The revolutionary mood of the late sixties wasn't down to any sudden shortage of these material goods but a disdain for materialism. Early models of rock that rolled off the conveyor belt mimicked the world of easy consumption in their simple design and motorised mobility. Krautrock offered not just a new music but another mode of living, in communes, an alternative to the options of nuclear family, national service and indentured labour, however well paid. The Krautrockers were never in a position, however, to effect any great Pol Pot-like wholesale social transformation. Instead, in occasional word and deed, they offered a satirical critique of a pitifully sated society, spiritually turned off and addicted to banal trappings. They sought to add a little spike to the 7-Up diet, as Timothy Leary and his cohorts, as we shall see, quite literally did in their one-off drug-fuelled recordings with Ash Ra Tempel.

When Krautrock descended to the everyday stuff of this world, it was with the amused detachment of visiting aliens on an anthropological scouting mission – hence Faust are never at their strangest than when mimicking in palsied, mocking vocals the modern-day consumer on 'I've Got My Car and My TV'. However, the relationship between Krautrock and commodity was more complex than a mere flight to the fields of spirituality from the plasticity of modern life. The likes of Pink Floyd, John Lennon and George Harrison preached against the trappings of the material world from the lofty perch of assured material comfort. There's thankfully little of that sort of hypocritical cant in the Krautrock canon.

They did, however, consider themselves to be engaged in art, rather than merely in the commercial pop business; even Kraftwerk, for all their talk of product and industrial processes. Despite appearances and their success, Kraftwerk weren't poppists, cheerfully and unpretentiously embracing the shiny stuff of modern life. Even as the group occupied the charts with their supposedly superficial paeans to models, radio sets and showroom dummies, Ralf Hütter declared his disdain for the ephemeral pap with which they were surrounded. The idea of Kraftwerk was high-minded: for everyday objects to be invested, à la Bauhaus, with the qualities of art – for material and things and function to be elevated, rather than the other way round, art reduced to mere commodity.

Can's very name reflected their interest in Andy Warhol, as exemplified on the sleeve of *Ege Bamyası*, featuring the Turkish tinned food product from which the album takes its name. Again, this reference to commodity as art is a plea, particularly to a German cultural establishment obsessed with 'high' and 'low', to understand that for budding classically trained musicians like Irmin Schmidt and Holger Czukay to forsake the classical work for rock wasn't a sellout on their part but an extension of what could be considered art.

Then there was Neu! (and later Harmonia), who in their titles, logo and sleeve art aped the visual language of the advertising industry, which had its headquarters in Düsseldorf. The satire is obvious, though well executed, with Dinger himself having set up an advertising agency of sorts and being versed in the dark arts of the business. But Neu! were also genuinely seeking attention. Dinger in particular really did wish to mainline directly into the popular consciousness. What's more, Neu! truly were as novel as it said on the tin – a product for their own times, and times to come.

Crucial to Krautrock's drive to lay new foundations was electronics, despite the sheer unfeasibility and cost of synthesizers in the sixties and seventies. The technology was there, in evidence on Walter Carlos's *Switched on Bach*, on Who albums like *Who's Next*, but as yet, synthesizers were too cumbersome and temperamental to be absolutely relied upon – they required patience and persistence. Klaus Mueller, publisher for Klaus Schulze, as well as working as a roadie in the 1970s, recalls the practical difficulties of setting up the equipment back then. 'At concert venues there was the problem that the equipment needed a steady temperature. Which meant that it had to be connected to the power and switched on at least three hours before the concert. Sometimes this was not possible. I remember the Berlin Philharmonic Hall, where Herbert von Karajan and the Berlin Philharmonic were still rehearsing onstage at seven o'clock in the evening, and [Klaus Schulze's] concert on that same stage was announced for eight o'clock.'

In popular music, only Stevie Wonder, in the early seventies, made extensive use of ARP and Moog synthesizers, working with programmers Bob Margouleff and Malcolm Cecil. Totally blind, immersed without distraction in the world of sound, he had the will and motivation, as well as the creativity to spare, that enabled him to make what have come to be regarded as among the greatest records of the era, bestselling electric-blue masterpieces which altered the fabric of future R&B and went some way to undermining assumptions about the 'soullessness' and inexpressiveness of synthesizers. Equally tireless were the Krautrock generation. However, unlike Wonder, their very German-ness and the unacceptable oddity of their creations reinforced the old equation of electronics and inauthenticity in the minds of some.

For Krautrockers, it was the continued, imitative use of traditional instruments played in the received, traditional rock 'n' roll manner that was most inauthentic. Hence their attraction to electronics, a carry-on from Stockhausen but also born out of a need to customise and modify. Synthesizers were actually a highly expensive rarity in West Germany at the time. And so, for the most part, the Krautrock groups had to make do with traditional instruments, onto which they would bolt on whatever devices they chose, from contact mikes to dynamic pedals designed to create echoes and delays, as well as sound effects and tape machines. So processed and filtered were the end results that they sounded like they'd been produced with banks of advanced technology, rather than improvised using cheap, makeshift gadgets. This was a music that originated in the here and now, rather than in the back then or the overseas.

'Product of West Germany', inscribed Kraftwerk on the sleeve of their album *The Man-Machine*, and this is true in a geographical sense. The physical landscape of Germany is a determinant in shaping Krautrock. As with America, the sheer space impacts on the music, and the journeys undertaken across it affect its sense of narrative. In the course of researching this book, I made most of my journeys by rail, quite extraordinary, long trips across a landscape both breathtaking and mundane, through forests and past distant little gingerbread towns but regularly sweeping past enormous industrial plants, great complexes of zig-zagging metal tubing, as formidable as outdoor art installations but integral to Germany's productivity and economic health.

Writer and editor of *The Wire* Chris Bohn has written about Germany as 'the one country to challenge American road mythology', and of the Neu! *motorik* experience as paradoxical – to travel along the 'exhilarating sweep' of those motorways is to enjoy at once a sense of freedom and breakthrough but also, as they trail on, the feeling that there is in fact no escape, merely a shimmering, utopian mirage. There's no comparison for this in the UK. Hit the road in England and its dull sprawl of conurbations, and within barely an hour you'll have hit a Derby, a Watford or a Doncaster.

Krautrock, however, was specifically a product of *West* Germany. The circumstances which gave rise and shape to it were to do with the condition of that temporary, federal state – prosperous, ashamed, liberal in many respects but clinging to conservative illusions, low in self-esteem, in conflict with its own youth, fragmented by national disunity, riven by traumas, disconnected from its past, having possibly sold both its soul and its identity for the dubious bounty of American materialism, in dire but unacknowledged need of cultural reinvention and replenishment. What of East Germany? Although there was such a thing as 'Ostrock' in the 1970s, groups like the Klaus Renft Combo, the Puhdys and Karat, some of whose members flirted with dissidence and showed courage in difficult circumstances, listening to them is a somewhat mouldy, hand-me-down experience, redolent of the dismal brown panelling of seventies pop culture at its worst. Unsurprising, really. They were postwar Germans who came up a different way, made fully conscious of Germany's fascist past, sent on compulsory school trips to concentration camps, but also faced with an official hostility towards Anglo-American rock 'n' roll which left the GDR's 'bad boys' in no doubt as to how to dress and play. Young musicians there had desperately little access to basics such as decent transport or even telephones, had few outlets or opportunities. It was far too much to ask that they have their own generations of Cans and Neu!s, their own *kosmische* or *motorik* music. How could they and why would they?

There's a strong sense of the identity of great cities in the Krautrock era, too, particularly at a time when Berlin had temporarily ceded its dominance as capital city to Bonn. Today it has reassumed its centrality but in the seventies it had a distinct outsider status, hard to get in and out of, an island within East German-controlled terrain. Other cities such as Hamburg and Munich assumed a rival importance of their own, the latter hosting the Olympic Games of 1972, for example, while the competition between the near-neighbouring, antithetical cities of Cologne and Düsseldorf was akin in some ways to that of Manchester and Liverpool in the early 1980s and evident in the contrasts between Can and Kraftwerk.

As significant as the cities are the rural heartlands and forests of West Germany, solaces of both romanticism and retreat. So vast are the dense recesses of forest in Germany that they have long been invested with myths and meanings of all kinds, by all German parties, prominent both as a geographical reality and a feature of the collective German imagination. The Nazis prudently commandeered them, placing great store on *Naturschutz* (protection of the forests), but they also appealed to artists like Joseph Beuys, who inaugurated his '7000 Oaks' project in the 1980s, designed to replenish the ailing woodlands as a process of healing and redemption. The forests could be seen as symbolic of a 'truer', forsaken German identity but also a vast refuge for the countercultural, for those who wished to distance themselves from the prevailing, urban-generated ideas and values of their own time.

Stockhausen had eventually made a home for himself in the forest; the members of Cluster would do the same, as did Klaus Schulze, while Faust were allowed to develop undistracted in a converted schoolhouse in remote Wümme. The danger of such a retreat to nature is the development of an agrarian, neo-Romantic aesthetic, and there's no doubt that Krautrock sailed close to that at times, but correctively, all of these artists were steeped in electronics. Apart from the practical or accidental reasons for fetching up in such far-flung places, and the misbehaviour they could get up to undisturbed, the sort of contemplation of nature in its stillness that the groups were able to engage in there was a necessary, healing corollary to their kinetic, *motorik*, noisenik tendencies – to achieve what Julian Cope termed, in reference to the music of Hans-Joachim Roedelius, 'a raging peace'.

It marked, also, their exile from the urban mainstream of German pop life. They were not ambitious entryists, like the punk generation. 'Why do people hark back to these bands?' says Portishead's Geoff Barrow. 'What makes them truly outstanding? I suppose it's the same as the way you could talk about King Tubby – they experimented, they're artists, and it doesn't sound as though they had a single commercial consideration.' Artists, indeed – landscape artists, depicting a real Germany and possible, physical futures.

There's a strong sense of horizontality about Krautrock. It was not about songs, those small, vertical structures. It was predominantly about texture, rather than text. There are very few conventionally great singers in its canon, and that is somehow a part of its strength, its identity. Powerful vocal performances are not what the genre is about. As she asserted herself within the male-dominated group, Renate Knaup of Amon Düül 2 laid down some fine vocal performances, able to express herself at last, but you get the feeling that the more she does so, the less it's Krautrock. The inadequacies of Ralf Hütter's vocals are not a weakness of Kraftwerk, but one of the group's key, defining factors. Had Tangerine Dream featured a Jon Anderson-type vocalist, it would have undermined one of the strong implications of their early work – that the cosmos is awesome and that, for all the ego and subjectivity of humans, it is indifferent to us. It's not all about us. If one little man, for instance, in recent history had not managed to place his own fanatical dreams, desires and loathsome prejudices at the centre of the world stage and persuaded others to buy into the cult of his personality, the world might have been a different place.

Faust's vocals are a mocking addendum – there are some great lyrics but they are like a Surrealist game amid their sound collages. Klaus Dinger semi-vocalised when he played with Neu!, but his main narrative drive was in his application of sticks to drumskins. Can boasted two great vocalists in Malcolm Mooney and Damo Suzuki but both were deeply unorthodox, tossed about in the mix like rag dolls, affected by the much larger instrumental forces at work in the group. Can could not and should not have been configured any other way. It was vital to the structure of the music that the vocalists and their centrality be downplayed. There were no stars, no icons in Krautrock, no frontmen, no frontwomen, no single focus of attention, merely communes of musical workers on an even plane.

There was German protest folk in the sixties, articulating in song the grievances of a generation, and that was fine. There was Ton Steine Scherben, who wrote angry, punkish anti-capitalist tracts in song and whose manager once tried to smash up a studio table with an axe following a heated TV debate with Krautrock entrepreneur Rolf-Ulrich Kaiser. They were fine. There was *Hörspiel*, a singular German tradition of radio plays in which artists like Rolf Dieter Brinkmann delivered savage sound poetry such as *Immer mit dem Scheissgeld* (1973), during the course of which he assaulted the microphone in an *art brut* frenzy, screaming, 'Everybody go to hell with your fucking reality,' and that was very fine. But this was not Krautrock. In Krautrock, there is nothing so on-the-nose as protest songs – and, in general, little or no reference to the Second World War, despite its formative influence on the music. There are exceptions to this – specifically Düsseldorf group German Oak's self-titled album made in 1972, recorded in an old air-raid shelter. With titles such as 'Swastika Rising', it is inevitably mistaken for a neo-Nazi exercise, but it is in fact a concept album tracing the rise and fall of the Third Reich, as further titles such as 'Raid over Düsseldorf' and 'Out of the Ashes' attest. It's a story told in the typical Krautrock instrumental shades – woozy keyboards, violent broadsides of crude electronics and documentary sounds, crashing percussion and wandering wah-wah guitar. It was disastrously received in its day, however, its subject matter alone precluding the possibility of getting the album stocked, or a wider airing.

Was it mere pragmatism that prevented the major Krautrock players from dealing head-on with the elephantine historical fact which they all acknowledged to be so integral to their very existence? Does it lay Krautrock open to the accusation of being just as amnesiac and escapist as the more popular, MOR Schlager it stood against? There may be some small truth in this. The pain, not just of moral regret but of victimhood, would have been felt at a personal, familial level by the musicians of this era, despite their given solidarity with the student generation in revolt. It is not a subject on which they wish to dwell for too long in interviews, and one or two, even now, would prefer not to talk about it at all. The convulsive vacillation in Krautrock between the axes of noise and beauty, metal and nature speaks about trauma and healing, destruction and rebirth, but at a subliminal, unspoken level.

Direct, overt political reference was less hard work artistically, however, than the more experimental approach undertaken by Krautrock, which was concerned with radically altering the very materials and structure of the genre, to open space for the flow motion of free thought. Denunciations of Hitler and Goebbels from across the decades would have been worthy but a little trite by comparison, and mere drops in an ocean of existing discourse. 'At the time, there were lots of people highly qualified to formulate the political situation in a clear way,' says Faust's Jean-Hervé Péron. 'Very clear, very knowledgeable. So the art didn't need to be that clear – we didn't need to take care of this situation. In the States, maybe someone like Dylan was needed, but in Germany and France we had a whole generation of young people writing pamphlets, books, essays, forming demos.'

In lieu of the tyranny of verse and chorus, Krautrock structures favour loops and repetition. Can's Irmin Schmidt was among those taken with the minimalist school of Terry Riley and Steve Reich, because he saw that music as an escape from what he calls the 'Stalinism' of twentieth-century twelve-tone music, and looked to apply similar structures within Can. Jaki Liebezeit of the same group rejected free jazz as ultimately bound by its own restrictions, finding a greater freedom in repetitive cycles. The constant turnover of Neu!'s 4/4 *motorik* beat, the brutal riffs of Faust, the prettier but circular melodic motions of Kraftwerk all so different, yet fundamentally so similar. But why?

'I remember talking to Ralf Hütter from Kraftwerk about this and he said it came from the electric train sets they had as children,' says David Toop. 'Which I thought was a typical Ralf construction – tantalising, appealing, slightly fictional. I had toys like that when I was a kid – toys were incredibly basic back then – two tin train wagons and a circle of tin track and the miracle of it moving around because it was electric – I suppose the combination of electricity and repetition is plausible as a first thought in formative years. And then, obviously the way that connected for them with all sorts of ideas about what constituted Europe in the postwar period. One of the ways to break free from serialism [a twentieth-century mode of composition involving a recurring series of ordered elements] was repetition, which Stockhausen detested as the worst possible thing, lower than human. The other thing was to have the opposite of that, in which, in theory, nothing was ever repeated, that is to say, improvisation. In a way, Krautrock had both those things. A nod towards blues structures, rock structures but without the same chord changes – an exaggerated repetition. And then the free stuff. If you wanted to kill the father, you had to do both – repeat, repeat, repeat but be anarchic at the same time. And be illogical. So much about the music is illogicality.'

The structures of Krautrock also laid it open to the charge of pidgin simplicity from some British journalists who had bought into the narrative of progressive rock, with its emphasis on baroque elaboration. 'I remember James Brown being criticised in the same era as Krautrock for making stupid, simplistic music – because of the repetition,' says Toop. 'Prog had taken on the idea that it was all about diversification all the time, most of it pointless. All that endless shuffling of time signatures. You listen to it and the only thing you can think is, why? It signified sophistication. Repetition felt wilfully stupid – but certainly wasn't stupid in the hands of a Jaki Liebezeit.'

In a sense, most popular rock music is repetitious, with its riffs and nagging grooves, but a release is found in the solo or a big, anthemic refrain. Krautrock offers no such ejaculatory relief. Its locked grooves afford all kinds of picaresque adventures – the ever-shifting, train-window scenarios of Kraftwerk's 'Europe Endless' or Faust's 'So Far' or Neu!'s 'E-Musik'. It's pure, almost infantile pleasure (anyone with small children will be familiar with the refrain 'Again! Again!'), but it also hints at an underlying, Sisyphean futility. There is a stasis, a fixation about it – we are travelling but 'going' nowhere at once. Endless, beginning, endless, beginning. The human, player or listener, at the centre of this process does not get to roam in subjective indulgence. They are tethered. The real 'business' is in the structures, the ambience, the flow, a larger ideal, a collective energy, rather than ego-driven individualism. It's not that sort of narrative.

Space and the East abound too in Krautrock, in common with the wider hippie culture of the day. The relationship, however, is more intense in Krautrock. No mere token 'spacey', Joe Meek-style effects but a headlong launch into an outer space which doubles up as inner, mental space. Meanwhile, in the music of Embryo, for instance, or Hans-Joachim Roedelius's fascination with Japanese culture, the East is more than merely holidayed in, to bring back souvenir plunder or a pinch of saffron; it is fully absorbed. In both instances, these could be seen as acts of cultural 'colonisation', not for exploitative, commercial ends but to expand the idea of what New German music could become. It's an escapism of sorts, an imaginary flight, but neither self-indulgent nor away with the faeries. It's about charting and incorporating new areas, new dimensions.

Considering that Krautrock is so shaped by the German experience, historical, cultural, geographical, it's perhaps surprising that one of the countries to have been least impressed by the music is Germany itself. It became popular in both France and the UK, and later the USA, Japan and points beyond. Less so its country of origin. 'A prophet is not without honour save in his own country,' says Amon Düül 2's John Weinzierl, and that has largely been the case with Krautrock.

Klaus Mueller summarised in a precise, numerical formula the overall response to the new seventies German music in its own time. It read as follows:

Ignorance: 90%
Laughter: 5% (some journalists)
Respect: 5% (some journalists)

It was like Krautrock never happened. As far back as 1980, I remember attending a house party held by my German exchange tutor. I got talking to a rather serious longhair friend of his, who was from Hamburg. Excitedly, I tried to engage him on the subject of Faust, who had originated in that city, and at whose name I expected him to swell with civic pride. He knew nothing about them, he said, loftily, almost boastfully. 'I am only interested in the important groups,' he told me, 'like Rainbow.'

Robert Hampson of Loop recalls, 'When we first went to Germany and I talked of the likes of Can to German journalists, they often had never heard of these bands. I was shocked. Considering that even Can had had a number-one single at one time with "Spoon", most journalists only ever really knew of Kraftwerk, and even then, only the period from *Autobahn* onwards.'

Simple Minds' Jim Kerr is equally flummoxed. 'Germans don't get it. I'll discuss the German influences, Faust and so on, with them, and they don't know what I'm talking about.'

Visiting Berlin, it is as if Krautrock's bid to drive out Anglo-American rock as a predominant force never really made a dent. There are posters for upcoming gigs by Bon Jovi everywhere. The only umlaut in sight is that atop the name of Motörhead, also touring. Trips to two different restaurants afford a soundtrack that is a veritable elephants' graveyard of pop songs long extinct in the UK – Alvin Stardust's 'My Coo-Ca-Choo', Terry Jacks's 'Seasons in the Sun', Nik Kershaw's 'Wouldn't It Be Good', Dire Straits' 'Sultans of Swing'.

None of this, however, is to suggest that Germans as a whole are too dumb to recognise their own cultural product. At a superficial level at least, there is an appeal in Krautrock of the Teutonic other, which, of course, means nothing to Germans themselves. Kraftwerk in particular fail to resonate the way they do overseas, in the Anglo-American market particularly. Partly this is because, not unreasonably, Germans have never considered there to be anything inherently amusing, or exotic, about being German. 'No German identified with the concept projected by Kraftwerk,' says Stefan Morawietz, who, it so happens, lives in Krefeld, birthplace of Ralf Hütter. 'It was fulfilling all the clichés everyone had about Germany.'

Morawietz knows all too well about Krautrock – he made a TV documentary about the German rock music of the era for German TV. However, he believes that critics from outside Germany are guilty of promoting a canon of bands as 'Krautrock' on the basis of electronic experimentation, whereas he believes the 'real' Krautrock consists of the groups who actually made a connection with local audiences in far-flung parts of Germany, well off the beaten track. 'The music was made in the early seventies, but most listeners weren't ready for that. It was only in the mid-eighties that German people started thinking that groups like Can and Amon Düül might be a good heritage for Germany. Before that, they meant nothing,' he says.

His own personal preference is for groups like Eloi and Jane. 'They were hugely successful – they were the groups people actually went to see. Although their sound derived from English bands – the early Eloi stuff is either more primitive or way more complicated than anything like Genesis or King Crimson. It's totally complicated, that's the classical influence you get with German musicians. Jane was fun music. Then the third group was Birth Control, originally from Berlin, later close to Cologne. Grobschnitt were from Hagen. They played in every bar that would open their doors to them. Amon Düül, Can, most of these electronic bands, you couldn't see these bands play. Kraftwerk you could only see in small venues around Düsseldorf, supporting better-known bands. No one in Munich would ever see Kraftwerk, though that changed after *Autobahn*.

'Even if these groups played progressive, it was not the same progressive as in England. The structure, the rhythm changes, dynamic changes were way more complicated than in English bands. That's one of the reasons why Grobschnitt started their set with jokes and comics – because their music was so difficult it helped them relax, to have a relaxation point during this complex music. But these were the guys that everybody listened to. They played the villages, where no big bands played. No English, no American groups.'

Morawietz makes an important point, one that's not to be sneezed at – that these groups, at hand, were the ones who in practical terms bolstered a sense of homegrown identity. That said, anyone who can get from one end of an Eloi album to the other is a better man than I.

Diedrich Diederichsen, formerly of the German magazine *Sounds*, is also a little wary of overpraising groups like Can and Kraftwerk, particularly for their vaunted links with the art world, links he believes are overstated. 'I think that there is a certain sensibility in Düsseldorf, for example, [that] informed what Kraftwerk was doing at a certain period, but they were not really close to the real art world, they were not close to the debates, they were not there. It was more like a superficial relation because they went, maybe, to the same bars.'

However, he does suggest that one difficulty in West Germany was the lack of a major music press, or lack of interest in any such thing, that would provide a framework, a discourse for the new music. *Sounds* was one such paper, ambitious in its aesthetic scope, and apposite for the new German music. It was named after a remark by Albert Ayler that the future of music would no longer be about notes, it would be about sounds. However, its influence was limited by comparison with the UK press.

'I remember when I started to write for German music papers in the late seventies that there were journalists of importance in the UK press. Then, Germany sold almost as many records as the British, in certain periods even more, but issues of music magazines sold were far fewer. *Sounds* was extremely small – the best-sold issue was forty-three thousand copies. And that was a very good month. So in Germany there was obviously a huge market of people who were buying music, but were not buying any information about the music. It was not the same in Britain, with magazines like *NME, Melody Maker*.'

The Bremen DJ and co-founder of the German TV show *The Beat Club* Gerhard Augustin recalled in a *Eurock* interview in 2002 how hard it was for underground groups. 'For new groups without a hit single it was very hard. Some of the old Nazis were still in control of the media so they would never give exposure to new experimental rock music.' And yet it was Augustin who was instrumental in the signing of groups like Amon Düül 2 and Can to Liberty/United Artists. The 'Altnazi' influence wasn't so strong as to prevent non-commercial Krautrock groups from being signed to major labels, perhaps precisely because of the culture gap between the out-of-touch executives and the music itself. It's quite astonishing that despite demo tapes of sheer, unabashed extremism, they were nonetheless signed to major German labels, with high hopes even entertained of Faust that they might cause a Beatles-style sensation. While Germans may never really have taken Krautrock as fully to heart as the rest of the world, its institutional postwar tolerance meant that the music was at least able to attain crucial footholds in its country of origin.

In the UK, meanwhile, a handful of journalists, bored with the increasingly leaden state of British rock in the 1970s, more frills than thrills, began to take notice of what was happening in Germany. Ian MacDonald at the *NME* was one, though he would later retract some of his praise and deplore the excess of drug taking that he felt clouded over some of the music. Richard Williams, then a writer at *Melody Maker*, was another. 'I came back from Berlin with all these albums – *Phallus Dei* by Amon Düül, Can – a whole pile of them. It was obvious that something interesting was happening. It sounded as if it was people who had heard Terry Riley, Velvets, free jazz. Nobody here at that time was influenced by the Velvet Underground – not until Roxy and Bowie. There was a darker side, drones and a sense of timelessness in the music, which they seemed to have a handle on. Quite a lot of them sounded as if they had studied with Stockhausen, even if they hadn't, which was very different from, say, Keith Emerson. That was refreshing to me because I hated prog with a passion, which set up some interesting tensions with me and *Melody Maker* writers like Chris Welch.

'For me, Nico was one of those who helped establish a founding mood. I loved the thing she added to what they were doing. She helped established this idea of coldness, which is quite important in all of this. Darkness and coldness nowadays have come to be seen as essential constituents of rock music. Well, for a long time, there was no darkness, there was no coldness. Everything was sunshine and optimism. You had sad songs but they were sad love songs. And then came this new wave of German music.'

As early as 1970, Williams reviewed Can's *Monster Movie*, and while he would doubtless not care to have every word quoted back many years on ('Mooney, a Negro, doesn't have a particularly powerful voice, but his wailing and screaming fits perfectly where a less reticent singer would obtrude') and while unable to hazard as yet an overall sense of why German music was emerging at this stage as a collective force, it's a prescient and shrewd analysis of the group's fundamental rearrangement of the rock elements, concluding simply, 'Nobody in Britain is playing this kind of music, which is well worth hearing.'

Needless to say, a penchant for German rock set Williams up for some philistine ribaldry from his office colleagues. 'Oh yes, absolutely. People didn't like experiments that went off on a tangent from the prog evolution.' Goose-stepping, combs pressed under noses and straplines filled with *Achtungs!*, Panzer and Luftwaffe references were all part of the merriment. 'You can tie that in with the Goons and Monty Python and sub-editors competing to get in with the most ludicrous puns.' Priceless examples of this tendency included the following straplines: 'Can: Ve Give Ze Orders Here' (interview by Nick Kent, *NME*, February 1974); 'Can: They Have Ways of Making You Listen . . .' (profile by Ian MacDonald, *NME*, November 1974); and 'Kraftwerk: The Final Solution to the Music Problem?' (interview by Lester Bangs, *NME*, September 1975, which was printed on a backdrop of an image of a Nuremberg rally). This tendency persisted, with almost calamitous consequences, into my own era as a *Melody Maker* journalist. Had I not spotted it at the last minute and hauled it from the presses, a 1990s Kraftwerk feature of mine would have appeared rejoicing under the headline 'STRENGTH THROUGH JOY'.

In America, Lester Bangs was the first notable journalist to introduce German music to a Stateside listenership, first singing the praises of Amon Düül 2 with customary Bangsian descriptive expansiveness and then, in more fraught and dubious terms, heralding the international arrival of Kraftwerk. However, it was France where critics proved the most amenable to Krautrock. Jean-Pierre Lantin's piece 'At Last: The German Rock Has Arrived!', published in *Actuel* in January 1973, not only provided a copious introduction to the still-burgeoning new scene but did so in terms free of the latent Germanophobia which so often characterised Anglo-American coverage.

Although he briefly presented the BBC music showcase *The Old Grey Whistle Test* in the early seventies, Richard Williams was, to his frustration, never able to get any of his beloved German groups on the show during his tenure. But then, in keeping with much of the music of its pre-video era, Krautrock is not the most alluring of visual experiences. Kraftwerk again, with their aspirations to *Gesamtkunstwerk* (a total, audio-visual work of art), are an exception, of course, and much of the sleeve artwork on labels like Ohr and Brain is vivid and arresting. Still, there's no getting around the fact that for all the sporadic efforts of postmodern retromaniacs, the 1970s was, in terms of appearances, the most appalling decade in living memory. Regardless of how kind nature had been to them, no one looks good hidden beneath acres of facial hair, bellbottoms and soul-sapping mixtures of orange and brown. Krautrock was not exceptional in this respect. One cannot stare very hard for very long at Amon Düül or Guru Guru. Meanwhile, its emphasis on the group over the individual means that it yielded few 'faces' (those parts of their faces that were not covered in whiskers), with Kraftwerk again the main exception. Klaus Dinger tried for, and would probably have liked to have achieved, iconic status, but his image is not seared on the memory like others in the rock pantheon.

All of which is to the good, in that Krautrock is the most 'visual' of listening experiences. The music is often applied, spontaneously, in the studio, rather than composed. It's music of colour, depth and dimension, of scale and contrasts, all of which draw your mind's eye. Gigs, not inappropriately, took place in galleries as often, if not more so, as in dedicated rock venues or concert halls. It is painterly, sculpted, wrought music. Despite Diedrich Diederichsen's caveats, the very proximity of Krautrock to the art world and its great twentieth-century traditions is striking by comparison to that of British rock, many of whose players went to art school but were ultimately stunted and hamstrung by a very deep-seated British fear of pretentiousness. 'In England,' Brian Eno once said, 'the greatest crime is to rise above your station.'

'I think Germans are really serious about things,' says Tim Gane of Stereolab, today a Berlin resident. 'There's no coyness like you get in England, "don't be too arty, don't make a fool of yourself". But in Germany, they're quite serious about art and music and deciding these things are worth doing.' Such seriousness was born not out of the country's deep-seated traditions but from the inescapable gravity of Germany's recent past.

*

> 'At school, breeding and order ruled. The headmasters, judges were ex-Nazis, who quite astonishingly had become "denazified" overnight. You weren't allowed to question your father about what he had done in the war, nor your grandfather. Naturally, we wanted to be free from this waste, this violent legacy.'
>
> Irmin Schmidt, Can

Those coming of age in the late 1960s in West Germany, whose memories of the Second World War were either of infancy or non-existent, would have looked pretty askance at their parents as they began to learn for themselves about the years 1933 to 1945. They were assisted in their enquiries by a handful of intellectuals, artists, writers and prosecutors determined to re-examine the enormities of the Third Reich, in which so many ordinary Germans must have been implicated, despite numerous and much-repeated protestations by the vast majority that they had no idea what was going on. On *Absolutely Free* by the Mothers of Invention, one of the more beloved groups of the European counterculture, Frank Zappa cried out, on 'Plastic People', 'Watch the Nazis run your town!' In West Germany, to say nothing of the 'Communist' East, this was less hyperbolic and a good deal closer to the truth than on the west coast of the USA. Take Altnazi figureheads like Kurt Georg Kiesinger, a paid-up member of the National Socialist party for twelve years, who during the war had worked in the German foreign ministry's radio-propaganda department. This did not prevent him from being elected as Chancellor of the Federal Republic of Germany by the Christian Democratic Union party in 1966, a position he occupied for three years.

The economic recovery alone was remarkable, given the utter devastation Germany had both visited upon itself and had visited upon it by the end of the war. From 1942 onwards, with America persuaded into the fray, it was pretty clear that the war was unwinnable. By 1944, the German population were weary, cynical and uncertain of what had hit them, and what was about to hit them. Reduced to the very bones of austerity, few bothered with the '*Heil Hitler*' greeting any more – it had been replaced by the more pertinent '*Bleib übrig!*' ('Survive!').

And yet the Germans fought on. This, despite the only prospect of victory existing in Hitler's increasingly deluded and addled mind as he pored over plans for the new Europa in his bunker, even as it vibrated to the onslaught of the approaching Red Army.

It would be wrong to suggest, however, that for the majority of Germans, their persistence was due to an overall fanaticism or credulity bred by the Nazi high command. No one believed any more the propaganda screeched across the airwaves. That said, those who did believe – the network of Volkssturmers, functionaries and 'little Hitlers' – were both brutal and futile in their effectiveness in subduing the majority. So instilled was the authoritarian mindset that, astonishingly, sailors in the German navy were put to death for desertion even after the formal surrender had been signed.

However, for most, a lack of resistance can be put down to sheer exhaustion, as well as a lack of options available in a totalitarian state in which, to his very last, palsied, hunkered down and bent on suicide, Hitler was absolutely in charge. Fear and helplessness were the primary emotions, anger a distant second, while any kind of sympathy for the victims of the Nazis' years of brutal supremacism was a speck on the horizon. Even as images of the Holocaust trickled out, even as the disgusted Allies frog-marched local Germans past the piles of skeletal corpses while they tried to avert their eyes, there was no immediate sense of shame. Many looked at both emaciated survivors and the dead, robbed of all semblance of human life, and saw not horror but affirmation of their ingrained belief that the Jews were, indeed, less than human.

Prejudices remained sullenly intact but the physical fact of Germany in 1945 was ruins: five hundred million cubic yards of them across the country, all told, so slow to be cleared initially that in Cologne they were actually topped with accrued layers of vegetation. Green on grey – this is an apt visual metaphor for Krautrock itself, organic growth arising from a foundation of rubble. For some of the older Krautrockers, such as Conrad Schnitzler, Irmin Schmidt and Hans-Joachim Roedelius, war and its aftermath provided the physical and sonic backdrop to their upbringing. Violent noise was not an aberration but a natural condition, while fragmentation, concrete and entangled metal, was their element. Echoes of this naturally resound through Krautrock; it's one of its subliminal energies. In the sleevenotes to the 2008 album *Axolotl Eyes*, Schmidt recalls his flight from Berlin with his mother. 'We travelled to Innsbruck. The night in the sleeper carriage became a key experience. The monotonous knocking rhythm of the wheels interrupted by crazy "drum fills" as we went over the points, the constant, changing whoosh of the movement into which I hallucinated choirs and murmuring orchestral sounds, the mysterious voices at train stations, sudden booming that would stop as abruptly as it had started . . . by the early hours of the morning, I started to cry bitterly from utter exhaustion, and through my sobs tried to explain to my worried mother that "no, there is nothing wrong – it was just so beautiful".'

To an innocent child there was a strange beauty in these circumstances, but the adult generation was afforded no solace. If ordinary Germans maintained an elephantine silence in the postwar years, it was because they wished to distance themselves not just from the crimes they had committed, from what they had done, but also from what had been done to them. Not just the trauma of guilt but of terrible victimhood. Of all the men born in Germany in 1918, for example, two out of three did not survive the war. Many women, and indeed their families, chose suicide rather than submitting to the rapacious cruelty of the advancing, vengeful Soviet army, attaching ropes to one another and throwing themselves in rivers. In Berlin alone, there were over a hundred thousand rape victims, some ten thousand of whom died, many having taken their own lives. Their cities flattened, their women raped, their men massacred, their country occupied, all for the crazed, intoxicating idea of their own national and racial superiority. It was too much to realise, to take on board, especially with the immediate problems of hunger, destitution and runaway inflation to contend with. Too much for ordinary, well-to-do citizens who until recently had enjoyed all the pleasures, the clocks and sofas, motor cars and clean linen of modern civilisation. People like us.

As early as 1944, US Secretary to the Treasury Robert Morgenthau had advanced a punitive plan which would have effectively reduced Germany to an agrarian state. Morgenthau's plan was rejected but its supporters did succeed in effecting a policy of 'denazification' in the postwar years, influenced by the Frankfurt school of thought that Naziism was not a top-down phenomenon but more like a virus which could be medically, systematically eradicated. Consequently, some two hundred thousand former Nazis were interned by the Western Allies between 1946 and 1949, as well as over 220,000 government and industry personnel.

Denazification, however, was a huge mistake, a case study in how not to handle an occupied people, one later repeated by the Americans after the second Gulf War in Iraq. Anti-Nazis as well as ex-Nazis felt alienated by their treatment at the hands of the Allies, with the British in particular guilty of regarding Naziism as somehow essential to the 'German character', a perception which added to the futility of their task – how to 'de-Germanify' the Germans? Efforts to weed out and expel from civil society all those civil servants and administrators who had been part of the Nazi apparatus foundered when it emerged that society had difficulty functioning without their experience and competence.

By 1951, denazification was abandoned, giving way to the more pragmatic Marshall Plan, in which the USA would provide billions generally for war-torn Europe but particularly West Germany, industrial heartland of the continent. West Germany's economic revival would be key to the recovery of Western Europe, which would be an effective future trading partner and a bulwark against future, Soviet-inspired communism.

The regeneration of West Germany took remarkably little time. Fuelled by American assistance, Germans threw themselves into the business of rebuilding their industrial base, sublimating the energies they were as yet reluctant to apply to acknowledgement of war crimes or repentance, to great effect. By the early 1950s, West Germans were enjoying the material boons of an astonishing boom and were once again well clothed and well fed. The country's moral nourishment was another matter, however. In 1951, a poll revealed that only five per cent of them felt any guilt towards the Jews. Brecht coined the aphorism '*Erst kommt das Fressen, dann kommt die Moral*' ('Eat first, morality later').

America's expansion of their Coca-Cola plants into Europe was reviled by some as a symbol of over-encroachment by Uncle Sam on Old Europe, the French in particular. However, consumption of all things American was rampant in Germany in the 1950s

– Irmin Schmidt was not the only avid consumer of cowboy stories. German-language paperback novels about the old Wild West became massively popular, selling in the tens of millions.

While this sort of transatlantic love-in might have appalled the French culturally, on a more practical level the French and Germans would move towards closer integration and form a common trading partnership which would lead to the foundation of the European Union. West Germany benefited from the leadership of Konrad Adenauer, whose conservative origins were in no way tainted with any unfortunate Nazi associations – he had been deposed as Mayor of Cologne when Hitler came to power in 1933. He was no radical, however. In 1957, he campaigned on the very un-Krautrock slogan 'No experiments!'

By the 1960s, Germany was aptly described as 'fat and impotent', dollar-fed, disconnected from its past, both good and ill. In a lecture series delivered in 1997 in Zurich, the late W. G. Sebald described the postwar state of West Germany as having 'developed an almost perfectly functioning mechanism of repression'. By the late 1960s, it was a materially comfortable society, economically fully regenerated, but one caught in a fog of voluntary amnesia, grey conservatism and the lingering clouds of the unacknowledged, unexpelled past. It was at once soft and authoritarian, peaceful but unresolved.

The generation that came of age in the 1960s was the first to be untainted by personal guilt but conscious as curious adults of the enormous war crimes in whose shadow they had been born. Many became politicised. Thousands turned out for demonstrations and sit-ins. Millions embraced Anglo-American rock 'n' roll, first as a rejection of the Teutonic values of their stiff elders, before later rejecting the overweening, imperial influence of America, though still living their lives to an Anglo-American rock soundtrack.

Krautrock represented a rejection of the musical response to the moral and material condition of the Fatherland. It was, in part, Oedipal. From Conrad Schnitzler to Klaus Dinger, there are stories of familial strife and rebellion that are common enough in their dynamic. Ralf Hütter doesn't speak of any turbulence in his own relationship with his parents, while the father of Florian Schneider (co-founding member of Kraftwerk), a famous architect, even helped them secure recording premises. That did not stop Hütter from once declaring, 'We have no fathers.' The mothers of the Krautrock generation often emerge, insofar as they do in their stories, as quietly sympathetic and encouraging, often musical themselves or having harboured creative ambitions which went unfulfilled in an age when women were supposed to stick to nurturing rather than self-fulfilment. The brutal, collective paternalism of the Third Reich under Hitler affected Krautrock's musical response, its composition. Although de facto leaders emerged among the groups, it preferred communal structures ('No Führers!' as Jaki Liebezeit puts it). It rejected the cock-rock posturing that blights so much sixties and seventies British-American rock. Its hankering for ambience and colour, for non-phallic structure, for openness and embrace, feminises the music to a great degree. It's as if part of Krautrock's undertaking is to reject the Fatherland and re-embrace Gaia, Mother Earth. (Although the relative lack of female practitioners, especially on the predominant, instrumental side, shows that Krautrock was not entirely ahead of its time, with commune life a depressingly sexist affair.)

No fathers, no precedents. The writer Italo Calvino suggested that a postwar society should proceed from a *tabula rasa*, a clean slate. In its desire for originality as a spiritual imperative as well as an artistic one, Krautrock was only reflecting what had been going on in the German arts as a whole since 1945. In the visual arts, Ernst Wilhelm Nay, formerly condemned as a 'degenerate' artist, would go on to co-found the Zen 49 group, whose purpose was to restore 'the spiritual orientation of abstract art'. Significantly, this group rejected symbolism, polemics, and sought recess in the meditative qualities of non-representational art – a visual forerunner of Krautrock in some respects.

One artist who would later have a direct bearing on Krautrock was Joseph Beuys, born in 1921 in Krefeld. In 1941, aged twenty, he enthusiastically joined the Luftwaffe, only to down his Stuka somewhere in the Crimea. There, he later claimed to have experienced something akin to the 1960s TV series *The Champions*, in which a trio of law-enforcement agents are miraculously healed and granted life-changing powers by an advanced civilisation living secretly in the Himalayan mountains. He said he had been restored to health by local Tatar tribesmen, neutrals in the war, whose ministrations included wrapping him in felt. This experience, real or imagined, seems to have proven an epiphany for Beuys, one which he processed into a 1974 work, *I Like America and America Likes Me*, in which he was transported by ambulance, swathed in felt on a stretcher, to the René Block Gallery in New York, where he spent eight hours a day for three days in the company of a wild coyote.

Beuys's artistic purposes were twofold. On the one hand, like so many avant-garde twentieth-century artists, he considered it his purpose to collapse the walls between art and life. For him, art wasn't something confined to dead, horizontal frames but something active and social, intervening in the lives of people – hence his involvement in Fluxus and the 'happenings' of the early 1960s, one of which earned him a punch in the face from a right-wing student when he took part in an installation commemorating the twentieth anniversary of the attempt on Hitler's life. However, he also had a faith in the shamanistic qualities of art, its supposed healing powers, the sense of mythology it invoked. It seems to have become his mission to heal the German trauma by means of art as 'alternative therapy'. This also involved a measure of self-dramatisation; his response to the 1964 assault was to pose, bloodied but unbowed, holding up a small crucifix to the audience in his left hand while extending his right arm in a Roman salute. The Artist redeemed through physical suffering, iconic, messianic, cultic.

What's mildly problematic about Beuys is that his ascent into self-mythologising, fabulism and the notion of art as somehow containing healing properties feels like an evasion, on his own part, of acknowledgement of his own Nazi past. Having been reborn, that Luftwaffe youth is no more, is another 'self'. For a long time he said little, and little was said on his behalf, about those formative years. In a biography published in 1987, the year after Beuys died, his wartime exploits are described merely as a 'learning experience'. Nonetheless, he would be a vital touchstone in the Düsseldorf arts scene, which in turn would assist in the nurturing of groups like Kraftwerk and Neu!. And it was as a response to the killing of Benno Ohnesorg that he founded the Deutsche Studentpartei (German Student Party).

Some of the country's finest literary minds, and consciences, such as the playwright Bertolt Brecht, had actually chosen to migrate (initially, at least) to East Germany following the war; others remained in exile. The Zen 49 group referred consciously to an earlier association, the literary Group 47, so named after the year in which they were formed. They celebrated, among others, the work of Heinrich Böll and his *Trümmerliteratur* ('the literature of the rubble') in novels like 1949's *The Train Was on Time*, which explores the trauma of ex-soldiers. His most famous work was 1972's *The Lost Honour of Katherina Blum*, which, in acid, satirical terms, depicts the tabloid-driven amorality and panic in the face of the activities of the Red Army Faction.

Although West German literature undoubtedly experienced its own upheavals in the postwar period, and its greatest authors such as Günter Grass took it on themselves to act as keepers of the public conscience (despite his own eventual unmasking as a member of the Waffen-SS), its trickle-down effects were slower, with the youth at the barricades disposed to more immediate insurrectionary literature – magazines, manifestos.

One of the tasks a new generation of filmmakers set themselves was to restore some sense of what it meant to 'be' German, how one identified oneself as such, other than by a stigma. These same concerns would later be central to the activities of the new vanguard of German music-makers.

In 1962, a group of filmmakers issued what would become known as the Oberhausen manifesto. It was a reaction to *Heimatfilm*, the predilection for Anglo-American cinema, in particular Westerns and the shunning of efforts to address the traumas of the very recent past. In line with European cinema in general, it called for a new aesthetic, a mode of non-commercial cinema in which the filmmaker was recast as auteur, able to execute a necessary set of intentions rather than merely be obliged to entertain.

'Film needs to be more independent. Free from all usual conventions by the industry. Free from control of commercial partners. Free from the dictation of stakeholders. We have detailed spiritual, structural, and economic ideas about the production of new German cinema. Together we're willing to take any risk. Conventional film is dead. We believe in the new film.'

One of the co-signatories of the manifesto was Alexander Kluge, who in 1961, along with Peter Schamoni, made the film *Brutalität in Stein* ('Brutality in Stone'). Just under eleven minutes long, it consists of a black-and-white Eisensteinian montage of neglected, abandoned but still imposing and not yet demolished architecture of the Nazi era, its off-white pillared corridors and staircases, as well as scale models of the Germania of which Hitler dreamed. The soundtrack, fading with abrupt transience in and out of silence, features old newsreels, propaganda, scratchy, stirring classical music and extracts from speeches by Hitler and the Nazi high command. Towards the end of the film, we hear Hitler call for the construction of emergency wood and mud dwellings for refugees, but not a single human being appears in *Brutalität in Stein*. It is a narrative told entirely in building blocks, one of edifices still existing. This signifies the stone-cold inhumanity of the Nazi regime, but also it is for us to picture the wretched victims of the concentration camps, whose fate is described in one chilling narrative passage as they are herded methodically to their deaths. By featuring no human beings, the film serves to rekindle the imagination of them. It is, in every sense, a masterpiece of structure, at once aesthetic and a commentary on aesthetics, a cornerstone of the New German Cinema. It also prefigures some of the more brutalist, abstract tendencies of Krautrock – the music of Conrad Schnitzler, for example, or the sonic, proto-industrial monoliths of early Guru Guru, full of implicit damnation.

New German Cinema matured and developed in various ways throughout the sixties and seventies, determined to develop its own distinctive visual language that eschewed the conventions of Hollywood with its predictable, too easily satisfying narrative arc and resolutions in which reality was distorted and put into soft focus to accommodate the star players at its centre. Again, there's a parallel here with Krautrock's rejection of traditional, Anglo-American templates. As well as dealing head-on with the social realities of postwar Germany, films like Kluge's *Yesterday's Girl* used Brechtian techniques that constantly reminded you of the cinematic format, never allowed you to bathe in the escapism of the silver screen. Wim Wenders's movies similarly employed alternative narrative devices. As such, in terms of both form and content, they sought to forge a new sense of German identity. The culmination of this was Hans-Jürgen Syberberg's seven-hour epic *Hitler: A Film from Germany*, infrequently broadcast since its release and hard to acquire. It is neither documentary nor biography exactly, but rather as near as cinema has come to the *Gesamtkunstwerk*, in which cinema, music, surrealist art, poetry, even puppeteering all come into play. This, however, was released in 1977, the year in which postwar cultural reflection was reaching a crest in West Germany, and Krautrock had come and gone.

In 1971, though, another movie of the New German Cinema had made quite a different sort of impact on the more stoner end of rebellious student youth. Werner Herzog's *Fata Morgana* was put together from footage shot in the Sahara desert, in what was initially intended to form the basis of a science-fiction movie about a dying planet. It consists largely of lengthy tracking shots of the desolate, intermittently verdant Saharan landscape, unpeopled until almost midway through the film. In the first section, 'Creation', actress Lotte Eisner recites extracts from the Creation text of the Quiché Indians of Guatemala, while in the second, sardonically entitled 'Paradise', a series of the conditions of this impossible-to-conceive state are listed: roast pigeons flying directly into mouths, wars stopped by women, 'plane wrecks distributed in advance', and so forth. The final section, 'Golden Age', commences with the bizarre and unexplained footage of a madame and a pimp playing what Herzog describes as 'the saddest music I ever heard', a duo playing a stiff cabaret turn on drums and piano, singing in muffled tones.

The film supposedly presents an unbearably bleak view of things: human beings attempting to thrive in impossible conditions, caught in the midst of a futile desolation. However, it's a film that can be greatly enjoyed, as a sheer sensual experience, and was by young audiences, often with chemical assistance. In its very rhythm and picaresque structure, in its emphasis on landscape rather than foregrounded human character, in the sheer, mournful, natural beauty of its footage, its sun-drenched blues, icy whites and vivid green undulations, charred with events such as red girder construction and the rotting carcasses of livestock, with its repetitions and loops (planes landing over and over, trucks driving in circles) it shares uncannily similar qualities with Krautrock, with its utopian/dystopian sound fields, surrealistic interventions and changes of direction and soberly dreamlike preoccupations with places and states outside the surly bonds of the here and now, imaginary possibilities. Certainly, on viewing *Fata Morgana*, and doubtless attracted by its use of the text from which they took their own name, the group Popol Vuh, led by the director's old acquaintance Florian Fricke, ended up collaborating with Herzog on future soundtracks.

In 1946, the Internationale Ferienkurse für Neue Musik (International Summer Courses for New Music) were set up in Darmstadt, in Hessen, central Germany, in the occupied American zone, by music critic Wolfgang Steinecke. These courses were very much underwritten by the Americans, and were part of a broader effort to re-educate Germans in proper democratic, anti-Nazi values. Among those whose work was showcased at the courses were composers Hans Werner Henze, Gottfried Michael Koenig and the man who is regarded as Krautrock's most prominent and vital ancestor, Karlheinz Stockhausen.

As a boy growing up as an impoverished son of the soil in a rural village in the vicinity of Cologne, Stockhausen (born 1928) used to lie in the fields and stare at the blue skies above him, watching propeller planes drone and wheel. They were harbingers of a war to come, of course, but they also inculcated in the young Karlheinz a desire to fly, one which he expressed in some of his most notorious works, including *Hymnen* and the *Helikopter-Streichquartett*, in which the string players delivered their parts from helicopters floating about above the area surrounding the concert hall. It was more than mere conventional, aviatory enthusiasm, but a longing to be un-earthbound, or even skinbound. Music would eventually be the means by which he would simulate this desire for ascension.

Stockhausen suffered as a result of the Nazi policy of euthanasia: his own mother, whose married life had been one long round of pregnancies, was institutionalised and eventually returned to her family as an urn of ashes by the authorities, who claimed she had died of leukaemia. His father died too, in combat in April 1945, a fate he had anticipated with equanimity – he feared the peace, and what would become of him under Allied occupation, more than the present conflict.

In the last years of the war, in his teens, Stockhausen worked as a stretcher bearer; he recalled seeing body parts strewn in the trees, chunks of charred human flesh, following the strafing of the planes. The sense of people reduced to their mere physicality by war, which, as he later put it, 'washes away the connection of man to the divine', was seared on his consciousness. He seems to have been aware of people making love in hospitals amid the dying: 'people become very physical living close to death'.

In the years following the war, he studied at the State Academy in Cologne, while playing piano in bars for tips, everything from Beethoven sonatas to sentimental standards. The end of the war coincided with a 'point zero' for modern classical music: Pierre Schaeffer was experimenting with musique concrète, new composers such as György Ligeti and Pierre Boulez were emerging to supplant the likes of Bartók and Webern, while in 1949 Theodor Adorno published his *Philosophy of New Music*, but it was in 1953, when Stockhausen went to Paris to become assistant to Herbert Eimert at the Electronic Music Studio of Nordwestdeutscher Rundfunk, that he truly came into his own as a composer, and, he felt, composition itself took a great leap forward. 'In the music written since 1951 there was an explicit spirit of non-figurative composition.'

This leap was thanks to the development of such manipulative, electronic devices as filters, modulators and magnetic tape. Although it would be years before music academics would take the sounds produced by these machine devices seriously (as late as 1975 the eminent German music critic Hans-Hubert Schönzeler wondered if Stockhausen's 'electrophonics' amounted to 'just plain effects'), Stockhausen understood that these instruments afforded the possibility of reducing sound to sub-atomic particles, the 'splitting of the sound', as he put it. Traditional, linear, representative composition with its reference to themes and conventional time scales was now obsolete; in a sanguine moment of futurism in 1953, he opined that twenty years hence, no one would be talking about Bach any more.

It wasn't just electronics which would define and liberate Stockhausen the composer but acoustic instruments also, albeit orchestrated according to 'aleatoric' principles (players allowed a degree of improvisation, compositions as zones of activity rather than strict, linear, preset tasks, with instructions to players, as in one case, not to commence playing until they had emptied their minds of thought). He also took on board world musics and their alternative scales – Balinese, Indian and Japanese. However, in works like *Gesang der Jünglinge* and *Kontakte*, written in the 1950s and '60s, Stockhausen developed a whole new set of temporal and spatial relations in his music; a 'moment form' in which processed sounds erupt, cluster, coalesce, recede, obeying the dictates of their 'inner lives'.

Initially, Stockhausen shared his senior colleague Herbert Eimert's predilection for a 'pure' form of electro-acoustic music, pristine and untainted by any association with this fallen, ruined world, in contrast to Pierre Schaeffer's musique concrète, which took as the stuff of its collages everyday sounds from the field of real life. This idea was reflected in Hermann Hesse's novel *The Glass Bead Game*, a futuristic work which debates the extent to which 'high' intellectual and cultural activity should remove itself from the world as it is. Stockhausen did incorporate musique concrète pretty quickly into his world; despite his reputation for seriousness, remoteness and eccentricity, he had a well-developed sense of humour and was generally well stocked with all the usual human passions. However, he saw the new direction of composition as away from the faded Romantic era, and its preoccupation with mankind, into more divine, cosmic realms.

This wasn't airy-fairy, wishful vagueness, so far as Stockhausen was concerned. He felt that it behoved human beings to maximise their physical faculties, in particular hearing, which he felt had been traditionally, woefully neglected in Western culture at the expense of the visual. Exposure to his own music, he trusted, would help restore the balance. He saw it as a plain, physical fact of the human condition that far from the cosmos being 'out there', its vibrations were bombarding us, every waking second of our lives – in the form of sunlight, for example – perpetually knocking at the locked door of our limited consciousness and understanding of our capability. One of his greatest works, *Hymnen*, an extended electronic piece of four 'regions' taking in mangled excerpts of the world's national anthems, crackles to a permanent blizzard of radio waves, palpable transmissions from the non-silent universe.

His visions for humanity were a mixture of the utopian and the dystopian – his future dreams included domestic utensils whose electronic whirrings would be so nicely attuned as to add a pleasingly euphonious dimension to everyday life. He also anticipated major apocalypse at the end of the twenty-first century. 'We have to go through these crises at the end of the century and the beginning of the next. There is no other way,' he told the American journalist Jonathan Cott in the early 1970s. He spoke of dreams in which he envisaged American cities being destroyed. (When the Twin Towers fell in 2001, the nearest actual approximation to his foreboding, he was quoted, albeit, he protested, erroneously and out of context, as saying the attacks were a major work of art.) However, from these purgatory experiences, this 'purifying shock', mankind would emerge the better for it.

Stockhausen became the poster boy for the postwar avant-garde, name-checked by Frank Zappa, appearing on the sleeve to the Beatles' *Sergeant Pepper* album. He is popularly cited as 'paving the way' for modern electronica. But he was always quite disdainful of anything to do with pop, however supposedly radical its leanings. He described pop art as 'shameful for mankind . . . garbage art, which celebrates material impermanence and decay, which is a disgrace'. Although not entirely indifferent to the work of his 'pupils' such as Can's Holger Czukay and Irmin Schmidt, as well as Kraftwerk, he didn't really see them as his successors. And when, in 1995, he was presented by Radio 3 with a pile of platters by new electronic artists such as Aphex Twin, Scanner and Plasticman, he dismissed their efforts as raw and repetitive, recommending them to listen more closely to his own masterworks.

Towards the end of his life, Stockhausen began to talk about coming from Sirius, the brightest star in the night sky. This was simply the logical conclusion of his artistic impetus to fly away from this world, one in the clutches of Lucifer. 'Today, we are in the opening period of a completely new era,' he said, back in 1971. 'But consider what babies we are when we think of the speed of the cosmos. In 1980, they want to go to Mars or Venus. Compared to all the stars that exist, what an embryonic state this is in the space age! Yet it revolutionises everything; our time concept, the concept of how long our bodies will have to last in order to travel several thousand light years. We must transform our bodies, which are completely relative nowadays; the human being has been made relative by its consciousness.'

In many respects, Stockhausen is comparable to Sun Ra, the bandleader and pioneer of electronics in jazz, who also ventured into the realms of the astral, with his singular brand of cosmology and claims to have originated from the planet Saturn. For Sun Ra, born Herman Blount in Alabama in 1914, such Afro-futurism was an imaginative and necessary mode of psychic escape from inescapably miserable times for black Americans. For Stockhausen, his bitter, formative experiences of war inculcated a similar longing, and a similar belief that through some untapped power of intense concentration, escape was possible – to reach a place out there, free of gravity, brutality, of charred flesh, conflict and the murder of parents.

In his pioneering use of electronics, his futurism and urge to create new forms impelled by the ruinous experience of war, Stockhausen was a father figure to Krautrock, no doubt, though he was only remotely conscious of the fact. However, he was a figure against whom two of his 'sons', ex-pupils Holger Czukay and Irmin Schmidt, would find it necessary to revolt.

A more obvious and everyday source of artistic revolt, if not inspiration, for young German musicians in the 1960s was Schlager, the pop scene whose middle-of-the-road banality represented their polar opposite. Schlager had its visual corollary in *Heimatfilm* ('homeland films'). Chocolate-box, fluffily Aryan affairs featuring recognisably Germanic types, *Heimatfilm* was generally shot in the clean air, amid the lodges, dairy herds and great outdoors of the Bavarian Alps, rather than the dust and rubble of postwar cities. These were pure escapist hokum, set in an imaginary, ahistorical, pastoral Germany in which there had somehow been no war, no Reich, no Jewish question, no bombs.

Schlager simply means 'hit', but it came to define a certain reactionary style, the music favoured by conservatives or *Spiesser* ('squares'). To listen to, for example, Lolita's 1960s hit 'Seemann, deine Heimat ist das Meer', accordion-tinged, docile, swaying to what barely qualifies as a pulse, let alone a rhythm, is to be hit by a Proustian waft of Euro-dreadfulness, not just of the past but of the present day – of tableclothed restaurants, replica pine, garishly orange plasticity, tacky Alpine souvenir shops, odourless, apple-cheeked intimations of a Nordic, mono-ethnic neverland that's uncomfortably close to the tableaux of Aryan fantasy. What in other national contexts might seem innocuous and wholesome struck many in the postwar German era to be wilfully, inexcusably anodyne, an aesthetic offence. Song titles often reflected a nostalgic wistfulness ('Memories of Heidelberg'), but this appeared to be a music defined by what it refused to remember, was determined not to know, or admit within its confines.

As a counterculture began to emerge in Germany, Schlager, as featured on conservative host Dieter Thomas Heck's show *Schlager-Hitparade*, became the focus of the ire of a new, restive generation of intellectuals. They condemned Schlager, or its close relative Volksmusik, as *Volksverdummerung* (brainwashing) and those who listened to it as demonstrating signs of 'intellectual retardation'. The culture gap between Schlager and those young people at the vanguard of political protest was most obviously pronounced in 1968, one of the most politically violent years of the decade, when students stormed the barricades in France and Germany, Soviet tanks rolled into Prague, and American cities burned in the wake of Martin Luther King's assassination. While all this was going on, the German charts resounded to the vacuous chirruping of one Dorthe Larsen, and her biggest hit, 'Sind Sie der Graf von Luxemburg?' ('Are You the Count from Luxembourg?'), which encapsulated the anti-zeitgeist as only Schlager could. Granted, in other countries there were those who fiddled while Rome burned – UK audiences at this time were enchanted by Des O'Connor crooning hits like '1-2-3 O'Leary' and 'Dick-a-Dum-Dum'. But in West Germany, pop whimsy seemed, to an angry, dawning new generation, to be not innocent but complicit.

Take Heino, from whom it could plausibly be believed the word 'heinous' is derived. Born Heinz Georg Kramm in 1938, Heino was first attracted to music by the strains of the accordion, an instrument which he practised in Düsseldorf restaurants. Signed up in 1965, he was an immediate, if improbable, success. His first single sold a hundred thousand copies and the follow-up, 'Wenn die bunten Fahnen weh'n', went gold. Since then, he has never looked back: his sales in Germany exceed those of the Beatles, and he is regarded as a cherished cultural institution by the *Spiesser*, young and old, and as a figure of more ironic worship by others; Heino took out a restraining order against the singer Norbert Hähnel after he opened for the band Die Toten Hosen with a parody of the veteran Schlager star, 'Der Wahre Heino' ('the true Heino'), in 1984. He was eminently imitable. With his dark, rectangular shades, 1970s catalogue polyester garb and helmet-like clamp of blond hair, Heino cut a figure that was so straight, so anaemic, it was outright alien – the MOR Man Who Fell to Earth. Indeed, there is a cult, calling themselves the Cosmic Order of Heino, who believe that benevolent aliens inserted a chip into the singer's brain enabling him to act for the betterment of humankind.

It is easy to see why this überstar could be regarded as überkitsch, a pricelessly garish, Eurovision antique. It is unironically disturbing, however, that he chose in 1973 to record a version of 'Schwarzbraun ist die Hazelnuss' ('Black and Brown Is the Hazelnut'), a nineteenth-century German folk song which was revived in the twentieth century and became a very popular Hitler Youth anthem. As well as the hazelnut, black and brown were the colours of the National Socialist Party, the colours which the song's protagonist hints that his *Mädchen* should sport if she wishes to be his girl. His version of the song was a great favourite with neo-Nazis and, in South Africa, pro-apartheid Afrikaaners. That this banjo-soaked arrangement, backed with a screeching choir of schoolchildren, should have been a huge hit speaks sinister volumes about large swathes of the record-buying public in West Germany in the early 1970s.

In fact, Schlager was not absolutely nationally and racially pure and, as with the German pop scene in general, it reflected a significant undercurrent of internationalism and exchange from a country with a surprisingly large pan-European population. Many of the Schlager stars were not German-born, such as the 1971 Eurovision Song Contest winner, Greek-born Vicky Leandros.

Prior to joining Abba, Agnetha Fältskog released several singles sung in German and targeted directly at the Schlager market, including 1968's 'Señor Gonzales' and 'Fragezeichen mag ich nicht' (1970). Nor could it be said that every pop singer was an apolitical airhead. Katja Ebstein represented Germany in the 1970 Eurovision Song Contest with 'Wunder gibt es immer wieder', but used her fame as a platform for political activism – she was a member of the 1968 student movement and was arrested in the eighties while taking part in a blockade of an American nuclear-weapons depot in Germany. It's further worth pointing out that Schlager did not exercise blanket dominance over West German radio – it coexisted alongside surprise interventions in the charts from the likes of Leonard Cohen, even Frank Zappa.

Certainly, West Germany did not remain untouched, or its youth unaffected, by the import of rock 'n' roll, with a similar ensuing moral panic as in the USA and the UK, as horror mounted at the apparent unbridled sexual liberation of a new generation affluent and confident enough to engage in unbridled hip-swinging and gratuitous consumption. In 1956, the *Berliner Zeitung* described the new music as 'nonculture', while elsewhere concern was expressed that young females in particular were dancing like 'wild barbarians in ecstasy'. Artists like Peter Kraus attempted a sanitised, homegrown teen-pop version of the new craze.

Even prior to rock 'n' roll, there was fomentation. The Federal Republic's policy of seeking to rearm, especially in the context of the Cold War, saw thirty thousand young people turn out for a peace march in Essen in May 1952. The police moved in to break up the march, and as they did so, a twenty-one-year-old demonstrator called Philipp Müller was shot dead. This wasn't to prove the catalyst for wider protest, however, and, without any articulate and active youth culture yet in place, both the media and authorities were able with remarkable ease to absolve the police, with *Die Welt* even going so far as to blame 'communists' for firing the shots.

The rise of rock 'n' roll led to a series of what became known as *Halbstarke* (beatnik) riots, which took place not just in West Germany but also Austria and Switzerland during the 1950s. These often followed screenings of films featuring James Dean and Bill Haley and the Comets, and were very similar to the sort of disturbances that occurred in the UK when the same films were screened, when not only were cinema seats ripped up but also, according to a disgusted *Melody Maker* news report, flower beds trampled in Croydon. There were further riots in 1962 in Schwabing, lasting days, following an attempt by police to halt a jazz concert which had overrun its curfew time.

For those peaceable young musicians who simply wished to make a career for themselves, or were looking for a place to earn their spurs, jazz was a strong option in postwar Germany – a pre-existing style which in an implicit, non-tubthumping way carried with it all the values desirable for progressives looking to take their place in the new Federal Republic. It was in keeping with the new friendship with America, but also a music that spoke of freedom and of sympathy with the non-Aryan, in which you could be as open and modern as you pleased – in theory. In reality, young German jazz bands were straitjacketed by conformist expectations from all sides. 'The jazz scene was very conservative; you played what you were asked to play – traditional, standard jazz,' said drummer Christian Burchard. Free jazz would detonate the shackles of the genre worldwide, with figures like Albert Ayler and Pharoah Sanders blazing a trail taken up by a more ambitious generation of German players.

Another option was simply to do as everyone else was doing in the early sixties and imitate the Beatles. With the rise of the Fab Four, an Anglophilia swept the German music scene, with England regarded as the *Beatmütterland*. Groups such as the Lords and Cavern Beat slavishly attempted to learn by rote the smart, elastic changes instigated by Lennon and McCartney, imitate their look and even try to get down pat their Scouse-tinged singing accents. Young German musicians would accost visiting UK beat groups of the day at concerts and try to scavenge tips off them as to how to perfect German beat-music replicas of their own. Venues like the Star Club and the Top Ten Club in Hamburg played host to this new beat invasion – Hamburg had, of course, been where the Beatles themselves had initiated their legend, if not yet made their name.

The further down south you went in West Germany, however, the more it was a different story. Much depended on whether you were playing to British or American GIs stationed in the country, whose tastes dictated the bill of fare in the concert halls, and who were catered to by overseas radio stations enjoyed by young Germans also. Groups like Xhol Caravan originated as soul covers bands, but this was not always to the taste of the American soldiers – some German bands found themselves pelted with rotten eggs for playing the music of black artists, with the GIs racially divided between lovers of country and western and those of Stax and Motown.

The trajectory of the counterculture in West Germany was, in many ways, very similar to that in the UK, America and much of Europe – the initial, rude stirrings of rock 'n' roll, anti-nuclear and civil-rights protests and, in the late sixties, student revolt. All of this took place against the backdrop of improving economic conditions, about which the likes of Herbert Marcuse felt ambivalent at best – surely the Coca-Cola creature comforts of capitalism merely sated and neutralised the proletariat? So they did – but as the historian Robert V. Daniels observed, 'Revolution is most likely to occur not when a society is in a state of hopelessness but when it is developing dynamically and enjoying rising expectations. It then experiences frustration and outrage as social and economic advance encounters obstinacy and entrenched government or custom.' So it was across the Western world, not least in consumerist West Germany.

Salvation for the student revolutionaries, however, lay not in any domestic music they could yet divine but a foreign variety: the explicitly dissenting sixties rock music emanating from the UK and America – the Beatles, the Stones, Dylan and Frank Zappa's Mothers of Invention. Although the older, intellectual leaders of the 'extraparliamentary opposition' among West German leftists were suspicious of rock's decadent tendencies and doubted the capacity of its shaggy, drug-addled followers for the rigour of revolutionary action, it was beloved by students who considered it somehow integral to the overthrow of the state and the freeing of the younger generation from the shackles still imposed on society by the Altnazis. This was encapsulated in a 1970 poem by Günter Herburger entitled 'The End of the Nazi Era', in which Mick Jagger was imagined as an avenging angel come to collapse at last the still-upright pillars of the past, and to do so on the site that rallied youth to far less utopian ends in the 1930s:

> When the Rolling Stones, in the rubble
> On the grounds of the Nuremberg Party days
> Finally begin to play and Mick Jagger
> Before one hundred thousand German students
> Sitting in flowers and sucking on grass . . .
>
> And in the mega-amplifiers, a singing
> Mick Jagger eats photos of Hitler and Hess . . .

In the mid-seventies, however, when it became clear how little chance the scenario of this poem had of coming to pass, thinkers like Rolf Dieter Brinkmann formally renounced such conventional, mega-rock music, disillusioned by its commercialism, its hedonism and its commodification. 'Sister Morphine, I get no satisfaction, let's spend the night together, and other melodies have been driven into the bodies of you and me, simply by a bunch of pop singers . . . who say a bunch of crap in discotheques around the world which resemble gas chambers.' And so Mick Jagger, who was most probably unaware of his status in certain febrile intellectual circles as a risen, then fallen messiah, was reduced from the scourge of the Nazis to the present-day handmaiden of fascism.

As naïve and overheated as such intensity of feeling might seem today, there was an additional edge to the German counterculture of the 1960s. These were not impoverished or underprivileged youth; quite the contrary. As one young woman told the writer Gitta Sereny during the 1960s, 'in West Germany, young people get everything on a silver platter'. Perhaps, however, this was out of guilt for the other things the elders were withholding from their offspring. Nothing was taught about history post-1933 in most schools, and at most homes the topic was never broached. For those West Germans who had reached adulthood prior to and during the war, those who survived would for the most part have been happy to shop, dine, garden, work, play and worship their way to their graves without ever making reference to the 1933–45 period. A fog of silence had settled nicely over the 1950s. However, thanks to the determined efforts of a minority of prosecutors, by the 1960s Nazi war crimes made their way to the top of the news agenda. Between 1963 and 1965, the 'Auschwitz trials' saw twenty-three men, mostly SS members, go on trial in Frankfurt, with some 273 witnesses called to testify to their atrocities. At last, this represented the beginnings of a public reckoning and an acknowledgement of responsibility on the part of the German people for the Nazi era, challenging the persistent myth that they had been captives of a clique of madmen operating in their name without their knowledge or consent. The first large-scale psychoanalytical study of the denial of postwar West Germans was published: Alexander and Margarete Mitscherlich's *Die Unfähigkeit zu Trauern* ('The Inability to Mourn'), which noted the astonishing lack of guilt and shame they felt.

As the filmmaker Margaretha von Trotta put it, 'We felt that there was a past of which we were guilty as a nation but which we weren't told about at school. If you asked questions, you didn't get answers.' And so, for Germans joining their American and European brothers and sisters in revolt, the rebellion was domestic as well as international – and unique in its totality. As the historian Tony Judt said, 'If ever there was a generation whose rebellion really was grounded in the rejection of everything their parents represented – everything: national pride, Nazism, money, the West, peace, stability, law and democracy – it was "Hitler's children", the West German radicals of the sixties.' Their anti-Vietnam stance was exacerbated by the sense that in their own way, their own parents, their own country had been culturally invaded by the Americans, albeit with the benefit of Marshall Plan dollars rather than bombs and napalm. 'The Yanks have colonised our subconscious,' complains a character in Wim Wenders's 1976 film *Kings of the Road*. They saw now why their parents had taken refuge in hard work, material gain, and how they had embraced the American dream so willingly, as a means of repressing the German nightmare which they had both perpetrated and endured.

The reaction of the young was paradoxical, however. On the one hand, they baulked at the repressive, neo-Prussian conservatism of the Adenauer regime, against dominant, institutional modes of repression, be they crackdowns on demonstrations or tabloid newspapers disseminating reactionary bilge to offset the growing tide of countercultural dissent. However, it was clear, up close to those young people in revolt, that all the fight had gone from their parents' generation; that they were, for all their industriousness and outward respectability, cowed and fearful of the shadows of the past. When young people scuffled, chanted, cursed the imperialists or even, in extreme cases, perpetrated acts of terrorism against property (and later citizens), it was as if they were reproachfully demonstrating to their elders a spirit of combativeness and resistance that had been wholly lacking in the German people of the 1930s and '40s; the very willingness with which they had been mobilised militarily indicated not their strength but their submissiveness. Although the wartime generation were largely unable to bring themselves to atone for, even acknowledge Germany's war crimes, this was not necessarily born out of stereotypical arrogance or sneering, strutting Teutonic pride but rather a profound lack of self-esteem; a feeling that any sense of national identity had been wiped out, along with any sense of sustaining myth or memory.

In 1961, the Sozialistische Deutsche Studentenbund – the Socialist German Student Union, founded in 1946 – was expelled from the SPD, the Social Democratic Party of West Germany. The new consensual brand of politics in West Germany meant that young people in particular felt they had no political or ideological choices. This was exacerbated when the SPD and the Christian Democratic Union joined parliamentary forces, united in a policy of rearmament. Having nowhere to go, they became instrumental in a new, outsider political organisation, the Außerparlamentarische Opposition (APO), and it was this that would form the basis for the student movements in Germany of the 1960s, which would eventually have such a bearing on youth culture and intersect with both Krautrock and, later, the terrorist movements.

No experiments? Yes, experiments. Drawing on Fluxus-style ideas of active intervention (sit-ins, demonstrations, a refusal to accept hierarchical norms), as well as a broader identity politics in which gay rights and sexual liberation were high on the agenda, the antics of the APO were not to the taste of the older guard. As one professor of Islamic Studies at the University of Hamburg remarked to demonstrating students, 'You all belong in concentration camps.' The professor had been a member of Hitler's brownshirts, one of the many reinstated following the failure of denazification. And therein lay the problem. The university establishment had undergone no process of postwar regeneration; its prewar status and privileges were preserved, its courses were fusty and antiquated, its hierarchy and structures were inflexible.

In common with other Western countries, meanwhile, there was a rise in the use of drugs in West Germany throughout the 1960s, not merely as an option for recreation and relaxation but as a culture in its own right. The German hippies, or *Gammler* as they were known, were the focus of media attention and consternation from the mid-sixties onwards, with *Der Spiegel* running a cover feature on them in 1966. They could be found in the seedier, more bohemian quarters of most major German cities, from the Reeperbahn in Hamburg to Kurfürstendamm in Berlin. It perturbed their elders that the *Gammler* rejected alcohol, the traditional, legitimate, bourgeois drug of laughter and forgetting, in favour of hash and other such Eastern options, or worse, LSD. It perturbed them also that they were looking to alter their minds with a view to raising their consciousness, as raised consciousness meant raising issues which had lain dormant since the 1940s. Bernward Vesper, son of the Nazi poet Will Vesper, put it best in his book *Die Reise* ('The Trip'): 'We have been anaesthetised since our childhoods. Drugs tear the veil of reality, wake us, make us alive, and make us conscious of our situation for the first time.'

The *Gammler* were looking to do more than get high; they presented a critique of the consumer society their guilty parents had laboured hard to bequeath them, as well as the work ethic required to maintain it. They were dropouts who refused to take their place in a capitalist system which presented itself as the sole alternative if they wished to get on. Their own consumption of narcotics was an alternative to mind-numbing, status-seeking consumerism. The drugs were acquired via American soldiers or Turkish *Gastarbeiter*, or simply by hitting the well-trodden hippie trail, but certainly, by the late 1960s, there was an ever-increasing traffic of narcotics flowing through West Germany. All of this was in advance of Krautrock, but it meant that there was a pre-existing group of longhairs, dissenters and altered minds who would enable the cognitive framework in which the music was made, and received. Growing sections of the country's youth were perfumed with the heavy toxicity of the counterculture.

The response to this insolence, manifested in beat music, politics, drugs and an aversion to the short back and sides, was brutal. 2 June 1967 saw the shooting of Benno Ohnesorg, a twenty-six-year-old German literature student, during the demonstrations that greeted the state visit of the Shah of Iran, whom the New Left regarded as repressive. Following the dispersal of demonstrators, Ohnesorg was shot dead by a plain-clothes policeman, Karl-Heinz Kurras (who ironically later turned out to be a Stasi spy), who was twice cleared of all charges brought against him. This only bolstered the suspicion that as far as the authorities were concerned, insubordinate hippies were all fair game. This event – another apparent act of state-sanctioned violence, which led to the formation of newer, more militant, eventually terrorist factions – had a pivotal, birthing effect at the moment new German music was just beginning to emerge and take shape.

1968 was, as across the world, violent and fateful in West Germany. The gap between the *Spiesser*, swaying in vacuous, mildly inebriated time to the Schlager hits of the day, and the students now tearing into the fabric of bourgeois life was conspicuous; it was hard not to take sides. Feelings of wistfulness among the older generation for the Nazi era were dying hard: a poll in 1968 revealed that while only a tiny number of people desired the restoration of a Hitler-style Reich, fifty per cent of the West German population believed that Naziism was 'a good idea badly executed'. Astonishingly, this was a higher percentage than when the same question had been put in the late 1940s. *Bild*, the Axel Springer-owned tabloid, a thinner, terser equivalent of the *Sun*, stoked moral panic at the feral, lefty longhairs now running amok in German society, with headlines such as 'STOP THE TERROR OF THE YOUNG REDS NOW!' In 1968, Rudi Dutschke, a former East German dissident projected as one of the leading activists of the West German anti-establishment New Left, a figure parallel to Daniel Cohn-Bendit, was accosted in a Berlin street and shot in the head by one Josef Bachmann, a house painter.

Bachmann explained in court by way of mitigation that he was on a mission to 'kill a dirty communist'. His lawyers argued that he had merely been a tool of 'more powerful forces'. Bachmann was a disturbed individual who lived alone in his apartment with only a poster of Adolf Hitler. He was also an avid *Bild* reader, and had taken to heart the depiction of Dutschke in the Springer press as a dangerous fanatic who needed to be dispensed with by 'self-help', as the paper put it. Bachmann was sentenced to just seven years, though he committed suicide in 1970, having engaged in correspondence, possibly remorseful, with Dutschke, who survived the assassination attempt but never recovered from his injuries. Dutschke died in 1979, drowning in a bath following an epileptic seizure. *Bild* blithely dismissed the pair of them as lunatics from opposite ends of the political spectrum and got on with business as usual.

During the demonstration at which Ohnesorg was killed, one Fritz Teufel was arrested and held until the following December, with students staging a hunger strike in protest. He had become a member of Kommune 1, founded in early 1967 in West Berlin. Kommune 1 was a further development from the APO, its fluid, open-plan living arrangements a specific reproach to the suburban model of small-scale, tight-knit domesticity, confined domestic cells of social conservatism, even fascism. Kommune 1's core members considered the very idea of the family, with its restriction on personal development, to be inherently right-wing. The personal was deemed political. Privacy was eschewed – the bathrooms had no doors and nudity was considered a political statement, one of absolute freedom and lack of sexual inhibition but, they claimed, also one of solidarity with the naked bodies of concentration-camp victims. Kommune 1 set up in the vacant apartments of a series of authors, including Hans Magnus Enzensberger. Although the group espoused Situationist ideals and had an anarchistic scorn for such concepts as property rights, they had a definite leader in the figure of Dieter Kunzelmann and charged to be interviewed or photographed.

Kommune 1 began to engage in acts of provocation that were more mischievous than terrorist, including the 'pudding assassination', a thwarted attempt to hurl pudding, yoghurt and flour at US Vice President Hubert Humphrey during a state visit in 1967. Hilarity, publicity and moral panic ensued (they were dubbed the 'communards of horror' by the right-wing press, who also insisted that the Vice President's life would have been threatened by an assault of cake ingredients). This was abetted by press conferences and a widely circulated photo of naked Kommune 1 members assuming the position against a wall.

This was the height of the group's political notoriety – by 1969, they had abandoned pranksterism in favour of more direct action against property, issuing flyers calling for the firebombing of department stores, and its various members were subsequently accused and convicted of terrorist activities, including attempting to bomb US President Nixon's motorcade. (An incendiary device had been planted at their commune by one Peter Urbach, a police spy, later found to have supplied a bomb intended to blow up a Jewish community centre in Berlin in 1969.) From the remnants of Kommune 1 would also emerge the Baader–Meinhof group or Red Army Faction (RAF). What was left of the Kommune was invaded and trashed by a gang of rockers in late 1969, as if to symbolise the disillusionment of the end of the decade. Kunzelmann was now lost to heroin addiction.

However, Kommune 1 intersected with rock history, not only when Jimi Hendrix dropped by to visit, but when they were joined by Uschi Obermaier, a model from Munich. She had lived with Amon Düül in their Munich commune, but soon she moved in with the communards of Kommune 1, in their single bedroom.

Countercultural forces were beginning to merge. The International Essener Songtage, a festival of 'politics, art and pop', was held in 1968, bearing the ominous subtitle '*Deutschland Erwacht*' ('Germany Awakens'), a suitably cheeky co-option of a nineteenth-century German nationalist motto, and featuring Floh de Cologne, Tangerine Dream and Guru Guru in its line-up. This would be an entirely different sort of awakening, albeit of German origin. The authorities showed their determination to suppress any dawning consciousness which they felt threatened the state. At the Songtage, Floh de Cologne had completed their set by exhorting the audience to squat and to steal food, as well as showing pornographic slides. They found themselves facing charges of blasphemy and procuration. This was also the year in which the Bundestag passed Emergency Laws designed to curtail civil rights in the event of what they deemed 'crisis' situations, such as revolution, whose petroleum smell was still in the air. This was the cue for massive protests across the Federal Republic.

The short-lived Zodiak Free Arts Lab, founded in Berlin in late 1968, was another example of music (or anti-music), politics and art co-existing in the same space. Its monochrome walls played host to jazz extremists like Peter Brötzmann and Alfred Harth, as well as to the younger members of the 'Berlin School', like the fledgling Tangerine Dream and Agitation Free. It was a sign that the air was alive with a new, electric noise, whose psychedelic brutalism blasted the writing on the wall for old-style singer/songwriter events like the soon-to-be-defunct Burg Waldeck festival. The volume had gone up several notches. The Arts Lab, however, quickly found itself under the cosh of the Berlin police – drug raids were frequent, and this eventually led the revolutionary group Zentralrat der Umherschweifenden Haschrebellen ('The Central Committee of Roaming Hash Rebels'), whose members included future terrorist 'Bommi' Baumann, to set fire to a police car in protest.

As elsewhere in the West, the idealistic fervour of the German counterculture petered out as its members variously grew up, sobered up, split up, succumbed to drug addiction, became disillusioned, or simply submitted to the need for a comfortable existence untroubled by the persistent attentions of the police. Although Chancellor Willy Brandt's administration was considered benign and conciliatory, particularly when he made a public and Nobel Prize-winning gesture of penitence, travelling to Warsaw and falling to his knees in front of the Warsaw Ghetto, it was his administration which in 1972 also introduced new statutory measures, the so-called Radikalenerlass or Anti-Radical Decree, in which no one with sympathies for far left-wing causes, in particular the Red Army Faction, would be allowed to hold public-sector jobs. The move, dubious and opposed as it was, succeeded in sapping the last energy from the tired Extraparliamentary Opposition, who were forced to disband.

As their popular support withered, the remainder of those sympathetic to the Baader–Meinhof axis hardened in both their attitudes and activities. The state often appeared at once heavy-handed and incompetent in their dealings with terrorism, as demonstrated in their desperately poor handling of the capture and eventual killing of Israeli hostages during the 1972 Munich Olympics. The terrorists' outrages culminated in the storming of the West German Embassy in Stockholm; the RAF ringleaders were imprisoned. Ulrike Meinhof committed suicide in 1976, Andreas Baader and Gudrun Ensslin in 1977.

Krautrock ran in tandem with this overall rise and fall of the far left. It, too, was ignited by the events of 1968; it too was pretty much defunct by 1977. But how much did they really have in common?

The Baader–Meinhof axis exerted a Bonnie and Clyde-like frisson of fascination then, and still does now. Their superficial, iconic appeal has a rock 'n' roll air. All that youthful, violent, gun-toting energy, and who's to know exactly what they got up to when they were shacked up between bank robberies or international outrages? A tag cloud puffs up in which the words 'revolutionary', 'liberation' and 'sexual' bounce tantalisingly up and down.

Gerhard Richter's cycle of paintings based on documentary photographs of the group, which he produced in 1988, only helped to ingrain them as valid fixtures in German culture. There was something romantic and reproachful about the rash of supposed suicides which brought the RAF to both their climax and their demise in 1977. 'The deaths of the terrorists, and the related events both before and after, stand for a horror that distressed me and has haunted me as unfinished business ever since, despite all my efforts to suppress it,' said Richter. Their blood sacrifice felt to some as if it were the ultimate countercultural gesture. In that respect, was it not hand in hand with the radicalism of Krautrock? Were they even in cahoots?

There are elements of wishful thinking at work here. In 2012, Courtney Taylor-Taylor of the group the Dandy Warhols produced a graphic novel, with Jim Rugg, entitled *One Model Nation*. It tells the story of a group, a Krautrock hybrid, who dress in buttoned, militaristic shirts and dark ties, use drum kits but with spanners in lieu of sticks, and operate giant reel-to-reel technology and keyboards as well as guitars. They resemble Kraftwerk more than any other group, though their hairdos belong more to the late nineties than the late seventies. They consort with David Bowie at parties but also with Andreas Baader, and, against the cartoon backdrop of a hyper-real Germany (it so happens that Karl Bartos, formerly of Kraftwerk, acted as an informal adviser in this respect), they play out what the author describes as a 'classic Greek hero's journey' narrative structure involving shoot-outs and explosions.

Another representation of Krautrock in popular culture is in the Coen Brothers film *The Big Lebowski*, which features a group entitled Autobahn. On the cover of their album, entitled *Nagelbett* ('Nail Bed'), the three, fronted by Peter Stormare as Uli Kunkel, aka Karl Hungus, pose in red shirts that unmistakably refer to Kraftwerk's *The Man-Machine*. When not producing affected 'Techno-Pop', the trio moonlight as somewhat risible hooded and black-clad nihilists who try to terrorise Jeff Bridges's Dude by introducing a marmot into his tub as he bathes. 'We believe in nothing, Lebowski, nothing,' they jeer in fey, Teutonic tones as they further threaten to return the next day and cut off his 'Johnson'. The Coen Brothers are generally at the clever end of Hollywood when it comes to hip referentiality, and *The Big Lebowski* is one of their greatest, funniest movies, but they betray a bit of age, conservatism and possibly the mildest, lightest touch of Europhobia in this broad parody, as well as some peculiar ideas about the politics of Kraftwerk. Their Euro-ness makes them utterly antithetical to the Dude, who projects all the shambling, easy-going values of ageing hippie America, in contrast to the neurotic, morally dubious modernistic stiffness of 'Autobahn'.

In reality it is true that there were some brushes between the loose affiliations and fleeting acquaintances of the radical political organisations and the communes that were home to the Krautrock groups. Peripheral members may have crashed overnight on the same premises. There are common figures such as Uwe Nettelbeck, who put together Faust but prior to that had worked for the same magazine as Ulrike Meinhof in her days as a journalist. Certainly, both Krautrock and the RAF belonged to the same spectrum of youthful disaffection, were both rooted in the same disillusion and disdain. The idea, however, that they formed any sort of alliance is a fiction. 'We never moved in the same circles as those with extremists, certainly not terrorists – the aggression in our music did not have the same direction of impact,' said Can's Irmin Schmidt. Ralf Hütter of Kraftwerk would never have thought of cutting off anybody's Johnson.

Like most ordinary progressive liberals, German music groups of the day were not a part of any groundswell of support for the RAF, who, once they had abandoned their initial policy of 'property, not people' and gone in for outright carnage, were regarded as beyond the pale by the vast majority of progressives, as well as the bourgeois. In the initial spirit of insurrectionary bravado of 1977, German punk groups declared their support for the RAF, while in the UK, Joe Strummer of the Clash naïvely wore an RAF T-shirt. The Krautrock generation did not, however. Indeed, retrospectively, it seems insulting that they should have felt obliged to disavow the organisation, as it would be to ask, say, U2 if they were in sympathy with the IRA.

However, that need to disavow arose in part from the fact that most of the new German groups tended, in the eyes of a watchful and paranoid police force, to fit the profile of terrorists. To wear your hair long and to dress in a neo-hippie style in West Germany in the late 1960s and early 1970s was to ostracise yourself from respectable, law-abiding, mainstream society, far more so than in the UK, as Krautrock groups discovered to their surprise when they first toured in Britain. Who was to say that you weren't 'one of them'? You certainly resembled 'one of them'.

Groups like Amon Düül (both 1 and 2) found themselves victim to low-level, stop and search-style harassment. In December 1971, the discovery of an unwashed car left absentmindedly in a town centre and traced back to them had led to the arrest of one of their number on suspicion of being part of a terrorist network. Hans-Joachim Irmler, meanwhile, recalls the time when the door to his room at the group's commune was kicked in and an armed policeman pointed a machine gun in his face, screaming at him to stand up and put his hands against the wall. He looked outside the window to see the converted schoolhouse ringed with more police, all similarly armed to the hilt, their guns trained on the building. He had been out driving with his girlfriend, who happened to bear a strong resemblance to the fugitive terrorist Gudrun Ensslin – certainly so far as the suspicious, squinting owner of a garage was concerned when they stopped there for petrol.

With a tabloid press led by *Bild* baying in the background, mischievously willing to tar all hirsute, free-thinking, commune-dwelling types with the same brush as a threat to the state, the distinction between aesthetic radicals and those who were plotting to kidnap businessmen or blow up aeroplanes was somewhat blurred.

As for the RAF themselves, they can appear to shimmer with revolutionary mythos in the blur of Richter's portraits, but sharpen the focus on their actual activities and they are revealed as psychotic incompetents, their often farcical ineptitude only matched by that of the West German authorities: one of their members was tried and sentenced in court, only to walk free from the building after he managed to swap places with a friend who was also heavily bearded; when the authorities realised their mistake, they had no choice but to let the friend go. What's more, the record collections of the revolutionaries don't stand up to scrutiny. When investigators came to clear out Andreas Baader's prison cell, they found no LPs by Kraftwerk, Can, Neu!, Ash Ra Tempel or Cluster. They did, however, find on his record player an album by Eric Clapton, his nondescript 1975 blues-rock effort *There's One in Every Crowd.* If Baader was evil, then, *pace* Hannah Arendt, here was a banal detail.

Krautrock and movements like the RAF certainly bore a sartorial resemblance to one another. Both had youth appeal – a 1971 poll revealed one in five West Germans under the age of thirty to harbour sympathy for the RAF and its members. Ironically, the likes of Cluster and Neu! would have killed for similar figures like that back then. But only metaphorically. Krautrock was not that sort of extremism. Rather, it represented the other, more covert but enduring extremism operating in West Germany in its day.

Much as the Baader–Meinhof group represented a small minority who went a great deal further than the vast majority of restive postwar youth in revolting against the repressive, Altnazi-ridden powers in 1960s Germany, so the likes of Can, Neu!, Kraftwerk and Faust were among a very few groups, all affected by the same cultural circumstances, who went to sonic extremes. The Baader–Meinhof group still generate a frisson as the most widely recognised symbols of postwar West German rebellion, remaining the subject of cinematic and iconic fascination, despite the fact that they are utterly spent as a credible political, moral, ongoing force. The Krautrock groups fall short of the recognition levels afforded to the terrorists, and yet their own music, which made few headlines in its day, has made for a far more enduring, fertile and universal legacy.

Krautrock was dissociated from the dull dissipation that enervated German youth in the 1970s; nor was it part of the broader feeling of hangover which clouded rock music in general in the aftermath of the 1960s. This was the time when it was just coming into its own. Lodged in the physical spaces allowed them, from old schoolhouses to galleries and forest retreats, the musicians carried on in a spirit of fresh innovation which ran counter to the bluesy, overwrought, decadent mood of their Anglo-American counterparts, from Zeppelin to the Southern rockers, whose music, albeit sensational, was becoming increasingly cumbersome, bloated and irrelevant with each passing year – a victim in many ways of its own commercial success and the impact that had on the lives of its makers. The Krautrockers were, in a sense, the beneficiaries of general apathy and indifference. It helped that, relatively ignored and untroubled by the industrial machinery of the music business, they had to fall back on their own resources, build their own machines. Krautrock was a product of its own times, yet way ahead of them.

Back, however, to the late 1960s, to a West Germany at its own particular gates of dawn, and, specifically, a disparate handful of musicians, unconscious of each other, of the word 'Krautrock', all of them in search of other colours on the spectrum beyond the blues, fed up of the Fab Four, past jazz, ignited by psychedelia, by the new electricity in the air, revelling in the uncertainty of youth revolution, seeking and discovering new ways of living, being and playing, in search of a musical voice that would ultimately speak louder than words. In Hamburg, Düsseldorf, Cologne, Berlin – but first, to Munich, and the first stirrings and most significant evolutionary steps of a new music from the primordial soup of the 1960s Commune movement.

1 Amon Düül and the Rise from the Communes

> 'The fifties and sixties were the time when everything was possible. Everything was hope. The major disappointments of technology had yet to happen. These days, I feel a lot of despondency. I think it's an industrial thing and a media thing. You're sitting in front of the television, this boombox and you're dependent, you can't switch it off. You feel helpless, unable to influence anything. But you can.'
>
> John Weinzierl, Amon Düül 2

Wearing a group T-shirt for recognition purposes, John Weinzierl greets me at a small station just outside Munich. It's the culmination of a lengthy rail journey from Hamburg, much of it spent in the amiable company of a young German student who, though a music fan (of the Red Hot Chili Peppers in particular), has, like so many of his young countrymen, never heard of any of the major names of the so-called Krautrock movement, certainly not Amon Düül, whose name I write for him on a napkin, double umlauts stressed and followed by an emphatically underscored 2, lest he confuse them with the 'original' Amon Düül. He politely promises to check them out.

Amon Düül are, for many, the Alpha if not the Omega of Krautrock – a term Weinzierl despises, will not entertain, pronounces with venomous spittle, regards as 'insulting' and those who bandy it as 'criminal'. A precondition of the interview is that I resist any attachment of the term to the group, which he is happier to label 'psychedelic underground'. However, it can sometimes seem as if Amon Düül, or AD 2, never happened. Their ideals and theories, which Weinzierl expounds over pints of wheat beer on an unfeasibly warm afternoon in a pretty, idyllic Munich *strasse* close to his new apartment, would strike postmodern, post-everything minds of the twenty-first century as hopelessly pre-Aquarian – he talks of Atlantis, of the descending phases of humanity, of the horrors of the mechanised age, of the alienation that has resulted from our refusal to sustain the example of communal living, with a conviction undimmed over forty years of achievement, disillusionment and revival. It's tempting to think not so much that he's lost the plot but that he's sticking to a plot that ran aground decades ago, before our present age of sophisticated fatalism. And yet their website's mission statement speaks with jolting pertinence in an age in which so many are transfixed by a matrix of iPads, phones and computer screens of 'the vision to escape the cosmic loop of stupid recurrence . . . and still free minds before they could be hypnotised into fatal despondency'.

The first incarnation of Amon Düül were barely musicians as such but a commune, who gathered first at drummer Peter Leopold's apartment in Klopstockstrasse, Munich, in 1967 before moving on to larger quarters in Prinzregentenplatz (from the balcony of which Hitler had once delivered a speech) as the commune gathered momentum and new members. Central to the commune were Leopold, his brother Ulrich, and violinist/guitarist Chris Karrer.

Karrer had followed the conventional rock 'n' roll trajectory, from blue suede to Beatles, before exposure to John Coltrane led him to immerse himself in free jazz, which made rock seem stunted and underdeveloped by comparison. However, when he first encountered Jimi Hendrix in 1967 playing at a small Munich venue, he was struck first by the number of girls at the concert, in contrast to the all-male world of free-jazz audiences, and then more forcefully by the firestorm of Hendrix's playing, after which he went home and smashed his jazz collection to pieces. Duly ignited, he chanced on the Amon Düül commune, which would later grow into an extended community of partners, sisters, children and assorted domestic animals.

Munich was one of the focal points of the German student revolts of the late 1960s; the young and disaffected would gather at such focal points as the Trikont Cafe, where piles of leaflets urged insurrection. 'The big revolution started in Munich,' says Weinzierl. 'The student thing took off here, coming together with Berlin. The K1 was based in Berlin and strictly political. People like Fritz Teufel and Kunzelmann were leading members of the commune. Whenever we were playing in Berlin, we used to stay with them. In the early days we never needed hotels when we were touring, 'cause we used to stay with one of the many communes spread all over Germany. Later Uschi Obermaier joined the K1. Not very long later the K1 ended.'

Chris Karrer found the Berlin commune to be a great deal less gentle than Munich. He recalled the time a group of rockers gatecrashed the place armed with knives and guns, turned the record player up to maximum volume and proceeded to punch out the protesting commune members, including Karrer himself, who suffered broken teeth. It turned out that another political party, who lived in the building and were also its landlords, wanted to attract lodgers prepared to pay a higher rent and, rather than abide by the formalities of due notice, had sent the rockers up to evict the commune.

'We were in the [Munich] commune and going to the university and academies the whole time, playing at teach-ins. It wasn't intended as a way of making a successful career, to make records at that stage,' remembers Weinzierl. Instead, the pre-musical Amon Düül would turn up en masse and provide a rudimentary, tribal, rhythmical accompaniment to the burgeoning rumbles of discontent, achieved on basic wooden instruments. 'The idea was, everyone is a musician. We'd give out bongos and tambourines to the audience so that they could play along. You didn't go along to the concert and watch the band; you came to the event and you were part of it. Only the music industry made us a band.'

Weinzierl, who according to *Tanz der Lemminge*, Ingeborg Schober's biography of the group, was a 'beautiful, blond teenager' when he joined the commune/group while still a schoolboy, today looks as vigorously good for his age as most of his German musical contemporaries, uncannily resembling Larry David of *Curb Your Enthusiasm*. Only a horrendous and persistent bout of hiccoughs betrays anything but rude health. He's accompanied this afternoon by Danny Fichelscher, who has played drums on and off for Amon Düül as well as Popol Vuh. Fichelscher always cut a slightly Nosferatu-ish figure but greets me with a handshake, a gleaming eye and a torrential monologue despite being due for an urgent dentist's appointment in twenty minutes. He is keen to congratulate the French for being the first to realise the true importance of Amon Düül.

'Always for us, there were highly educated, intellectual people involved in the music – from art school – the movement, the melting between the music and the mind, of ideas, was what made it beautiful. France was very important and very good for us. In their development, they have always been people of the word, very intellectual. If you read the first critics and what they wrote about our music, it was beautiful, crazy, amazing, so good for us. If they like something, they find a good reason, with words.'

Weinzierl recalls the students from the Paris commune who dropped in, curious about their German counterparts, though, despite such attentiveness, they didn't really generate a large-scale music scene of their own, equivalent to that which was blossoming all over West Germany. But then, young Germans like Weinzierl were born into very different geocultural circumstances, first seizing on, then with equal violence rejecting, Anglo-American music as a model.

'I formed my first band, the Merseygents, when I was fourteen,' he tells me as Fichelscher whirlwinds off in a flurry of apologies towards the dentist. 'This was the way out. Then you realise, you don't want to copy this, that you have your own tradition. And because of having music lessons in school, we are able to learn about this. So our music is based on more symphonic principles. People said we played these long numbers because we were stoned and couldn't stop. They were wrong.

'I actually split from my family from school and went to Amon Düül at the age of seventeen. I didn't return to them for seven years. The way I was treated in the family, the idea was that I would come back and see them in a big car, and I did – a Cadillac. But my parents never got the message. Others did, not mine. My parents knew me from the papers. I remember one gig and seeing my mother in the audience, thinking, "Oh man, this is a bad trip . . ."'

For Weinzierl, born in 1949, although the fifties and sixties were times of great hope and expansion, he felt the full, brown-panelled joylessness of a postwar German upbringing. 'I was raised Catholic and had to pray to Mother Mary every evening in the month of May.' It wasn't exactly unmusical – his father had been a zither player, his mother a dab hand on the accordion. But this stifling soundtrack only intensified his longing for a rock 'n' roll portal to freedom.

'Our way out was hearing AFN, the American Forces radio, and Radio Luxembourg. At home, we had Badische Rundfunk, very square stuff – there were *Kunstlied* [art songs], there was Fritz Wunderlich [a famous tenor, notable for German renderings of operatic classics, who died at the age of thirty-five while on a hunting expedition] – there was only this one station, my parents always listened to this. When I was sick, my mother made me a bed in the dining room and this stuff was belting out – all this operetta stuff . . . I can't stand it today. It just felt so bad. I like classical music very much. But the minute they start singing I switch off. Years later, it so happens, I had a relationship with the daughter of Fritz Wunderlich.'

Weinzierl was at boarding school in Hohenschwangau with Jürgen Rogner, brother of future Amon Düül 2 organist Falk, sneaking out by night and driving to Munich to liaise with the other Düüls, who themselves had attended boarding school together. 'At school, the Nazis were still there. The Nazi stench. All this drill, all this bullshit, it was all still there and we rebelled against it. It wasn't what they said. But you could smell it. You could sense it about them – the discipline, just for discipline's sake.' Children, he says, asked about the war and the role of their teachers in it but found themselves fudged. 'The word "Jew" was never mentioned.'

With adolescence, however, came acute consciousness and dawning realisation. 'We were young enough to feel something higher. It wasn't like today's scene, it wasn't about ego, lots of fucking, lots of drinking, just to satisfy the ego – we wanted something better. We wanted to get out of that, and this, Amon Düül, was the result.'

Sporting long hair in 1960s West Germany didn't simply mark you out as a typical young specimen of the day but practically as an outlaw. It was not so much a case of 'swinging' as avoiding being swung for. 'It was not easy to walk around by yourself, especially with long hair,' recalls Weinzierl. 'We had to go out in numbers, eight or nine. You couldn't get served in restaurants at all. Unless after an hour of sitting there you started breaking things to get attention.'

As for America, which had seemed to be the font of material freedom in earlier, adolescent years, it was dawning on Weinzierl and his peers that it was no benign, international uncle. 'We didn't realise what it really was. People only see what they want to see. We realised that these nice guys, these nice Americans only brought their companies here so that we would eat their shit. They destroyed our food, they brought this hardcore industry.'

The very name Amon Düül ('Amon' was an Egyptian sun god, 'Düül' a variation on the word 'dyyl', coined on an album by a Canadian group entitled *Tanjet*) had been conjured up to evoke exotic, mythical connotations, rejecting both the Anglo and the German, speaking of ancient and future. 'We had to start from scratch,' says Weinzierl. 'We felt international. You have to learn English in German schools, and that's a good thing. We can talk to all our Western friends. I think a sense of German identity got lost during the war and after it. Nobody wanted to be German. When I was five years old I made a trip to Yugoslavia, the first time I had been abroad in my life. And it was then that I was shocked to learn that I was a murderer, a mass killer. People would come up to me and talk about this. "You killed sixty million people." As a young boy this was very hard to understand. So, you learn this early on. We have the burden of our fathers, which we carry, of course.'

Confusion still lingers as to the incarnations of Amon Düül, not helped by the fact that nowadays even group members themselves habitually drop the '2'. Back in 1966, according to Chris Karrer, there had been Amon Düül 0, featuring Karrer on guitar, Lothar Meid on bass and drummer Christian Burchard, an experimental jazz trio in the days prior to Karrer's Hendrix epiphany. Amon Düül 1 were the next generation, the commune in which the Leopold brothers featured strongly, particularly Ulrich, and they were given the chance to play at the Essener Songtage festival in 1967 and to make their vinyl debut. 'It was one commune. And they had an offer to come to Berlin and record an album. Then came the first Essen Song Festival. A big opportunity. Two days before this, however, there was a massive fight and the two groups didn't talk to each other.'

The precise nature of the argument that ensued is unclear; 'just some personal bullshit', says Weinzierl, and perhaps the truth is lost in ancient clouds of dope. Certainly, however, it seems that there were two Amon Düül factions – the few that could play, the large remainder who could bash bongos onstage – and it was along those lines that a split occurred. According to Chris Karrer, the libertarian conditions were hardening into something unpleasantly ideological, with 'free sex' now mandatory for the men. 'They asked me, "You haven't fucked for four weeks – are you gay, or impotent?" I had to take a woman and fuck her there on the floor, where twenty people could see.' Musical development was considered hostile to a declared ethos of amateur incompetence, while life at the commune was becoming cultic and controlled, with even the smallest purchases having to be run by the commune's 'cashier'. Renate Knaup had joined the commune following a stint as an au pair in Muswell Hill. 'It got to the point where I had to ask the others for five marks to buy a new pair of tights, because we had put all the money in one cache,' she told *Mojo*'s Andy Gill in 1997.

The recording session in Berlin, conducted by the relatively non-musical faction of Amon Düül, was a disaster. 'They couldn't even set their amps up the right way,' says Weinzierl. Peter Leopold would eventually rejoin Karrer and co. To further muddy the waters and the ears, however, a series of recordings were produced under the name 'Amon Düül' over the next few years, including *Psychedelic Underground*, *Paradieswärts Düül* and *Disaster*, all of which were derived from the 1968 sessions, considerably tidied up, it is alleged, and overdubbed by producer Peter Meisel as a cash-in. This caused considerable confusion to early lovers of the group.

'We made the big mistake of simply adding the 2 to the name,' says Weinzierl, 'and this led to the misunderstanding that it was all one thing. I'm very surprised when people take one of these rubbish albums and say it was quite good.' Lester Bangs, in a famous 1971 profile of the group, actually went so far as to lambast himself for pomposity as he recalled describing *Psychedelic Underground* for *Creem* as 'the kind of clattering "space jam" that is likely to result anytime you get a bunch of amateur musicians together with huge amps and too much dope even for them to say something musical by accident. Lots of percussion and one-note guitar.' He then admitted to owning a couple of copies of the album himself. His more affectionate, modified verdict is close to that of many towards these amateur extended jams – that if you place yourself in the correctly indulgent mood, chemically or otherwise, they are a listenable reminder of the rude clay origins of German psychedelia, like an extended, grainy, sepia-tinted old snapshot. Milestones perhaps, but not masterpieces.

At the second Essen Song Festival, the last four bands were Tangerine Dream, Pink Floyd, Amon Düül and the Nice. 'I played bass with Tangerine Dream and guitar with Amon Düül,' says Weinzierl. 'It was fantastic, a very vivid memory. Dave Anderson was playing with us, all the big bands were there – Rory Gallagher, Deep Purple, Fleetwood Mac, Free also. All the bands worked together, back then. They put their PAs together to make one giant PA. That would be impossible today because of industry shit. It was all one thing. I remember we were tripping on the day of our concert. I remember Dave Anderson going down the stairs onto the stage. It felt like half an hour of him simply going down the stairs.'

Unlike Can's Irmin Schmidt, Weinzierl always felt a closer affinity with British music. 'There are only two albums you need to buy from the twentieth century,' he asserts: '*Sergeant Pepper's Lonely Hearts Club Band* and Pink Floyd's *Piper at the Gates of Dawn*. Everything else is variations, with sugar, with milk, without.' He never felt any strong leanings towards the Grateful Dead. And yet it was they who paid Düül the ultimate, visionary compliment when they played together. 'Grateful Dead understood us. RatDog [Bob Weir and Rob Wasserman] told us, "You are not a hippie band!"'

1969 also saw the opening of a club in the bustling, lively

Leopoldstrasse called PN, run by a fellow who was two decades older than anyone in Amon Düül but who understood, tolerated and took money at the till from a new generation who were clearly steeped in something a good deal more intense than the faddy world of beat music and needed a place in which to indulge their acid-fried extremism. Talking to *The Wire*'s Edwin Pouncey in 1996, Chris Karrer recalled one particularly committed fan, a bald Russian named Anatole. 'He used to dance to our music in a very extreme fashion. Once I saw him at the front of the stage with this naked old woman and he was shoving his Vaselined finger in and out of her backside to the rhythm of the music while ringing this bell at the same time.'

The first Amon Düül 2 album proper was *Phallus Dei* ('God's Penis'), which was released following extensive gigging on the part of the new group, who sought to make a professional go of things without abandoning their founding idealism. They were signed by Siggi Loch, head of the German wing of Liberty/United Artists. Karrer, Knaup, Leopold, Weinzierl and Rogner were joined by English bassist Dave Anderson, drummer Dieter Serfas and Chris 'Shrat' Thiele on percussion and vocals.

'We believed in new ideas, communication, completely new ideas – world, tribal-based,' explains Weinzierl. 'It was about "communication", not being pop stars, but translating into proper music. It was not something like the non-musicians and the musicians. It just happened there were four of us who did play an instrument and the time came for us when we needed to make money. But we were not like the Scorpions, listening to American hard rock and copying. We didn't allow ourselves to listen to Clapton or that American or English Mickey Mouse music. It was about listening, seeing what comes, what could be done, what could be done differently – especially as we had this identity clash, as the world told us it was no good to be a German, you must not be a German, you must not go to war again. Of course, you hear this stuff and you look inside yourself, asking, "Where is my war virus? My vicious virus?" But of course it's not there.'

Phallus Dei opens with 'Kanaan' and, while impressive in its psychedelic march, it feels a little overshadowed by the influence of Pink Floyd, with its reminiscences of 'Careful with That Axe, Eugene'. Only when the pace quickens do you sense a group anxious to go places of their own. 'Dem Güten, Schönen, Waren' ('To the Good, the Beautiful, the True') is something altogether more disquieting, with Karrer's electric violin hanging high and spectral in the mix, and its mock-shamanistic, whooping vocals and the following lyric in particular:

Wir tanzten zusammen Ringelreihen
Und sangen ein wunderschönes Lied
Die jüngste fing an, nach der Mutter zu schreien
Ich durchbohrte sie sanft mit meinem Glied.

('We danced ring-a-roses together and sang a wonderful song/The youngest began to cry for her mother/I softly penetrated her with my member.')

This lyric needs – dear God, does it need – placing in context, if not in some sort of long-term quarantine. This isn't some endorsement of child abuse as a form of initiation into a new, untrammelled world of free love; the rest of the group chant disapprovingly in the following verse, calling for the execution of the gloating protagonist ('*Hänget ihn auf, den geilen Moloch!*' – 'Hang him high, the dirty Moloch!'). But who is he, exactly? Is this God, wielding his 'member', his phallus? The intimations of ritual, religious abuse are prescient, but would undoubtedly be considered too near the knuckle to be bandied about in our own times. Certainly, the song as a whole leaves the listener in no doubt that we are now in a psychedelic land of folkloric horror, far away from the gentle meadows of Donovan or the idyllic haze of the US west coast. The cover, depicting the bare twigs and crow-lined branches of a deciduous tree set black against a turbulent blue sky, certainly feels apposite.

'Luzifers Ghilom' is still less lyrically distinct, suffused with distant howls, abruptly bisected by an Indian chant, and with a general roughness that consigns it to the enigmatic mists of psychedelic antiquity. 'It comes from having no good instruments. Not the right instruments. Not to grumble but we didn't have the best instruments and we didn't give a fuck, we didn't want it to be polished so sometimes it sounds weird,' says Weinzierl. However, on the title track, filling out side two and stretching to almost twenty-one minutes, Amon Düül give the fullest indication of their provenance, range and potential. Its dank opening recalls postwar composers such as Luciano Berio, the British free improvisation group AMM and the gaudy, faded colours of some 1960s swords-and-sorcery B-movie, before the pace again quickens and it is as if the animal Düül has crawled ashore from the primordial waters of the European counterculture, slowly sprouting wings as colour spews from the skies. It messily ranges the landscape from rock to folk, from modern classical to free jazz, to the rhythms and snake-charmer pipes of Eastern music. The influence of Zappa is clear, his effortless ability to juxtapose high and low cultures, but unlike Zappa, who was always altogether too overtly smart, Amon Düül feel more magical, infernal, closer to the earth's core. When it settles into a rock jam it doesn't feel quite as essential as Can, with their premeditated restructuring of rock's very DNA, but its roughness is a virtue – there's a violent primal energy, a feeling of new worlds erupting from the old, about the way Düül regurgitate their extensive influences and musical traditions.

The album was completed in just two days, though not without some friction with its sound engineers. 'They didn't know a thing,' snorts Weinzierl. 'They were used to playing with Bavarian orchestras. They would try to tune us right down. They couldn't handle us, so they left us alone. And there was no multitracking, it was done on a shoestring. When we made *Phallus Dei*, we'd do twenty-minute tracks. If someone goofed in minute eighteen, you couldn't do an overdub, you had to start again. And we had the album completed in two days.'

Andrew Lauder, who was Liberty's head of A & R in the UK, was sufficiently intrigued to give Amon Düül a UK release – they were certainly a remarkable change from the normal fare punted to him by the German wing of the label, mostly abysmal Schlager or light MOR which, to the persistent chagrin of the Germans, he would turn down. 'Amon Düül were the first of those new groups I heard – before Kraftwerk,' he tells me. 'They'd been signed by the guys in Munich. *Phallus Dei* came as a finished album, a finished article.'

The album sold well and would prove a gateway for other German music of the era, including Can, Neu! and Kraftwerk. When Amon Düül 2 eventually toured the UK, Weinzierl was surprised and gratified by the relatively easy-going cultural climate of the country. 'When we came to England we couldn't believe it. We were allowed in hotels. You couldn't stay in hotels in Germany. It was "Hello, love!" and "Come in, love!" We thought, "What's going on here?"' They would support Roxy Music at the Greyhound, in Croydon – some double bill – and record the *Live in London* album there.

By the time of *Yeti*, their follow-up album, Amon Düül felt established, out of the water and on dry land. They were able to record on sixteen-track, though to their intense annoyance their old-school engineer Willy Schmidt insisted on recording on eight-track, to show off his abilities to make do. There was also a reconciliation of sorts with Amon Düül 1, two of whose members – Rainer Bauer and Ulrich Leopold – joined in the session that produced 'Sandoz in the Rain'. It is the cover art, however, created by Falk Rogner, that is most disquieting and enduring. It's a collage, depicting former commune member Wolfgang Krischke as the Grim Reaper, wielding a scythe against a backdrop that is part azure, part fiery orange.

Krischke had eventually sided with Amon Düül 1; however, it had been Krischke who had warned Rogner and Knaup, meeting them at the station following a break they took from the commune in the South of France, to be prepared for an interrogation for having left it without permission. He died just months after the group split, having returned to his parents' home, where, following an LSD trip, he stumbled outside into woodland and died of hypothermia. Looking hurt and sullen as he stares out of the cover of *Yeti*, Krischke himself is the *Schnitter*, the Reaper, of folklore: his own life cut down, now a martyr-like figure, a symbol of the impending cultural harvest to come.

Yeti is more polished and tidy than its predecessor. 'Soap Shop Rock', composed by John Weinzierl, is segmented into four parts that last between three and six minutes, as do the majority of the tracks. As such, it is for many a more digestible proposition, and opener 'Burning Sister' is relatively conventional and lucid by Düül standards, a blazing, rocky crowd-pleaser. Renate Knaup's background vocals often feel more like she is simply trying to make herself heard as a woman in a man's world.

'The problem I had in the beginning was self-confidence,' she said. 'It was difficult to be the only woman involved inside this macho musical mafia. *Phallus Dei* had no words for me to sing. I only did these oohs and aahs for the vocals. I wanted to be a soul singer, in the same way that Hendrix was a soul singer.'

On this album, however, she comes into her own on her self-composed 'Archangel Thunderbird', which would prove to be one of Amon Düül 2's most popular songs, one which pricked up the ears of UK music journalists like *Melody Maker*'s Richard Williams. She determinedly rehearsed the song, based on an old hymn of her childhood, for two days, and, when she came to lay her track down, did so with a resounding thwack that made her fellow band members jump. 'This was always a man's band and if any of them could have sung properly they would never have chosen me, a girl, to be their vocalist,' she said.

She was probably right to be suspicious of the men, particularly in the lax, sexist climate of the day. Even in 2012, John Weinzierl described to me being in a rock band as 'a mate's game. The minute you have a lady it is all different. It's like having your mother on tour. I remember Renate chasing the groupies away, saying, "Go away, we don't want you here!" And the rest of the group came out and said, "What are you doing?" The boys liked Renate, not the girls. That's how I felt.'

Elsewhere, despite its relative audience-friendliness, *Yeti* still feels like an album dissolving in itself, in a molten state somewhere between solid and liquid, not yet set. It is aeons away from Pink Floyd, now gliding into their magisterial, pacific, some would say complacent phase. More seems to happen in a restless, shape-shifting Amon Düül minute than in a Floyd half hour – on 'Eye Shaking King', for instance, which Lester Bangs described as 'overpowering the listener and turning his brain to the resinous extract of Burroughsian Mugwump spinal fluid'. Or 'Cerberus', which begins with a slurp and gallops into a heated twelve-string guitar segment, replacing the precision of the Mothers of Invention's 'Nine Types of Industrial Pollution' with fingertip-shredding passion, before phasing into a state-of-the-art electric guitar jam. Finally, there are the improvisations, such as the title track, in which the group, who were increasingly turning up at the studio with solo compositions, got to revert to their 'tribal' selves.

These culminate in 'Sandoz in the Rain', on which an olive branch was extended to members of Amon Düül 1 – Ulrich Leopold plays bass and Rainer Bauer contributes somewhat wayward vocals on this lovely, weightlessly pastoral piece, with Thomas Keyserling adding a flute that skitters over the acoustic surfaces like a dragonfly across water. Paradise regained. The Swiss company Sandoz, in whose laboratories LSD was discovered, supposedly wrote to the group enquiring as to whether their name was being taken in vain in the title, but the group feigned innocence. 'Of course, I cannot confirm the rumour that we were all on acid while we recorded the song,' said Weinzierl. (They weren't – at least, according to Falk Rogner, the only time they recorded on acid was for 'Wie der Wind am Ende einer Strasse' on *Wolf City*, after which they decided it was a waste of time to spend five hours recording five minutes of music.)

Yeti was followed swiftly by *Tanz der Lemminge* ('Dance of the Lemmings'). In its mix of high musical pretensions, its tracks subdivided in the grand classical manner, and its mock-grandiose titles, it's once again tempting to invoke the Mothers of Invention circa 1967–8 as a point of comparison. Again, however, while Frank Zappa always ran a tight ship, *Tanz der Lemminge* is, wonderfully, all at sea, yielding all kinds of booty and wreckage on its travels: 'Planets rise out of the ash/It's coming down with a terrifying crash.'

Whereas the likes of Yes and Genesis tended towards conjuring elaborate lands of make-believe in which Lewis Carroll and Tolkien were touchstones, Amon Düül's musical drama appertained to very real and rotten things in the soul of man. As Weinzierl said, the album's title 'stands for the mechanical way of living that leads to destruction, which seems to be a result of the abnormal psyche of man nowadays, and shows that the only way out is awakening'.

'Syntelman's March of the Roaring Seventies' makes swift transitions from stringy folk to jazzy accelerations, an apocalyptic tumble, stylistically a collapsing tower of Babel, funnelled through with whooshing electronics, noodling guitar solos crashing and burning like comets, and not a caravan in sight. The sense of communal chaos and the frantic ransacking of cultures and traditions continues on the 'Restless Skylight-Transistor-Child' suite, featuring subtitles such as 'A Short Stop at the Transylvanian Brain Surgery', with Knaup continuing her struggle to be heard amid the multiplicity of instruments and sardonic vocals. Despite the classical-style formalism of these pieces, the effect is of a shambolic spree that seems to create new noise hybrids. As Bangs put it, 'Amon Düül's assimilation and synthesis of all major twentieth-century musical idioms is so astonishing that you sometimes don't know exactly what you are hearing.'

The side comprising 'The Marilyn Monroe Memorial Church' sets forth into the cosmos demarcated by Pink Floyd on the live disc of 1969's *Ummagumma*, a seemingly routine space-rock mission. But then they become stranded and suspended in feedback, echo and a ghostly white extremism of their own making. '*Tanz* is an opera,' says Weinzierl. 'I wanted to make "space" music but realised it was impossible because you can only draw on your terrestrial time. People talk about Pink Floyd. You can make "spacey" music, yes, but space music, no.' It's peaceful, transfixing, yet strangely bleached and hellish, as if they are traversing some gigantic spiritual void. The meandering sound of a honky-tonk piano some eleven minutes in ought to provide some solace but adds to the nightmarish air, confirmed when it leaps out of the mix at you Keith Tippett-style, 3D-style. As with so much music to which the word 'lysergic' is attached, 'The Marilyn Monroe Memorial Church' is probably best listened to stone-cold sober and in daylight as broad as possible. The final side, by contrast, relatively orthodox psych-rock fare, provides the relief of waking up back in your own bedroom.

Tanz der Lemminge was not the last great Amon Düül album – as musicians they actually improved individually over the next few years. Renate Knaup was given an increasing role as vocalist but having deplored the shambling, noisy beginnings of Amon Düül, it was clear that her ambition was to be a professional vocalist of the sort the experimental German music of the 1970s found it hard to accommodate. Eventually, she would come into her own in the more formal setting of Popol Vuh, leaving Amon Düül, where she was only able fitfully to flourish.

'With *Phallus Dei*, with Renate it is just oohs and aahs. The voice is like an instrument for us,' said Weinzierl. But as the seventies progressed, the smoke began to clear a little. Subsequent albums were very solid indeed – *Carnival in Babylon* boasted another formidable performance by Knaup on 'All the Years Round'. However, the ranging ambition, the lengthy improvisation of yore was now giving way to a more compact and codified approach to songwriting. It was only 1972, but there was no way back to the sixties.

'The whole thing started collapsing when the soccer players started wearing long hair. At that point, we should have dropped out,' says Weinzierl. Indeed, the fabulous barnets of such West German football stars as the allegedly leftist sympathiser Paul Breitner, who probably never had any difficulties gaining admittance to hotels, was a sure indicator that the culture was moving swiftly on, and the counterculture being assimilated. On *Wolf City*, Amon Düül augmented their sound with the magnificent Moog synthesizer played by Florian Fricke, producing a grand, choral sound. While the likes of 'Deutsch Nepal' inspired a later dark ambient group of the same name and could hardly be counted as mainstream, Amon Düül would hereafter gradually be sucked, album by album, towards the pop centre, to Weinzierl's retrospective chagrin.

'The three-minute thing is an industry thing. In the beginning, I thought record companies were all musical experts, people who liked music – until you realise it's just some fucking jerk in Switzerland with too much money thinking to himself, "Maybe I'll start up a record company." These disappointments all came with time, but early on we did have belief in it. The times did change – living in the commune we didn't realise so much. Other people came to us, like moths to a candle. The nice days finished, but Amon Düül didn't finish. After our first eight albums we were conned into doing more rock, more conventional songs, because that's what the producers wanted. Do you give in at this stage? No, you grow into it. You think, "Well, it's all about communication," so you think, "Okay, well I'll speak this language."'

Leap forward to 1975. Amon Düül 2 have signed to Atlantic Records, their contract with United Artists having been terminated following *Vive la trance*. 'Our first manager when we started told us that we could be as big as Pink Floyd. To us, the idea was ridiculous – we didn't want to be big, we just wanted to play. It was hard enough just to live, let alone play.'

However, to herald this major-league transfer to possible transatlantic glory, they recorded perhaps their most ambitious, explicit and grandest conceit – the double album *Made in Germany*, a sort of cross between Syberberg and Tim Rice/Andrew Lloyd Webber, a rock opera satirically taking in the recent sweep of German history, complete with orchestral overture, lavish and intricate arrangements and pop-friendly tunes referencing everyone from Kaiser Wilhelm to Fritz Lang to Ludwig II to Hitler. It is by turns lovely, dated, audacious and ill-advised, a magnificent flying machine finished to a high polish that unfortunately did not fly.

'*Made in Germany* should have been our way to Mecca. We wanted to hire a Zeppelin and land in New York,' recalls Weinzierl wistfully. What did not help, it seems, was the group's decision to pre-empt mid-seventies conceptions of the Teutonic by satirising them to the max. The word 'Kraut' rebounds with bitter irony around the album, in lyrics about 'zer Krauts coming to the USA' or in titles like 'La Krautoma'. They also featured a spoof interview between an inane American DJ and Hitler, whose 'responses' take the form of snippets of his speeches. This was one of a number of tracks expurgated at the shuddering behest of the American record label.

'Using some of these things, deliberately, like the Hitler speech, you can tell how ridiculous this is. Whenever you came as a German it was assumed you were a Nazi sympathiser,' recalls Weinzierl, who styled himself as 'John von Düül' in preparation for the grand American invasion. 'We signed with Atlantic, under Ahmet Ertegün. But he said there was no chance of releasing this album, even though it was satirical. So just the single album came out. This should have been our big Coming to America album – but it was shot down.'

Weinzierl may rue losing the chance to make it Stateside, but others in Düül regarded *Made in Germany* as a nadir, including Falk Rogner, who, ironically, contributed some of its best moments. He later described it as Düül's worst concept album, a folly which producer Jürgen Korduletsch (later responsible for a slew of disco remixes) had a large hand in orchestrating. There had even been wild talk from the German branch of the company of renaming the group Olaf and his Swinging Nazis, though thankfully this idea was squelched at the outset. It began to appear that, having covered a vast amount of terrain in a short space of time, Amon Düül had reached a terminus, left with only quantum leaps of desperation as options. As a parody of the notion of 'Krautrock' uninitiated outsiders might have taken it for, *Made in Germany* does have immense curiosity value, even kitsch possibilities, as well as genuine merits.

Chris Karrer once said of Amon Düül 2 that they were 'trying to find the point of intersection between two parallels in the infinite'. That sense of trying to reconcile the irreconcilable beset Amon Düül from the moment of their first split. In their earliest days music was a metaphor for absolute democracy – anyone could play – but then a rift developed between those who really could play, and wished to develop creatively, and those who weren't capable of much more than bashing out a dissenting, joyful noise, a lump hammer to stake their place in the countercultural scheme of things, to the growing irritation of the musicians.

They extol, and continue to extol, the virtues of commune living, in which resources increase through sharing and a support network provides constant moral encouragement and a reminder of common humanity. 'Let's make a commune again, for young and old, a forum to introduce new ideas to young people,' Weinzierl urges. 'Look at the situation you have with dementia, all those lonely old people in their own houses. It should not be like that. In our first commune as Amon Düül 2, we lived in a house with twenty-eight rooms, a dozen cars, everyone paying a hundred a month. It could be the same now.' However, from the band members' own accounts, it was clear that this 'free' mode of living quickly developed into something more sinister, as strong and autocratic characters inevitably took it upon themselves to impose 'freedom' on others. Moreover, Amon Düül themselves suspended commune living when they found that they became weakened through overdependence as individuals on the collective.

The current state of play is that the group, whose nucleus are in touch at the time of writing, are living in a 'virtual' commune. That might sound wishy-washy but the great thing about Amon Düül 2, who initially split in 1981, is the very fact that there is a current state of play with them. Despite internal rifts and periods spent apart, the band remain active today. (Their website, amonduul.de, is a very useful gateway to their present schedule of engagements and reissues.) For Weinzierl, however, it is not simply a case of seeing out their own days. 'We are overdue the next step. Do you read the Bible? The story of Noah's Ark? The description of the Ark is a description of human beings – the body, the emotion and the mind. The flood of then is like the Babylonian flood now. When the dove comes back, times will be better. The same then as now.'

Sometimes he despairs at the present acquiescent cultural conditions, as depressingly far as is imaginable from those of the late sixties. 'I find it very sad when I see eighteen-year-old guys growing their hair and playing hard rock. Today, it's just consumption,

consumption. We were absolutely not about that idea, that if you do not consume, the world will go under. Economic growth is one of the nails in Christ's hand.

'There are certain times in this life when people are more prepared to perfect themselves, to step outside their lives than others. Such a time was up until the end of the 1970s. We are not living in those times now. There were things in the air like understanding, development of man. It was a time of being, not being afraid – but full of hope. One feels one has to be so much more careful.'

And yet the esteem in which they are held by subsequent generations often surprises the group themselves. 'We played with Slayer at a festival in Sweden,' laughs Weinzierl. 'We thought of ourselves as a fairytale band of the past. How strange to play with all these metal guys – we were like the "goodies" among these two-metre-tall Viking guys. They strode over. We were thinking, "Please, don't hurt us!" but they just wanted to say, "You inspired me!"'

2 Can: No Führers

'We completely refuse to make a judgement about what is beautiful and what isn't. We make something, that's all, and the scope of possible sounds is immense. We're not musicians, we're universal dilettantes.'

Holger Czukay, 1972

Jaki Liebezeit, drummer of Can, still active in his seventies, has toured all over the world. He's astonished to find appreciative audiences in Bolivia, Poland, Brazil, Serbia, Turkey, fans who greet him like he's stepped out of the tapestry of legend, begging him to sign their Can albums. In Cologne, Liebezeit, one of the architects of modern rhythm, goes about quite unmolested and unnoticed.

'I am not a local hero. But then the local heroes in Cologne are only heroes there – even in Bonn, or Düsseldorf, they are not known.'

The Dadaist and Surrealist Max Ernst, born in Cologne, wrote of the city, 'Here, the principal currents of Europe meet: early Mediterranean influences, Western rationalism, Eastern tendencies towards Occultism, Nordic mythology, the Prussian categorical imperative, the ideals of the French Revolution and much besides.' Twinned with the similarly independently minded Liverpool in the UK, Cologne is a fortress town with a distinct and defiant identity which has survived being bandied between the French and the Prussian empires, both of whom attempted, ultimately in vain, to subsume the city. It's a proud Catholic stronghold – the dominant spires of its cathedral, among the finest in the world, reach black and upward towards heaven, barnacled with gargoyles, studded with Gothic embellishments and curling, elaborate tracery. Its interior boasts the rich accumulation of centuries of artistry, culminating in the stained-glass feature by Gerhard Richter. And yet it's always been a bristling hive of dissent, a cultural and secular oasis. Look closely at Cologne City Hall and you'll see beneath the statue of the querulous Konrad von Hochstaden, thirteenth-century Archbishop of Cologne, two prominent buttocks mooning in the general direction of the city's enemies. As for Ernst himself, the Museum Ludwig features his blasphemous artwork *Die Jungfrau züchtigt das Jesuskind vor drei Zeugen*, in which the Virgin Mary takes supposedly sinless infant Jesus across her lap and administers a good spanking to his bare buttocks.

Cologne cocks a vivacious snook at its more austere near neighbour Düsseldorf. Beer and football are the modern theatres of warfare. In Cologne, they drink Kölsch, in small two-hundred-millilitre glasses so as to preserve the freshness of the brew; in Düsseldorf they knock back Alt. In Cologne, they know how to live, especially come Carnival time just before Lent, when the normal rules of piety and religious observance are temporarily suspended as the citizens pour onto the streets in masks, led by the riotous Prince, a gold-chained, peacock-tailed creation known as 'His Madness', whose float is the climax of the annual parade. Cologne is in the industrial heartland, for sure – to its north lies the Bayer chemical works, which look like some vast, abstract cultural representation of German electronic sound art. It also has strong hints of the pastoral, girdled by a green belt and with forests upriver where, on the boat ride, you can today see shepherds leading their flocks to sip in the waters of the Ruhr barely a mile from the built-up city centre.

After the First World War, Cologne had a good Weimar period under the mayoral leadership of future Chancellor Adenauer. In terms of town planning and social housing, it was a model of civic development. It was also relatively resistant to the Nazis (or so they like to think), despite the tireless efforts of Gauleiter Josef Grohé, with Adenauer ordering the taking down of anti-Semitic hoardings that the local Nazis erected in the run-up to 1933. Had Germany as a whole voted as Cologne did, the Nazis might well not have acquired the key percentage of the electorate they needed to come to power and then do away with elections altogether. At the end of the war, Grohé, from hiding, urged his fellow citizens to resist the Allies as they overran the city, until they had shed every last drop of blood. Following a brief internment, he lived on in Cologne until 1988, a local businessman, open and unapologetic about his Nazi beliefs until his dying days, a living symbol of the lurking failure of denazification.

Which is not to say that Cologne is today a city that has failed to come to terms with its Nazi past; its former Gestapo HQ is now the site of the EL-DE (Leopold Dahmen) Museum, which presents a vivid history of the city, told in photos and exhibits. That said, it only became a museum in 1979, after a student protested that the building was still being used as an administrative HQ, with those who had been victims of the Nazis forced to revisit the site of their torment whenever they had to deal with the city's bureaucracy. Moreover, Cologne boasts one of the largest Jewish communities in Germany and excavation work is currently ongoing to unearth the city's old Jewish quarter and synagogue. However, the sense of a city riven by corruption, at least in terms of its building work and contracts, was exacerbated in 2009 when it suffered one of its most poignant disasters – the collapse of the building housing the Historical Archive of Cologne, which had survived the Second World War intact, but now lost thousands of irreplaceable documents going back centuries. These included the founding charter of the University of Cologne, signed in 1388, along with the documents that established Cologne as a free imperial city under Emperor Friedrich III in 1475. Also among the treasures lost was the 'Golden Book' of the city, in which, according to Jaki Liebezeit, the members of Can had written their names. 'Every five years the book is full and they put it in the archive,' he says. 'Our names were in one of the books that disappeared.'

Picking me up from my hotel in a mauve compact vehicle of some vintage, in keeping with his policy of using cheap but functional everyday technology, Can's drummer Liebezeit drives me out to his studio on the edge of Cologne, the former site of the chocolate factory which now serves as an arts centre, with multiple working spaces for musicians, visual artists, dancers. In his mid-seventies but mobile and spry, he still rehearses in the studio he keeps there, on a customised set of drums without cymbals ('no need for their white noise these days'). We sit at a table arrayed with oriental and African percussive devices whose influence has over the years subtly inflected and informed his cyclical playing style, which has always been resistant to Western notions of progression.

He is rather gloomy about Cologne currently – its financially parlous state, the corruption of local government, and also the fact that, while FC Cologne recently dropped to the second division in the German football league, their rivals, Fortuna Düsseldorf, ascended the other way, gaining promotion to the first. 'It's a mirror for the city,' he remarks, drily. 'Culture-wise, I think it went down in the 1970s and '80s. It has two faces, Cologne. You know, if you are not born here, you are considered an "*immi*". Even if you are from Düsseldorf, you are considered an "*immi*".' And yet it is home to Liebezeit, along with the many other '*immis*', including an extensive Turkish population who, despite or perhaps because they felt like outsiders, have had such an effect on the character of the place.

Born in 1938, Liebezeit's movements in his formative years are a little vague – even his fellow Can members know little in this respect, as he has chosen never to discuss this very early part of his life or his family background. ('I sense a very heavy experience,' says

Can keyboardist Irmin Schmidt.) 'I am not very rooted. I was born in East Germany in a village near Dresden, then moved to another place with my mother (my father no longer lived with us), then another place, then another, so I have no real roots. Later, I went to Lower Saxony, in Kassel – one of my grandmothers lived there.'

As a youth, Liebezeit was conscious of American rock 'n' roll: 'There was "Rock around the Clock", "Tutti Frutti", and of course Elvis Presley. I listened to it but wasn't interested in playing this kind of music – also, there weren't many other rock 'n' roll musicians.' That said, his first gigs saw him play rock 'n' roll covers for the GIs stationed in West Germany. 'Kassel was in the American zone, so you could hear American music there. There were American soldiers' clubs – even when I was still at school, I played at the NCO club – they would go there with their families, children. I came in contact with American music culture that way.'

Liebezeit first took up jazz when he met Manfred Schoof, who had attended the Music High School in Cologne. 'Once I visited him in Cologne – I thought of going to the Music High School to study drums there, but their idea of drums was not the same as mine.' However, he was more amenable to jazz. Schoof had put a group together. 'They were already playing modern jazz. I very much liked Art Blakey and the Jazz Messengers, Max Roach – I tried to play just like Art Blakey. I came to Cologne, I started a band here. One day, I was about twenty, we went to Munich to play at a club – my first professional job, four weeks. We did covers of Art Blakey and the Jazz Messengers. We were quite a success, because maybe people didn't know it was a copy! We ended up staying for months. One night, the whole Art Blakey band came to the club, because they were in town. The band all wanted to play, except Art Blakey, so they asked me to play in his place. I was so happy – I knew all their records, I knew exactly what to play. And Art Blakey was in the audience, I was so afraid. But very happy to have this chance. I was very proud.'

Shortly after this, Liebezeit received an offer to play in Spain. 'We played in Barcelona – I was there for seven months, not a single day off, can you imagine? Two dates a day. There was a law that for every foreign musician, a Spanish musician must be employed. And so every night I played from twelve to one in the morning, then two till three, alternating with this local band, in this club in the old town.'

It was while in Spain that Liebezeit experienced the epiphany that eventually would have such an impact on the structure of Krautrock and all that succeeded it. 'In the same building as the club was a flamenco club. I was impressed by the rhythm, and I thought, "They play with much better rhythm than the jazz musicians." Also, when I was in Spain I could receive North African stations on the radio. So I listened to Moroccan music, all kinds.'

Liebezeit's interest in musics outside of both the American and the European traditions, be they pop, jazz or academic, was further piqued when in 1961, some years in advance of the Beatles, he developed a fascination for Indian music. 'I bought a record – over fifty years ago. It was called *The Music of India*. This was before hippie times, no one knew about Indian music. This was in a music shop, they had special records for ethnological research. I was so impressed. So I was listening a lot very early on to North African, Indian, also Turkish music, Iranian music. More than jazz or rock, I was interested in these rhythmical musics. Jazz and rock to me were European, they had nothing to do with all this.'

Returning to Cologne, however, and hooking up once more with Manfred Schoof, Liebezeit discovered that jazz had evolved from its bebop phase into the avant-garde, under the influence of Ornette Coleman's *The Shape of Jazz to Come*. 'We played free jazz. That was something completely new for me. They told me, "You have been away in Spain, you have been sleeping, this is how things have moved on."'

Liebezeit adapted but, after a while, found himself in a quandary.

It was not that the new music was too difficult. 'It was not so hard.' However, after some eighteen months, he discovered that what was considered structurally 'free' in jazz in fact represented a terminus, a point at which further progress was impossible – the condition, many insisted, that classical music had formally reached under the aegis of Schoenberg and the twelve-tone system. 'I only played free jazz for one and a half years. But I was bored. There was no development. What can happen? It was finished.'

This was key. Free jazz was, for a certain wing of German musicians including Peter Brötzmann and Alexander von Schlippenbach, a potent metaphor for freedom of thought, for untrammelled self-expression, which borrowed from the American tradition, naturally, but to which they added a European dimension that made it their own and reflected their particular cultural upbringing. But, for Liebezeit, these excesses did not represent the road to the palace of wisdom.

'When Can started I was finished with free jazz. I was not satisfied, they were not satisfied with me. In free jazz there was no future, everything was destroyed. Repetition was not allowed, but for me, repetition was one of the basic elements in music. In free jazz, they said, all tones are equal. That's okay for human beings – all human beings are equal, true, but I don't think the same thing for tones!

'In the European system, you think in bars – you can fill this bar with anything you want,' explains Liebezeit. 'Fill the next bar with anything you want. But I prefer music where you think rhythmically in cycles . . . with a cyclical rhythm you cannot change it, you have to obey the rhythmical movement. You can change some things but you must keep the basic shape of that rhythm.'

Liebezeit has also spoken about a chance encounter with an individual who, after a jazz concert one night, solemnly intoned in his face, 'You must play monotonously!' This was very possibly a reflection of the concertgoer's stoned condition, but it turned out that Liebezeit was thinking along the same lines and it helped crystallise his thoughts. He had seized on a paradox – that real liberty in music arose from the strict and rigid imposition of order, regularity. Such strange watchwords, in the cultural context of 1960s Germany, but they worked. If Western avant-garde music had suffered from over-development, now it was necessary to go back and begin again, to make new time, create new intervals and changes.

Cologne, however, had been the fulcrum of the new music in the 1950s – it was here that Stockhausen had founded his electronic music studio. In glass cabinets of the Hochschule für Musik are exhibited the wonderful pieces of hands-on analogue kit on which he created masterpieces like *Gesang der Jünglinge* and *Kontakte*, before the university declared them obsolete in favour of the less romantically antique digital equipment of contemporary computer technology. The radio station WDR (Westdeutscher Rundfunk) broadcast orchestral works by the postwar classical school, including Pierre Boulez. High classical, high jazz hung high in the ether, virtuous expressions of civic regeneration, marking a gaping cultural lacuna between themselves and the Schlager pop scene way below.

Cologne was, as Irmin Schmidt says, a 'very lively place' at the time. Schmidt and Holger Czukay were both pupils of Stockhausen. Czukay, who had been born in Danzig, Poland, and was a refugee during the Second World War, was the more technically minded of the two – his first interests had been in radio repairs and in engineering, which were on the point of becoming creative musical skills in the impending era of the studio and the editing suites as instruments in their own right as opposed to just recording spaces.

Czukay, who in person has about him at all times a humorous twinkle in his eye that brings to mind Salvador Dalí (as well as a predilection for recurring motifs in his work – the French horn, samples of Pope John Paul II, shortwave radio extracts), had also about him an element of the 'outsider', even in the higher echelons of academic music study. 'I was always being thrown out of music colleges,' he told Richard Cook in 1982. 'Stockhausen took me in – he asked me if I was a composer and I had to reply, "I don't know."' Yet of the two, he was the one who was most taken with the rigidity of Stockhausen's teachings, the more scrupulous disciple. He was less taken with rock music, which failed to engage him until 1967 at the earliest, but when he first encountered Malcolm Mooney and then Jaki Liebezeit, with whom he would enjoy a pugnacious relationship in the rhythm section, he was the most open to persuasion that Can could be a pop proposition, one which would earn the band their pensions as they rolled out smash pop hit after smash pop hit.

'Stockhausen denied repetition!' says Czukay, speaking from his studio in Cologne, where he lives and works. 'He thought it was a weak point. Jaki said it was a strong point. For me, by repeating something, you create something new in it. This idea occurs in Buddhism. Don't think too much! Not while making music!' This would be one of many arguments Liebezeit would have with Czukay. To the average listener, Czukay's playing sounds reserved, open-ended, discreet. To Liebezeit's pained ears, however, it could feel as invasive as Spinal Tap's Derek Smalls's bass soloing on his 'Jazz Odyssey', compared to the ideal of single-note purity he harboured. Less, less, less, Liebezeit urged, with such exasperation that he once chased Czukay around the studio with an axe that was lying fortuitously to hand. 'Yes, I did that once,' chuckles Liebezeit. 'But of course I would never have hurt him. He provoked me so much that I wanted to make him afraid. He believed that I might have hit him with it!'

*

July 2010 – the Schlossfestspiele, an annual classical event in Ludwigsburg, just outside Stuttgart. In the impressive concert hall, which bears comparison with the Royal Festival Hall, the last night's gala performance is dedicated to Irmin Schmidt, who conducts an orchestra including Markus Stockhausen on trumpet and Gerd Dudek on saxophone. They play a selection of the TV and film music he has composed over the years, for Wim Wenders and the like, as well as delivering a brisk, hilariously effective version of one of Can's biggest hits, 'Spoon'. The audience, most of whom look either too old or too young to have appreciated Can the first time round, gasp appreciatively as, with collaborator Kumo (aka Jono Podmore), Schmidt punctuates the proceedings with jolting outtakes from their *Masters of Confusion* album, in which breakneck keyboards and stabs of electronica serve to light up the venue like indoor lightning bolts. Wenders, in spectacles and a big, boxy demob suit, delivers an affectionate and funny *Laudatio* to an equally informally attired Schmidt. In Germany, there are formal distinctions between *ernsthafte*, or serious, music, and *unterhaltungs* music, which is mere entertainment. *Ernsthafte* music gets you a higher royalty and legal protection. In this swooping and stooping performance, Schmidt delivers a masterclass in subverting the high with the low and the low with the high. ('We didn't accept any of this hierarchy,' he tells me. 'We were as serious as we were funny.')

A *Kapellmeister* (director of music) at the Theater Aachen in his twenties, Irmin Schmidt had looked groomed and destined for a career in mainstream academic German music as a trained pianist and conductor. However, as he told Wenders, although schooled in the music of Luigi Nono, Berio, Boulez and so forth, he had come to form the opinion that it was African Americans like James Brown who were making the real 'new' music. From a young age, forever at war with his father in particular and the expectation that a good, well-trained young German would take up a respectable position in the subsidised world of *Hochmusik*, Schmidt fought at some level against the career path mapped out for him, even as he followed it. He was a master of his craft, staging performances by the likes of Mozart and Hindemith, and even in the early days of Can attempted to live the dual lives of a jobbing classical conductor and an experimental rock musician. Eventually, however, the sheer physical strain was too great. He could not be two, three people at once.

'It didn't work because Can needed wholehearted commitment. I was teaching at an actors' school, doing theatre music in Munich, giving concerts – I did several things at the same time at the beginning but it was impossible to maintain. Sleeping on the plane, it was impossible,' he tells me. 'Of course, when I started with Can, I had colleagues ask, "Why are you wasting your time?"'

From the early sixties onwards, however, Schmidt had seen in the American wing of postwar art and music a minimalism, a simplicity, an openness to indeterminacy and the environment with which he identified far more than with what he bitterly describes as the 'Stalinism' of twentieth-century classical-musical dogma and the imposition of techniques like serialism. He was an avid observer of Fluxus, taken with the ideas of John Cage. Like Czukay and Liebezeit, Schmidt is a little older than his peers in the music scene of the late sixties and early seventies. Although they didn't impact on that scene until after the Fab Four had split, these three Can members are all older than the oldest Beatle. As such, he has distinct memories of war and its aftermath – the ruins, the stench, the rubble of cities he had been just about old enough to remember before they were bombed. The sense of structure that came with his training, the placement of things in time and space became intertwined with a deeply felt desire, commonly held with a handful of other musical visionaries at the time, to rebuild, to plant something he felt was his own, which he had helped forge and nurture, rather than musical forms imposed from outside or from above.

Schmidt first met Czukay in 1965, when both were studying at the Darmstadt International Summer Courses for New Music together. In 1966, he made a trip to the USA, in which he met the minimalists Terry Riley, La Monte Young and Steve Reich, as well as Dick Higgins and Nam June Paik of the Fluxus movement. All of this helped reinforce his urge to 'start anew', to get back to some sort of first principles. He saw Warhol's *Chelsea Girls* and, on a later trip, would be impressed with the 'Ur-rock' of the Velvet Underground. All of this he contrasted with the pitifully inadequate German beat scene. He initially thought of trying to work with local Cologne beat group the Lords, fusing his classical chops with their borrowed rhythmical know-how, but all they succeeded in doing was getting very drunk. He was, however, taken with the Manfred Schoof Quartet, one or two of whose number he had already worked with on film projects, including drummer Jaki Liebezeit. But surely this Liebezeit fellow was too steeped in the remote intricacies of free jazz to be of relevance to the project germinating in his mind?

Paradoxically, although Schmidt looked to America for inspiration, it was precisely in order to reject the Americanisation of German popular music, particularly the blues derivations so popular in Europe. This wasn't out of any contempt for the blues, but because it was geographically inappropriate. 'For us, the blues didn't mean much, except that it was a phenomenon of the twentieth century that gave birth to John Coltrane and Charlie Parker – and you can only create in this tradition if you can be a part of this tradition. There were wonderful blues singers – Lightnin' Hopkins, wonderful. But as a European, as a German, it's a lie to try to play pure blues.'

What Schmidt absolutely rejected was the post-Beatles influence, itself once removed from the source of things, America. 'We were never at all influenced by the English. The Velvets, the Stooges, James Brown, Sly Stone. And Captain Beefheart, yes.

Actually, my revelation was Jimi Hendrix in a way. "Hey Joe". That was something which had a big influence on me. The way he plays guitar is like the creation of a new instrument. Like Charlie Parker made a new instrument of the saxophone.'

Schmidt found himself pushing at open doors. Czukay had independently discussed forming a beat group with a young Swiss guitarist friend of his, Michael Karoli, whom he brought on board and with whom Schmidt formed an instant bond. He then made the happy discovery of Liebezeit's disaffection with free jazz and his own desire to play something with a more fresh and open rhythmical foundation befitting the time and place they were in. 'Holger was also fed up with classical, Irmin was fed up with classical, I was fed up with jazz,' says Liebezeit. 'We wanted to do something completely new. This was 1968, the year of revolution in Germany. Pop revolution, student revolution, build a new society, make everything better.' And, for Liebezeit, this rejection of the past meant also a rejection of the immediate past of twentieth-century classical music. 'Atonality – maybe it was to express what was happening after World War I – but for me, this music sounds very destructive, like just after a war. It's creative, but to only play this kind of music . . .?'

Also included was a composer and flautist, David Johnson – he can be heard soloing on Can's 2012 restoration of unreleased material *The Lost Tapes*, on the track 'Millionenspiel', laid down when the embryonic group still went by the working title of Inner Space. He had also filmed some of the running street battles of the 1968 Paris riots, which were used as a backdrop to Can's earliest live performances. Johnson didn't really fit in, however, and, disillusioned by the rock direction the group were taking, drifted away.

They secured the exclusive space necessary for their fermentation as a group through an art-collector friend, Christoph Vohwinkel, acquiring a room to rehearse in in Schloss Nörvenich, a castle near

Cologne which today is an art gallery. The isolation of Schloss Nörvenich and the lack of any outside influence in terms of commercial and artistic direction, sound engineering or production meant that they had absolute freedom to become whatever they saw fit to become, with no preset plan or pre-written material.

Then along came Malcolm Mooney, an American sculptor, the very personification of indeterminacy. He was introduced into the world of Can by Hildegard Schmidt, wife of Irmin and later redoubtable manager of all things Can. She met Mooney in Paris, visiting one Serge Tcherepnin, a student of Stockhausen. It was June 1968, in the immediate aftermath of the student riots. Mooney was on his way back from India, after an abortive attempt to find spiritual enlightenment. 'He went out to India to meet a guru, only to be told that the guru was in the USA at the moment,' says Liebezeit. Mooney was also in flight from the Vietnam War and was loath to go back to America himself. Initially, Hildegard had thought she might use her husband's connections in the art world simply to find a place to paint and sculpt. However, on visiting Schloss Nörvenich, Mooney decided to join in rehearsals and swiftly found himself a member of the group.

Then, as now, black singers were commonly expected to act as signifiers for the authenticity of their people, delivering artless but immaculate soulfulness, poured like molasses directly from the heart. They were not supposed to act as absolutely free agents. Mooney had been a member of an a cappella group. However, to the consternation of those first exposed to Can music, his vocal performances felt quite distressed, weatherbeaten, fixated. He didn't merely front Can – it was as if he was subject to it, thrown this way and that by the music, his narratives affected by both its repetitions and its abrupt changes.

'His singing was completely rhythmical,' says Liebezeit of Mooney. 'Everyone thought it was terrible, but no, it was a phenomenon like that of Louis Armstrong. It was not a "nice" voice.

Now everyone realises that Malcolm, like Louis, has a beautiful voice. He sings in a gospel choir, you know. Once, in New York, I met him there, and he told me we could not meet on the Sunday, he said he had to sing with his gospel choir. He was very enthusiastic about that, every Sunday.'

'This thing of repeating a sentence, a banal sentence – but repeated about seventy, eighty times – it's pop art like having 150 cartons of Brillo by Warhol,' says Schmidt. 'In a way, it's the same idea, the repetition of this banality, it becomes something else. Can are not a pop group. It's pop art. It's art music. It's part of a tradition but maybe the difference is that it's part of a new tradition, not the pop or rock tradition.'

The first fruits of Can's jamming were collected on a tape named *Prehistoric Future*. 'Can never wrote anything, not on paper,' says Liebezeit. 'We thought, "Today we don't have to write on paper, like Beethoven or Mozart – we write on tape." We had no sound engineers. Holger Czukay was our sound engineer because he had some idea of technical things – he could repair a radio. Also, he had been a student of Stockhausen, so he had some idea of electronics.'

However, says Schmidt, 'Although we created a sense of freedom, there was intense concentration and discipline. Michael and I came from totally different directions – I wanted that. I had the education in new music, Ligeti, Stockhausen, and the accumulation of hundreds of years. Holger had much the same sort of education, but I wanted to have a brilliant jazz musician and a classical musician and a rock guitarist – three phenomena of the twentieth century – and bring them together, see what happens when these persons meet, see what happens when these people, with all their abilities, start from scratch.'

With the exception of the younger Karoli, then, who had a background in beat music and the look of a customary rock star, everybody else in Can was deliberately departing from their own background and training, be it classical, jazz or, in Mooney's case, doo-wop. Everyone was an enabler of the group as a whole. No one was there to demonstrate their virtuosity, to show off their soloing chops. It would have been easy enough for Schmidt, for example, to venture on bedazzling keyboard runs, or for Liebezeit to channel the spirit of Max Roach and Elvin Jones on the drum kit, but this would have been wholly irrelevant to the purpose of Can, to the space, structure and energy flow they were looking to establish.

'Jaki did not play like Billy Cobham,' says Schmidt. 'It's very easy to create a big, romantic, huge sound, but the harmonies of prog rock are so banal. Banal romanticism. It was different with the Beatles, who were much more intelligent. But simple harmonics only make sense in James Brown, or the Stones. Prog rock is kitsch. Punk is not kitsch. That's the difference. Hip hop is not kitsch either, certainly not the backing tracks.'

Although at times maniacal in his pursuit of purism in the studio ('Jaki was eerie, he gave me the creeps, I thought he was a murderer, or someone capable of committing a murder,' says Michael Karoli of the drummer), and forever exhorting Czukay to shave down to ever more minimal degrees of minimalism ('one single tone, that will suffice – to me, this was a novel idea' – Czukay), Liebezeit insists that there was 'no boss' in Can. 'We were a pure collective. Nobody had the chance to become the "leader" – the Führer! No one was allowed to become Führer!' The political implications of this hardly need unpacking. 'Yes, I agree, it was a political structure,' says Liebezeit. 'Some English paper once wrote, "Can means 'Communism, Anarchism, Nihilism'"! But it was political by doing, rather than words. A group with no leader means everyone is the leader, everyone is equally responsible. Initially, with the Beatles, I always thought they were like this, four equal friends. Then I found out that for songwriting, it was always Lennon/McCartney.' Can's collective spirit would also extend to composer credits and payments, which were distributed equally among members on all tracks regardless of their particular input. 'The composer was always Can.'

'With early Can, the fact that we worked without any hierarchy made a big difference,' says Schmidt. 'It's something which educates you as a musician in a different way. All of your senses have to be open to the other musicians. What makes, I think, a piece of art, whatever, paintings, sculpture, music, literature – it defines a historical moment. It's made, say, in 1971. What makes it last is that when it succeeds, it's because of a presence of mind that includes in it future possibilities.'

That Can effectively conjured themselves out of thin air is one of the great mysteries of modern musical alchemy. To what extent did the group have conversations, planning meetings to establish what they were looking to achieve?

'There was not much discussion,' says Schmidt. 'When you start improvising, a groove, a riff, an atmosphere appears, and you think, "That might be the essence." It can occur even in the first minutes. There is a phrase from [French writer] Paul Valéry – in an interview, when he was asked about inspiration. The first phrase comes from "up there", and the rest is shitty work. There is the potential. And then it is about concentration, to get to the essence. And that's why these pieces get so dense and concise.'

For Can, the creative process did not just involve listening to each other but to the very space in which they were working, as Schmidt meticulously explains. 'From the beginning we would often spend hours, sometimes days, transforming the studio, the space, into a sound installation. A microphone, a speaker and maybe a bit of delay would be enough to make the room resonate. Every little noise, every sound became meaningful: steps, a chair, a few words, an accidental sound created by touching an instrument. Playfully, unintentionally but at the same time highly concentrated and alert, we would explore the space, the sound of objects and movements – more attentive listeners than players.

When we were lucky a magical sound-atmosphere would appear, the room, everything around us, the ambience became music – the Can version of ambient – a school for magicians.'

One track on *The Lost Tapes*, 'Blind Mirror Surf', illustrates this more potently than any of the material released during Can's lifetime; it was recorded in a ballroom at Schloss Nörvenich which was awaiting renovation, effectively a heap of rubble. Come the evening, however, and the rays of the setting sun cast through the windows lent it a peculiar, ghostly atmosphere. Although it's an extreme piece, atypical of Can in its amorphous blend of drones, clanking and single, spare instrumental notes spiralling about the room, punctuated by the noise of shattered glass, it's a fine metaphor for the spirit of the group arising beauteously and forming from a cultural condition of neglect and ruin.

Liebezeit puts it more prosaically. 'We went to the studio and started jamming. And then we would throw in ideas. We would play, then record it, listen. If it was no good, we would keep going until we got something. We would develop it in the studio.'

Had Can's debut album, *Monster Movie*, been their only one, it would have assured their place in the history of German music and of rock as a whole. Whereas it would take Kraftwerk several years and albums to 'become' themselves, Can put their principles into practice with immediate and immaculate effect. This isn't to say that they were already the finished article, for the very principles they had set in place allowed for the possibility of subsequent development, in which they would take on all manner of shapes and colours and hues. Still, *Monster Movie* rolled into 1969 like a boulder from an unanticipated futurequake – or so it feels in retrospect.

The title of opener 'Father Cannot Yell' could be interpreted as a reproach to the guilty silence of a previous generation, for which the present generation was loudly compensating: 'Woman screams "I am fertile" and the father/He hasn't been born yet.'

But it was never Mooney or Can's style to invest such value or meaning in lyrics. Mooney's approach was in keeping with the improvisation of his fellow instrumentalists, textural rather than textual, fixating, riffing on phrases.

The opening rapidfire, Morse-code organ tones of 'Father Cannot Yell' recall, despite Schmidt's protests that Can were in no way influenced by English groups, Pink Floyd's 'Astronomy Domine'. However, within a few bars, it is clear that Can have ideas of their own about 'progression'. In the mid-section, where a west-coast American outfit might have felt obliged to let rip with a twaddling solo, Can appear deliberately to get stuck in a groove, as if their feet are nailed to the floor, attacking it over and over. Moreover, Schmidt, hammering away and sustaining single notes, suddenly plunges the track into a change of direction with a karate chop-like blow to the keyboard, an application, perhaps, of the methods of American pianist Frederic Rzewski, whose virtuoso pieces contain within them borderline acts of violence to the instrument.

Then there is 'Yoo Doo Right', almost twenty-one minutes long, which rumbles into being on a slow tide of Liebezeit rhythms as if he has replaced his sticks with caveman's clubs, before clambering to the next level on a recurring series of bass runs from Czukay. Mooney's lyrics feel like he is in the grip of an epiphany ('You made a believer out of me'), but one which is causing him some deep internal pain which he somehow cannot resist. It's as if he is bearing the burden of the group, risking the damage, suffering the affliction that is Can. At around the six-minute mark the track begins to rotorblade away, to levitate, sustained by Karoli's guitars and Liebezeit's cyclical but increasingly tumultuous percussion, before dropping back to a soloing Mooney, still mulling over the same lyric, accompanied only by Liebezeit, a human metronome, before the whole track comes alive again, refreshed and mutated, but still hammering away at the same locked door, discovering a strange liberty in confinement, infinite variety in repetition. As Mooney produces a spectacular vocal effect, Czukay, bearing the stern injunctions of Liebezeit in mind, sticks rigidly to a two-note bass utterance and Karoli uses his guitar as a sheer conduit for the flow of electric energy. A sense of the infinite groove Can had established is confirmed by Malcolm Mooney's recollection of the 'Yoo Doo Right' session in an interview with *Eurock*'s Archie Patterson in 1983. 'The recording, which started at about 11 a.m., ended at 11 p.m. It was quite a session. I left the studio at one time for lunch, when I returned, the band was still playing the tune and I resumed where I had left off.'

The achievements of *Monster Movie*, of which just five hundred copies were initially privately pressed, only seem more remarkable, as opposed to diminished or dated, many decades on. However, the initial response to them in Germany was confused and derisory. Far from embracing them as national saviours, listeners tended to measure them by the standards of Anglo-American rock and as such found them wanting. As would often be the case, Germans were the worst critics of German music, rather than its most ardent supporters. The very name of the group, meanwhile, was a gift to stinging German humorists, as Liebezeit recalls.

'Can back then was not really noticed. We were considered not to be as good as English bands. It was difficult for Can in Germany in the beginning – they thought of us as a band who were trying to make rock music because they "Can't". You see? "Can". "Can't". What we were doing was simply not recognised as rock music. But that was the idea, not to copy English or American bands but to find our own way, which differs from other countries. In England, when we first played, they enjoyed it for that. In Germany, they thought the same thing – "It doesn't sound English" – and hated it!'

It was only when they earned the respect of overseas audiences and critics that Can were feted in their own country. One step towards such recognition occurred when they came to the attention of Andrew Lauder, the twenty-three-year-old British head of Liberty's A & R department whose passion was west-coast rock and who would later be influential in signing key pre-punk and punk groups, and later the Stone Roses. Having worked in Munich, he was conscious of groups like Amon Düül and a burgeoning underground German music movement. For a brief time, Abi Ofarim, musician and husband of Esther Ofarim, who had represented Switzerland in the Eurovision Song Contest, tried his hand at group management – and among his early clients were Can, though the arrangement came to grief and resulted in years of dispute. He did, however, albeit in a perfunctory way, introduce Lauder to Can.

'Can came to Liberty in a strange way,' Lauder recalls. 'Abi Ofarim was there on some other business, a lunch appointment, and at the end of it, he handed me this record. I really don't know if he knew very much about it – felt like he was just the messenger, doing someone a favour. Why him of all people? Anyway, I was taken by the cover, which was truly bizarre, so I put it on straight after lunch and it was absolutely mindblowing – like "What the hell is this?" I blasted it right up till the building shook.'

Can would go on to tour and gain a measure of international success as a result of *Monster Movie*'s distribution. Initially, however, their main audiences were of the artistic rather than mainstream rock persuasion. They occasionally put on gigs at Schloss Nörvenich, soundproofing the studio with dozens of army surplus mattresses as the audience, perched on the stairs outside, listened in through the open door. Though by no means the leader, singer Malcolm Mooney was a vital, driving force in the Can line-up, whose performances had persuaded Holger Czukay that Can could be more than a temporary academic experiment. 'Malcolm was important in pushing us forward. Malcolm knew how to do this. He came from the world of painting, the visual arts, the world he returned to.'

However, it was an interaction with the art world that led to one of the more unfortunate incidents in Mooney's brief, blazing and tempestuous career with Can. In November 1969, the group were in attendance at the opening night of a local exhibition of the French sculptor Armand. Mooney decided to funk up the typically staid and formal air of proceedings by climbing onto a stack of the multiple parts of the main exhibit, and announcing that they were for sale at the knockdown price of fifty marks each. This caused rather a stir among the dealers, critics and socialites in attendance, who, alive to a bargain, at once began to toss money in Mooney's direction. Arman watched aghast before descending into hysterics. The police were called, and Mooney, pockets bulging with coins, was hastily shepherded outside by Hildegard Schmidt and into Irmin's waiting car, in which they made a getaway. The incident was reported in *Der Spiegel*, with Mooney apologising, returning the money he'd accrued to the gallery's proprietor and thanking him for the opportunity to stage his performance.

To say that Mooney was a loose cannon in his time with Can is to strain the capacity of both the words 'loose' and 'cannon'. The spontaneity which served him and Can so well in performance did not work as effectively when applied to everyday life. On another occasion, as if unaware that the hostilities of the Second World War had ceased, he attempted to crash through the border control that separated Germany from Switzerland. Irmin Schmidt received a call late at night, greeted with due stoicism, from a guard at the frontier at Basle informing him that they had a tearful Mooney in their cells, where he had refused to speak for four hours. They had found a scrap of paper with Schmidt's number on it and were hoping that he would take delivery of the errant singer. Schmidt made the three-hundred-mile round trip without demur. It turned out that Mooney's girlfriend was visiting friends in Zurich for the weekend and Mooney, deciding he needed to see her immediately, had impulsively grabbed the Can Volkswagen, a battered vehicle lacking both number plates and insurance, and made off, minus licence and passport, only to come up against an inevitable wall of bureaucratic objection, to which he took exception.

Eventually, it was as if the psychic stress of being a lightning rod for Can's innovations, their spontaneity and repetition, became too much for Mooney. In one of his last performances, he arrived ten minutes late and, as was his wont, took an event in his sightline as the basis for his lyrical improvisation. This method had worked admirably in the past to lock Can's performances into the here and now on tracks like 'Waiting for the Streetcar' on *The Lost Tapes*, prompted by someone ordering a taxi from the venue. On this occasion, he saw members of the audience sitting on the steps and struck up the mantra, 'Upstairs, downstairs, upstairs, downstairs'. After an hour or so of this, however, it began to feel less like an incantation, more evidence of an onstage nervous breakdown. Even as the rest of Can took a break, Mooney kept up the chant incessantly, eventually collapsing in exhaustion, still burbling the words 'Upstairs, downstairs' as he was borne away.

Shortly after this, he was advised, on psychiatric grounds, to leave Can. He later spoke of feeling very much apart in the group, a black man among white European men, and while he clearly wasn't the victim of overt racial prejudice from anyone in the group, one can understand his sense of cultural rootlessness, his loneliness and the uniqueness of his situation and how hard it must have been to bear in 1968. One of the very last tracks he recorded with Can features on the *Soundtracks* album. On 'Soul Desert' he sounds parched indeed, gasping – a compulsive performance, but maybe that of a man out of his element, at the end of his tether.

'He was just homesick,' surmises Liebezeit. 'It was nothing to do with drugs. Everybody was trying a little LSD, grass, but that was quite normal at the time. Yes, some people got a little crazy but they were already crazy.'

'When he left, in my eyes, the band concept fell apart,' said Michael Karoli, years later. 'I thought the band concept had finished.' An attempt to replace him with Lee Gates, another African American vocalist, didn't quite work out – he was a more accomplished singer but had none of the outrageous, combustible qualities possessed by Mooney.

A serendipitous encounter with a young Japanese busker called Damo Suzuki would be the remaking and reconstituting of Can. According to Czukay, it was the evening of a show in Munich at the Blow-Up, in Franz-Josef-Strasse. He had been impressed by the way Suzuki carried himself and suggested to Liebezeit, who was with him, that he front the band that evening. Initially, Suzuki sang in the airily pacific, lilting way of his that would become familiar to Can fans, but then, in Czukay's words, he 'let a horde of Samurais out of the loudspeakers', erupting like a Krakatoa of atonality. According to legend, the patrons of the Blow-Up fled in droves, not before one or two of them had sought to express their disgruntlement with their fists. Among those left were thirty Americans . . . and, Czukay insists, David Niven, who expressed bewilderment as to whether what had taken place had actually been a musical event. It seems too tall a tale to swallow, the suave, ageing English actor happening by a seventies disco and maintaining a very English, quizzical reserve as all about him charged for the exit doors. He doesn't touch on the episode in his extensive memoirs. However, it's such a wonderful juxtaposition, it deserves to be true.

Can Mark II were born, and, in the wake of Suzuki's weightless vocals, they would be a more airborne proposition than the heavily rhythmical, prehistoric futurists of *Monster Movie* – from 'Father Cannot Yell' to 'Mother Sky'.

It turned out that, like Mooney, Suzuki was an international fugitive. Mooney was on the run from the USA and chanced on Can via India; Suzuki had run away from his home in Japan at sixteen and arrived in Munich via Moscow. 'Damo was more abstract,' says Czukay. 'He made melodies, so Michael Karoli became more important to him. But . . . the words could be anything.' According to Schmidt, 'Damo often sang in a sort of Dada-speak – a mixture of English, German, Russian, Japanese or utterances that belonged to no language. That was great – there was no message, only sound. Lyrics were completely uninteresting.'

In late 1970, work would begin on what would be Can's third album release, in which the concept of inner space, of the group as a collective incantation, the working together of strands from the various avant-gardes of jazz, rock and classical was realised in a quite frightening, even sprawling manner. At times, on *Tago Mago*, the Can members are like so many latter-day Benjamin Franklins, flying their kites in an electric storm of their own making. Tago Mago is a private island off Ibiza where Liebezeit had holidayed in the summer. Named after the ill-fated brother of the conqueror Hannibal, its name happens to bear the meaning of 'rock magician', the sort of happy accident that appealed to Can's sense of serendipity. *Tago Mago* could never have been made with Malcolm Mooney, whose presence would have had an earthing effect on the disparate forces at work in the studio. With Suzuki at the mike, airy and aeriated by turns, things are less gravitationally bound, flying and pinging about, in and out of the loop, supercolliding.

Opener 'Paperhouse' doesn't sound like such a departure, with its familiar, helicopter-like mid-section as the group collectively take flight, but there's a subtle difference in Suzuki's placement in the mix, riding the silvery, scaly tail of Michael Karoli's melody rather than working off the percussion. This only frees up Liebezeit, however, rather than making him redundant; now it's as if a jetpack has been attached to his drum kit. 'Mushroom' cinematically marks a shift to a different, harsher film stock as Suzuki's mood really begins to swing, while 'Oh Yeah' fluctuates against the distant, swaying mountainous horizons of Schmidt's keyboards. 'Halleluwah' is a prolonged intensification, still in the tradition of 'Yoo Doo Right', as Czukay almost drops from sight, Liebezeit's percussion marches on in a rigid but irregular twelve/thirteen-step, and Karoli and Schmidt colour in with violins, saffron flourishes and, from the keyboardist, harrying interventions like military aircraft hoving and rumbling, as if about to drop acid from their bomb-bay doors. The nearest precedent or musical cousin to all this is electric Miles Davis – his *Jack Johnson* album was a similar mix of lilting, minimal, funky riffs and brutal, churning electronics.

It's on the second disc, and 'Aumgn' in particular, that *Tago Mago* really steps into the next chamber. The title is taken from the teachings of Aleister Crowley, the dark, Satanic inverse of the word 'Amen', which is recited three times at the end of the Gnostic Creed. It is Irmin Schmidt, rather than Suzuki, who takes up the 'Aumgn' chant, which, vari-sped and drenched in reverb, coils in a slow, serpentine manner throughout the mix. Can were never as earnestly or morbidly fixated on Crowley as, say, Led Zeppelin's Jimmy Page; their brazen adoption of this holiest of unholy words is, in its own way, as blasphemous an affront to subscribers to Crowley's Gnostic Catholic Church as it is to the conventionally pious. Karoli, however, was shocked at Schmidt's 'irreverent' use of the chant, convinced that it was unwise so blithely to toss a black magical incantation into a sound mix. Then there is the hyper-sped, Munchkin frenzy of 'Peking O', the hallucinatory, lysergic chatter of talking rats who have found a way to trigger a drum machine just by running on a wheel.

The disc is a masked ball of improvisation, realised in the sumptuous Schloss Nörvenich, in which the forces of yin and yang, light and shade, commingle and battle like fighting seahorses. Nothing supernatural is happening; rather, this is Can exploiting their extraordinary human resourcefulness, spontaneous creative powers and advanced understanding of how to navigate your way around studio space using your wits rather than state-of-the-art technology. It's also a creation of the editing suite; scissors, again, are one of the key instruments.

'Collage is one of the main principles of twentieth-century art – Picasso, Schwitters, Rauschenberg,' says Schmidt. 'And we used it in all kinds of possible ways, in editing a tape, or on "Aumgn", where we splice together the elements. Snippets, overdubs. There's a lot of collage. Eisenstein. Film basically is collage.'

'Aumgn' is a feat of splicing, of various happenings, musical and non-musical, including previous group rehearsals surreptitiously recorded by Czukay. It wasn't entirely premeditated; according to Michael Karoli, he, Czukay and Suzuki had played their way towards a 'supersoft, microscopic' sound, a most delicate and exquisitely soft vibe, a prolonged moment they were in and which they were in the process of committing to tape when Irmin entered the studio like a bull in a china shop and, in what was a bloodyminded but calculated act of creative intervention, started to smash a wooden chair to pieces. 'I could have killed Irmin,' he later said. In the ensuing, deliberately provoked chaos, a boy in the building rushes into the studio and chants along, mike stands topple, dogs bark, disciplined musicians screech and do violence to their instruments, percussion runs haywire, circuitry is cheerfully broken.

Tago Mago might never have come about as a double album, its second disc of 'silliness' allowed to moulder in the vault, had it not been for Hildegard Schmidt, who adamantly persuaded Siggi Loch of its worth. (She was also the early driving force behind the *Lost Tapes* project.) On *Tago Mago*, Can turn themselves inside out, spill out the guts and wires and organs of their internal workings, reveal the monsters and mischief of their inner space that belie the serenity of tracks like 'Bring Me Coffee or Tea'. The group never worked to a programme or agenda – what happened in the studio happened, and they enabled it. However, *Tago Mago* does capture a hint of what 1970 was about in its tussle of light and shade and hints of future Can tracks to come. Bumps in the night, scratching in the corridors, that long stretch in the small, pitch-black hours when the frolics of yesterday seem so long ago and tomorrow feels like it will never arrive. *Tago Mago* sits on the cusp between the dead sixties and the unborn seventies.

Certainly, its temporal and spatial awareness impressed their former mentor, recalls Schmidt. 'Yes, after *Tago Mago* came out, they convinced Stockhausen, who was reluctant, to do a blind test of listening to five German groups. Four of them he rejected fiercely, saying, "Come on, this is shit." But then he listened to all of "Aumgn". And he said, "That's really great." He even started to listen to it a second time and make a very precise analysis of certain parts, saying, "That's really intelligent." Then when he found it was Can, he said, "Ah, no wonder, they are my pupils." He observed things about the harmonics and so on that we had never thought about.'

*

Francis Durbridge was a British playwright and crime novelist who in his native country is remembered, if he is remembered at all, for the Paul Temple series, which starred the suave Francis Matthews in its early 1970s TV version. Durbridge specialised in murder mysteries in elegantly appointed surroundings, and from the late 1950s onwards his work was hugely popular in West Germany, so much so that there was outrage in 1962 when a comedian blurted out in a newspaper interview the name of the murderer in Durbridge's latest made-for-German-TV adventure. From that point on, all those involved in Durbridge productions were contractually sworn to secrecy regarding the outcome of the series – including Irmin Schmidt, who, through his film and TV connections which were a handy revenue stream for the group, had secured for Can a spot on Durbridge's *Das Messer*, which went out in 1971. As is often the case, music which would be considered too abrasive and uncongenial to mainstream ears if presented as a pop proposition was much better received in the context of a fraught, visual drama. So it was with 'Spoon', whose clipped, brass-like motif recurred like a police flashlight through the credits of the series, imposing itself on the public consciousness. It did nothing as a single in the UK, but in Germany it sold three hundred thousand copies.

Success at last, but Can had already made waves abroad. 'After the release of *Monster Movie*, there was a certain build-up of estimation,' recalls Schmidt. 'It helped that our first appearance in England was a real success, in 1970, I think. With the second tour, the public was crazy about it – not many people, only seven, eight thousand, but very enthusiastic and the press loved it. That, of course, helped, the enormous acceptance in England. And France, later, we had a fantastic reception. From the very first concert, which is considered legendary in France, which was a sellout, we had to play another concert for the extra one thousand waiting. Both nights were incredibly successful.'

It was only this success that had persuaded the initially chortling 'Can't' brigade to take the group seriously at all in Germany. Now, they were practically pop stars. Liebezeit, sceptical of their newfound fame, found the black lining in the silver cloud. 'It was one of the biggest TV hits of that time, everyone saw it. We had big concerts in Germany. After a while, people slowly got it. But at first they were thinking, "Ah, they are quite successful, so they must be good."'

Others came out of the woodwork, including their 'manager', Abi Ofarim, from whom the group had barely heard since Mooney had left. 'He was a completely useless manager,' recalled Karoli, who thought that the wealthy popster, dressed like a cross between a flower-power relic and a fugitive from a Spaghetti Western, didn't even look like a rock manager, let alone act like one. The final straw came after he had booked a concert for Can in Munich, and when they had rung Ofarim's office to ask the whereabouts of their hotel, they were told they would have to drive back to Cologne the same night. Hereon, Hildegard Schmidt would take charge of the band's affairs, though in West Germany at that time band managers were not officially allowed; such business was supposed to be handled by the art agency of the Federal Employment Office.

There was further stress as Can found themselves under pressure to finish recording their next album, 1972's *Ege Bamyası*. Michael Karoli fell ill, possibly a psychosomatic reaction to the impending deadline, which created in him more anxiety than it did in Schmidt and Suzuki, who spent much of their time playing chess.

Can were no longer at Schloss Nörvenich but had now moved to a disused cinema in the idyllic town of Weilerswist, south of Cologne, which they soundproofed with mattresses and upgraded with new equipment purchased by Czukay, digging into his savings. Yet, despite all this turmoil, the much-underrated *Ege Bamyası* sees Can in absolutely mid-season form, perfectly integrated and floating free. On 'Pinch' you can hear distant refractions of Miles Davis and Curtis Mayfield, but those remote comparisons are as near as it gets to what was going on in 1972. At their best here, Can sound perfectly in tune with the world, pan-global in their consciousness, yet aeons ahead of anything else happening in it. Can were post-rock even at a time when rock's narrative was in full blaze, engaged in a discreet long-distance relationship with funk before terms like 'fusion' had even been coined. 'Sing Swan Song', prefaced by the sounds of natural running water, is like an open window to the bucolic tranquillity of their immediate surroundings, the infinite, organic continuum of their sound thrumming in perfect rhythm and accord with nature itself. On 'I'm So Green' the harmonic understanding between Michael Karoli and Damo Suzuki is unparalleled.

If there are unfamiliar flavourings, it is due to the continuing, pervasive influence of African and Far Eastern music, with which all the Can members were profoundly familiar. Jaki Liebezeit, of course, had studied the patterns and cycles of Indian and North African music; Irmin Schmidt and Michael Karoli shared an interest in Balinese and African music, while Holger Czukay had recorded 'Boat-Woman Song', an early exercise in sampling, based around an instrumental loop with the vocals of Vietnamese women, in all their apparently discordant beauty, fluttering around the foreground.

Can also had their 'Ethnological Forgery Series' (as featured on the album *Unlimited Edition*) – they were refuting a phenomenon years before it even occurred, that of the rise of 'world music' in the mid-eighties. World music would became a deeply irritating, albeit well-meaning affectation on the part of Western musicians, a token of authenticity. If Paul Simon could be forgiven for using Ladysmith Black Mambazo as a backdrop on *Graceland*, then Mick Jagger's brief dalliance with Moroccan music in the late eighties felt more like an attempt to acquire a fashionable ethnicity by osmosis. Peter Gabriel, founder of WOMAD, and David Byrne in particular (who in 1999 wrote a memorable and acute editorial entitled 'I Hate World Music' for the *New York Times*) developed a scrupulous knowledge of the 'genre' which enabled them to reach a much wider audience, but at the same time, it was as if they were so awestruck by the excellence of African, Brazilian and Far Eastern musics that they themselves were debilitated as artists.

Elite rock developed an ambivalent relationship with world music – on one end of the spectrum, the condescension of Live Aid and the representation of Africa as an electric guitar; on the other, a preoccupation among white audiences who suddenly felt rather culturally anaemic by comparison with the authenticity of 'world music', which, paradoxically, impelled them towards a sort of token adoption or tourism which Can deplored. 'You summed it up perfectly – tourism,' says Czukay, recalling the laughter of the Vietnamese villagers when he took up their instruments and played alongside them. 'That's how it ended up. For us, it was humour. We are not Africans, we are not Asians.' And yet that lack of cultural pretence, the open declaration of inauthenticity declared in the naming of the 'Ethnological Forgery Series' – they neither exploited nor envied the music of other continents, but rather learned from it, and used it to enhance their sense of cultural identity rather than throw a smock or poncho over it. As Schmidt puts it, 'Forgery also has a lot to do with alchemy. It is, so to say, a melting of these things. The term "Ethnological Forgery Series" is an ironic name, not a persiflage.'

Breaking down Can's music at this time into its constituent parts is near impossible – it's all things and none, derived from every category from classical to pop yet falling into none of them. *Ege Bamyasi*'s title track is an exquisitely blended and flavoured stew, cooked from torn-up roots in a giant, metal, cylindrical melting pot. And then, with 'Soup', the pot is hurled from the stove. The track was only included to make up the album as otherwise it wouldn't have been long enough. Some three and a half minutes in, what has been a deadly build-up of Can at their rockiest, a throwback to the tempestuousness of the Mooney years, suddenly begins to disintegrate. Schmidt drops keyboard notes like a flurry of drips from a rusty basement pipe that has sprung multiple leaks. Karoli's guitar squeals in panic, Liebezeit ratchets up the percussive heartbeat, Czukay has apparently fled behind his console to take up operations there. Then, as if suddenly convulsed by the channelled spirit of Tim Buckley circa *Starsailor*, Suzuki breaks into a non-verbal vocal frenzy, as barely identifiable sheet waves of viciously serrated noise strafe and circle in the mix like an aircraft burning up in a tailspin. It's like some recreation of an early Dada theatre event, with Hugo Ball declaiming his phonetic poetry as all around him fellow artists concoct a cacophonous parody of the chaotic paroxysms wrought by the First World War, with someone having found a way of miking and maxing up the Futurist Luigi

Russolo's noise intonators for the event. It's a cathartic release of the palpable tensions that always kept Can simmering, of nameless rage, of abstract protest, and what those pop pickers who bought the album on the basis of the hit single 'Spoon' made of it is a matter for speculation. 'We all had the potential of violence in us and it was brought out – but in the music,' says the personally peaceable, artistically combative Schmidt. 'Some of the live performances were so violent, extremely violent. But this experience of the second half of the twentieth century – all of this violence, it had to be brought out. It was not idyllic.'

That said, Can's 1973 release, *Future Days*, is intensely, almost blindingly idyllic, so painless it hurts. As the metallic, cricket-like effects of the title track increase in volume over its nine and a half perfect minutes, it's as if we're on the point of gladly being swallowed up by the sun. The album benefited from a general good mood in the studio, as the members returned fresh from holiday, enjoying the boost of a hit single, and the comfort zone it afforded them. The strife and anxiety that had made life so difficult during the *Ege Bamyası* sessions had abated. It's often supposed that great art requires adversity to thrive and is starved by tranquillity; Orson Welles's speech in *The Third Man* about four hundred years of peace and prosperity in Switzerland merely producing the cuckoo clock has a lot to it. On *Future Days*, however, Can crucially turn this assumption on its head. Czukay described it as Can's 'ambient' album, but its ambience is that of the year 2050, a dappled landscape of lapping, glittering waters and shimmering mirages, but whose beauty quickens the heartbeat, heightens the desire to engage with what's happening around you, rather than lull you into falling asleep in its bath. Liebezeit is a one-man rhythm factory on 'Bel Air', Czukay tracking him in lengthy single-note runs, while Karoli in particular trails and blazes all over the canvas on the album he personally considered his finest achievement. *Future Days* stands as a paradigm of perfect integration and functionalism, quietly scotching the ideal (ironically a driving one in the actual Bel Air, adjacent to Hollywood, California) that Utopia is arrived at by allowing the ego to run untrammelled in pursuit of its own exclusive desires. On *Future Days*, all ego is sublimated. Can is the thing, the organism that shines.

Then there is 'Moonshake', whose robotic discipline and 'solo' of scrapes and whirring cogs might have made it seem like a pleasant little R2-D2-style curiosity in its own time but can now be seen as a prototype for the sequencer-driven regularity that underpins so much modern, machine-driven music – *Future Days* indeed, as revealed in 1973, the missing link between Jaki Liebezeit's anti-free-jazz epiphany and the electronica of our own time.

As for Suzuki, he wafts swallow-like about *Future Days*, a living embodiment of its antigravitational push – except at the beginning of the title track, when, in a literal exercise in immersiveness, his vocals are recorded underwater. All was heaven in Can-world – and then, Suzuki found God.

According to Czukay, Suzuki 'met a girl who was firmly bent on marrying the most famous singer in Germany'. She was also a Jehovah's Witness, and, having bagged a smitten Suzuki, persuaded him that he would have to give up his career as a singer. At the height of his powers and success with Can he duly did so. 'They told him he could not carry on with his hippie career – he must be a good husband. So he left Can – which was a big mistake.'

So it was that Suzuki was drawn back into the life of domestic obligation from which he had made such a dramatic break as a youth, out of the Can framework which had allowed him absolute free play. His story almost had a tragic ending when he fell gravely ill soon after leaving the group. 'One day his wife called me and said, "Come to the hospital, Damo is dying,"' recalls Liebezeit. 'I said, "This is nonsense, he's a very strong man, he's not dying." Of course, Jehovah's Witnesses are not allowed to have blood transfusions – but he asked for one and was completely cured. This was in 1975. He divorced soon after. He worked for a Japanese company for a while, near Cologne. He had a very good job there. He worked there for over ten years, but quit to make music again. He lives in Cologne but I never meet him. I don't know if he feels bad for leaving Can.'

Suzuki resumed his music career in 1983. Nowadays, he is permanently on the road, engaged on a non-stop tour in which he plays with local pick-up musicians, driving his own destiny, determined to make up for the lost years but with very little indeed to say about his time with Can. 'I wasn't really thinking about many things,' he told Mike Barnes of *The Wire* in 2004. 'I was part of the band, but actually not really part of the Can, because for me it didn't matter. It's just something that happens, because I was just a hippie – I didn't really have any kind of opinions.'

After Suzuki's departure, Can didn't wait for serendipity to strike a third time and handled vocals themselves, with Karoli and Schmidt sharing. 1974's *Soon Over Babaluma* was their last great album; on 'Dizzy Dizzy' (featuring Karoli on violin) and 'Come sta, la luna' Can have absorbed the entire topography of world music to their own, unique ends and hint at Jon Hassell, Fourth World Funk dreams that would later inspire David Byrne and Talking Heads. However, it's on side two of the album, in 'Chain Reaction' and 'Quantum Physics', that Can's sense of space and craft fuse to make something like a spacecraft. 'Chain Reaction' begins with a gypsy wedding-style dervish before, in true Can style, things begin to lift off, culminating in 'Quantum Physics' and the gaping, cosmic tones of Schmidt's Alpha 77 synthesizer, as the group recede into space, with Czukay as bass pilot, Liebezeit's drums slowly reduced to a distant patter. 1975's *Landed* featured the track 'Unfinished', an extension of 'Quantum Physics', akin to the assemblage of a space station, commissioned but never used, whose meaning and purpose, like that of Can themselves, would remain unexplored for years to come.

None of the Can members have ever lost their creative touch, their relevance or prescience – but Can itself began to suffer the fate of all organic progress and started to deteriorate from the mid-seventies onwards. There was one more bright moment in the popular firmament, however: in 1976, they had a hit with 'I Want More', on which their structural, rhythmical logic converged fortuitously with the impending disco boom. They appeared on *Top of the Pops* in August 1976, in what seem the rather gloomy studios of that barren pop time, following Robin Sarstedt. Noel Edmonds, every sartorial inch the epitome of 1976 and the crying necessity for punk, introduces the band, chortling implicitly at the band's Germanic origins but resisting an '*Achtung*'. Painfully, he cannot resist a pun, wondering aloud if Can have a chance of making the 'Top Tin'.

Unfortunately, as Schmidt recalls, the full Can complement was not available for the performance, with a little fellow with a bubble perm who patently isn't Michael Karoli taking up guitar duties. 'Michael was in Africa. We were suddenly number four in the charts – we all went on holidays after its release, not expecting it to be a hit. The rest of us were in Yugoslavia, Jaki at home, so we could fly over. But Michael was uncontactable – he was on safari. We told them the story. We asked him to announce that Michael is hunting lions in Africa because everyone knows how Michael looks and this little guy was so different – but they didn't.' After all, the *Top of the Pops* producers doubtless thought to themselves, 'What's the difference between one German musician and another?' Certainly, they were entertaining, but a transient European group, surely, like the Dutch group Focus, destined to have a single hit but then never trouble the all-important British Top Tin again. But then, to this young viewer, Noel Edmonds was the last word in style and pop omniscience.

*

Can in their prime took a very hands-on approach to their studio work, with the editing a key aspect. It's one of their ironies that the fluency and naturalism of their infinite jams were actually artificially created effects born of the editing process. 'Holger edited,' recalls Schmidt. 'He was the technician. But the editing was shared by the rest of us. The decision-making as to how the collage was constructed was down to Michael, Holger and me. Jaki didn't like the editing thing at all – but he had a very important role. He listened to it and if we had fucked up the groove it was not allowed. We had to, when we made edits, make sure there was a continuity of the groove. It could change, but it had to make sense as a groove. It couldn't speed up for no reason, for instance. The architecture was done all together.'

Can made no bones about this, nor any secret of the fact that despite what Schmidt once described as their 'telepathy', their working relationship was not one of frictionless, mutual agreement – unlike Kraftwerk, they were unabashedly public about their behind-the-scenes tensions and arguments, chuckling about them like a couple in a long-term relationship, reminiscing on their last big bust-up, secure in the knowledge that there would be more in the future. 'Yes,' says Schmidt. 'Of course, it's impossible to have four bandleaders, five with Malcolm in the group. Of course there were disagreements. There was no leader. So we could discuss things.'

Can's gradual demise in the late seventies wasn't so much due to intolerable differences as to the inevitable onset of multitrack technology, which the group reluctantly embraced, but which meant that they were no longer communicating with one another in real time, musically. 'Technology is always overestimated,' believes Schmidt. 'There is an industry which is there to sell instruments. If people think that technology makes a difference, it doesn't.' Hitherto, they'd been recorded by Czukay on a two-track machine. 'When sixteen-track came in, we had to learn everything from new again,' says Czukay. 'A group is a living organism. A band should be like a gang, everyone steaming from the same horn. At this point, everyone became more individual. Which is fine, no problem. By that point, we had our own "musical families" – we drifted away from one another.' Certainly, this was the case for Czukay, increasingly estranged from the rest of the group, less and less interested in playing, with Can at any rate.

Moreover, the new musicians they felt obliged to recruit, such as Rebop Kwaku Baah, did not always fully get with the Can ethos, the discreet generosity it involved, and particularly their payments scheme (in which monies for recorded tracks were split evenly between the group members, regardless of their creative input into them), which was unfamiliar to them as seasoned music-industry players. The last four seventies Can albums, *Saw Delight*, *Flow Motion*, *Can* and *Out of Reach*, have their moments but often they feel to be flowing through the motions indeed, no longer pushing at the envelope, the musicians alive but Can the organism dying. The eventual demise of the group was greeted with equanimity; Liebezeit saw it as quite normal, according to his belief that a band's natural life is 'about the same as that of a dog'.

Can and Kraftwerk, Cologne and Düsseldorf, chalk and cheese. Kraftwerk 'were reaching for something exactly the opposite of what we were', says Schmidt. 'We are expressionists, very German expressionists. It's like comparing Bachmann to Mondrian.' Whereas Kraftwerk have always kept a firm metal lid on their interior lives, Can's ethos is to unleash theirs, on the audience and each other, making it a point of artistic principle to drive each other to distraction. Kraftwerk are about determinacy, Can about chance. Kraftwerk are abstemious, Can embraced drugs and life's good things; a 10.30 a.m. interview with the group in 1997 saw Michael Karoli order his first beer of the day. Kraftwerk embraced the functional logic of twentieth-century technology, Can embraced magic and were undone by technological advance. Can naturally perished, Kraftwerk have carried on, with the durability of metal.

And yet, while Kraftwerk continue to exist as a structure and a continually modified spectacle of light and design and sound, it is the members of Can, with the exception of the late Karoli, who have continued to generate new and original material through the years. Holger Czukay followed Can's demise with *Movies* (1980), in which his childhood love of shortwave radio prompted him to create a patchwork of the sonic detritus of East and West ranging from the sublime to the silly. Pieces like 'Cool in the Pool' and 'Persian Love' anticipated the widespread use of samplers by several years. He went on to work with David Sylvian, Jah Wobble and the Eurythmics, among others, an old master floating over a new ambient/electronic seascape. As well as continuing his career as a composer of soundtracks, Irmin Schmidt has created the monumental opera *Gormenghast*, and worked with his son-in-law Kumo, aka Jono Podmore, on albums in which middle and late avant-garde twentieth-century techniques cross jagged swords. 'Most older musicians don't make challenging music because they surround themselves with admirers,' said Schmidt in an interview with *Stereotype* magazine in 1999. 'Admirers are boring, unless they're very rich or pretty young women. If you want to stay creative, you have to find younger musicians who can blow some fresh air into your mind. I'm always looking for people who have skills I don't have, so I can learn something.'

As for Liebezeit, he has puttered continuously and undimmed through the decades. While the group took breaks during gigs in the 1970s, Liebezeit would set up a rhythm on a drum machine to fill in the interlude, for the dancing or atmospheric pleasure of patrons. It is as if he has been the steady heartbeat of Can during their busy life and afterlife. He lived in the Can studio in the countryside for seventeen years after the group split up, only moving back into the centre of Cologne when the price of petrol forced him to. He has continued to develop and disseminate his theories of percussion, working in combination with fellow Can members or the Berlin-based Burnt Friedman on a series of albums. 'In the nineties, I started to play more electronic music – sequencers, synthesizers. I started to think like a machine very early on but it took a while to get rid of these ideas, until the nineties, when I started to think in a different way from rock and jazz playing.'

He understands, however, the malign role machinery has played in the modern music industry, as an instrument of cost-effectiveness. Even Schlager has its own man–machine relationship nowadays – the singer, the karaoke backing track.

'It's easy to copy something with a machine. And cheap. It costs no money to make music. One person can make a full orchestra. You don't have to hire a drummer, just put everything together onto the computer – it's perfect, no mistakes. You don't need expensive studios, you can sing perfectly using the computer – no need even to buy tape.'

And yet there is still something radical about human beings playing like machines.

'Yes. In a way, you have to be able to play like a machine. But you can be better than a machine because of the human ear – you can hear what else is going on.' Such was the joy of Can – their openness, their attentiveness to one another, to conflict as well as communion, a channel for the very electric energy of life itself, in all its variegation, its unpredictability, but also, when ears were open and egos suppressed, its potential for a harmony of which life itself has fallen short. Can were not just a group but a way of being, a way indeed of living forever, an infinite, organic continuum. Said Michael Karoli, three years before he died, 'The soul of the entire thing was not composed of our four or five souls but was a creature named Can. That is very important. And this creature, Can, made the music. When my hour comes, I'll know that, apart from my children, I've helped create another living being.'

3 Kraftwerk and the Electrification of Modern Music

> 'Our parents were bombed out of their homes. Their main interest was to reconstruct a life for themselves. They became obsessed with material things and went over the top. In the sixties our generation reintroduced consciousness and a social conscience into Germany. Music didn't exist and we had to make it up.'
>
> Ralf Hütter, talking to Mark Cooper, 1982

> 'Much as Germany had to rebuild after the war, so we had to build up everything new from scratch.'
>
> Ralf Hütter, talking to the author

In April 2012, New York's Museum of Modern Art played host to Kraftwerk. Interest in the event, described as 'the first synthetic retrospective of Kraftwerk's oeuvre', was intense and black-market tickets were changing hands for hundreds of dollars, with the paying audience limited to 450 per night. The almost painfully hip attendees, posing and peering, included a smattering of celebrities such as Michael Stipe and ranged in age from fifty-somethings who had worshipped Kraftwerk in high school to youngsters for whom they were the stuff of ancient synthpop legend rather than the soundtrack to their lives. The whole affair felt like a Conference of the Futurisms: robots, constructivism, throwaway 3D glasses to view the performance, speculative, holographic technology, neon lighting, digitisation.

Why such curiosity? Despite coy hints of new material in the pipeline, with which enthusiasts had been periodically fed since *Electric Cafe*, their last album 'proper' back in 1986 (discounting 2003's *Tour de France Soundtracks*), this was an elaborate package of their classics – over eight consecutive nights, they would play eight of their albums in full. It was hardly a comeback or reunion – despite their increasingly reclusive airs, Kraftwerk had been touring pretty much every year of the new century. Only one of the original Kraftwerk members remained – Ralf Hütter, with Florian Schneider having left the group for obscure reasons, though very possibly the arduousness of touring. In the late 1990s, Schneider looked distinctly uncomfortable when waylaid by a pop journalist for a Brazilian TV channel, that trademark, almost leering smile looking a little careworn, politely fending off her queries with the most basic, monosyllabic responses. Perhaps the prospect of Kraftwerk as a touring installation is no longer congenial. Now, alongside Hütter, it was Henning Schmitz, Fritz Hilpert and Stefan Pfaffe.

The excitement and attendant flurry of press derive from Kraftwerk appearing at an art museum – as if they have finally received admission into a higher aesthetic realm, established, as one enthusiastic punter put it, as a 'cultural institution'. Nothing so crass as the rock 'n' roll Hall of Fame for Kraftwerk. In taking their place in MOMA they could at last claim that they had realised their long-declared intention to make of themselves a *Gesamtkunstwerk*, the sort of total art dreamt of by Wagner in which music and visuals and theatre were fully integrated.

Of course, MOMA benefited from this event too. The museum's directors are not averse to attracting attention by featuring artefacts of popular culture – they had previously exhibited an Apple computer, possibly less concerned about the category error this might have represented than the publicity that ensued. Moreover, while the fates of contemporary avant-garde art and contemporary avant-garde music have differed wildly since the beginning of the twentieth century, the one hugely popular, the other obdurately languishing in obscurity, sound has become an ever-increasing component of the art galleries, affording them a new lease of life, a certain contemporary electric relevance.

That said, Kraftwerk, who by this point as a group were over forty years old, sat in strange, if triumphant relationship to the year 2012. In his one-piece black unitard, modelled on the artwork from their *Electric Cafe* album, Ralf Hütter, by now in his early sixties, looked like some senior admiral from an enemy federation in *Space: 1999*. It is frequently, and rightly, said of Kraftwerk that they were essentially responsible for the electrification of modern music – the cables of post-punk, industrial, techno and hip hop all lead back to *Autobahn*, *Trans-Europe Express* and *Computer World*. It's also said that, having initially, patronisingly regarded them as a novelty – Euro-Smurfs on stylophones – the world eventually caught up with Kraftwerk and revered them. Even the staid, stadium likes of Coldplay and U2 pay due honour to Kraftwerk, with Bono feting them as 'a great soul band' and Chris Martin recycling the riff of 'Computer Love' on 'Talk'. (Kraftwerk granted their permission with a terse communiqué reading 'Yes'.) And yet, in 2012, they retained the air of belonging to some bygone astronaut era, veterans of an abandoned space project. The fact that they produced so little material after 1986 only exacerbates this sense. For all their *gesamt*-ness, their totality, their completeness, it is as if they proposed something that, like jetpacks or flying cars, somehow failed to materialise. It's as if the world never did live up to the architectural blueprint that they laid out, with its deft pen-and-ink depictions of a serenely functional and reconfigured new world.

For while so many of the highways and byways of modern music lead back to Kraftwerk, no one is quite like them. Although the likes of Underground Resistance and Drexciya have continued to pay homage to the precise, railroad rhythms set down by Kraftwerk on *Trans-Europe Express*, elsewhere electronic beats have gone through a whole host of mutations, from acid house to dubstep. Moreover, who has come close to approaching the flat, fey vocal stylings of Ralf Hütter? Their immediate electropop children, the Human League et al., tended to replace their gentle, surface complacency with a slightly overwrought sense of angst. And who still employs four people to do the job that two or even one could quite easily do?

Kraftwerk, then, have retained their original sense of oddness – populist and yet brazenly concealing their true selves for the sake of some higher, enigmatic artistic purpose. In a *Culture Show* interview in 2009, Ralf Hütter dispatched one of the robots to be 'interviewed' – more of a comical signifier of a robot, closer to a ventriloquist's dummy than a state-of-the-art specimen of Artificial Intelligence. In answer to questions, Hütter delivered Kraftwerkian aphorisms via a voicebox, verbal capsules of bland concealment. ('Technology through advancement. Think first.') There are reminders of the US group the Residents, who refused to identify themselves at all from the very beginnings of their career, thus removing themselves as personalities entirely from the artistic process – but that option was never open to Hütter and co., who started out in the 'ordinary' alternative stream of Krautrock, long-haired and musically meandering and trying to make their mark, before they 'became' Kraftwerk. For a more pertinent comparison, you'd maybe have to look at the art world to which Kraftwerk have been admitted as honorary guests – specifically to Gilbert and George, two very public and yet very private artists, for whom privacy isn't just a matter of personal temperament but a conceptual imperative, the better to preserve their 'selves' as the work of art. Impeccably besuited, anti-anti-establishment, as unfailingly polite as they are unforthcoming to the impertinently nosy interviewer, the comparisons are myriad. Moreover, watch Gilbert and George perform their 'dancing sculpture' on YouTube, zig-zagging about jerkily to Dave Dee, Dozy, Beaky, Mick and Tich's sixties hit 'Bend It', and you're reminded of Kraftwerk doing their own 'mechanical dance' in the video to 'Showroom Dummies' – just as stiff and formal and hilariously uninhibited, and, improbably, quite clearly accustomed to dancing. But who is the joke on?

Ralf Hütter was born in 1946, Florian Schneider a year later. In subsequent years, they were fond of saying that they had 'no fathers' or, given the fact of the war, had 'no incentive' to respect their fathers – but this is perhaps taken as metaphorical rather than autobiographical, a general remark about the generation who, collectively, had to begin again. Hütter was the son of a doctor and enjoyed a comfortable, untroubled upbringing conditional only on his living up to the expectations of his class and educational background. Schneider's father was much more prominent. Paul Schneider von Esleben (1915–2005) was a noted architect, examples of whose work can be seen in Berlin and Munich – sleek, functional, discreet, modernist, affording ample light. He also designed the headquarters of the Mannesmann Steel Corporation in Düsseldorf. When interviewed by Glenn O'Brien in 1977 about the attitude of their parents towards their music, Ralf Hütter remarked, 'They would like to prevent us from doing what we do. We are doing business, but we should be doing office business.' But if Schneider senior was disgusted or dismayed by his son's choice of career, it didn't stop him from going so far as to secure the rental of the property in Bergalee which would be home to Kling Klang, Kraftwerk's legendary base.

Hütter and Schneider met at the Düsseldorf Conservatory in 1968 on, of all things, a jazz-improvisation course, where Hütter played electric organ and Schneider the flute, an instrument he played in a jazz group with various future members of Amon Düül. They played together in the Fluxus-inspired milieu in which student life, high art and free music intersected, playing at galleries, parties and colleges, eschewing (or being eschewed by) the conventional pop circuit. Schneider had briefly been a member of a collective which went by the name of PISSOFF, made up of Düsseldorf musicians and alumni from the Joseph Beuys school, including artist Eberhard Kranemann, who later went on to collaborate with Neu!. In keeping with their name, PISSOFF played three-hour sets of ultra-loud noise with an aversion to pitch and melody, a primal roar of 1968 protest.

Hütter and Schneider decided to form a group, the Organisation, with Basil Hammoudi, Butch Hauf, Fred Monicks and others, using an array of instrumentation including glockenspiels, gongs, maracas, plastic hammers and tambourines, the full armoury of the hippie improv collective of the time. The producer Conny Plank, a former jazz musician and sound engineer on the lookout for groups who were looking to forge a distinctively new sound, took the Organisation under his wing and enabled them to record their first album, *Tone Float*, in 1970.

Hütter and Schneider would doubtless no more care to listen back to *Tone Float* than they would to look back at photos of themselves at the time as raw young hippies. The only real hint of the Kraftwerk to come is in the name, which, although faintly redolent of communal music-making, implies a businesslike formality, as well as a Stockhausenesque sense of an apparently 'free' sound field actually operating under preset conditions. There's the gentle, punning humour of the name (the organ – see what he did there?) and, perhaps, an equally gentle intimation of which of the Organisation's members was ultimately calling the shots.

Not that *Tone Float* really feels like that. The cover artwork is a particularly garish example of the misguided expressionism of 1970, a side profile of a colourfully hirsute hippie Übermensch staring with solemn purpose into the black distance, as if wary of the decade to come. It's been maligned for its indulgence, its lack of focus – a spoiled broth, a druggy free-for-all. But in its intricacy and irregularity, its multi-instrumentation and ethnological borrowings, it represented some of the best ideals of the time – no ego, no gratuitous demonstration of virtuosity, no lazy relapse into the leaden commonplace blues-rock clichés which were all over the place in 1970, no privileging of one genre over another.

It's by no means absolutely novel – the influence of the live side of Pink Floyd's *Ummagumma*, released a year earlier, is palpable. But accepted for what it is, *Tone Float* is a pretty decent outing, making up for its lack of conceptual intent with its intelligent workings around the sound palette. Recorded in the unlikely confines of an oil refinery, its centrepiece is the twenty-odd-minute title track, emerging from a rustle of bells and percussive rolls and chimes resounding from all angles in the mix, before settling into a pseudo-ethnic loop. Hütter's electric organ slowly but surely sidles to centre stage and the players reach a clangorous crescendo, before settling into a subdued, shuffling groove which is the first intimation of the sort of rhythmical underpinning you'd more usually associate with Kraftwerk. Eventually, Florian Schneider and his treated flute emerge from the tropical thickets, all animalistic wails and cirrus trails of echo.

'Silver Forest' is the most notable item on side two, Hütter's organ leaving spindly glow trails as, modified and filtered, it ascends into impossibly high registers, while on 'Noitasinagro' Hütter's organ paces about with the measured tread of a cleric as an electric violin weaves faltering signatures like a Bonfire Night sparkler.

Thanks to producer Conny Plank's clout, the album secured an international release, but sales were poor. Whereas Can, in particular, had immediately found their collective mojo and interlocked as players, *Tone Float*, for all its merits, is the work of musicians who have yet to discover who they are and what they're about. There exists a single clip of the Organisation, playing an early version of 'Ruckzuck', recorded at the Second Essener Pop and Blues Festival in 1970. You would think from this that the star of the group was the kaftaned fellow on the bongos playing with a gusto that seems only chemical in explanation, from whom the cameraman can barely tear himself away. There are segments of Schneider wailing into his flute, and barely a glimpse of Hütter, save for his fingers working the far right-hand side of the keyboard. For a group who later, quite properly and indignantly, dissociated themselves from the Krautrock genre, here they look like an almost too on-the-nose parody of it, splendid as this clip is.

The Organisation's other members melted away and Hütter and Schneider decided to carry on, self-determining and taking on outsiders only where and when necessary, rather than subsuming themselves into a wider collective. Like many of their fellow musical innovators, they saw the advantage of shutting themselves away in order to begin again more effectively. Hence their hire of what would become Kling Klang, a rented property in one of the less salubrious areas of Düsseldorf. Then, it was at the hub of the city, within sight of the main power station, whose industrial, artificial glow would inspire the group's name – *Kraftwerk*, German for 'power station'. Kling Klang was an exclusive space in which Kraftwerk could determine and develop their own sound and identity, but also set very much within the context of urban, industrial Germany, still in the last throes of postwar regeneration and rebuilding. Düsseldorf was the industrial heartland, the Ruhrgebiet, of Germany, even of a greater Europe, but it was all formidable glass and steel in the finish of its appearance, thanks not least to architects like Schneider's father. Here they set about soundproofing the place and installing tape machines, in preparation for rehearsal work on their debut album.

'We were able to shut out the distractions and define our own identity,' Hütter told Simon Witter in 2005. 'We were in our studio, with the doors closed and there was silence. Now what is our music, what is our language, what is our sound? We realised we had to start from zero. It's an amazing opportunity . . . We didn't have to reject anything. It was an empty space. And that same feeling was everywhere. The different artforms, literature, film and painting were everywhere in Germany in the late sixties, they were blossoming.'

One of the dominant features of *Tone Float* had been generous downfalls of free percussion, reaching monsoon levels on 'Rhythm Salad'. On *Kraftwerk 1*, they would employ two different drummers – Andreas Hohmann and Klaus Dinger, one of Krautrock's more volcanic personalities, who would later co-found Neu! – as they looked to rein in such tendencies. Wild, jazz-driven frenzies of sticksmanship were quite the rage of the day, as Werner 'Zappi' Diermaier would demonstrate to colossal effect in Faust. However, Kraftwerk were in search of a drummer who, like Jaki Liebezeit in Can, would willingly 'underplay'.

These issues aren't quite resolved on the album, which oscillates between passages of percussive fury and rhythmless, amorphous experimentalism, but does represent a significant step in Kraftwerk's evolution. 'Ruckzuck', featuring Hohmann on drums, is the standout track, in which Schneider attacks his flute with the breathy fury of a Roland Kirk, within the linear restraint of a looped, varispeed drum cycle, while Hütter occasionally breaks up the progress with almost petulant gales of electric organ. Conny Plank is at the controls and you sense his guiding hand in the elegant fading in and fading out, and the clever use of stereopanning, which anticipates Neu!'s 'E-Musik'.

'Stratovarius', meanwhile, an early addition to Kraftwerk's pantheon of corny English-language puns, is in its fragmentary structure more like some outtake from *The Faust Tapes* – a coiling, circling, heavily filtered organ intro is superseded by some desultory musique concrète clatter and a spare dialogue between a nagging, guitarish violin and stomping percussion, again receding in the mix, the sound equivalent of a camera slowly zooming out.

After this, Hohmann left the group and was replaced by Dinger. He's not immediately employed on 'Megaherz', which, after a squally opening of treated organ, settles into a reverie of keyboard and flute and gentle, regular flurries of wind chime, at times verging on a sort of pre-dawn silence. Tracks like this are maybe the reason why Kraftwerk disowned the album, as it apparently bears no relationship to their later, more foursquare, self-knowing and brilliantly functional pop work. But the album does overall offer a picture of the experimental hinterlands from which Kraftwerk logically emerged. In fleeting passages it also prefigures, of all people, Boards of Canada, whose misty, pre-distressed instrumental works, soaked in grainy analogue, are the epitome of 'hauntology', that very British and imprecise attempt to replicate or recapture the ghost lost in the machinery of early synthesizer music, be it in pop records or as used in public-information films, schools programmes or BBC jingles. And yet Kraftwerk themselves sound as if they are caught up in a proto-hauntological longing of their own, shot through with an imprecise yearning for some lost Arcadia.

Florian Schneider described this period as 'archaeology', but his playing is one of the most distinctive features of Kraftwerk's earliest albums. 'Maybe at some point they should release those early albums,' says Michael Rother. 'Not these bootleg albums with these badly balanced mixes and my fuzzy guitar . . . but the ones with the great stuff Florian does on the electric flute. He played a very rhythmic, dirty, distorted style, playing it through an effects unit – but the sound engineers at the TV and radio studios didn't see the significance of those elements and put him too low in the mix.' As it went, it could be argued that the story of Kraftwerk is the gradual marginalisation, and eventual removal, of Florian Schneider.

The album does conclude on a quite startling note. In later musical life, Kraftwerk would become renowned for their synthetic transcriptions of modern, mechanised life. On 'Vom Himmel hoch' ('From Heaven Above'), the first few minutes are a literal electronic simulation of the sound of aircraft swooping and shedding their bomb loads, which then transmogrifies into a workable jamming rhythm, with Dinger at last getting to exercise his sticks. The opening passage is, however, a rare, direct reference in the Krautrock canon to wartime, whose traumas and experiences generally play a much more suppressed and subliminal role in the music.

Although once he had departed Kraftwerk Klaus Dinger made a disparaging remark about having 'split with the millionaire sons for social reasons', according to Hütter Kraftwerk existed in relative penury at the time, shuttling about to wherever concerts would take them, anything from college venues to galleries to factory works dos and youth clubs, though their scope was restricted – they did not play beyond Dortmund. Hütter did recall their playing at an art gallery, jamming with Holger Czukay and Jaki Liebezeit of Can in an impromptu session one night. However, Liebezeit himself has no recollection of this event, which probably reflects Kraftwerk's position in the pecking order at the time, relative nobodies on the scene. Kraftwerk were still a rough, ready and hirsute proposition at this stage, their line-up unsettled, casting around for other musicians who might help enable them to realise a vision that was still murky to them.

They lured Michael Rother away from Spirits of Sound, another Düsseldorf-based group which also featured Wolfgang Flür, who at that point did not figure in Kraftwerk's plans. This was the end for Spirits of Sound, but Kraftwerk's own future looked by no means assured. Bassist Eberhard Kranemann, the old PISSOFF compadre, came and swiftly went; then, Hütter himself departed the group, under pressure to pursue his studies in architecture, which his family might well have regarded as an inevitable fallback once the boy had got this longhaired rock folly out of his system. Nonetheless, during this curious hiatus, Hütter remained in touch with Kraftwerk, coolly describing his break from the group in terms of a trial separation from a marriage. As ever with Kraftwerk, if there were any internal musical disagreements, they were strictly not for public consumption.

And so Kraftwerk were reduced to a trio – Michael Rother, Klaus Dinger and Florian Schneider. In a clip from a performance they gave on the German TV series *The Beatclub*, we see Rother, resembling George Harrison in his *All Things Must Pass* phase, face wreathed in curtains of hair, bearded and moustached, Dinger in shades and diaphanous-sleeved white shirt and, to the right, Schneider. Prefaced by a primordial brine of filtered electronics and chirruping feedback and a visual drench of wafting blues, neon purples and melting greys, Schneider breathes stertorously into his flute before the first, tentative chimes of melody take up, then the cumulative, prototype *motorik* groove, accelerating in pace and volcanic intensity, before some *kosmische* curlicues from Rother. Schneider is almost peripheral, his flute buried in the mix. (It's the same story on another clip, from WDR, recorded in the same year, with Dinger's drum kit set at centre stage and the more withdrawn Schneider drowned out in a thunder of percussion and wah-wah riffing.) Only his workman's dungarees, unfashionably short hair, the pop-art traffic cones and the stencilled KRAFTWERK logo in the opening credits of this appearance remind you, conceptually, of who or what this group is – with Rother and Dinger working each other into a riffing frenzy, it's a 'Kraftwerk' spiralling off into an alternative and parallel universe. Had they done so, then the Kraftwerk we know today might well have burned out before they were conceived. Had Ralf Hütter decided, or been persuaded, to stick full-time with his architectural studies, in fulfilment of his bourgeois destiny, then it is most likely that Schneider too would have dropped away and we would have been left with a Kraftwerkless Krautrock. An entire template for contemporary pop music might have gone unwritten.

As it turned out, it was Rother and Dinger who jumped first, fed up with the life of a jobbing band well down the bill, with no roadies and playing second filtered fiddle at festivals to touring overseas bands like Leicester prog rockers Family, and making the logical decision to launch Neu!. 'When the atmosphere wasn't right, the sound wasn't right,' Michael Rother told John Doran of

The Quietus in 2010. 'I think it was quite terrible and apart from those good times on stage there were a lot of arguments, especially between Florian and Klaus. They were arguing a lot. So we tried to do the sessions for the second Kraftwerk album in summer of '72 and that failed because it was quite clear that we were dependent on some rough live atmosphere to make us create that enormous noise and heavy beat that we did. So it was just natural for us to separate.' Ralf Hütter rejoined the band, now reduced to a duo, unencumbered by other musicians who were out of sync with their own aims. They retreated to their studio, and, armed with oscillators, tape echo and filtering devices, as well as organ and guitars, they made their second album, *Kraftwerk 2*.

'Atem', with its slow, amplified respiratory noises, could have been lifted from the later 'regions' of Stockhausen's *Hymnen*, whose vast, orbital exploration of national anthems from around the world and electro-acoustic simulations of a post-apocalyptic landscape give way to the sound of breathing, the ultimate representation of all human existence. The rusted, broken guitar chords of 'Strom' (which would have sat perfectly on any twenty-first-century Warp Records release, no questions asked) give way to the similarly broody 'Spule 4' and its ultimately anti-climactic conversational strumming, and 'Harmonika', whose accordion-like, wet-afternoon-indoors drones are reminiscent of the harmonium music of the Armenian spiritual teacher George Gurdjieff – or, if you prefer, two profoundly bored musicians stranded in the very early seventies, sitting around waiting for Brian Eno to open the doors to ambient music.

The real business end of the album is the opener. 'Klingklang', following a soft-focus intro of chimes and bells, suddenly ignites electronically into life. The rolling bassline, later reprised on 'Autobahn', the incessant, minimal patter of Hütter's keyboards, Schneider's breathy, smudged, treated flute phrases, the unsettling moments of varispeed would all be recognisable as Kraftwerkian/

Conny Plank tropes. However, what's striking, like the earliest, sputtering ignition of electropop, is the skittering undertow of drum machine, an instrument not entirely unknown to popular music (Can, Sly Stone and Robin Gibb on 'Saved by the Bell' had all used the device by 1971) but here looking set to play a key role as part of a new, eerily Meccano-like pop structure.

It was around this time, according to Ralf Hütter, that in a happy moment of inspiration at a dance party at a Düsseldorf arts centre he more or less invented modern dance music. 'I had this old little drum machine,' he would later recall. 'At a certain moment we had it going with some echo loops and some feedback and we just left the stage and joined the dancers. It kept going for an hour or so.' This prefigured the discovery by pioneering 1970s New York DJs like Kool Herc that by using two turntables and switching from the instrumental breaks of one funk twelve-inch to another, they could extend the dancefloor groove infinitely. But Kool Herc and Ralf Hütter were, at this point, continents and cultures apart, Superfly and Schnapps in the public consciousness.

1972 was a year of taking stock for the Kraftwerk duo, significant in that they acquired their first synthesizers proper, the ARP and Moogs that were being put to revolutionary and immersive popular use by Stevie Wonder on albums like *Music of My Mind* and *Talking Book*. Schneider, who though less gregarious than Hütter in interviews was the more sociable of the pair, also met Emil Schult, violinist and visual artist, whom he introduced into the Kraftwerk set-up. Schult, with his strong aesthetic sense and broader sense of cultural context as well as musically popular touch, would be a valuable collaborator as Kraftwerk slowly made the transition from generic early-seventies Krautrock, a visual and aural mess of colour, hair, flares, stacked instruments and cable and furious soloing, to a more spare and singular identity of their own. 'I had an influence on everything,' he would tell Pascal Bussy, author of *Kraftwerk: Man, Machine and Music*.

This was immediately evident on the cover of their 1973 album, *Ralf and Florian*, in which, for the first time, a certain high sense of effete kitsch enters the Kraftwerk lexicon. The Christian names of the partners are rendered in Gothic font on either side of the traffic-cone logo, and the effect is surely a homage to Gilbert and George, already familiar to denizens of the art-gallery scene like Hütter and Schneider (though Hütter would later deny the connection). However, it's only halfway there. Schneider was always the more consciously striking and imposing member of Kraftwerk to look at, and nowhere is that more evident than on this cover. He's gone the full distance with his immaculately tailored suit and non-kipper tie, hair lacquered and short, in 1973. Real *Spiesser* (square) stuff – he could be a young Prince Charles being introduced to the Rolling Stones. It is Hütter who lets the side down a little. Though his ears are visible, his glasses are askew, his hair lank, his jacket nondescript, his shirt unbuttoned, and he looks quite the pudgy, passive-aggressive scruff next to the dapper, urbane Schneider. It's as if the latter is leaning into his ear and whispering, 'You might have made more of an effort. A tie, at least.' These things would come to matter greatly with Kraftwerk.

The album, too, though one of the great lost treasures of what Hütter describes quite distinctly as part of Kraftwerk's 'early phase', reflects this sense of incomplete transition. Opener 'Elektrisches Roulette', characteristically heralded by a buzz of abstract electronics like some old valve machine in the throes of warming up, is fast-moving, *motorik* in miniature, as if some of the influence of the departed Klaus Dinger has left its trace. Hütter attacks the keyboards with an almost Dr John-like boogie-woogie frenzy that contrasts with the elegant, recurring ARP motif. 'Kristallo', named after a local hotel, is spindly and metallic, a further hint of shapes to come, a hissing and spitting rhythm box at odds with the simulated harpsichord strains that hang over the mix like a chandelier. This is the paradox of 'elegance and decadence' which Kraftwerk would later revisit. 'Tanzmusik''s unruffled, arpeggiated patter is in step with a characteristically halting, shuffling drum-machine rhythm, caught in a constant loop of beginning again and again, and also features what sounds like a vocal choir moaning with polite ecstasy into the rafters.

But then there are strong intimations of the earlier Kraftwerk, signified by Florian Schneider's flute, which, after *Autobahn*, would essentially cease to be a feature of the group's sound fabric. It may have been extreme of Julian Cope to have declared that Kraftwerk were effectively finished after 1973, but certainly the flute strains of 'Tongebirge', for whose wistful sweetness it's hard to find cross-comparisons (David Liebman's flute solo on Miles Davis's 'He Loved Him Madly' on the *Get Up with It* album?), feel like a loss when they eventually disappear altogether from the Kraftwerk canon. It's as if Arcadia was deliberately sunk – though perhaps sublimated is the better word. 'Heimatklange' ('The Bells of Home') contains a resonance that would hereafter be reduced to a barely tangible undercurrent in Kraftwerk. The longing for a sense of *Heimat* is one of the strongest emotions in German popular culture, as represented in film and Schlager, and here Kraftwerk offer their own take on it, both ironic and deeply felt, its tinkling pianos and multi-tracked flute evoking slow mists moving over beautiful, stagnant waters shadowed by the branches of dead trees – an ahistorical, melancholy, pastoral idyll, nostalgia, perhaps, for a time and place that never was, or has long been laid irretrievably low.

The album's lengthy centrepiece is 'Ananas Symphonie', which in its skeletal/baroque, minimal/luxuriant flourishes of silvery synth occupies a grand place of its own in the Kraftwerk back catalogue. Rustling and glistening, its flourishes resembling country-and-western slide guitar, it's quite unlike anything Hütter and Schneider had recorded before, or would record again, except that it features a new innovation – the vocoder. Again, this had been popularised, in particular by Stevie Wonder on tracks like 'Girl

Blue' on *Music of My Mind*, in which he uses it as a soulful cipher rather than a gimmick. Its use here is no less portentous. Though it's only used to utter indistinct vocal phrases, it's as if Kraftwerk's expressionist, silent era is over. Now the machines talk.

All the same, to gauge just how far Kraftwerk still were from the neon-lit precision of their future onstage four-man model, one only has to look at a clip of a studio performance they gave of 'Tanzmusik' in 1973 on the German TV show *Aspekte*. It's introduced by one Michael Stefanowski, who bleakly recites from an autocue as if reading out a press statement from a terrorist group outlining the conditions for the release of their hostages. The enervating gravitas of the intro is exacerbated by the stage set, which essentially consists of a brown pleated curtain. Again, it's Schneider who has made the effort, with his suit and period microphone, while Hütter is slumped over his organ, hair lank, apparently wishing he were somewhere else, picking out a melodic line in an error-prone manner. He's surrounded by unkempt boxes containing various modified devices, while behind him in a corner is dumped a grubby traffic cone.

However, Hütter and Schneider are now joined by percussionist Wolfgang Flür, formerly of neo-popsters the Beathovens, then later Spirits of Sound, from whom Kraftwerk had recruited Michael Rother. His introduction was the first phase in establishing the Kraftwerk line-up that springs iconically to mind today. Here, like Hütter, he is not quite the sartorial finished article, sporting a large black moustache, and tapping effectively away on a customised piece of electronic percussive equipment which looks like a tray of chocolate biscuits with their silver foil peeled back.

Still, these were the very final days of Kraftwerk as a peripheral, unremarkable-appearing drone on the outlying cerebral wing of seventies German rock. They were about to go global.

Side two of *Autobahn*, their 1974 breakthrough album, saw Kraftwerk continue in their tendency to fill out albums with a series of flotilla-type tracks, very much supplementary to the main event. The title track, however, which covered twenty-two and a half minutes on side one, would define Kraftwerk with an expansive exactness that's quite remarkable given their lengthy gestation period. All of Hütter and Schneider's preoccupations about the cultural colonisation of Germany by the USA, their desire to supplant American pop with a newly minted equivalent that was German in origin, were realised in urbane, spectacular fashion on 'Autobahn' – the moment at which the Kraftwerk project truly rolled out into the world.

While Kraftwerk's 'phase one', their recorded work hitherto, painted electronic pictures, they were impressionistic, open to interpretation. My own take, for instance, on 'Heimatklange', all that talk of dead trees and still water, might not be the mental image evoked in or meaning taken by another listener, or indeed Kraftwerk themselves. With 'Autobahn', however, in terms of the picture it paints it is as vivid and figurative and indisputable as Emil Schult's eerily bright, deceptively banal and depthless, faintly Hockneyesque cover artwork. It is, at surface level, a brilliantly evocative sonic depiction of a car journey, using a paintbox of chromium-plated melodies and sweeping synthstrokes, all of it based on a shuttle series of motorway journeys they made to glean noises and sensations they could rework into music using their newly acquired sequencer, which enabled them to achieve precision and clarity. The shutting of the car door. The ignition, the hooter. The gentle grinding through the lower gears. The steady negotiation of the minor roads out of the city, or suburb, travelling hopefully. The left and right turns, conveyed in swerving Moog flourishes. The exquisite monotony. And then, looking right and left at 3:17, joining the major road itself, the '*graues band*', bowling along at a swift but unhurried pace, the lush scenery reflected in Schneider's reverberant flute (making its last ever appearance in the Kraftwerk *oeuvre*) and the modified strings of guest guitarist/violinist Klaus

Röder. Then, a darker, busier Moog passage, in which the traffic gets more hectic, with overtaking, indications and bumper-to-bumper tension, horns, cars flashing back on the other side of the carriageway. Finally, sixteen minutes in, a pleasant fatigue sets in as the shadows of the day lengthen, and the journey wends hastily to its weary end, along bending, sodium-lit ring roads.

As if all this is not literal enough, there are Kraftwerk's very first lyrics, penned by Emil Schult and delivered in a deadpan chant by Hütter and Schneider. The English translation does not do justice to the rhythms of the original German, or such details as the pun on the Beach Boys' 'Fun, fun, fun' in '*fahr'n fahr'n fahr'n*', ('travel, travel, travel') or the gently explosive, lyrical joy of the word '*Glitzerstrahl*' ('glittering rays'), giving the lie to the notion that German is inherently, phonetically unsuitable for pop verse. However, it is all surface and description, like a school child's essay. The song describes, in plain and unaffected terms, the wide valley that lies ahead, the glittering sun shining down approvingly on the tableau; it notes the greyness of the highway, as well as the green which offsets it, and, of course, the whiteness of its stripes. And now, we are switching on the radio.

There it all is, deadpan, unambiguous, and doubtless proof to some listeners of the engaging naïveté of foreign would-be pop stars speaking in their second language. It is about what it is about, and that seems to be that. But beneath this disingenuous, Fluxus-like simplicity lurk a host of implications. Who celebrates a motorway in pop music, and why? Cars, yes, as desirable, phallic, chrome and fender objects in their own right, and for picking up girls, the revving of the engine as a measure of potency and purring desire. But the motorway, the journey, the scenery? How blandly European. Where's the male pulse, the full throttle, the roaring, tearaway passion, the faintly non-sanctioned feeling of getaway from the bourgeois, rabbit-hutch confines of the 'burbs? None of that is intimated on 'Autobahn', least of all in the choice of vehicles on the cover

– a black, somewhat authoritarian Mercedes and a small family Volkswagen. What gives? Hütter's recommendation that you listen to 'Autobahn', then go out for a drive on the motorway to 'discover that your car is a musical instrument', only added a Cageian twist.

Then there is the loaded subject of the autobahn itself. For many, it carried implications of the Nazi era, as did the Volkswagen, the 'people's car' favoured by the Führer and, as it happened, Kraftwerk themselves. Work on the autobahn network was greatly escalated (with forced labour) under Hitler, who had hoped that it would be useful in mobilising the military and their equipment, as well as enabling Germans to travel freely about their unified country, connecting via long, unspooling grey ribbons what was not so long ago a fragmentary collection of mutually mistrustful principalities. Were not the autobahns fraught with such associations, the concrete dreams of the Third Reich still in our midst? Surely to trill uncritically about the autobahn, carved monstrously across the verdant landscape in a brutal, violent imposition of modernist authoritarianism, was to be guilty of gross, wilful naïveté?

As it happens, the autobahns had originally been dreamt of in the Weimar era, and the first small stretch of motorway, which travelled the short hop from Cologne to Bonn, opened by future postwar Chancellor, then Mayor of Cologne Konrad Adenauer, in 1932, proved too structurally weak to be of much use bearing heavy machinery such as tanks, which had to be conveyed by train. However, there was still something funny-smelling about Kraftwerk's apparently odourless, synthesized tone poem. In blues/rock 'n' roll, the road was fraught and picaresque, dusty and precarious, in which hopes and fears were bundled up in a man's knapsack or loaded into the back of his beat-up vehicle. On Canned Heat's bluesy 'On the Road Again', the road was the only lonesome option available to an abandoned child, rootless and forced to move along, the only American way, the freeway.

Stevie Wonder, meanwhile, who was perhaps Kraftwerk's closest relation instrumentally, undertook a fraught journey of his own on 'Living for the City', the boy from 'hard-time Mississippi' making his way by road up north to New York, barely off the coach before he's immediately and lucklessly caught up in a drugs bust and sent down for ten years. Then there was Bruce Springsteen on 'Thunder Road', which is couched in an inflamed, desperate optimism – the only radio is that of Roy Orbison singing for the lonely, and the last chance for them to meet their destiny is to climb into a car with a 'dirty hood', armed only with a guitar: 'We got one last chance to make it real/To trade in these wings on some wheels.'

Guitars, babes, authenticity, thunder – it's an altogether different kind of journey from that taken together by the young men of Kraftwerk on the peaceable stretches of 'Autobahn', just one of their many such travels by road. Springsteen, as ever, is preoccupied with keeping it 'real', yet his febrile lyrical visions are sheer rock 'n' roll mythological hokum. Kraftwerk may look and sound 'inauthentic' but at least 'Autobahn' bears a closer resemblance to life as it is lived.

All of this might have made Kraftwerk appear amusingly insipid and ephemeral in 1974/5, one-dimensional Teutonic chancers who would be blown away by the first hot gust of raw rock 'n' roll passion. But beneath the smart lapels of their well-tailored exteriors beat a profound sense of artistic purpose with long-term consequences even they might not have anticipated.

For Kraftwerk, celebration of the autobahn was not mere bourgeois cheerleading but a return to the prewar Bauhaus principles in which art and technology were melded in a single purpose; another branch of the broader project of twentieth-century art to connect art with life as lived by the great mass of people who had left behind centuries of peasant ancestry for the new world. 'Our roots were in the culture that was stopped by Hitler,' said Hütter, 'the school of Bauhaus, of German expressionism.'

The 'expressionistic' aspect of Kraftwerk would become more muted, more implicit from here on in, but nevertheless the point stood. There were excellent reasons for singing and playing about the autobahn: to counter the somewhat agrarian strain of technophobia which was still a commonplace of post-hippie rock, and certainly of early Krautrock, with its tendency towards rural, communal retreat; to assert the aesthetic value of function in the machine age, rather than choose to recoil in postures of alienation from all that metal and concrete and automation that did, after all, form the basis of modern existence for the lucky ones; furthermore, to claim for Germany a central artery of rock 'n' roll mythology – the road.

Route 66 has always been the predominant stretch of rock 'n' roll highway, its Santa Monica Boulevard end in particular strewn with points of iconic interest, from motels to gravestones, involving everyone from Linda Ronstadt and the Doors to the Eagles to the Ramones. It's been celebrated in song – '(Get Your Kicks on) Route 66', composed by Bobby Troup in 1946 and later covered by Nat King Cole and Chuck Berry, among others, 'The Long Red Line' by Mary Cutrufello, 'Used to Be' by the Red Dirt Rangers and '2200 Miles' by the Mad Cat Trio all pay homage to the freeway. Its lineage is as old as the blues itself. Stretching from Chicago to Los Angeles, it's become symbolic of the American dream and of destiny, for those traditionally longing to escape the flyover dustbowl of the midwest in search of the sunlit fertility of the west coast. Travelling along it in today's more prosperous, homogenous times, it doesn't feel like an escape to any place that different – rather a long, long journey deep into America itself. So it is with the autobahn – a lengthy journey that takes you no place but deeper into Germany itself. (Eerily, some old stretches of the autobahn remained uncompleted after the war – these 'ghost highways' are still visible from the perspective of orbit, if not to travellers on the ground.) It can't boast the cluster of reference points of Route 66, but thanks to Kraftwerk, it has an enviable, perhaps unparalleled visibility in the popular-music canon.

It was, of course, as Kraftwerk admitted themselves, an idealised, even pastoral view of the autobahn, which in reality is an increasingly congested and contested artery of the German transport system that might more realistically be soundtracked by some compressed, high-turbo piece of Euro-techno. Strangely, there is, even at this stage, a sense that Kraftwerk were not so much embracing techno-modernity as taking deep draughts from the clean, inspirational air of the countryside, the vast interior of Germany which had been the cradle for so much new German music. On side two of the album, the two treatments of 'Kometenmelodie', one rendered in wispy, electric charcoal, the other in bright neon, the nocturnal atmospheres of 'Mitternacht' and the almost field-recording-like simulations of dawn birdsong and the pan pipes of a glad spring morning that light up 'Morgenspaziergang' ('Morning Walk') are minor musical matters, but they do significantly reflect a lingering bucolic strain, perhaps the result of recording in Conny Plank's new studio in a remote countryside location outside Cologne. This, however, would be the last time Kraftwerk would take inspiration from the rural. Hereafter, all would be not green, not hippie, not Krautrock, not *kosmische* but *Technik*. No more flutes.

Initial reaction to *Autobahn* in Germany was muted, despite a junket in which selected members of the press were invited to career along the motorway in hired cars with the album blaring out. This would illustrate once again the natural point that what is considered Teutonic and Other by foreigners is considered pretty mundane by Germans themselves. For them, there was little apparently alluring about a German group singing about driving on the road, any more than there was for UK rock journalists listening to Jasper Carrott singing about riding on his moped.

However, Kraftwerk's fateful break occurred when an edited version of the song started receiving extended airplay in Chicago and then across the USA. Reduced to a four-minute version, 'Autobahn' was not bowdlerised but served as a prototype for a new form of electro-pop which was pure radio contagion. After several years of paring and probing, Kraftwerk in 1975 were overnight sensations.

Their record company immediately capitalised on this success and an American tour was quickly organised as Kraftwerk, now with the addition of Karl Bartos, swiftly remade themselves as a draft version of the cropped, Teutonic, audio-visual electropop four-piece they would spend the rest of their career refining. Among the first fruits of the Euro–USA culture collision, between a country and a continent that had long distantly regarded each other with a mixture of fascination, suspicion and misapprehension, was an interview with Lester Bangs, one of the brilliant, if by today's standards gaseous, keepers of the Rock Critical Conscience. Prefacing his piece with a meditation on the hidden role of the machine as far back as Chuck Berry, Bangs worries about the onset of 'total passive acquiescence to the Cybernetic Inevitable'. He credits Germany with the invention of methamphetamines and their contribution to US culture, from the beats to Lenny Bruce on to Blue Cheer and Velvet Underground, and all in all greets the arrival of Kraftwerk on American shores with a mixture of apocalyptic fear and excitement. He portrays Florian Schneider as looking 'like he could build a computer or push a button and blow up half the world with the same amount of emotion'. Teutonic, war-derived clichés abound amid the cerebral fever – he describes Kraftwerk's build-up of equipment at Kling Klang as being 'for the eventual rearmament of their fatherland'.

Bangs raises with Ralf Hütter the spectre of machines developing their own consciousness, becoming the 'players' themselves, to which Hütter happily plays along. 'Yes. We do this. It's like a robot thing, when it gets up to a certain stage. It starts playing . . . it's no longer you and I, it's It. Not all machines have this consciousness, however. Some machines are just limited to one piece of work, but complex machines . . .'

Hütter ploughs audaciously on, playing up to the stereotype

of the Germans as boffins with a superior handle on technology but unbalanced by any regard for normal human emotion. 'We want the whole world to know our background. We cannot deny we are from Germany, because the German mentality, which is more advanced, will always be a part of our behaviour. We create out of the German language, the mother language, which is very mechanical, we use it as the basic structure of our music. Also the machines, from the industries of Germany.' By the end of the piece, both are egging each other on in a coy game of advanced stereotyping. Bangs wonders aloud 'If they would like to see it get to the point of electrodes in the brain so that whatever they thought would come through a loudspeaker,' before a moment of woeful, almost tumescent crassness:

> 'Yes,' enthused Ralf, 'this would be fantastic.'
> 'The final solution to the music problem?' I suggested.
> 'No, not the solution. The next step.'

Kraftwerk enjoyed America greatly, and their dealings with the press, passing off such 'whoppers' as telling one reporter that one of the reasons their music was so mechanical and rhythm-based was because 'in Germany there are no live groups'.

In the UK, in that pleasantly nondescript pop year between the Twilight of the Idols and the onset of punk, *Autobahn* was also a hit. Their chart entry was marked by an unusual appearance on *Tomorrow's World*, the Thursday-evening show which hungry British pop fans were forced to sit through prior to the weekly half-hour dose of guitars and glam that was *Top of the Pops*. In the item, a standard-issue BBC narrator explains how Kraftwerk create their 'machine music' in their 'laboratory' in Düsseldorf, where they make synthetic, replicated sounds based on the noises they experience while driving, which they recreate onstage 'with the minimum of fuss'. We see footage of the four-piece Kraftwerk playing a version of 'Autobahn' in a rehearsal studio. In some respects, the visual ambience is as dowdy and seventies-bound as their earlier appearance on *Aspekte* – once again, the backdrop includes a light-brown curtain, apparently a mandatory feature of the decade. Bartos and Flür, meanwhile, though besuited, look like nervous young comprehensive-school teachers as they bash out rhythms on their electronic percussive pads, which still have a scruffy, skiffle-ish appearance about them.

However, things have moved on in other respects. Each band member is denoted onstage by his Christian name, in neon lights. Florian, in particular, has grasped a sense of Kraftwerk's benign but ominous theatre of kitsch, leering in a rather over-friendly manner into the camera at the end of the piece like a benevolent sea serpent rising surprisingly from a loch. The voiceover tells us that, having eliminated all conventional instruments, Kraftwerk planned to go one step further and eliminate their keyboards, instead 'building jackets with electronic lapels that can be played by touch'.

'Very – numerical,' concluded quintessential 1970s BBC linkman William Woollard at the end of the item, with the air of one who did not expect to be troubled by 'Kraftwerk' again for the rest of his life. Unlike Bangs's piece and the end-of-the-world-as-we-know-it overtones it generated, *Tomorrow's World*'s take on Kraftwerk sat with their general view of the future as something that would be conducted as an orderly affair, with new developments in transportation, cybernetics and so forth created for the convenience of busy commuters and housewives rushed off their feet. Most of *Tomorrow's World*'s predictions about the way the world would pan out tended, in hindsight, to be somewhat wide of the mark – the jetpacks and robot housemaids they predicted in the 1960s and '70s did not materialise, as they misread the trajectory of technological development entirely. After a while, a sense that these were 'just for fun' speculations become ingrained in the tone of the programme, which, broadcast at that time of the evening, did not seek to be excessively scientific or to cause alarm among viewers of a nervous or British disposition.

In one respect, Kraftwerk followed in this tradition – the electronic jackets, like the jetpacks and robots, never materialised either. Considering what harbingers they were of the actual existing future, their own promises and predictions, many probably delivered tongue-in-cheek or as diversions, very often failed to come to pass, as in this case. At this stage, it might have been safe to add Kraftwerk to a pile of apparent one-hit-wonder electro-oddities of the era, which also included Hot Butter ('Popcorn', 1972), Space's 'Magic Fly' and Landscape, also featured on *Tomorrow's World* to demonstrate the electronically modified stylings of their 1981 hit 'Einstein a Go-Go'.

The feeling that Kraftwerk had shot their bolt was bolstered when 'Kometenmelodie' was issued as a hasty follow-up to 'Autobahn' but failed to chart. Nonetheless, Kraftwerk were now the most notable and well-known export of new German music, coming into their own just as the Krautrock scene in general was beginning to wind down.

That said, their follow-up would see their pop profile descend once more, at least in the US and the UK, while remaining among their most provocative and prescient releases. *Radio-Activity* arose, according to Wolfgang Flür, from Ralf Hütter's fascination at the number of radio stations, many of them privately owned, in the USA, as Kraftwerk did their extensive publicity rounds there. The very idea that one could have one's own private mode of radio transmission delighted Hütter. In a sense, it was as close as his imagination, or anyone else's for that matter, came to the idea of the internet.

However, the title also indicated a confluence with the idea of nuclear power, and it was hard not to suspect that as part of their flight from the dirty, the hippie, the ecological in search of cleaner, more modernistic options, Kraftwerk were inclining towards a bland endorsement of nuclear energy, a similar aesthetically and spiritually celebratory delight in its disseminating properties to that expressed by Salvador Dalí in his 'nuclear mysticism' era. Press shots taken around the time of them visiting a nuclear power plant, suitably dressed in protective footwear and white coats, looking on at the works in admiration, did nothing to diminish this impression. They seemed deliberately to be putting themselves on the side of the *Spiesser*, ethically untroubled by even the more alarming aspects of technological progress, and very much in opposition to the longhaired, agitated '*Atomkraft? Nein, danke!*' tendency.

Even had the album not involved a nuclear dimension, Kraftwerk's choice of theme and artwork was still potentially troubling. As with *Autobahn*, their notion of modernity was idealised and dreamily nostalgic, rather than bang up to date and realistic. So, no FM-receiving transistor radio for them but an older model from their childhoods, the sort on which they had listened to avant-garde broadcasts from a radio tower in nearby Cologne. However, once again, the radio that features on the cover of *Radio-Activity* is contaminated with negative associations – in this case, the preferred instrument of Nazi propaganda. In the EL-DE Museum in Cologne, dedicated to the history of the Nazi party in the town, there is exhibited a propaganda poster bearing the slogan GANZ DEUTSCHLAND HÖRT DEN FÜHRER ('The whole of Germany listens to the Leader'). At the centre of a large, attentive crowd looms a shortwave radio set with a round speaker face, very similar indeed to that used by Emil Schult in his design for *Radio-Activity*'s cover artwork, the Deutscher Kleinempfänger, developed in the late 1930s.

Of course, it was Kraftwerk's intention precisely to decontaminate the wireless from such associations, but their deadpan, below-the-radar subtlety meant that their intentions were not always abundantly clear, and it is hard not to suspect at times that that is the way they liked it, as they dallied playfully with Teutonic iconography. Yet it would come to horrify Kraftwerk that the inaudible satire and double-edged meanings of the title track's lyrics ('Radio-activity/Is in the air for you and me,/Radio-activity – discovered by Madame Curie') had been missed by many, and for their 1991 remix album they felt obliged to insert a somewhat clumsily explicit disclaimer of their updated version of the song, which now urged '(Stop) radioactivity', and included a vocoderised litany of nuclear disaster sites: Chernobyl, Harrisburg (Three Mile Island) and, of course, Hiroshima. While one might appreciate the political gesture, you can't help but feel this attempt at correction is something of a small aesthetic blot on Kraftwerk's otherwise pristine canon.

Either way, Kraftwerk were hardly in a position to influence the drift of Western energy policy. Musically, it was an entirely different matter. It's only possible retrospectively to assess the colossal size of *Radio-Activity* as a milestone in electronic music, one that marks a precise and signal midpoint between Stockhausen and Depeche Mode.

As the preambling tick of 'Geiger Counter' fades away, in drifts the title track, on synthetic, choral tide clouds courtesy of Kraftwerk's latest toy, the Vako Orchestron, a sort of Gothic mood generator which Hütter and Schneider would put to great use before it became obsolete. But it's the thudding sequencer pulse, the one that would subsequently cable through the electropop of Orchestral Manoeuvres in the Dark, the Human League and others, which really marks the beginning of a quiet electric storm. As the track solemnly unwinds, radio interference cascades like a bounty from heaven in all directions – or is it some sort of benign atomic reaction? – but there can be no doubt that in this new world into which we are stepping, the primacy of the acoustic instrument is no more.

'Radioland', with its signals fluttering about the mix like fireflies, further establishes the somewhat wispy, wistful mood of the album, as if to imply purely in its textures that this new world, albeit brave and unthreatening, is one in which the 'human', like the voices straining in the vocoder, is trapped, even alienated. 'Airwaves' is brighter, with its gentle, rhythmical shuffle again a harbinger for the sort of nimble synthpop that would be ubiquitous some five years further down the line. But then 'News' is rather more sombre, with its sample of a bulletin announcing the building of a number of new power stations. As a pop moment, it brings to mind Simon and Garfunkel's 'Silent Night', in which their rendering of the carol is backed up by a newsreader bringing the latest grim tidings from the Vietnam War.

'Antenna', with Hütter's voice rebounding indistinctly in an echo chamber, also adds to the faintly dystopian air of the album, its sense of existing in the shadows of transmitters, pylons and cooling towers. It's followed by 'Radio Stars', which is ostensibly about the sort of people video would eventually kill, according to the Buggles, and which the author for a long time chose to interpret as a tone poem to the excruciating human toll taken on those whose lives are lived out in electronic media, trapped in the holograms of their celebrity selves. The lyrics are, in fact, a paean to distant galaxies and stars, implying the connection, of which Stockhausen would have been fond, of radio interference (essentially, the echo of the Big Bang) and the wider cosmos. Kraftwerk had no wish to be associated with the *kosmische* elements of Krautrock, but at times they couldn't help themselves. 'Transistor', on which Hütter dusts off his Farfisa organ, is further proof that Kraftwerk had still not quite shed their old skin at this stage. 'Ohm, Sweet Ohm', despite its pun, sees out the album as we proceed into the sunset of the future in strangely downbeat mood, initially at the pace of a wake before the backbeat picks up.

Radio-Activity was not a huge hit, except in France, where the title track was picked up for use by a TV programme. Although it lays the cable for the first synth-wave of post-punk, it lacks the precision and clarity of *Autobahn*'s title track, in particular. It shows that Kraftwerk had yet to sublimate all their avant-garde energies and instincts into remaking themselves as a techno-pop paradigm. It's Kraftwerk at their most monochromatic, uncertain, shaded, atmospheric (both Reiner Werner Fassbinder and British filmmaker Chris Petit used *Radio-Activity* as soundtrack material), better perhaps for not being fully realised, perhaps even rushed in its making. It captures the zeitgeist, the feeling of pop and society itself teetering uncertainly on the cusp of a new era in which technology would not be romantic and novel but insidiously permanent.

In Germany, Kraftwerk were gaining respect by virtue of having gained respect abroad, in the rock 'n' roll fatherlands of the US and the UK. But there was another, blunter view of them also, in the mid-seventies. Says writer Stefan Morawietz, 'They were considered idiots, machine people – proto-disco. Today, they're the grandfathers of dancefloor. But in the 1970s, there was no worse music to German people than disco.'

Come 1976 and disco was already beginning to form a regulatory grid over the dance scene. The dominance of the sequencer, the primacy of the 4/4 rhythm had come to drive a girder into the sassy heart of old-school funk with its irregular beats and chops. The likes of George Clinton complained bitterly; disco was 'like making love to one stroke', he said. Even Stevie Wonder, who had been so helpful in introducing synthesizers into pop, would find himself sidelined – *Songs in the Key of Life* would ultimately be his last major hurrah. Others got with the programme. From New York lofts to Studio 54 to *Saturday Night Fever*, for good or ill, disco would be the new thing. Arguments about artifice versus soul, machines versus real instruments, accusations of plasticity and elitism would ensue. As they found their way onto the dancefloor, Kraftwerk would find themselves at the centre of these exchanges.

In the void that was 1975, that nothing, in-between year, they had appeared to be floating about like an impending weather front emerging from overseas, electric and amorphous but perhaps destined just to fizzle out. But by 1976, they were just one of a number of fresh propositions which would change the nature of modern music for good. Disco was one, for sure. But there was also punk, which initially seemed like an acne burst of obstreperous disaffection but whose implications would be more profound. And then there was another wing – Brian Eno, whose forays into ambient music, a modern-day adaptation of the ideas of Erik Satie and to an extent John Cage, sought as eagerly if more quietly than punk to remove the old-style Rock Star from centre stage and instead lay stress on form, texture, colour.

Since leaving Roxy Music, Eno had explored a solo career but also made forays into production, working with David Bowie during his Berlin era. Bowie was at his brilliant, flailing, damaged best in the mid-seventies. Accused by some of being a fickle changeling, a trend-follower and parasite on the originality of others, this was to misunderstand his genius, which was to catch the invisible tail of what was in the air, the dialectical motions of the pop times, and, craftsman that he ultimately was, convert it into a tangible pop narrative, a public psychodrama which mirrored the drug-addled volatility and uncontrollable momentum of his private/public life as the pop superstar of the 1970s.

By 1975, he was done with his plastic soul phase and decided to relocate to Europe. On one level this was out of necessity, to shake off the plethora of pushers and hangers-on that he had accrued in the US. His fascination with Europe, specifically Germany, was in part morbid, poseurish and facile. It wasn't just that he led the affected look-I'm-in-an-imaginary-film lifestyle of an Existentialist Abroad while in Berlin, living modestly, drinking coffee and eating Turkish food, exploring the city's decadent underbelly. He had been caught at customs in Warsaw with a case full of memorabilia of Hitler, a figure he found fascinating (in 1974 he had described him as 'the first rock star') and steeped in forces other than sheer racist vileness. He would suggest around this time that declining Britain was in need of a fascist dictatorship to knock it into shape. For all this, the emergent National Front in their magazine *Bulldog* hailed him as 'the Big Daddy of Futurism'.

Unlike Eric Clapton, who made ugly, anti-immigrant onstage remarks in support of Enoch Powell around this time, Bowie would subsequently and repeatedly apologise and atone for his flirtations with the far right in this period. He had been stupid, yes, but also isolated from reality by his star status and impelled by a need to be more controversial in more unreconstructed times than our own, not to say screwed up on drugs.

No doubt Bowie's fascination with Kraftwerk, as well as groups like Cluster and Neu!, was faintly lurid – he saw them as Teutonic creatures, something he would like to 'be', or to be by osmosis, for a while. However, his embrace of these groups, if a little opportunistic, was also visionary and shrewd and certainly did them great favours. It is hard to overestimate the awe with which Bowie was regarded by serious-minded male fans in particular in the 1970s. His charm wasn't rooted in any sort of blokeish empathy or easy likeability. He had about him the qualities of an extraterrestrial, fallen to earth, not down to earth. At my school, there was an older pupil who cast himself in the role of 'Ziggy Hero' – a glorified Bowie impersonator, Bowie by proxy. But no one thought this was in the least bit sad. Younger boys would flock around him agog every time he appeared in the corridor in his latest, Bowie-inspired mutations, or lend moral support in numbers as a teacher attempted to chide him for his outlandish garb.

For Kraftwerk, Bowie's patronage was deeply flattering on a personal level but also conferred on them a legitimacy they could use against those who found them risible. For there was a necessary, not inadvertent, comedic element to Kraftwerk. Paul Buckmaster, who worked with Bowie at this time, summed up the correct response to Kraftwerk rather well, his own and Bowie's: 'We both enjoyed their records very much indeed. We kind of took them seriously, but we kind of laughed as well.'

Kraftwerk were feted by both Bowie and Iggy Pop, whose worship of Kraftwerk was reciprocated by Hütter and co. Iggy and Kraftwerk hung out in bars and cafes, and even went shopping for asparagus together. The Stooges were one of the very few groups for whom they had ever admitted a liking. Detroit and Düsseldorf had a natural connection as areas with a history of heavy industry. Bowie had clearly been listening to the new German music in advance of *Station to Station*, released in 1976 – the clanking, metal regularity of the opener and title track betrays that, while the stereopanned simulation of a locomotive engine might well have implanted an idea in Kraftwerk's own heads. The most explicit tribute, however, occurs on 'V-2 Schneider' (from the album *Heroes*), a reference to Florian, though its pulse and thick layers of processed sax and keyboard sound more like exuberant Eno than Kraftwerk. It's also a little unfortunate that one of Kraftwerk's members should be linked with one of the Nazis' most lethal weapons – clearly, even for a visionary like Bowie, easy Second World War associations died hard.

There had been talk of Kraftwerk supporting Bowie, even of Bowie and Kraftwerk collaborating, but none of this came to anything – Kraftwerk were wise enough to maintain a distance and autonomy, rather than play the role of Bowie's protégés, or worse, temporary playthings, while the imperatives of Bowie's own career, and further mutations, meant that his Berlin phase would come to an end soon enough. But their association, as far as it went, was a great success, reinvigorating and transfusing the Bowie persona and adding lustre to Kraftwerk's image among fans and critics who hitherto had been uncertain of them. Bowie, he say yes.

Kraftwerk would unabashedly reference their meetings with

Iggy Pop and David Bowie in a way that left no room for misinterpretation – 'meet Iggy Pop and David Bowie', ran the lyric – on their 1977 album, *Trans-Europe Express*, for many their greatest achievement. Although generally objective and impersonal by lyrical nature, more outward- than inward-looking, on this album they would reflect on their newfound lives as public icons and absorb the experience into their material in a way they would never do subsequently. For all its perfection, the album yokes together, rather than integrates, two themes: Europe, as experienced by rail, and the spectacle and nature of pop and celebrity, with all its illusion and artifice, which at once mesmerises and pains Kraftwerk, certainly Ralf Hütter. The latter was dealt with on two tracks, both of which deserve a place in the corridors of pop permanency.

'The Hall of Mirrors', rendered to the slow, regular clank of electronic percussion and glossy spirals of synth wheeling about uncontrollably, not unlike the effect of reflections of your own reflected images arcing off into infinity, is the more affecting for Hütter's almost amusical vocal styling. As he rises to the chorus, 'even the greatest stars/discover themselves in the looking glass'. Here, one's reminded a little of Marlene Dietrich, darling of the Weimar era, musing fatalistically atop a stool. The harpsichord-type accompaniment, reminiscent of John Barry, adds a frisson of cinematic decadence.

A masterpiece of sobriety, a perfect sculpture of glass and metal, 'The Hall of Mirrors' encapsulates all of Kraftwerk's concerns about self-representation in art, the dangers of being personally invaded, captured and ruined by celebrity and the public gaze, the need to objectify and control the process. 'The Hall of Mirrors' confesses that this is a fraught undertaking, one which Kraftwerk would develop strategies to deal with, in interviews, onstage, sharply separating their private selves from their robot doppelgängers, a division which has become more pronounced in recent years.

'Showroom Dummies', based on a review in which they were thus described onstage, continues the theme at a much more upbeat pace, and shows a brilliant knack of making lemonade from the critical lemons handed to them. (To this day, critics level accusations of inertia and mechanistic tendencies at Kraftwerk as if expecting them to be wounded.) It culminates in a fantasy of the 'dummies' breaking out of their glass confines and making their way down to a nightclub to dance the night away, specimens of horrifying inauthenticity dominating the floor. It's as if they are saying to their detractors, 'Yess! Plastic! Scaryy! Fools, what are you afraid of?' It plays lightly on exaggerated fears of automation, *Doctor Who* fantasies of the Cyberman of the imminent future coming to get us. It's a witty celebration of artifice and its potential for authentic pop brilliance. For, like the rest of *Trans-Europe Express*, and unlike 99.9 per cent of the pop or indeed rock of its day, much of which has gone the way of all flesh and blood, 'Showroom Dummies' remains a thing of imperishable, indestructible perfection.

The remainder of the album was given over to Europe, with the central mechanical motif, following on from the car and the radio, being that of the train. The opening, 'Europe Endless', proceeds with clockwork imperturbability, sunlit and unburdened with any of the emotional baggage or brooding anxiety often associated with the sound of the locomotive, from Futurist paintings such as Umberto Boccioni's *Those Who Go/Those Who Stay* to the fadeout sample of the Beach Boys' 'Caroline No'. 'Europe Endless' has all the comfort of a first-class carriage, the synths ringing out like a hymn of praise to an unfurling, wholly absorbing landscape. Only Hütter's lyrics offer any hint of irony or duality: 'Elegance and decadence . . .', 'Real life and postcard views.' It would be for the Interrailers of a post-punk generation, doing the Grand Tour on the cheap, rucksacks full of T-shirts, cheap wine and paperbacks, to examine in greater depth just how fraught late-seventies/early-eighties Europe was at close hand, as reflected on the agitated, clattering whiplash of Simple Minds' 'I Travel' (1980) ('In Central Europe men are marching . . .'). 'Europe Endless' would establish the continent as the extensive site for a new rock 'n' roll psychogeography.

This would be reinforced on the album's centrepiece, the title track, segueing into 'Metal on Metal', one of a handful of the most influential tracks in the entire canon of popular music, on a list that would include Louis Armstrong, Elvis Presley and the Beatles among a very few. Again based on field research into the sounds of trains, which they then simulated using their upgraded range of kit, including the Orchestron and the Synthanorma sequencer, it's underpinned by the steady, curving, stereopanned shuffle of electro-percussion, but infused with a mountainous sense of drama lacking in 'Europe Endless'. Onward, upward and around the train hurtles, cold and sleek, indifferent to its surroundings, bowling through manmade carvings in the Alpine rock. There's a sinister moment as it plunges into extended darkness, prompting thoughts of Friedrich Dürrenmatt's Kafkaesque short story 'The Tunnel'. This is 'Metal on Metal', and the pounding, percussive anvil work of Flür and Bartos has an infernal quality; retrospectively, in *Energy Flash*, his 1998 study of rave and dance culture, Simon Reynolds described it as 'a funky iron foundry that sounded like a Luigi Russolo Art of Noises megamix for a futurist discotheque'. It's as if something did change, forever, in these few moments of darkness. Then, with an Orchestron burst, the train roars into the blazing light, with the force of the engines in Zola's *La Bête humaine*, dripping and glistening with fresh energy and impetus that carries it through to its terminus.

Relative serenity follows with 'Franz Schubert', on which, against a cycling, arpeggiating backdrop, Hütter embarks on an extended Orchestron solo, simulated classical strings, whose sweeping, robotic brushstrokes pay homage to Germany's monumental musical legacy. This is a further reminder that Kraftwerk's heads were never set entirely futurewards – rather they sought, as Hütter put it, to meld future, present and past into a single unbroken continuum, tracking over and reconnecting that which had been abruptly disconnected in Germany's recent history.

On the sleeve of *Trans-Europe Express*, the four men of Kraftwerk again pose provocatively, out of keeping with the times and 1977's rock norms, playing up superficial perceptions of Teutonic camp, and even the wistful imagery of right-wing German idealism. On the cover, they stare with ardent piety into an artificial light, immaculately suited, like some old-world portrait of Germany's four most successful young industrialists. On the back, they sit around a cafe table, bathed in the colourised soft focus of a typical *Heimatfilm* scene, high up in some rural and secluded spot, where the air is cleansed of the turbulence of political history. It's ironic, it's ridiculous, but at another level it is reclaiming for Germany and its popular music a sense of poise and unapologetic confidence. The four young men fix you with benign gazes, as if daring you to say something at their expense.

As the tallest and most distinctive member of Kraftwerk, it is Florian Schneider who dominates on the sleeve, his wide mouth set in an enigmatic smile. However, it is noticeable on the compositional credits that he contributes relatively little. He gets a co-credit on 'The Hall of Mirrors', most likely for its spiralling synth effects, as well as on the very brief 'Endless Endless', in which he provides the vocoderised chant of the song title which sees the album out. It would be some three decades before he chose to leave the group but already an imbalance in the Hütter–Schneider partnership was evident as their sound took a more minimal, nuts-and-bolts turn, less reliant on the embellishments of their earlier years.

'Trans-Europe Express' would prove to be a hit at the discos, much to Kraftwerk's approval. As they were anxious to demonstrate on the 'Showroom Dummies' video, they were keen and unselfconscious dancers, longtime lovers of nightclubs, in which they felt entirely at home. As Hütter himself recognised, disco, along with punk and Eno's retrospectively influential ambient work, was doing its bit to undermine the centrality of the rock star: 'In the disco, the spotlight is on everybody,' he said in a *Melody Maker* interview in the late seventies. 'Unlike concerts where you see only the star of the show and everyone else is in the dark.' A new *Volksmusik*, in which man and machine harmonised, a new cult of impersonality – what was there for Kraftwerk not to love?

However, it was an Italian, a relatively jobbing and unheralded figure, who was truly responsible for propelling dance music into the supersonic era. Giorgio Moroder's previous credentials had been as co-writer for the hit 'Son of My Father' by British group Chicory Tip, which made extensive, if not exactly revolutionary use of the synthesizer and was a hit in 1972. The song's assistant producer, Pete Bellotte, later recalled that he'd first been introduced to the Moog, 'a humungous machine with chords everywhere', when he met the German composer Eberhard Schoener. Bellotte was only able to access the Moog when the composer was away, as he took a dim view of his valuable machinery being used for the purposes of generating popular music, like some glorified Wurlitzer. Later, Bellotte and Moroder hitched up with Donna Summer, who had settled in Germany having starred in the touring musical *Hair*. They enjoyed a hit with the sensual, extended 'Love to Love You Baby', in which the principles of prolonging the dancefloor break and prolonged lovemaking were conflated, to highly controversial effect.

'I Feel Love' was similarly, minimally ecstatic, but also futuristic, the culmination of a suite of songs intended to reflect music through the ages. In order to achieve its effects, Moroder and Bellotte engaged the services of Robbie Wedel, the engineer who had first shown them what the Moog could do, to help them produce a track that was entirely Moog-based. 'He said this meant we would need to lock or sync the Moog to the Studer [tape machine], and when we asked, "What do you mean, sync?" Robbie replied, "Well, whatever you play now will then play in perfect time with the first take,"' recalled Bellotte, interviewed by *Sight and Sound* in 2009. 'We said, "How's that possible?" and he said, "It's something I've figured out that even Bob Moog didn't know his machine was capable of, and now I've told him how it's done . . . here's how. First, we need to record a reference pulse on track sixteen of the tape, and from that we can then lock in the Moog so that the rest of the tracks are perfectly synchronised."'

The resultant sound was like nothing that had been heard before in pop – a fast-cut, pneumatic regularity that was quite inhuman, yet somehow more than human in its remorseless capability. 'I Feel Love' was a massive and instant success. Its sheer fast-forward impetus defined supersonic '77, ominously upping pop's ante the way *Star Wars* did for Hollywood.

Kraftwerk's 1978 album *The Man-Machine* suffers just a little in that on certain tracks, including 'Spacelab' and 'Metropolis', they were playing catch-up with Moroder and Wedel's innovation, mimicking the multitrack Moog effect with which mass audiences had been familiar for over a year. They could hardly ignore it, but it was evidence that they were no longer the sole pioneers in their field. That said, Kraftwerk retained a far greater conceptual sense of themselves as *Gesamtkunstwerk* than any of their peers (certainly Moroder, with his moustache and thick-rimmed spectacles, was painfully lacking in the visual department). The cover of the album was their most arresting to date, the image which dominates popular perception of the group. It's a deliberate homage to the era of constructivism, to Bauhaus, to Suprematism, to artists like El Lissitzky, who, in works like *Beat the Whites with the Red Wedge*, dealt in functional blocks and lines of black and red, who had sought to marry art and actual existing socialism at state level, in propaganda, typography, architecture.

Kraftwerk respected these ideals; they saw themselves, in part, as a throwback to this era in art, when it was believed that the embrace of new technologies, new aesthetic forms, could actually assist in the development and improvement of society as a whole. Their notion of the man-machine was of a working relationship between the two. Inevitably, however, the geometric pose they struck was taken to be one of man becoming machine-like. This was an era in which the fear of the human cost of increasing automation abounded, not always unreasonably. One of the more poignant stories of this era was the closure of the Imperial typewriter factory in Humberside and subsequent protests. Hard for those thrown out of work to embrace with great gladness new technologies such as the electric typewriters and PCs just around the corner.

There was also the fear of 'robot workers', already introduced in the 1970s, eventually taking human jobs, and a fear as old as Charlie Chaplin's *Modern Times*, of human beings becoming cogs in a larger, indifferent industrial machine. Conversely, there was a lot of talk in the late seventies of the 'micro-chip' radically transforming society, precluding the need for a great deal of manual labour, but generating wealth for the common good, enabling the vast majority of people to enjoy far more leisure time. As computer scientist James Martin put it in his book *The Wired Society*, a year before *The Man-Machine*, 'Imagine yourself transported to a city ten or twenty years in the future. There is almost no street robbery as most persons carry little cash. Working from home is encouraged and made easy by videophones . . . industry is run to a major extent by machines . . . the work week is three and a half days.' This was the sanguine, *Tomorrow's World* vision of things, and, given that such devices as the washing machine genuinely had reduced the daily hours of drudgery humankind was forced to serve, women in particular, it did not seem entirely implausible.

In the 1970s, then, an increasingly mechanised future felt impending, looming, uncertain, as it had since the beginning of the century; now, however, it seemed an imminent prospect. At the time of the release of *The Man-Machine*, Kraftwerk were pivotal. Jon Savage had cited them, along with other Krautrock bands such as Faust, in a fractured, prescient piece he wrote under the banner of 'The New Musick' in *Sounds*, in 1977. 'Amon Duul/Can/Kraftwerk/Faust (a few). Nico. Moving to mirrored isolation/mesmerisation – no feeling . . . Looking for a TV plug after the bomb's dropped . . .' Figures such as Daniel Miller, Thomas Leer and Robert Rental were revving up a DIY but highly effective prototype of electro-pop. 'No feeling' was important – Kraftwerk's emotionlessness, their purposefulness, their compactness would be a paradigm for future operations; no more the frilly, open-necked, open-hearted, autobiographical indulgence of the over-Americanised, histrionic rock star. This, among other things, would put them in sympathy with the post-punk movement.

On *The Man-Machine*, Kraftwerk represented a conscious, deliberately constructed aesthetic offence to traditional rock values, particularly American ones, where a sense of unbuttoned maleness, of hair and heart and emotive authenticity was paramount, and suspicion of Anglo-European artifice, 'haircut bands', would persist throughout the 1980s and '90s. Pouting in rouge lipstick, top shirt buttons done up, red shirts – hell's sake, Kraftwerk were the anti-Springsteen, indifferent to escaping with Sally or whoever to the woods, morbidly devoted to technology. Machines, so far as American rock was generally concerned, were not things with which you formed a compact but things which you raged against. Furthermore, just in case anyone was in any doubt, the back sleeve of *The Man-Machine* featured the gratuitous piece of information concerning its provenance, 'Produced in W. Germany'. It was indeed – geographically, but also a product of West Germany's circumstances.

And so, the electromagnetically irresistible 'The Robots', commencing with that now signature 'Kraftwerk calling' synth motif. All jerky right angles and clockwork motions, there's not an ounce of flesh on its moving metal frame. The vocal is entirely vocoderised, the deceptively banal lyric a statement of intent – Kraftwerk were now reduced to pure function. Total memory wipe, blood replaced with oil. 'We're functioning automatic/And we are dancing mechanic.' As with 'Showroom Dummies', there's an element of deadpan sarcasm, a response to critics who thought the joke was at Kraftwerk's expense, rather than their own.

However, there remained a sheen to them, a strangely romantic, auratic resonance that amounted to way above the sum of their electronic parts. This was evident on 'The Model', a retrospective hit for the band, released to capitalise on the synthpop wave it had anticipated back in 1978, squeezing in at number one in the UK in February 1982 between Shakin' Stevens and the Jam, a paradigm of electropop. On its immaculate surface, with its old-world, John Barry-esque elegance, 'The Model' might have come across as in keeping with the licensed narcissism of 1982 and the New Romantic times, but Kraftwerk actually harboured quite stern views about the celebrity gaze in pop. 'A lot of the music around is pap, with the same values as pornography. Those are the values that turn "The Model" into a robot,' snorted Hütter.

'Neon Lights', meanwhile, bathed in the sodium of the nocturnal landscape, again showed their ability to transcribe perfectly, in minimal yet vivid electric strokes, facets of modern industrial society considered beneath the attention of most of their peers. Celebrated, contemplated thus in the mediating force of pop music, Kraftwerk achieved a fusion between humankind and the artificial world they had created for their betterment. With the closing title track, meanwhile, it's as if the robots have achieved some sort of human empathy: playful, joyful, like the flower-carrying cybernetic creatures in a Fernand Léger portrait.

Over the next few years, Kraftwerk would produce two more albums 'proper' – 1981's *Computer World* and 1986's *Electric*

Cafe – with the single 'Tour de France' sandwiched in between. Released in the same year that IBM launched the first PC, *Computer World* represents Kraftwerk at their most perfectly clairvoyant. The album dances to the new digital/binary configurations of the coming age, shuffling and pinging industriously, immaculate in its design and exuding Kraftwerk's trademark synthetic aura of absolute assurance. Yet it also reveals a shrewd sense of human design; on the title track, a litany of agencies such as the FBI, Interpol and Scotland Yard indicates that Kraftwerk are perfectly aware of the capacity of computers to be used for surveillance purposes. (Proposals were already afoot in the early 1980s to introduce a computerised system of ID cards in West Germany.) Then there's the pink neon heart-throb of 'Computer Love', which sweetly anticipates the capacity they are also likely to possess as a means of finding romance – fast-forward thirty years to Match.com.

It had been three years since *The Man-Machine* and, with a putative album project with the working title of *Technopop* shelved following a serious accident suffered by keen cyclist Ralf Hütter while out on the road, a further five years would pass before *Electric Cafe*, an immaculate album which refined and revisited all of Kraftwerk's key themes, with some 3D holographic imagery thrown in to denote progress. In truth, however, by this time Kraftwerk's work was done. The electrification of pop music was complete. Synthesizers were an integral part of the Lycra fabric of popular music; they denoted neither inspired futurism nor synthetic mediocrity but, like the electric guitar, could be used for better or worse. The thawing of the Cold War had allayed fears about the imminent annihilation of mankind, victim of its own technological overdevelopment, the terror of which had lent a chill dimension to the post-punk era. By the mid- to late eighties, people were settling into a less anxious relationship with a modern world developing at a manageable pace technically, albeit in ways unanticipated by most of the futurologists of the 1960s and '70s. Even Germans making popular music was no longer a novelty, but part of the routine cross-Channel cultural traffic yielding the likes of Nena's '99 Red Balloons'. When I asked Ralf Hütter what they had been doing during this period, he explained that they had been involved in building software and converting their studio into a digital operation, which, while that would certainly take time, felt like displacement activity for a group who had simply run out of major themes and ideas.

Once a harbinger, Kraftwerk settled into a role that was part anachronism, part international treasure, part baffling oddity, fully revered. They have been mostly a touring proposition, refining and modifying their onstage spectacle, but not fundamentally altering or decommissioning their core *oeuvre*. I saw them in 1991 at Brixton Academy and loved them; a friend, however, pointed out that they had put on almost exactly the same show back in 1981. There has been talk of new material and, on the fleeting occasions when it has emerged, such as their theme for Expo 2000, it has exhibited an undimmed assurance of touch. Really, however, what is there left for them to say? They said it, and it happened. Their 'silence' is a logical one, like Marcel Duchamp's conscious decision to stop making art for the last forty-five years of his life.

And yet Kraftwerk have carried on. They took a ten-year break from touring in the 1980s but have spent much of this century on the road. Schneider was rumoured to find this onerous – he is no longer with Kraftwerk. But Hütter finds the very idea of stopping odd. Kraftwerk, he told me, are 'always a work in progress'.

*

'James Brown could never have come from Belgium,' Henry Rollins once jeered in a stand-up routine, extolling the exceptional cultural qualities of the USA. The emergence of Kraftwerk to occupy at least as influential a role in popular music as the Godfather of Soul seems equally improbable. It was, however, no accident, of geography or otherwise. Kraftwerk were revered by a post-punk generation because, like them, they set themselves against the American dominance of rock music, were bent on reinventing pop and rock in a way that mirrored the provincial reality of their own experiences and represented Europe as a rival cultural and continental wellspring to that of America. Kraftwerk influenced electropop and the neo-glam New Romantic movement, from Gary Numan to Steve Strange, because of their androgyny, their rejection of 'rockist' mores and its conventional set of representations of the 'human' in music. Kraftwerk saw the value of artifice, of manufacturing your being, of art as a form of presentation rather than earnest, ostentatiously heartfelt autobiographical self-expression, of becoming rather than being – as the writer Simon Price would put it, to 'tear up the hand of cards you were dealt' and remake yourself.

That Kraftwerk were fated to provide the girders for modern dance music is most astonishing of all, but again, not so far-fetched. When Afrika Bambaataa and the Soulsonic Force adopted elements of Kraftwerk's 'Trans-Europe Express' and 'Numbers' in 1982 to create 'Planet Rock', he and producer Arthur Baker were only taking down something that was already in the air. Recalled Ralf Hütter in 2005, talking to Simon Witter, 'I remember we went to a loft club in New York around the time of *Trans-Europe Express*, and the DJ had pressed his own record, using our tapes of "Metal on Metal", but extending it on and on and on. It was the beginning of DJ record making, and we were fascinated. It was just in our direction, because that's what we would do in our studio, establish a groove and play it for hours and hours. Maybe go out and come back hours later, and the machines would still be playing. So we were both surprised and pleased.'

Kraftwerk had resonated with African American music lovers

since the days of 'Autobahn'. However, the release of 'Planet Rock' represented the formal inauguration of 'electro-funk', which anticipated both techno and hip hop. Hitherto, electronic music had been regarded as a frigid, Caucasian conceit. It was generally considered antithetical to the spirit of jazz; Miles Davis was considered a sellout rather than an innovator in his electric phase, while Sun Ra, who had been availing himself of unconventional and electronic instruments from the 1950s onwards, was regarded as an eccentric loon, feted by a handful of longhairs and Europeans. Funk was a different matter – George Clinton and Parliament had used synthesizers extensively, as did Stevie Wonder, but neither were especially 'cybernetic' in their approach. Clinton detested the monotonous, too easy regularity of disco, its lack of sass and licks, while Stevie Wonder's great seventies albums generally saw him use a standard drum kit.

Why, then, should Kraftwerk, who, like the rest of the Krautrock generation, had been predicated on the need to seek alternatives to American blues and rock, make such a natural connection with black audiences, one that was strengthened further when they were taken up by the likes of Derrick May and Kevin Saunderson in the mid-eighties? 'They're so stiff, they're funky,' said Carl Craig, while in Simon Reynolds's *Energy Flash*, Juan Atkins spoke about the natural connection between Detroit and the midwest and the harsh, steely clank of modern European electro – the industrial beat of the Motor City, in which blacks and whites were employed side by side, fought for their rights as workers side by side. As for the question of soul, well, Ralf Hütter was adamant when I put this to him. 'Our machines have soul,' he replied, firmly.

The real attraction may have been the modernity of Kraftwerk. Notions of heart and soul, of sensuality and authenticity tend to be fondly invested in black music by white listeners, who have often preferred its distant, unthreatening, boogie-woogie past to its more unsettling present-day mutations. You don't have to cast your ear very far, be it in the direction of *Later . . . with Jools Holland* to the retro-soul of Adele or the late Amy Winehouse, for example, to see that there is a significant appetite among white audiences for African American music in its more antique forms.

There is generally a strong inclination in white popular musical tastes towards the nostalgic, the retrograde. This is less the case for black popular music, which is more impatient for innovation. So it is that since 'Planet Rock', electronics, new production techniques and, especially, rhythmical rearrangements have all played a starring role in the proliferation of state-of-the-art genres – hip hop, contemporary R&B, drum 'n' bass, dubstep, footwork, from Detroit to the pirate stations of the early 1990s, who played, as William Orbit remarked, wall-to-wall Kraftwerk. It makes sense – if you are African American or Black British, the sounds of the sixties and the seventies do not have the rose-tinted connotations they do for white audiences, still less so the fifties, forties or thirties. Discrimination, humiliation, the struggles of the Civil Rights movement, to be treated with parity and basic human dignity – what's there to be nostalgic about?

Kraftwerk talked about Year Zero, but they were by no means immune to profound feelings of nostalgia, and a desire to reconnect with Germany's great traditions and its active role in early twentieth-century culture. Their most recent shows are filled with digitalised, retromaniacal Super 8 images of advertising hoardings for eau de cologne and so forth, taken around Düsseldorf. However, from the late 1970s onwards, their primary emphasis was the present and the future, as reflected in their fearless attitude towards new technology and their drive towards an increasingly rhythm-oriented, machine-like approach to music. All of this was bound to strike a chord with black music-makers and audiences, in flight from the trauma of their past, their hopes and dreams of better prospects invested in the future, starting today, getting moving right now. A twitchy, hypermetabolic impatience for structural change in the mode of music was a reflection of their hunger for social change. 'Certainly, all my friends were into futurism,' Jeff Mills, one of the founder members of the Kraftwerk-influenced, Detroit-based collective Underground Resistance tells me. 'Not Afro-futurism but in a technological way. We were interested in how we were going to live tomorrow. We learned a lot through science fiction, books. People were much more open back then. Technology had a lot to do with that – for black people, so long as it was funky . . . it wasn't just Kraftwerk, it was Visage, it was Gary Numan. The Clash is another ['This Is Radio Clash']. But it was Kraftwerk's track "Numbers" that sealed the deal, followed by "Tour de France".'

Today, there are those, particularly the likes of Heinrich Müller of the Underground Resistance axis, who continue to keep the faith with the specific metre and patter of Kraftwerk's trademark rhythms, as laid down between 1977 and 1981. Mostly, however, Kraftwerk serve as an example of the need for upgrade and development, of the need to establish a sense of place and of identity through sound that has materialised in musics which physically have little in common with *Trans-Europe Express* or *The Man-Machine* other than that they are achieved by primarily electronic means. From IDM to Burial, from Timbaland to Wiley – so prolific and diverse and ubiquitous is this music that it is hardly necessary for Kraftwerk, their leader Hütter now in his sixties, to blaze a trail, light the way.

And so, paradoxically, what they have encouraged in others, Kraftwerk have ceased to practise themselves. Following a period of drastic evolution, they have become a permanence. And all that they have done, in terms of presentation, software and so forth, is to seal that permanence. That's their forward mission from here on. Which is fine; they owe us nothing further. No longer in a state of forward-moving flux, except in the visual development of their stage shows, they can be contemplated all the more clearly in their fixed, idiosyncratic, logical strangeness. There are things about Kraftwerk. Here are some of them.

RALF HÜTTER LOVES THE WORD 'LITTLE'. It was dotted throughout his interview with me, and throughout their discourse. The 'little' melody he discovers, to his enchantment, he can play to the lyric of 'Pocket Calculator'; the 'little mechanical dance' he and the rest of Kraftwerk enjoyed performing when out nightclubbing; his 'little' machines and 'little' electric keyboards. Kraftwerk demonstrated how big, industrial-sized machines could be played on tiny, hand-held devices, but Hütter, you sense, is slyly conscious of how mainstream rock, with its penile tendencies to dramatic self-aggrandisement, is very uncomfortable with the word 'little'. The emasculating effect, the snip-snip frequency of his use of the word is an intentional, pocket-calculated assault on Big Guitar.

KRAFTWERK ARE NOT ABSOLUTE, UNCRITICAL TECHNOPHILES. They prefer, for example, the train and bicycle to the plane. Let Brian Eno create *Music for Airports*; give Kraftwerk a velodrome any day, like the one in which they legendarily performed in Manchester in 2010. 'We prefer the tempo of the autobahn,' Hütter told me. 'We love cycling, we love the speed of cycling, the cinematic experience. The same with driving. In a plane, you are too dislocated from what is going on around you.' This is key to understanding Kraftwerk. '*Mensch – Natur – Technik*'. No futurist fantasies of jetpacks or flying cars for them; we already have the machine, the mode of transport in which the human being and the environment are perfectly matched – the humble pushbike, on which, between them, the Kraftwerk members have been known to clock up hundreds of miles a day. Hütter even professes an ecological consciousness. 'Of course. With complete destruction, the relationship between man, machine and environment is completely finished. We are very much aware of this.'

Few groups have been as 'environmentally conscious' as Kraftwerk. As Wolfgang Flür put it, the windows of their attentiveness were open to 'trains, planes, even the rustling of the wind', and all this fed into their music, adding to their overall Doppler effect. Kraftwerk were tuned into everything.

Kraftwerk regard technologies not as objects to be glorified or fetishised, but as functional – and neutral. 'It's always been the same,' says Hütter. 'Since they invented the knife, you could either butter your bread with it or stab someone in the throat with it.' However, they take a scalpel to the flabby, passéist sensibility of those who took refuge in the string-soaked, sentimental tropes of a long-dead classical past. At the time of its release, Hütter deplored the John Williams soundtrack for *Star Wars*, in all its crowd-pleasing, epic, orchestral tonality, revealing it for the cosmic Western it essentially was.

What's more, Hütter suspects that aesthetic Luddites aren't always motivated by a proper Huxleyan suspicion of technological development at the expense of man and his soul but by hidebound prejudice, fear and loathing, even hypocrisy. 'Yes, we were attacked, strangely enough by people who expected the latest and most up-to-date equipment when they went to the dentist,' he told me. 'They would not have liked to have had their bad teeth pulled out with pliers but they attacked us for being too mechanical. When it comes to music, they wanted old guitars from the fifties.'

THE PARALLELS BETWEEN KRAFTWERK AND BAUHAUS ARE STRIKING. Not the Northampton post-punk group of the same name, I should hasten to stress, but the art movement of the 1920s, to which Ralf Hütter has frequently referred as an influence. 'We knew them from the art scene in

Germany; they were the basic programmes of our education. The ideas reflected in our work are both internationalism and the mixing of different art forms, the idea that you don't separate dance over here and architecture over there, painting over there. We do everything, and the marriage of art and technology was Kraftwerk right from the beginning . . . we broke down the barrier between craftsmen and artist, we were music workers.' (There was some resentment among the 'workers' regarding this title, incidentally, particularly from Wolfgang Flür. 'I was not a music worker!' he protested, in BBC4's *Krautrock* documentary.)

In this respect, as in others, Kraftwerk are actually a throwback. Architect Walter Gropius founded the Bauhaus movement in 1919, with Germany having just experienced the trauma and ruin of a wartime defeat. Amid the rubble of despair and shortages, everything seemed up for grabs – the Berlin wing of the Dada movement entertained serious hopes of working in league with the Communist party who briefly held power in the city. Gropius had similar dreams of art transcending itself, calling for a unity with craft, technology, the state (a 'Republic of the Spirit'), with life itself. The Bauhaus movement sought to do this not through music but through design, in every area, ranging from household implements to town planning. Artists could no longer be regarded as detached aesthetes with all the spurious distinction that implies but, as Hütter also puts it, as workers. The iron and glass tubes, the symmetry and right angles of Bauhaus design are like a visual transcription of the Kraftwerk sound – spotless, minimal, metal surfaces, to replace the ancient, baroque follies of the discredited old world, with all its old errors and unfitness for purpose. No more such hand-me-downs from a ruinous past. Bauhaus reflected a need for national reinvention, in which art would play a starring role. Bauhaus, too, suffered from criticisms of coldness, spartan remoteness.

KRAFTWERK'S RETICENCE IN INTERVIEWS IS UNDERSTANDABLE, EVEN NECESSARY. It's said that Kraftwerk rarely do interviews – however, Hütter in particular has conducted many, many interviews over the years, even if these have tapered off a little in recent times. What he has always refused to do is divulge any information which journalists might find useful about his private life, or what goes on behind the scenes, or off-duty at Operation Kraftwerk. Their secretiveness is a further sign of the aloofness they project in their music, as far as their detractors are concerned. And there were many who took great pleasure in the publication of Wolfgang Flür's *I Was a Robot*, in which he divulged a few vague, mildly salacious tales of post-gig, backstage life with the group. This humanised Kraftwerk, some felt – the robots caught with their pants down, hairy limbs revealed. Kraftwerk were furious and wanted the book suppressed, a censorious reaction which cast them in a negative light.

However, one can sympathise. Not unlike Gilbert and George, Kraftwerk are very conscious and careful about where, and how, they place their selves in the scheme of things, about the relationships between their actual selves and the Doppler selves that function as self-signifiers onstage. They are not up and out there in a self-revealing, self-celebrating capacity but as visible functionaries, a working model of the man–machine relationship. Their refusal to play the role of conventional rock superstar has another provenance. 'The whole ego aspect of music is boring. It doesn't interest us. In Germany in the thirties we had a system of superstardom with Mr Adolf from Austria and so there is no interest for me in this "cult of personality",' Hütter once said.

Coming as he does from a well-to-do background, it might be suspected that Hütter wishes to conceal his bourgeois and privileged origins, which run counter to the idea of him as, in a particular sense, a 'self-made man'. Kraftwerk have never quite attained the sort of superstardom that would attract the morbid attentions of the paparazzi or tabloids to any particularly invasive degree. Despite Kraftwerk's fame, Hütter has managed to preserve his privacy. Again, it's fair to assume that this is simply a rational and sane thing to have done, rather than because he has some terrible secret to withhold or seeks to cultivate an air of mystique.

He has hinted in interviews that his family may not have approved of his bohemian musical adventures, particularly in his longhair, obscure early days, as well as remarking vaguely that in his early teens he felt somewhat withdrawn and disconnected from the world. However, Hütter's choice not to expand on all of this, nor to feed the beast of celebrity curiosity, which has grown ever more ravenous, for its own sake is one that should be respected, even admired. Sometimes Kraftwerk's eccentricities are explicable in terms of their background – Iggy Pop was rather taken with Florian Schneider's fixation on asparagus, and shopping for the correct, white asparagus, as if he were in the grip of an arbitrary culinary fixation. However, in the Ruhrgebeit, when it's in season, it is considered eccentric not to take an interest in asparagus, which plays a dominant role on the dinner plates of the region. *Ganz normale.*

KRAFTWERK ARE FUNNY. Their trick has been to offer themselves up as the butt of Anglo-American humour, the amusing foreigners, with their naïve grasp of the English language and their jerky, gauche attempts to create English-language pop music, and, of course, the robots, which these days have all the subtlety of Wii avatars. But it is Kraftwerk who have had the last laugh, riding out those early years of Second World War-related captions and critics breaking into German accents in mid-review. Humour and music do not easily mix; it is almost impossible to make music that is intoxicating and immersive but also raises a wry smile. One generally has to be sacrificed for the other. Kraftwerk buck that. It is to do with the precise nature of their humour, which isn't exactly satirical, or exactly self-deprecating, but somehow derives from their precision, their simplicity and unaffected lucidity. Or, as Hütter puts it, 'It is a sort of bland humour – smiles, rather than laughs. It is not so much humour at the cost of someone else but a liberating humour, that involuntary smile when things become transparent, when it clicks and everything is ideal.' Kraftwerk are so magnificently antithetical – they stand in an orderly line and go about their business methodically, in contrast to the daft, agonised guitar wranglings of rock as parodied/celebrated by Jack Black and Tenacious D. As Hütter puts it, 'Our drummers don't sweat.'

KRAFTWERK ARE NONCONFORMISTS. In these times in which rock 'n' roll has been corporatised and corporations have been rock 'n' rolled, in which its energies have long since been absorbed and commodified, in which every mission statement must boast of a 'passion' for whatever commodity or service it is providing, the sheer, static cool of Kraftwerk, who once declared that they 'believe in anarchy and self-rule', remains exemplary and unnerving. It's a commonplace that in the DNA of any band with pretensions to modernity to have emerged since 1977 can be found ancestral traces of Kraftwerk (to the extent that Liam Howlett of the Prodigy was compelled to protest that he 'never liked Kraftwerk' in an attempt to stake out an alternative lineage for the group). However, Kraftwerk's success, and the reason why it has been necessary for them to maintain the spectacle of themselves through touring, is to have preserved the fact of their oddity, even in relationship with a twenty-first-century soundworld in which technology is, if anything, over-familiar – a square peg calmly slotted into a round hole. Their rejection of the guitar, of the dirt of the soil, of the male stance and gaze and phallic, egotistical thrust still so obstructively central to the rock tradition and experience is, for all Kraftwerk's air of eccentric, pacific robo-androgyny, among the greatest and most discreet triumphs in rock history.

IT'S NOT JUST ABOUT TECHNOLOGY. Quite simply, in word, melody and gesture, Kraftwerk, and in particular Ralf Hütter, have always known exactly which buttons to push. And there it is, and there they are.

4 Faust: Hamburg and the German Beatles

> 'When you think about Faust, when you consider that they're the strangest "manufactured" group ever – they've all been yoked together, pulled off the street, and yet each of them has a great talent for something. It's hard to believe they were seven average people who happened to be on the music scene in Hamburg. Or maybe they were a product of the times . . .'
>
> Tim Gane, Stereolab

'Hamburg is a totally different scene from Berlin, which has a different vibe, or the Cologne scene. Hamburg has always had a scene of its own,' says Hamburg resident and Faust founder member Jean-Hervé Péron. 'The press, film, Polydor International. The Beatles ignited their career here – there's been a lot of British influence in its development.'

The Beatles arrived in Hamburg, formerly in the British occupation zone, in 1960, in the raw days when they were famished, pill-popping young rockers urged to *Mach schau!* – put on a show – for a salty audience of drunken sailors and local, sleazy thrillseekers, rocking and rolling about in the licensed squalor of the place. They form part of the town's heritage today – there are Beatles walking tours which take you past the old Top Ten Club on the Reeperbahn, where the Beatles played ninety-eight consecutive nights, on one of which Paul McCartney and Stuart Sutcliffe had an onstage fistfight over remarks McCartney made about the latter's girlfriend, latently jealous of his doomed, static cool. There is a statue of Sutcliffe, one of five that make up the pre-Fab Four Beatles. He's a little detached from the rest of the pack, fated not to share in their eventual success, yet somehow the abiding embodiment of the Beatles spirit in this period, as photographed by Astrid Kirchherr.

For all that, however, in their actual time in the town, the Beatles did not exercise any direct influence on the cultural shape and destiny of Hamburg, or Germany. Back then, they were just a bunch of slovenly, Brylcreemed, leather-clad herberts reeling around between venues, bars and seedy digs. It was only when they returned home to England to be cleaned up, recast as mop-tops and resold around the world that they would truly revisit West Germany as an arguably overbearing hegemonic force. As elsewhere, they dominated the charts not only with their own universally popular string of hits but also through German imitators; groups like the Rattles. Hamburg had its own beat scene, featuring the likes of Udo Lindenberg, Marius Müller-Westernhagen and Otto Waalkes.

Jean-Hervé Péron greets me, flanked by two amiable, woolly hounds, at the Clouds Hill Studios in the Rothenburgsort district of Hamburg, a spectacularly well-appointed space set over two floors in a converted warehouse overlooking the River Elbe. Even here there is the faintest of Beatles connections; it is the only recording studio in Germany equipped with a vintage Neve 8078 console, the audio mixer that Beatles producer George Martin commissioned Rupert Neve to manufacture in 1978. John Lennon also did some of the recording here for his last album, *Double Fantasy*. Its fixtures and fittings include pillars and carpets that make it feel more like some avant-garde stately home than a conventional recording space, while it commands spectacular views over the Elbe landscape. Look out of the studio window and in the far distance is an imposing, metallic industrial estate, a reminder of Germany's still formidable manufacturing base. In the nearer distance, however, below the waterway, is a small green belt of idyllic parkland. The visual schism is uncannily similar to that of

Faust's own music, in which brutalist modernism and hankering pastoralism are adjoined.

A feeling of cultural cringe still permeates modern Hamburg. Despite boasting of its status as a 'free and Hanseatic City', able to forge its own commercial destiny, set its own laws and maintain its own army, a local guidebook is equally proud to note the immense popularity of musicals like *Cats* and *The Phantom of the Opera* in the city. In the late sixties, however, the musicians who made up Faust were among those who were beginning to baulk at the occupation of their own minds by the Fab Four. Frank Zappa, who with the Mothers of Invention had lampooned *Sergeant Pepper's Lonely Hearts Club Band* with such scabrous, dissecting brilliance on 1967's *We're Only in It for the Money*, certainly caught the imagination of young Germans, as both an American and anti-American, but the real change for German musicians wasn't in the mode of music, says Péron, but something fomenting within themselves. No more imitation.

Faust would be the break away from the Beatles. A small step in Hamburg, a potentially giant leap for rock music.

'By this time, groups were mostly busy with themselves,' says Péron. 'There was something in the air, something special at this time. It was more visceral, it was inside. It wasn't the Beatles. There was indeed a vacuum in Germany – not only a physical vacuum, with all these areas being bombed, all these anti-spaces – there was also an intellectual and emotional emptiness which needed to be filled. And this is what happened. So, there were many groups enjoying the rock 'n' roll and blues, like groups all over the world. But there was also a minority, a strong and intense movement, busy with themselves, making new harmonies, new ways, new conceptions.

'There was a similar thing happening in France with things like Magma, but not as much as in Germany. It was a traumatised country – but on a heap of shit you get the most beautiful flowers. Things were fermenting, pushed by the '68 movement from France, which was highly political. All these tectonic forces were at play and we were lucky enough to be young back then, to pick up those vibes and turn it into art.'

In 1968, Hamburg was the centre of a German record industry that was becoming conscious of a new struggle for national and cultural identity rumbling beneath its feet. The success of groups like Can and Amon Düül had surprised some executives at Polydor, who had assumed German music to be so crippled by lack of self-esteem that it was incapable of purveying much more than Schlager and light-orchestral future-kitsch such as James Last – music for a national listenership keeping their heads determinedly down the middle of the road of continued prosperity. The international wing had spotted the potential of new German music sooner than its domestic department, seen how it had a cachet in other European territories, including, vitally, the UK.

This, however, was as far as the major record company's shrewdness extended. It was suggested to them that they could create a customised German superstar group of their own, a Teutonic equivalent of the Kinks, maybe, or a Beatles equipped for the seventies. After all, what was the difference between developing a new rock group and developing a new top-of-the-range car?

The man who had proposed that such a thing was doable was Uwe Nettelbeck. A small, primly dapper man of exquisite tastes and used to high living who managed to contain any revulsion he felt at the slovenly fug of hippie mores, Nettelbeck was a journalist who had worked for a number of the underground magazines that had flourished in the countercultural scene of the late 1960s, including *konkret*. He had even incurred the displeasure of Ulrike Meinhof, during her days as a writer on the same magazine, who accused him of being a counter-revolutionary snake in the grass – or so the story goes.

'With Faust, you have Nettelbeck and then you have the band.

They were in different worlds,' says *Sounds* journalist Diedrich Diederichsen. 'Nettelbeck was an important and influential writer in the sixties. He was a prominent writer on counterculture in his early twenties, when such a thing was unheard of. He knew about all the parallel cultural movements, art movements who weren't even aware of each other, similar movements in different cities – the Viennese Actionists, the Destruction in Art Symposium in London. He knew of all these things and was the first person to write for *Die Zeit*, but he was also a radical leftist, and that was not tolerable for *Die Zeit*. Then he became editor of *konkret* for a short period, the same time as Ulrike Meinhof, but his falling out with her is exaggerated; they had little in common. He was a well-known figure – and it was with this authority that he came to Polydor and sold them Faust.

'What's astonishing is that Polydor let him do it, but also that someone who had such a name like him was connected with this weird band,' says Diederichsen. 'This was something that had not happened before – this well-known critic and intellectual and this formless, progressive rock. This had not existed before, this combination.'

'"The new Beatles!"' laughs Péron. 'I'm not absolutely certain if that's what they said to Uwe, but certainly, after we were put together, I heard this expression. I have a friend who was the son of the man who gave Faust the green light. Uwe himself was not looking for the "new Beatles" – he felt what was happening, this vacuum. He felt this. He said, "It's such a shame there is such a huge amount of money being spent on pop, on Schlager, the best equipment – why not allow an experimental group to have a better start, not to have to worry about studio costs, about food – why not give them the chance?" And he managed to trick Polydor. He managed to get a big budget. We were the one in a million. Polydor thought they were investing in successful popular music, maybe even Schlager. So for Herr Vogelsang, big boss at Polydor, it was all about the numbers – "We sell so many albums, spend so much money promoting them, let's see if it works."'

Via Hamburg filmmaker Hellmuth Costard, whose *Besonders wertvoll* had starred a talking penis, Nettelbeck made contact with Péron, who was playing with a song-based group called Nukleus alongside guitarist Rudolf Sosna and saxophonist Gunther Wüsthof. They in turn knew another group, a more noisenik, maximal outfit who operated under the slick banner of Campylognatus Citelli and who included among their number Werner 'Zappi' Diermaier and keyboardist Hans-Joachim Irmler, from the Swabian region of southern Germany. These two polarised musical propositions were promptly soldered together and carried out their first rehearsals in the dank confines of an old air-raid shelter – essentially a long, dark corridor which led nowhere. In terms of symbolising Germany's past and present cultural situation and its uncertain but intriguing future, it could not have been more apt.

Faust were duly birthed, their name a pun on the German for 'fist', a skeletal representation of which would eventually appear on their debut, transparent-sleeved album, but also referencing Goethe's Faust, who makes a compact with the devil in exchange for freedom to explore the sciences on earth. The parallel with Faust the group and their deal with a major record company was obvious, but under the aegis of the crafty and open-minded Nettelbeck, Faust were able to cheat the devil, for a while at least, while availing themselves of facilities including, crucially, Polydor's in-house producer Kurt Graupner. Faust were a fabulously accidental product – if they say that a camel is a horse designed by committee, then Faust were a magnificent, misshapen beast begotten by misconceived corporate design.

It's all the more extraordinary since the group were green-lit on the basis of a demo, recorded in late 1970, that included 'Lieber Herr Deutschland', into whose four-minute collage are compressed all the chaos and militant determination of the extended post-1968 moment, from its opening, power-to-the-people chant to its skronking abandon, as if the ceiling of their air-raid shelter had caved in, followed by the mock-formal reading of a piece of factory blurb extolling the virtues of a labour-saving, fully automatic washing machine, then a solemn tolling of metal bashing before a lurching, tumultuous, strangely beautiful echo-drenched jam in which indistinct vocals bob and drown. It's an exploded transcription of a Situationist fantasy. It does not remind you of the Beatles or the Kinks.

'Every day there was a demonstration in the streets,' says Péron. 'Even at the time, we were into field recordings, which was not a term used at the time. It was a testimony of the vibes. We recorded the sound of hammer ramming – the washing-machine stuff – it was an acoustic collage. These days, having field records mingled into recordings is much easier in the digital world. Maybe the demo was for Uwe. Who knows? He was a very clever man. Maybe Polydor never heard it.'

For all their naïve designs it's to Polydor's credit that at this stage they not only waved Faust through with a shrug and an 'I expect you know what you're doing' but also financed the building of a new studio for the group in a former schoolhouse in the small village of Wümme, some twenty-five miles outside Hamburg, with producer Graupner seconded from Polydor's Deutsche Grammophon.

Faust had some acquaintance with Amon Düül but were less aware of the parallels between themselves and Can, and vice versa. Both had retreated from the city, from the potentially malign influence of the German urban everyday, shut themselves off in order to begin again. Both were preoccupied with the idea of Germanness, not out of any desire to restore patriotic pride, with all that that entailed, but with the aim of reflecting their own situation, of working as musicians with the tools and traditions of countries with which they had no association.

'As far as content is concerned we are realising the particular situation a German band is in, by not having any roots in rock music, but on the other hand knowing all the stuff because our record shops are just the same as yours, there's no difference. But it puts you in a strange relation to the stuff because you neither speak English nor have any connection to anything in it. It's a second sort of reality,' Uwe Nettelbeck told *Melody Maker*'s Karl Dallas in 1973. 'So we try to make an amalgam from all the material which comes to us to form something which goes beyond quotations. The material should be altered, shouldn't stay the same, never, and this should be combined with sounds.'

The members of Faust were by no means pawns in Nettelbeck's game and Polydor's naïve schemes, but strong, diverse characters steeped in music, culture, the fine arts and the raging political debates of the day, all of them having followed mazy paths to Faust and Wümme. Jean-Hervé Péron was actually French, a busker who had found his way to Germany following a romantic pursuit. Hans-Joachim Irmler was a multi-instrumentalist, a graphic designer who had a highly developed understanding of the relationship between noise and music. Rudolf Sosna was part Russian, a boozer and a poet who drank himself into oblivion, discovered dead in his bath in 1997. He was the tragic keeper, perhaps, of Faust's soul. 'Rudy is in my opinion the genius of Faust, the everything of Faust,' says Péron. 'We all had aspects, but he had them all. He played guitar, piano, trumpet. He was an excellent painter. And a lyricist. When he talked to you, he would unravel these long sentences, you'd get lost in them. He was always either heavily drinking, or drinking nothing, or eating nothing and heavily drinking – he was intense that way.

'We were a gathering of eight people, with Uwe and Kurt [Graupner] – and eight such different people!' says Péron. 'Yet we were all looking in the same direction. And I think this is what is unique about Faust. You had Uwe, who was a visionary, a sharp, extremely educated man, despite being kicked out of school – a good sign! So many connections. Kurt Graupner with the black boxes, a genius.

'Then there was Gunther Wüsthof, typical of the dry humour and systematic thinking of the northern German. He was extremely logical in his creative approach. He used maths – taking a word, taking the first, third, fifth, seventh letter of this and see what word comes. He did the same thing with music also, on saxophone. It's not free jazz what he's doing, he's following some pattern. He's following something in his head that I can't follow. He would bury sheets of metal and let them lie for twenty years, then dig them up. This is art. He comes from a region of north-east Germany where people are supposed to be very slow and stupid but of course they aren't, and he certainly is not.

'Werner "Zappi" Diermaier, our drummer, is very naïve in a positive way. He isn't touched by intellectual thoughts – he is very straightforward and is the one who has maintained most of the vibes. He never asks questions about the nature, quality and direction of the music. He's the best and the worst drummer. He synthesises everything and everybody and keeps things going. That takes a lot of openness, disparateness – don't question things, just take it in.

'And Irmler, south German, a fantastic brain for electronics and conceptual music. Then Arnulf Meifert – he did not fit in the cocktail. He was a bit too serious.'

On the strength of their debut album, the group to whom Faust seemed most closely related were the Mothers of Invention, led by Frank Zappa. Faust's use of tape collage, abruptly splicing between electronics, spoken-word passages and passages of chamber rock, their facetious iconoclasm and scathing humour all recalled early Zappa albums like *We're Only in It for the Money*. Drummer Diermaier's nickname of 'Zappi' came about because of his love of the LA-based composer who was both a key player in the west-coast rock scene and disdainfully detached from it. Faust's debut album could be condescendingly mistaken for a shambling, amateurish attempt on the part of semi-comprehending Germans to create a Teutonic Mothers.

There were, however, key differences. Zappa was driven initially by an anger which, as his career progressed, degenerated into a satirical and hollow sneer. His arrangements, amalgamated pastiches of rock, doo-wop, jazz, classical and musique concrète, were breathtakingly finished, dazzlingly executed, but often seemed to be pointed demonstrations of virtuosity, a baton with which to beat the less advanced pop in all its earnest banality. Every passage in Zappa's *oeuvre* feels like it's in inverted commas. As a bandleader he was a disciplinarian to the point of being a martinet, and he was far more of a social conservative than he was often taken for. His vocals are not so much sung as spoken, sardonic and always above it all. What one finds hard to locate in Zappa and the Mothers of Invention is that intangible, haunting and haunted quality you might call soul.

Faust, by contrast, had no obvious leader and were socially ultra-liberal, with nudity and riotous living going hand in hand with their radical politics and music-making. And, despite their name, Faust most certainly had a soul. There is about their playing a sense of urgency, of restlessness and necessity, and, as a corollary to their roiling turbulence, a profound sense of pining. As with Can, as with Kraftwerk, as with the avant-garde project of the twentieth century in general, their deconstruction of existing conventions is all part of a process of reconstruction, of reassembly, at some level a vain effort to rediscover something that was once whole and pure. The dissonance in Faust is exhilarating, challenging, but also has echoes of the tragic.

Wümme was more than a conveniently detached retreat in which to record. It was a way of living, working, playing and being. Ground rules were established which essentially dictated that there should be no rules, often the most exacting and rigorous code by which to live. It had the potential for contradiction and conflict – as Irmler put it, 'Everyone can live out their preferences, yet has to stand his ground against the other five.' It required cultural isolation: no radios, no TVs, no record players, none of the potential contamination of the mainstream – think for yourself, from zero, from the beginning.

For all that, however, Faust were not exactly spartan. Prior to their arrival at Wümme, they spent a few months at the large, secluded house of Nettelbeck's wife Petra, in an indolent, luxurious haze of sunshine and dope. 'We did nothing,' confessed Péron. 'They gave us a big house in the middle of the countryside. It was a training centre for the army. We were surrounded by Panzer tanks, soldiers in camouflage. All this while they were getting Wümme together, getting all the gear in.

'Petra is one important figure of Faust – she had a very important role. There is always a woman in the back of all this. Women – I would be nothing without women keeping me up – for Rudolf it was Marita, absorbing so many of his problems. And Petra, understanding the group, understanding Uwe, the problems within the group – and dealing with these things, as women do.'

Even when they reached Wümme, and despite a set-up which enabled them to record at any time of day or night, from their beds if they were so inclined, Polydor were rather nervous as to whether their young charges were actually producing anything of commercial value. Arnulf Meifert, perhaps the most conventionally conscientious of the group, tried to crack the whip, urge the collective to work harder, rehearse more – for which he was eventually dismissed by the group, following a mock show trial, which Péron today agrees was most unfair.

Arnulf 'would talk politics and have serious discussions about contracts. He would discuss every aspect of the contract whereas we didn't give a damn. Just let us sign it and make music. And that would get in the way of Uwe, who liked to move fast. It was cruel to Arnulf, fuck yeah. He didn't mean it badly. There was a latent generational problem. He was older, he was more serious politically and musically – he was an intellectual. We kicked him out. But not really being aware of how cruel that was.'

Life at Wümme, remembers Péron, was a strange mixture of the monastic and the merry. 'We worked, but not in a spirit of working. We had fun all the time. We would live there, we didn't have TV, newspapers – I think we had a telephone. No women around while recording, just us and our dogs. All we did was cook, make music, talk, cook, make music, sleep. The village was several kilometres away – just a few houses. One was sort of a bar, one room within a farm that they opened in the evening for local farmers to gather, have a beer. We would visit that regularly, just so that we had some sort of social life. There are beautiful pictures of the big man, Zappi, in only his pink baggy underwear. You lose all sense of time when you are totally free. You dress or don't dress. Mostly we were naked – so for us, putting on underwear was really quite an effort to dress up! Nobody minded, though, they accepted us – it was a privileged time.

'Some of us worked in the day, others were night people – you might get up and hear Joachim Irmler play on his organ in the middle of the night, or playing from his bed, having run a cable through to his room. None of this is myth, all of this is true. I'm sure you could do such a thing nowadays – in those days, so much more hardware was required. We were extremely free. The whole scene, not just Faust.'

Peter Blegvad, an American expat languishing at Exeter University, lived briefly at the commune and toured with Faust, invited over to Germany by his friend Anthony Moore of Slapp Happy. 'In the evenings, they would repair to the local town, to a seedy discotheque which played oompah music, and occasionally they would bring back drunken townspeople and jam – but these people were seldom musicians, so the results would be drunken harangues over rock 'n' roll,' he told *Mojo*'s Andy Gill in 1997. 'I remember a tape we were all impressed by that featured the local Elvis impersonator – not so much a profession, as a delusion by which he would be gripped after sufficient quantities of alcohol – who one night recorded the entire Presley *oeuvre*. He was shouting, with a thick German accent, all those famous words, with Faust backing him.'

The record company were not reassured by the dribs and drabs of taped music that emerged from the compound – yodelling, mock waltzes, musique concrète collages using the revving of a van, and so forth. However, sound engineer Kurt Graupner was an ingenious enabler who made the most of the simple eight-track machines and mixing consoles Faust had been given to work with, and who was versed in the art of treating the studio as a musical instrument, in terms of processing, echo, spatial location, all of which would add depth and dimension to the soundworld in which Faust operated.

He built mixers into the units that would allow them to pan from speaker to speaker in real time. He assigned each group member a metre-long box with twenty controls. These 'black boxes', as they were ominously known, allowed Faust to modify their own and each other's output, enabling them not just to play but to spontaneously engineer at the same time. 'We got the black boxes, we each had three channels – we could do quite fancy things,' recalls Péron. 'We could distort, use ring modulators – we could interfere with what other players were doing. You could be playing guitar and someone else had decided to change the sound of it as you played. There were some splendid moments.' Hence the marinating, bubbling, mutated, distorted quality of Faust's music, a quality that would be wiped away in a future era of digital recording. 'We went into the studio not knowing at all what we were going to do. You start playing, so there's a skeleton, a body, a drawing – and then, you try to get to the essence of what you've created.'

This was not just sonic adventurism for its own sake but philosophically crucial to Faust. Drums, guitars, all the beat-music tropes, none of these should be accepted as they were – everything had to be cut up, processed, modified, to reflect their own times, their own place, their own hands-on involvement. Nothing could be taken as given. As Joachim Irmler puts it, it was necessary to make their instruments sound as unlike themselves as possible.

'Faust was never about being professional, expert musicians,' says Péron. 'We never wanted that, or weren't able to have it. We had this Dadaist idea in mind, this feeling of being extremely serious about not being serious, or not being serious about serious things.'

Finally, with Graupner toiling on through the choking clouds of second-hand dope smoke, an inspired, indolent, intense, inebriated, inchoate jamming sprawl of ideas was reduced to Faust's debut album. It may not be their finest but it is their truest, in reflecting the conditions in which they lived and worked – the billowing stuff of absolute freedom, pared and shaped in the editing suite. It's been argued that it might have benefited from more rehearsal, more refinement, but to what end? What key roughnesses, edges, idiosyncrasies and snags might have been planed away for the questionable sake of achieving a professional finish? Opener 'Why Don't You Eat Carrots?' is explicit – samples of the Stones' '(I Can't Get No) Satisfaction' and the Beatles' 'All You Need Is Love' are ritually set alight in a crackling conflagration of electronics, the beat-group era consigned to yesteryear. It's a flaming, flagrant example of sampling as quotation, years before the practice became commonplace, with all its attendant copyright problems. However, says Péron, 'At the time, the rule was that if you use fewer than four bars of a song, you can quote anything.'

What follows has the feeling of being carried out on charred terrain, ground zero. It could be anything; here, it's a stilted piano fanfare, a tinpot parody of light orchestral music, James Last recreated as an expressionist theatrical soundtrack, interrupted by processed choral vocals rearing ghostlike from the mixing desk. Then, at the signal of a trumpet, a quickening of the pace and a hectic, eerily banal procession of fuzz guitar and brass, a lyric conceived by the 'exquisite corpse' Surrealist technique in which random phrases are juxtaposed by collaborators, as massive broadsides of electronics blacken and eventually overwhelm the track. A sudden, cinematic shift and we're down in the U-Bahn, eavesdropping on a private conversation, before the group suddenly reappear, playing like some anarcho-collective who, to their surprise, have seized control of Ruritania and now must compose a new national anthem.

'Meadow Meal' begins with the snake rattle of modified keyboard and percussion, before the song proper abruptly strikes up, trailing through folk-rock fields buffeted periodically by gigantic foghorn blasts of electronics. The lyrics once more connect at some serendipitous, subconscious level ('A wonderful wooden reason'). A brief fuzz-guitar orgy ensues, then back to those fields, silent and empty, visible only through a screen of thunder and heavy rainfall, and then, rising like a cathedral mirage, a sober, meditative procession along the organ keyboard by Irmler, a self-confessed player of limited ability. This is the sort of affecting, arresting simplicity undreamt of in the world of the Mothers of Invention, for whom the organ was another instrument on which to play dazzlingly and put lesser musicians to shame.

Flip onto side two and 'Miss Fortune', sixteen and a half minutes of terrain over which the Faust collective range with neither inhibition nor indulgence, strumming, screeching and wah-wahing, driven on by the earthsplittingly powerful percussion of Werner Diermaier. The opening few minutes are an extended figure eight of a loop, almost cheesily fuzzy, yet drawing you like quicksand into its jam, before accelerating into an oblivion marked by the mammoth wail of Wüsthof's sax and a radioactive dribble of downtime electronics, as if contemplating the vastness of a levelled landscape yet to be rebuilt. A chorus of inebriated but impassioned cod-operatic vocals strikes up as Diermaier galvanises the energy levels with a monsoon of percussion, and fuzz guitar and treated organ revive and swell like glow worms. Somewhere in the background a grand piano abides, like old Europe, occasionally breaking into a boogie-woogie run. Then there's a malevolent cackling of evil vocal sprites, before a wheezy three-note organ motif on which the aim seems to be to break the needle on the wah-wah monitor, as well as to do its bit in further dabbing and cleansing the jaded palate of decades of increasingly moribund and second-hand, blues-based Anglo-American rock. I still recall hearing this organ 'solo' and remember the sheer, ectoplasmic delight it visited on my budding musical senses. I considered these quite definitely to be the greatest sounds I had ever heard.

Finally, a spoken-word passage involving angels, queens, Voltaire and garlic, which reminds one of the poetry of Hans Arp and Tristan Tzara, early Dada texts set against a similar explosion of both art and the everyday, the fragments falling where they may, whose violent energies were a disgusted parody of the everyday destruction on Europe's battlefields.

The difficulties of presenting the Faust assemblage live were highlighted when, at the hasty insistence of the record company, Faust played a concert at the Hamburger Musikhalle. The group designed a surround-sound system involving eight loudspeakers stationed around the venue. 'We planned to create a sound that hovered in the room,' recalled Graupner. The idea was for guitars, keyboards, noises to whizz around the hall in a manner akin to Stockhausen's *Kontakte*, but there simply wasn't the time to execute this ambitious project, especially as the equipment arrived late at the venue on what was a cold and icy day. With the roadies unable to provide assistance, the group ended up soldering their own wires, even shopping for cable, right up to the point at which the gig began. Other major features of the event were a giant wall of tin cans, prematurely tumbled over by Diermaier, and several colour TV sets.

The audience, most of whom were probably not paying punters but a mixture of journalists, guest listers and people hauled in off the street, eventually received with equanimity what turned out to be an improvised shambles of backfiring stunts and fitful musical performances, being sent out to the bar more than once while the group tried, and ultimately failed, to set up a reliable sound system. Zappi Diermaier then stepped forth to deliver a volley of a cappella vocals, probably not playing to his greatest strengths, and eventually the audience came up onstage, co-played the instruments and toyed with the tin cans lying around and chatted with the group. Eventually, the hall janitor tapped his watch and drew proceedings to a close in the small hours, and everyone went home in good humour, with the exception of the Polydor delegation, before whom visions danced of all their hopefully invested Deutschmarks flying south.

'If they had given us three months to prepare for the gig,' Graupner later reflected in frustration, 'we could have created a revolution.' Péron's eyes gleam with wistful amusement at the memory. 'Our first concert was a very creative disaster. A splendid, magnificent disaster. In our minds, we were in our studio. We behaved as if we were in the studio onstage. If things didn't work, we'd stop, have a chat, roll a joint, have a coffee. But live you're not supposed to do this.'

For the second album, in 1972, Faust were under pressure to release material that at least had the contours of conventionality, some semblance of rock form. *So Far*'s all-black artwork is a pointed contrast to the transparent cover of the original, as if to underscore their new resolutions. However, one senses more than a dose of sarcasm in its opening track, 'It's a Rainy Day, Sunshine Girl', Diermaier's percussion tolling obediently to what Faust biographer Andy Wilson describes as not so much a 4/4 as a 1/1 beat. If David Lynch's film *The Straight Story* is a consciously tongue-in-cheek repudiation of his reputation for the outlandish, then this is Faust's Straight Song, perhaps the most deadpan, caveman-like rock recording of all time.

'It's a rainy day, sunshine baby,' chant the group dolorously, with someone chipping in an Elvis-style 'uh-huh', over a single-note saloon-bar piano and a single stringy guitar chord. So it proceeds, until gradually the skies darken with electronics, pterodactyls and flying serpents wheel about overhead, a blues harmonica courses over the horizon and, finally, the arrival of Wüsthof's saxophone solo. Julian Cope described it as his favourite sax solo of all time – an extravagant yet strangely understandable reaction, given its perfect placement, unexpectedly 'finishing off' the track's wonderful, wooden, tantric experience. 'We played this at a concert in Paris, and Gunther didn't play the solo at the end – I don't know why, he refused,' remembers Péron. 'And there was one big journalist, the one in Paris who would make or destroy a group. And he refused to talk to us afterwards because Gunther failed to play this solo. This is how this song affects people.'

The album is punctuated by brief interludes: 'On the Way to Abamäe' is Faust in enigmatic, bucolic mode, its gentle acoustic guitars reminiscent of the sort of music that accompanied the Test Card in between mid-morning schools programmes, straining like a bud at bursting point with an exquisite pastoral melancholia; 'Picnic on a Frozen River' is a spare, formal conversation carried out between instruments in single notes of piano, guitar and woodwind, while 'Me Lack Space . . .' sounds as if Faust had converted one of the Futurist Luigi Russolo's noise intonators, or perhaps a hand-cranked What the Butler Saw machine, into an exquisite-corpse lyric generator, spitting out Dada-verse like 'Hey

Miss Brown, object to the oak . . .' Other, more extended tracks sound informed by the Mothers of Invention album *Absolutely Free*. 'I've Got My Car and My TV', delivered in a vocal that oscillates between silly falsetto and baritone, lampoons the banality of the comfort bubble and imagines a punitive finger appearing from the heavens and a godlike voice declaring, 'Those guys are right,' before haring off into a cheesy, extended three-way jam of guitars, sax and keyboards. '. . . In the Spirit' suggests Zappa's 'America Drinks and Goes Home', whose depiction of a cabaret singer trying to sate a late-night crowd in the throes of a drunken frenzy so brilliantly caps *Absolutely Free*.

Two further dark, towering moments match 'It's a Rainy Day . . .'. The title track, after a cat's cradle mess of guitar, settles down into an unsettlingly MOR riff, another parody of 'straightness', topped by a two-note brass motif, a too-banal-to-be-true tableau of light orchestral pleasantness. 'We wanted to create a locomotive action,' says Péron, acting out the dynamics of the song in semaphore gestures. 'Then big waves – boosh, wooaaaaa! Then another tsunami. We still love this piece because you can improvise within it, invite guest artists, play this groove and get them to improvise over it.' It's an unnerving journey along the middle of the road, through flat *Heimat* territory, akin to Kraftwerk's later journey on *Autobahn*. This journey, however, is swiftly assailed by swathes and shards of black analogue electronics like bats or Hitchcock's birds – anguished, throbbing, serrated broadsides, hoving shadows, murders of crows. It's as if the green and pleasant land is yielding its ghosts, dreadful, suppressed memories rearing up in reproach to the amnesiac pop escapist.

If *So Far* can be seen as a way of using the disruptive tools of sheer uncompromising noise to excavate the oppressively neat and tidy surfaces of German pop culture, then 'Mamie Is Blue' really brings out the heavy equipment. The simple chant at the heart of the song, 'Mamie is blue and Daddy is too', could be fancifully regarded as a sharp take on an older generation guarding their secrets and sorrows. If so, they are laid horizontal and subjected to a brutal noise therapy here, as Faust make full use of their black boxes to create a grim battery of psychic trepanation – drilling, remorselessly treated guitars and scalding, pitch-black noise. 'Mamie Is Blue' prefigures by several years the savage metal deconstructions of Einstürzende Neubauten; indeed, Faust were using industrial machinery onstage long in advance of Blixa Bargeld and co.

Given the spectacular variance between Polydor's commercial hopes and expectations of Faust and the reality, it is remarkable that they were allowed to release a second album, a tribute to the times in which record companies operated speculatively, in the dark, with relatively scant pop sensibility and an openness to the Next Big Thing, regardless of what improbable shape that might take. However, they were also guided by numbers, and when the sales figures came in, the plug was pulled on the Wümme project. A protracted legal dispute followed between Uwe Nettelbeck and Polydor as to the ownership of the compound – it mattered little, as when Faust left they took with them every last fixture and fitting, so that when a heavy-metal band from Berlin came to record in the studio following Faust's departure, they were enraged to find nothing left but floorboards and walls. Faust had supreme faith in themselves, but few if any of their countrymen had any sort of critical handle on what they were trying to do.

Once again, England was more appreciative of new German music than the Germans themselves. Briefly, having been dropped by Polydor, Faust found themselves destitute and forced to live on dog food. 'In the history of Faust there were ups and downs,' says Péron. 'Even the bad times at Wümme – we enjoyed eating dog food! Well, I liked it, but it's not everybody's thing.'

However, thanks to the enthusiasm of John Peel and the *NME*'s Ian MacDonald, among others, Faust had a reputation in England. 'And then, Uwe managed to get us onto Virgin. Don't ask me how he managed it, but that shows how visionary they were. They were looking for new horses.'

Once again, Faust found themselves landing butter side up, this time beneficiaries of the young Richard Branson, whose empire then extended merely to the fringes of seventies rock. Péron recalls a meeting with Virgin's Simon Draper, when the deal was sealed, in which the group made their musical pitch. 'He had a thing of playing with his pen, up and down. He sat and listened to us for thirty seconds and said, "Okay, enough, it's crazy enough, it could work."'

Faust would decamp to the Manor studio in Oxfordshire – cradle also to *Tubular Bells* by Mike Oldfield, another Virgin hopeful – to record *Faust IV* in 1973. Before that, however, would come *The Faust Tapes*, comprising the music the group had been working on since *So Far*. Nettelbeck and Draper cut a singular deal in which they agreed to hand over the tapes for nothing, and Virgin agreed they themselves would earn nothing from the release. It was duly issued as an introduction to the band – a full album for 49p, the price of a single. In the days when shelling out for an album represented a far more significant outlay than it does today, the very cheapness of this offer was both novel and irresistible to 1970s UK record buyers and guaranteed Faust sales of upward of fifty thousand copies.

Péron recalls *The Faust Tapes*, a series of short, disjointed and largely untitled pieces, as being 'eighty, eighty-five per cent the work of Rudolf Sosna. Drums, guitar, everything.' To the Faustophile, it is a headphone cornucopia of considered trifles, a fast-cut, zig-zagging backtrack through the Wümme years – even the banished Meifert features on a couple of pieces. The flights of inspiration, the lateral leaps from one idea to another, the filthy stormclouds of analogue synth, the ludicrous choral pieces, or 'All on Saxes', a veritable primate's blowing session, broken up by extended passages of acoustic lucidity like 'Flashback Caruso', amount to a photo album of a unique period of record-company-sanctioned absolute liberty, a liberty taken to extremes. To the average, speculative 1970s purchaser, however, whose tolerance for extremes was neither high nor often tested, *The Faust Tapes*, without context, would have been as alien as a foreign language, and very possibly a made-up foreign language at that, despite the fact that Faust sang in English. This wasn't like the sort of studio indulgences that had been granted to the Beatles late in their career, when they were bored with each other and could commit to vinyl practically anything they pleased. This was unlicensed jesting, this abortive mess; these sweepings from the cutting-room floor of some German madhouse represented a waste of grooves. To those who didn't understand that 'free' amounted to more than extended guitar solos or growing your hair long, *The Faust Tapes* was 49p poorly spent. Certainly, it's debatable as to whether it introduced Faust to a wider audience or warded off the general public for good. Péron, however, regards the release as altogether positive. 'I heard so many stories about people using it as a frisbee – which is good, no problem. It had a huge impact for us, in fact. It had many people talking about Faust. Yes, it was cheap, so a lot of people bought it for that reason, but it had great impact.'

Andy Gill, future *NME* journalist, was one of those who were lured out to see Faust, having invested his forty-nine pence in the group. He recalled a concert they played at the Sheffield City Hall in late 1973 which reflected their singular fluid approach to how or how not to stage a concert. The event took place in almost total darkness, save for the light afforded by the cathode rays of two TV sets and a pinball machine. There were armchairs and sofas, not the usual fixtures and fittings of a rock stage. On them sat various members of Faust, strumming in a desultory and oblivious way, before 'Zappi' Diermaier struck up with a primitive, percussive groove, with which the guitarists joined in, a single chord, over and over. One of them got up to play some pinball, as if the riff had established its own momentum regardless of his participation, watched a little television, then took up a power tool and set to work on a piece of concrete, a deafening, abstract, electronic intervention which tore across the monotony of the riff. Gill pertinently places the concert in the tradition of the great Futurist and Dadaist theatrical outrages of the early twentieth century, in which the object was that the affronted bourgeoisie storm the stage, their provoked anger a necessary part of the artistic proceedings. The Futurist leader Filippo Marinetti had been disappointed when he brought his show to London only for it to be received with polite approval. At the Sheffield City Hall, however, Faust had better luck – as the sparks from the concrete flew upwards, the hall lights went up and the venue manager stormed to the front and bellowed to the audience, 'That's quite enough of this! This is not music!' as the group looked on, grinning with satisfaction. However, as a chorus of boos grew – at the stuffy manager, not the group – the gig resumed, in defiance of the manager's self-appointed efforts to define the nature of art in the twentieth century.

'We never knew what we were going to play,' recalls Péron, who found himself in ironic agreement with the irate hall manager. 'Maybe Zappi and I would go onstage because we always wanted to play. But the others would be backstage, not giving a damn – Gunther might come on and play the pinball machine, or come onto the sofa onstage and read . . . but this is what our music was all about. This is not music. It's the audience making the music, sharing the experience, coming onstage. We wanted to provoke. We wanted reactions. We wanted to grab the people, that's for sure.'

At the Manor studio, Faust were less happy. They were far from home, far from the hermetic, womb-like environs of Wümme, and having to deal with in-house sound engineers. 'It was designed for rock bands,' Irmler complained of the studio. Moreover, having had to endure the miseries of eating dog food back in Germany, they now had to subsist on the still worse fare that was 1970s British food. Recalling the memory of it thirty years later, 'Zappi' Diermaier conveyed his lingering memories of the woeful, greasy, underimaginative, overcooked cuisine he suffered with a series of hacking noises and nauseated expressions which spoke more eloquently than his limited English.

Meanwhile, Irmler and Nettelbeck were beginning to have instinctive doubts, perhaps borne out in the long term, about Virgin boss Richard Branson. Was he sincerely a force for countercultural good or just another capitalist profiteer? A mistrust grew between Branson and the group, Nettelbeck and Joachim Irmler in particular. 'I began to talk to him in my heavy Schwabian dialect,' Irmler told me, out of anger at Branson's inability to speak even a single word of German. The relationship deteriorated as Branson, like Polydor before him, pressured the group into finishing an album and even took it upon himself to offer unsolicited advice as to how they could boost the commercial potential of their sound. There were disputes on the road, too: Chris Cutler of the group Henry Cow recalled an incident at London's Rainbow Theatre in which Péron, an unabashed nudist, threatened to take to the stage naked from the waist down, having been told by Branson they were only getting half the money they were expecting. 'You pay us half the money, I play in half my clothes,' he reasoned to aghast Virgin representatives in the wings.

In the midst of all this, however, came *Faust IV*, an album whose strength and serenity belie the conditions in which it was made. It opens, with quite wonderful Faustian sarcasm, with 'Krautrock', cheerfully eating up the English term so many German musicians found hard to swallow whole and regurgitating over its eleven or so minutes a paradigm of the supposed genre, rolling down a dirty, untravelled road of bass pulsations, cyclical rhythms, churning up clouds of electronics like exhaust fumes. No chorus, no verse, just heavy, infinite rotations of rocky detritus, ploughing on and on to an unknown horizon. It goes nowhere and reaches out everywhere; whole micro-worlds of activity can be divined within its apparently static, monochord monotony.

It's followed, in stark contrast, by 'The Sad Skinhead', a cartoonish musical and lyrical tableau bristling with cheesy fuzzbox, poking gentle fun at the existential quandary of the hooligan: 'going places/smashing faces/What else could we do?' Such a many-headed beast was Faust, as further evinced on 'Jennifer', one of the late Rudolf Sosna's most beautiful creations, a paean to a girl who made a fleeting appearance at the Manor studio. An echoing bassline melts and thuds like a heavy heart, percussion rolls gently in the distance as an electric guitar glides like a lonely black swan over the song's marine surfaces. An affectingly inadequate vocal mumbles nerdy petals of praise to the woman with the burning red hair, until finally a tornado of electronics slowly whips up and the track is consumed in an infatuated agony and ecstasy of white-out/wipeout. It's the sort of liberty few other than Faust would have dared take; it anticipates the sensual blizzards of My Bloody Valentine by decades.

The album's flipside recalls some of the looser spirit of the first Faust album: 'Just a Second (Starts Like That!)' is a seemingly desultory track which over its several minutes undergoes drastic mutations, like fish sprouting limbs, while 'Läuft . . . heisst das es läuft oder es kommt bald . . . läuft' takes as its title a misunderstanding as to whether the tape is running or not, before developing into a deceptively substantial and silvery ballad. Finally, there's 'It's a Bit of a Pain', which encapsulates the sublime practical joke that Faust play on the rock format; a drowsy, introspective acoustic ballad which jolts alive with a mainline, thousand-volt burst of electronics, resumes, then is shaken up once more by another high-level dose of electrocution. An incongruous radio transmission of spoken word follows, like a cutting from *Le Figaro* slapped by Picasso onto one of his canvases, before a whale of a wah-wah solo gobbles up the track whole. The proportions are all so joyfully wrong it could only be Faust.

This, however, was 1974. Mike Oldfield's *Tubular Bells* was the Virgin horse that came through commercially, the peak of rock graduation as far as the general public were concerned. It would be easy to lampoon Branson, who would later give good enough reason to be cast as a ridiculous, even hateful and overimposing icon of modern capitalism. At least, however, he had given Faust an opportunity to record. Faust were ahead of their time but, as Péron admits, they had something of a high old time while at Virgin, at the label's expense, not least at the launch for *Tubular Bells*, where they hung out with rock aristocracy like the Rolling Stones. Today, he looks back on his younger self and his colleagues with a somewhat wry shake of the head.

'The problem was us. We were dilettantes. We were not lazy but we did not take things seriously. We pushed things over the top. We abused Richard Branson's generosity, I guess, in the silliness, in the blindness of our exuberant youth. We were probably impolite and disrespectful. We would have a good time with his secretaries, abuse his telephones, go to restaurants and have orgies and put the bill on Virgin – it was not very intelligent. So he decided, "This far and no more." Also the philosophy of people in the band towards Richard – there wasn't a fit. We went on tour, Zappi and I, with Peter Blegvad, but others, like Irmler, for different reasons said, "No, we don't want to do that shit."'

Faust were finished at Virgin. Even Nettelbeck had finally given up on his protégés, decamping to Germany. One after another, the rest of the group followed. There was one further coda to Faust mark I, however. At Irmler's suggestion, they reconvened at the Musicland studios in Munich. Technically, they were still a 'Virgin band', even if the label had made it clear they would under no circumstances be financing any further Faust adventures. On that flimsy basis, recalls Péron, 'We walked into this fantasy hotel, who also owned the studio where we were recording – we said, "We are Faust, we are on Virgin, give us your best rooms."' They recorded and lived grandly on room service for several days, until the management, suspicious of these longhairs running up a tab, demanded payment of some 30,000 Deutschmarks. Unable to oblige, the group grabbed what tapes they had made, and attempted to escape the hotel by smashing through the gates of an exit in a van. They failed, and ended up in jail, as the women to whom Péron paid aforementioned tribute in the history of Faust once more came to the rescue – in this instance, their mothers, who paid their outstanding bills.

On that bathetic, some might say pathetic, note, Faust's seventies odyssey ends. Some might regard their story as a homily to the perils of over-indulgence; others see them as particularly cosseted specimens of the sixties German generation, the sort at whom author Jillian Becker wrinkled her nose in *Hitler's Children*, her study of the Baader–Meinhof phenomenon – the children of a generation who had rebuilt from nothing, who had worked hard to provide them with material comforts they themselves had never known, lazy, undisciplined beatniks who only stirred themselves to bite the hand that was feeding them. Péron's own reflections on the group in their younger days suggests that in terms of their behaviour, Faust weren't quite every inch heroic countercultural warriors.

Of all the major German groups of the 1970s, Faust is still the one many have the hardest time taking seriously. Their mock vocals, their propensity for cheap fuzzbox guitars, their onstage antics, their major-label patronage and the memory of the 49p album gimmick mean that they are still regarded by some as Krautrock's 'novelty' band, a curio of the times. Conversely, their collage-like arrangements of sound, constantly and abruptly interrupting itself, make them inimical to the listener who prefers the relatively tranquil and assured *motorik* repetition of Neu! or Kraftwerk as they bowl along the electric highway.

Yet Faust have proven to be among the most enduring groups of their generation. The recordings they made in Munich did not emerge as a proper release until the late 1980s, at which point they had lapsed, individually and collectively, into near-total inactivity, returning to their homes, in some cases raising families. In 1980, however, their profile had been partially restored when their first two albums, long unavailable, were reissued in a limited edition of six hundred by Chris Cutler's Recommended Records label. Although they sat out the 1980s, the Faust legend would slowly marinate throughout the decade – cited in *NME* interviews with post-punk icons here, a reference point in more historically conscious reviews of Einstürzende Neubauten there – until by 1996, in his *Krautrocksampler*, Julian Cope declared, 'There is no group more mythical than Faust.'

'I was confronted with the punk wave at Virgin and I was mighty impressed by their energy,' says Péron. 'Actually, I'm not quite sure what post-punk is. Faust were never concerned with what was happening around us musically. In the eighties, we disappeared, we were busy with other things. I never analysed the music scene, these genres are a bit difficult for me to pinpoint.

'As for Einstürzende Neubauten, yeah, I've been thinking about this. Years ago I was thinking, "Fuck, man, these guys are reproducing what we're doing." Now I think, "Well, we captured something in the air, and we were pioneers, but I don't think they were copying us." So now I'm at peace with that. Some time ago I was listening to some music and I thought, "These guys are copying us, it's a disgrace." So I looked at the CD. It was AMM. "Later during a Flaming Riviera Sunset" – from 1966. After this, I became much more reasonable. So yes, Faust are extraordinary. One in a thousand. But not the only ones . . .'

They began to find favour with nineties groups also; when interviewed for a Kraftwerk tribute piece, Tim Gane of Stereolab was happy to oblige but remarked that the group he was most keen on from that era was Faust. By the early 1990s, with the last sputtering cough of grunge, the rock narrative had about run its course; with the likes of My Bloody Valentine and Nirvana, all that could be done within the conventional bounds of the genre had been done. It was at this point that Faust tentatively stepped back into the fray, with concerts at the Marquee and the Garage in Islington, in which they energetically took up where they left off. Playing to packed venues, they introduced metal grinders and live sculpture onstage, an anti-digital riot of primitive and electric energy that seemed like it came from aeons ago, yet was still aeons ahead. They played huge, ambitious events, musical equivalents of landscape art, such as the 1994 Long Distance Calls event in Death Valley in California. For this, group members plus guest artist Japanese guitarist Keiji Haino placed themselves on sand hills miles apart from one another and, having assembled record equipment (boards, directional mikes) during the day, waited for night to fall and then attempted to communicate with each other, in a series of 'Ur sounds'. The event did not go quite as planned, with various mishaps, such as Diermaier burning his bare feet in the sand and one of the few sounds to succeed in being transmitted being a Turkish pipe actually blown by a member of the intrepid audience who had sought out the event. 'The only thing that worked was the wind!' laughs Péron. However, it showed the monumental scale on which Faust now worked. They had prefigured this on the tapes that would eventually be released under the title of *Munic and Elsewhere* in 1987. If Kraftwerk were Krautrock's neo-Bauhaus group, then Faust were its neo-Dadaists. That was key to their strategy on their debut album and on *The Faust Tapes*. 'Every man his own football', as the Berlin Dada publication of that name had it, while allusions to 'Dr Schwitters', aka Kurt Schwitters, the artist who specialised in meticulous collages and vocal pieces such as the *Ursonate* ('Ur Sonata'), in their song titles confirmed that they were quite conscious of their artistic forebears.

'I agree about this one hundred per cent,' says Péron. 'Some of the group were well educated, knew about Dada and Fluxus and Stockhausen. Zappi and me, not so much. It's only with hindsight that I have discovered all of these things. But we were living Dada. It's so obvious, so natural, so enriching. Dada doesn't exclude seriousness. Or Fluxus. Everything is art and art is everything. Why just music, or music and a light show onstage? We paint onstage, we have poets onstage, we cook onstage, wash our feet onstage, children onstage . . .'

However, if early Faust is a facetious, intense explosion of the old norms, from Beethoven to the Stones, the charred space in which they found themselves subsequently was vast, stretching from one end of time and space to the other. Though recorded in 1974, *Munic and Elsewhere* hints at this new terrain. Reviewing the album for *Melody Maker* at the time, I remarked that Faust were now 'specks on their own landscape'. This was a reflection on tracks like 'Munic/Yesterday', with its limping, relentless groove, jamming onward and onward without logical beginning or end, overtaken by black floods of dub noise, inconsequential vocal chatter, searing guitars and red-alert electronics. Or 'Knochentanz', similarly linear and picaresque, prefaced by an Ur-sound, as if from a wind instrument fashioned from a jawbone, the First Trump. Like Can, Faust had already reached the condition of post-rock long in advance of the coining of the phrase, the parched, beautiful, blackened terrain that came afterwards, stretching as far as the ear could hear.

Vastness of space, noise and its intimate corollary, silence – these were the concerns of the New Faust. In Berlin, Péron remembered a gig in which they achieved what he terms the 'conquest of the silence'. 'At the end we managed this magic moment of having silence, and the audience still listening. There was no music but still the people were listening. It was a kind of magic for one minute – no movement, no sound. We practised this – to freeze, to freeze inside and also to make the audience freeze.'

In accordance with a tradition followed by many seventies groups, there are currently two versions of Faust: Hans-Joachim Irmler leads one, while Péron leads the other. It feels like a working agreement to disagree. 'Irmler is extremely important [in the Faust story], but on a human level we don't seem to be able to cope with each other,' says Péron. 'I'm very happy that we're doing it this way – respecting each other, splendidly ignoring each other, which is good.'

Today, Péron, who also goes under the artistic moniker of Art-Errorist, co-organises the Avantgarde Festival at Schiphorst, described by Chris Cutler as 'three days of Utopia' and celebrated for its policy of having no backstage area for artists – performers and the performed-to relax and talk together. He also tours with his own version of Faust.

'We are about to go to the States. The gigs we are playing are all sold out now. I wish that had happened twenty-five, thirty years ago. Our approach is basically the same now as then. Why now, and not twenty-five years ago when we were young and wanted to show the world? We are not getting younger and this fire that is inside us, it's not the same eruption. Even if I feel that huge fire, my head tells me, "You're not twenty, don't burn like this" – words like "It's indecent, it's inappropriate" come to my mind. But we have retained the spirit.'

5 Riding through the Night: Neu! and Conny Plank

On his blog on the BBC website, the filmmaker Adam Curtis put together a video collage, drawn from the BBC archives, of people of all ages, nationalities and backgrounds simply dancing. A mum and dad in a 1970s suburban living room, mountain-based rebel soldiers at play, an Afro-Caribbean in front of his bedroom mirror, native Americans in line formation, Twiggy, an ageing cabaret star, punks, go-go dancers. The soundtrack chosen by Curtis, a man of advanced musical tastes, was Neu!'s 'Hallogallo', a variation on the German word for 'wild party'. Yet nobody is going wild, or working themselves up into a dervish frenzy. Everybody is moving tidily, soberly, as much obeying a natural function as experiencing joy. Although it has ancestry in music history, 'Hallogallo' is rootless, sleek, evolved, a new piece of machinery. Its very placelessness gives it a universality, reflected in the unwitting subjects of Curtis's movie collage, who are, as he puts it, 'all together in the dance'. 'Hallogallo' roves beyond the mountainous, vocal drama of rock's customary ranges of ups and downs, euphoria and rumbling, no-satisfaction, to cool, sunlit flatlands where can be found a profound and perpetual satisfaction. In Wim Wenders's *Wings of Desire*, a lonely and very elderly man plods tiredly across the war-scarred terrain of Berlin, burdened with memories, and wonders to himself why 'no one has so far succeeded in singing an epic of peace'. Perhaps 'Hallogallo', albeit instrumental rather than sung, is that epic of peace.

'I always lived near water,' said Michael Rother, in a BBC4 documentary on Krautrock. 'In Pakistan at the seaside, Düsseldorf near the Rhine – I feel comfortable near water – it has an effect I can't quite explain. It has to do with the passage of time, it also moves along like music itself – there are some parallels.'

Curtis then went on to set the same dance footage to a dark ambient soundtrack, to illustrate the sense of isolation we often feel from one another, and there is a similar duality about Neu!, personified in its primary members, Rother and their volcanic drummer Klaus Dinger. 'It's hard to imagine two people being more different than Klaus and me,' says Rother, speaking to me from his studio retreat in the forest near Hamburg. 'My mother was a classically trained piano player but she never had the chance to play her music in the 1930s and 1940s – I don't have to explain further. It was very difficult, economically difficult. She had to support the family, work in an office. My mother died in 2003. I remember her as always being very supportive of anything I had in mind with music. There was no fight. That is very different from Klaus Dinger. I met his father in the beginning when we started as Neu!. He had to fight him, to follow his dream. My father died when I was fifteen. So that prevented a fight, because I'm sure he would have had different ideas about my professional life. My mother was afraid I might find it hard to make a living but she didn't share her fears – she believed in my strengths, my ability to get on.'

Despite their contrasting temperaments, however, Rother and Dinger represented the perfect synthesis – violent pacifism. 'With the music, Klaus and I were in nearly a hundred per cent agreement,' says Rother. 'People get the wrong idea about that. They think, "Oh, you guys must have been forever fighting in the studio – 'I want to have a quiet song, no I want to have a loud song!'" It was never like that.

'I refused to serve in the military – I was, and still am, a complete pacifist. Klaus was certainly not a military man, quite the opposite. I think an important element of the Neu! music is that along with the beauty there is a portion of dirt. And that's something that separates Neu! music from Kraftwerk, in my own understanding. There is a contradiction in our sound.'

Michael Rother's father worked for the German airline Lufthansa, and when Michael was a child he moved about from Hamburg to Wilmslow in England, and, when he was nine, to Pakistan, where he lived for three years. 'They started a Far East route in 1960, and he was in charge of overseeing it in both West and East Pakistan, as it was then. I do remember being completely fascinated by the strange sounds of Pakistani music as a child – snake charmers, local musicians playing at the gates to get some money. This music that seemed to go on and on, with no structure that I could make out – just an endless stream of melody and rhythm, like a river. I've always had a soft spot since then for Indian and Pakistani music – it's the music I play to soothe the nerves and find inner balance.'

Rother grew up amid an ambience of European classical music, thanks to his mother's playing. However, he experienced further epiphanies with the advent of rock 'n' roll. His older brother introduced him to the 'fast-forward, surging music' of Little Richard, unlikely trace elements of whose influence can be found in Neu!'s canon. Visiting Rother in Pakistan, his brother also brought with him a copy of the Shadows' 'Apache', a single of colossal, often unacknowledged influence on the avant-rock canon – only this version was by a Danish guitarist, Jørgen Ingmann.

Meanwhile, Klaus Dinger, a few years senior to Michael, had emerged from a suitable apprenticeship for a master percussionist, studying first carpentry for three years and then architecture. He would later describe himself as a 'working-class hero'. He first started drumming in a school band, but came into conflict with his music teachers, whom he found too authoritarian. He then joined a swing combo, before joining a group called the No, in thrall to the sixties art/mod tendency of the UK.

Rother was also devoted to British beat music ('which I later tried to forget, but you can't – there is no "erase" button!') and formed a series of bedroom combos with similarly guitar-obsessed friends that were stoically endured by his mother. In Düsseldorf in 1965 he joined Spirits of Sound, the crucible for future Kraftwerk member Wolfgang Flür. However, he quickly chafed at the tapered, monochrome musical ambitions of the group. 'I remember becoming more and more frustrated with Spirits of Sound in the sixties, trying to improvise, to add more to the basic ideas of the group, but it didn't work.'

Opting out of national service, Rother worked for a while at a hospital, in the psychology department. Here he met fellow musicians and for a while flirted with jazz, 'to get away from the rock and pop structures, but that was not me, not my personality'. Studies into psychology also assisted Rother in realising that as a young man coming of age in Germany in the late 1960s, he could not be impervious to the cultural, social and political forces ranging at that time, all of which would have a profound impact on his musical identity. He rejected out of hand the burgeoning violence and 'lunacy' of terrorist movements such as the Baader–Meinhof group, whom he regarded as on the wrong road altogether. At the same time, the horrors of the Vietnam War acted as a jolting reminder of the need to wrench oneself away from Anglo-American hegemony, to create oneself as a personality anew. 'You cannot separate the music from all of the political events, the student uprisings, the changes happening in film, art,' says Rother. 'We were all exposed to this virus of change, and what you came up with depended on your own creative potential. Everyone might have the wish to do that, but some just cannot.'

It was at this time, at the very dawn of the 1970s, that Rother fortuitously met Ralf Hütter of Kraftwerk in Düsseldorf and at last realised his own creative potential. 'There was a guitar player at the hospital I worked with and he had an invite to do some film music at the Kraftwerk studio. I didn't know who Kraftwerk were but decided to join him. I don't know what happened to my guitarist friend – maybe he left. But I picked up the bass and Ralf and I jammed. It was obvious to everyone in the room – Florian and Klaus were listening – that we had a very similar idea of harmony and melody. We just clicked. A short time afterwards, Ralf decided he needed to continue his academic studies, so I got a call from Florian and I was in Kraftwerk.'

The real good fortune, however, was that Klaus Dinger was also in attendance at the sessions. Rother was at once impressed, although at another level disquieted, by his reckless aggression on the drum kit. 'I admired the power of his drumming. I remember when we first played live with Kraftwerk, he broke a cymbal, he hurt his hand, there was blood everywhere, but he never stopped playing for a second. That tells you so much about Klaus's attitude. That permanent sense of opposition, the struggles with his family, blaming society for some of what were his own failures.'

And yet, for all that maniacal recklessness, Dinger's playing was underpinned by a sense of exactitude, as his widow Miki Yui observes. 'I think, from childhood, if you see his childhood drawings, he always had a strong visual sense – he also studied architecture, and this has a huge influence on his drumming. He knows what is "straight" and what is "not straight". Someone like me, I'm a fluid person; if something is two millimetres out, that's okay, but not to Klaus. You hear it on what people call his "hammerbeat" – he did three years of carpentry training, prior to his architectural studies, and learnt to be very good with his handwork and in using his tools. All of these things came together in his playing.'

For a short while, as Ralf Hütter temporarily left the group to resume his academic studies, Kraftwerk were essentially a trio, working live and consisting of Dinger, Rother and Florian Schneider. They played a handful of gigs, including one with a Swedish laser artist ('Everyone got very high,' Dinger later recalled). Excerpts from shows such as *The Beat Club* reveal a prototype Neu! at work, with Dinger hammering out what was later termed the *motorik* beat but which he himself termed the 'Apache' beat. 'The drummer was playing in a way that when he played, it allowed your thoughts to flow, allowed emotions to come from within and occupy the active parts of your mind,' recalled Iggy Pop years later. 'The guy has found a way of freeing himself of the stupid tyranny of blues, rock, all the conventions I ever heard – some sort of pastoral psychedelicism.' Speaking to John Doran of *The Quietus* in 2010, Rother suggested that, whereas Kraftwerk had taken their rhythmical inspiration from Germany's transportation networks, Neu! took theirs from another field of endeavour in which the West Germans conspicuously shone in the 1970s – football.

'I'm not sure that we thought it had anything to do with transport. I remember that Klaus and I never really talked a lot about theories – we just both really enjoyed playing soccer. You know football, running up and down and everything. We even had a very good team with me and Klaus and Florian – he could run very fast. I remember on one tour there were some British bands there at a festival and we met them on the field. We played against the English band Family at one festival. We all loved to run fast, and this feeling of fast movement, forward movement, rushing forwards was something that we all had in common. It was part of what we were trying to express in Neu!.'

The notion of Neu! with their dynamism and forward thinking outpacing and out-thinking representatives of England's muddy, moribund, hippie/blues early-seventies orthodoxy is too tempting to discard, though whether Neu! outscored Family on the day remains unrecorded. Certainly, the West German international team were as dominant in the indisputable, meritocratic field of football, winning first the European Nations Cup in 1972 and then the World Cup in 1974. Few dared to argue until decades later that German rock music was similarly dominant during the same period. When West Germany beat a hidebound, clueless England

3–1 in 1972, it was a humiliation that once again scotched cherished notions of inherent English superiority.

The return of Hütter, coupled with incompatibilities between Dinger in particular and Schneider, meant that Rother and Dinger never recorded under the Kraftwerk banner. Having grown up in the blue-collar district of Unterrath, Dinger considered there to be an insuperable barrier between himself and the upper-middle-class Kraftwerk duo. It galled him also when they turned up at the studio with a Farfisa drum machine, which they described as the 'world's fastest drummer'. It was the first inkling of their 'man-machine' phase to come – Dinger suspected that Hütter had distanced himself from Kraftwerk to gestate this reincarnation of the group. He himself was a great believer in 'handmade' music – he later named an album by La Düsseldorf (the group he founded after Neu!) *Individuellos* as a riposte to the new Kraftwerkian ethos. In 1971, however, enjoying the guidance of producer Conny Plank, they parted company with Ralf and Florian and began trading as Neu!.

The name was an inspired piece of branding, the brainchild of the enterprising and subversive Dinger – one of the most potent and memorable in the Krautrock canon. It functioned as a brash, almost punkishly direct statement of futurist intent, but was also neo-Situationist, appropriated from the sloganeering language of the advertising agencies, so many of which were based in Düsseldorf.

'It was a protest against the consumer society but also against our "colleagues" on the Krautrock scene who had totally different taste and styling if any,' Klaus Dinger told Chris Bohn of *The Wire* in 2001. 'I was very well informed about Warhol, pop art, contemporary art. I had always been very visual in my thinking. Also, during that time, I lived in a commune and in order to get the space that we lived in, I set up an advertising agency which existed mainly on paper. Most of the people that I lived with were trying to break into advertising so I was somehow surrounded by this NEU! all the time.' Dinger also conceived the artwork, in which the Neu! name leaps out of the sleeve with the impact of a Lichtenstein *WHAAM!*, with Rother's initial misgivings at its brashness overridden.

'Michael was a very good guitarist but a bit on the sweet side,' Dinger told journalist Michael Dee in 1998, when the pair were still at loggerheads over the prospect of re-releasing their back catalogue, and he was less fondly inclined towards his former musical partner. 'He was also very conventional and traditional in his thinking. He was basically against all the things that made Neu! groundbreaking and revolutionary. In those days I took a lot of LSD and he didn't, and as you can imagine, that made a big difference.' (Dinger was on record as having consumed over a thousand tabs of LSD.) 'We never had any loud arguments but he was always so reluctant, always saying: "Do you really think so?" Conny Plank was invaluable as a mediator. He gave me the freedom to fly high and wild. Michael was also very reluctant about the name. He didn't want to call the project Neu!, but it was perfect to describe our music which really was "new".'

Despite their utterly different temperaments, Dinger and Rother gelled almost immediately, their musical understanding an unspoken one. 'Klaus always talked about this,' recalls Miki Yui. 'He said that he and Michael had a "blind understanding" – outside of that, they didn't socialise, or go out together.'

There was a brief, early period of musicians' block, but this was broken as Dinger plucked away 'like a typewriter' at a Japanese banjo he had brought to the sessions. The instrument features, in heavily modified form, on 'Negativland'. Not that he took overall credit for founding the Neu! sound: he recognised that Michael's guitar work was crucial for him to feed off – on 'Negativland', for example, which was born out of a Rother bassline. Driving duties were shared. 'I believed in his originality from the beginning. It was very obvious,' said Dinger.

'We didn't want to impose specific ideas or emotions,' says Rother. 'We never discussed music. It was just the result of two guys with their talent – or non-talent! – struggling to find something that fascinated us, and of course, Conny Plank. We owe Conny Plank so much. He was, in a way, crazy. He was open to everything. It couldn't be crazy enough. I think his father was a church-organ player, so he had a very different background. He said some of my music reminded him of his father in its earnest attitude. He had the skills, the right mind and sensibility.

'We went into the studio without any rehearsal tapes, anything. We would start to play, he would pick up our ideas – on "Hallogallo", "Negativland". He had to memorise the parts we were playing – there was no computer-aided mixing back then. So when we played "Hallogallo" over twelve minutes on eight-track, I was amazed how sure he was at picking up the best elements and memorising them. I'm sure I couldn't do that with someone else's ideas. He could remember if the second verse wasn't that great, the organ was off after four minutes thirty-six seconds. I don't know how he did that. He organised the final sound. And when you take into consideration the limitations of studio technology at the time – he had a tape machine to create delays, an echo chamber, and that was about it. To come up with those colours . . .'

'Without Conny Plank, I don't know . . .' sighed Klaus Dinger, interviewed shortly before his death. Dinger, like everyone else who worked with him, understood that Plank was more than a mere recorder, engineer and producer. He wasn't there to knock artists into commercial shape and, in so doing, knock the vitality out of them or stifle them with a radio-friendly glaze. He wasn't there to hamper talent or to stamp music with his own overbearing imprint. For the right artist he was a co-conspirator, a radicaliser, someone who, had he been less idealistic, more ego-driven and blinkered, might have chosen to go it alone as an artist himself. As it was, he understood that he could make more happen by enabling other talent, showing them how things worked, using his boundless ingenuity not just to maximise but to multiply the possibilities available in the studio to those willing to go with him, to improvise and create on the spot. It's entirely to his credit that there is no such thing as a 'Plank sound' – he was a human window of opportunities for others. He was a godsend to German music of the era – without him, opportunities would have gone begging, colour been lost, groups split asunder.

'He had the possibility to get people to work together who were rather problematic with each other, in a group – like with Klaus Dinger and Michael Rother, who were infamous for having a problematic relationship,' says Plank's son Stephan, who is now the keeper of his father's archive and, when I spoke to him, in the middle of preparing a documentary about him. 'He would mend this and use this energy to give them the chance to record.'

Conny Plank died of cancer in 1987, aged just forty-seven. Stephan Plank was only thirteen when his father died, but he has come to learn all about his legacy, of which he was dimly aware as a child, with the family home adjacent to Plank's studio outside Cologne. He recalls his fascination at the spectacle of the recording space, particularly the elaborate lengths Plank went to in order to create tape loops. 'I remember I wasn't allowed in the studio when they were doing this, but they were so, so interesting and I would have loved to touch them! There were loops around microphone stands – they would go around the studio around all of these bobbins – it would be turning and you could see it was like a long conveyor belt which went through the studio. For a five-year-old, it was really interesting. But you were not supposed to touch it!

'I was rather young, but the works were part of my upbringing. People today talk about "far out music" – for me, it was just the normal background.'

Born in Hütschenhausen in Kaiserslautern in 1940, Conny Plank began his working life as a sound engineer – he is often said to have worked with Marlene Dietrich, though while this would link him rather neatly to Germany's early pop heritage, Stephan has been unable to find any verification of it. What is certain is that he worked with luminaries of twentieth-century composition, such as Mauricio Kagel ('Kagel gave me a lot of ideas about sounds,' said Plank of the Argentine composer whose works contain instructions for harpists and cellists to create knocking sounds on the wooden sides of their instruments) and, particularly, Karlheinz Stockhausen. (Stephan has unearthed a number of twenty-four-track recordings made by Stockhausen which he intends to digitise – 'It's five tapes, they were obviously serious about something.') Plank, then, was not only a bridge from the musique-concrète pioneers but had a first-hand familiarity with how they littered their soundscapes. '[Edgard] Varèse was one of the first composers who used normal noises not made by instruments. He used metal material, wood blocks, all kinds of material like tin buckets and he called it musique concrète,' he said, in an interview he gave to the magazine *Electronic Musician* in 1987, shortly before he died. 'We go on developing these ideas, using just normal everyday sounds, in the streets, the workshop, and we make music out of it.'

Plank was also conscious of the wider ramifications of new music in Germany. 'This is one of the points, one of the reasons they invented Krautrock, they had to rethink and restart,' says Stephan. 'And they decided that they are a part of German history, but they are not going to connect with the music that happened in the Third Reich. There was a saying in Germany in the seventies: "Don't trust anybody over thirty."'

Plank himself turned thirty in 1970 but he was more than worthy of the trust placed in him by a generation of German musicians whose radical approach put them beyond the commercial pale and who were therefore too hard up to purchase the latest equipment. Plank would, in time, put such equipment at their disposal. Failing that, in the spirit of precursors such as Varèse and Pierre Schaeffer, he would use everyday objects, strategically placed or deployed, to create effects that on record came across as ethereal transmissions from the furthest reaches of the cosmos. He would use pencils as makeshift spools for tapes. He would place speakers inside grand pianos to pick up the harmonics from the vibrations of the strings, or insert microphones into drums to alter their sound. He would convert his mixing desk into a prototype sampler by looping isolated notes on tape, then replaying them via the console, using the faders. His studio was a converted barn, but the sounds he achieved were never agricultural.

More than a wizard around a pencil and a console, however, he had a way with people that really produced results – so long as he liked you. He had that habit, occasionally associated with Germans, of being direct in his opinions. Towards the end of his career he passed up the opportunity, taken up eventually by Brian Eno, of working with U2, having made a snap but firm judgement of their lead singer, Bono. 'I cannot work with that man,' he said. 'He was into analogue processing; processing the people,' is how Stephan puts it. 'He wouldn't get himself too much in the songwriting; he would set the mood and get the people to do what they want, not influence them in a way as if to say, "Can you please do it like this?" He wouldn't do that.

'What he looked for in the musicians he worked with was a quality of authenticity. He would turn down productions where everyone would say, "Are you mad? You just lost a lot of money." He would say, "I couldn't work with this. I couldn't be authentic, so I couldn't do it."'

'I'm more in the function of a medium and not as a creator who has a character and impresses this character on every note,' Plank himself said. 'I'm not a musician. I'm a medium between musicians, sounds and tape. I'm like a conductor or traffic policeman.'

Listening to 'Hallogallo', the opening track on Neu!'s debut album, it's tempting to surmise that the duo have already accomplished their mission. The *motorik* principle has been immediately and forever established. This is the sound for which Neu!, even Krautrock itself, has become shorthand for subsequent generations. They could have packed up there and then. Although playing without a mandate, driving on guided by sheer lack of inhibition and instinct as curious young musicians of their generation, this is the potential sound of a new Germany – modern, open, at ease with itself, thrumming with assurance and optimism for what lies beyond the horizon. Not just a new Germany but a new world, sanguine, chrome-plated, energetic.

There was always a great deal more to Neu!, however, than the signature *motorik*. Their shadows are more complex. 'Sonderangebot' ('Special Offer', a continuation of the mock advertising motif) is beatless, a sandstorm of stereopanning cymbals and a desolate, pealing note, hanging like a condor in the mix. It's as if the car has broken down on the desert road and the noonday sun is piercing, throwing up mirages, rearing up and receding. With 'Weissensee' ('White Sea'), however, the beat resumes slowly, in crashing, quenching waves, as the dreamscape shifts. Suddenly we're at sea. You sense the understanding between Rother, wah-wah guitar casting about in a wild surmise, and Dinger, doing the heavy work, propelling the raft on some imaginary, drifting water. These are the ambient, ambivalent realms to which *motorik* propels us, an uncertain, unrealised beyond. Music, particularly the sort of inflected, informed rock music practised by Neu!, was always the most effective way of depicting these imaginary worlds, more elusive than the banal precision of Roger Dean's sleeve artwork yet too vivid to be considered abstract, not quite a whiteout.

'Im Glück' ('Lucky') is the first part of a trilogy, 'Jahresübersicht', which opens and closes with a rather grainy recording of Klaus Dinger on a rowing boat which his girlfriend Anita Heedman made in the summer of 1971 when they travelled around Sweden in a

Ford Transit. It's captured like a fleeting moment already trapped in the sepia past. Rother's guitars throb, caught in an intense stasis, more two-bar grill than four-bar blues, reminiscent of Robert Fripp's later work on *No Pussyfooting* with Brian Eno, but also of a sitar warming up for a lengthy raga.

'Negativland' follows, Faust-like in its violence, with its brutalist, jackhammer opening, a sample of applause at a Kraftwerk concert and then a black churn of tubular noise circulating over an open drum and bass riff. In short, this is Joy Division minus the vocals, eight years in advance. 1971, and an unmistakable signpost to post-punk has already been staked.

Finally, 'Lieber Honig', in which Rother picks out the sparsest of melodies as Dinger delivers an almost wordless paean of love to his girlfriend Anita, so magnificent in its painful inadequacy, as if infatuation has robbed him of breath as he grasps vainly for a register just beyond his reach. Retrospectively, it's shadowed by the ill-fatedness of the relationship. Perhaps Dinger has a terrified inkling it may not last. Krautrock never laid stress on conventionally strong vocals, and here is one of the genre's most magnificent examples of turning 'weak' singing to an advantage, no less so than Nico or Marlene Dietrich in their different ways previously.

'We were very economical,' said Dinger, of the sessions that led to *Neu!*. There are no spools and spools of lost tape or lengthy jam sessions from which the album's material was drawn. What you hear is largely what they laid down. By the same token, and despite its repetition, there is no filler on this debut album. Each track is a telling precedent – this is the sort of music that launches a thousand albums. 'Hallogallo' is considered emblematic of Neu!, and fairly so. As Adam Curtis's video realises, it speaks immediately and joyfully to everybody from across the ages. But it's almost incongruous with the rest of the album, on which Rother's sense of limpid, ambient beauty lies perfectly atop Dinger's undercurrents of emotional turbulence and sublimated rage. *Neu!* maps out a sort of musical-existentialist quandary, and is caught in an intriguing stasis, as if having arrived early at uncharted shores. What begins as a wild party drops you many, many miles from where you set out, with no map home.

'I am a great admirer of Can, especially Jaki Liebezeit,' says Rother. 'But I think there were differences in the extent to which the German groups really moved away from rock 'n' roll. For me, the guys who were really dedicated to leaving Anglo-American music behind were Cluster, Kraftwerk and Neu!. Even with Can, perhaps with having an American singer, there were still some known elements . . .'

Later considered one of the foundation stones of Jon Savage's 'New Musick', and subsequently of a post-rock generation, in its own time *Neu!* sold only moderately well, and certainly did not trouble the progress of the Anglo-American mainstream. They did, however, feel confident enough as a group to invest in more instruments, while Klaus Dinger made the perverse, ambitious suggestion that they record a single, off their own initiative, at a studio Conny Plank had found in Munich. This was a bolder idea than it might seem nowadays. Much as, in the UK, the likes of Led Zeppelin and Pink Floyd did not condescend to release 45 rpms for a market they considered immature and unbecoming of their immense scale, so musicians of the Krautrock generation tended to regard singles as the province of the Schlager brigade.

They recorded 'Super'/'Neuschnee' ('Fresh Snow'), which was released on the Brain label. A seven-inch copy is currently available for $99.99 on eBay. In 1972, however, this propulsive, party-friendly pellet of chant-fuelled *motorik* was destined for a white elephant's graveyard. The public disregarded it; the record company, who hadn't sanctioned the project, refused to promote it. 'What we were fighting with at that time may seem a bit ridiculous now, but it was just a loss of money and a loss of time, and not very supportive for no perspective coming from that point,' recalled

Dinger. 'We were quite frustrated.'

When they entered the Windrose-Dumont-Time studios in Hamburg to cut *Neu! 2*, Rother and Dinger were richer in terms of equipment but would find themselves financially embarrassed midway through the recording. Side one reprises the moods of their debut album. 'Für Immer' ('Forever') celebrates and reiterates the ground they broke with 'Hallogallo', taking up with fresh knobs on where that groove left off and heading out alone on their own freeway towards the ever-distant horizon, flanked by the neon trails of Rother's guitar. It's the very soundtrack to travelling hopefully.

'Spitzenqualität' ('Top Quality', continuing the lampooning of West German ad-speak) follows, and it's as if they've entered a tunnel, and another quandary, as Dinger's drumming slows to an ominous halt amid arcing studio effects like the indifferent sound of traffic whooshing past as you stand by your broken-down vehicle. Once again, the sanguine spirit of the opening track suffers a puncture. By the end, it's as if Dinger is not so much drumming as hammering a dashboard in frustration.

On 'Gedenkminute' ('Minute's Silence') the scene shifts, the beat is blown away, replaced by a gale and a tolling bell. The beat revives, however, with 'Lila Engel' ('Lilac Angel'), which with Dinger's half-formed vocal chant and Rother's scathing waves of guitar marks the midpoint between punk and the enigmatic drum-and-piano madame-and-pimp duo filmed by Herzog in a North African brothel in 1971's *Fata Morgana*.

Now came the real quandary. By this point, Neu! had simply run out of money to record any further material but had a whole side of an album to fill. Side two, therefore, consists of tape-manipulated variations on the unjustly neglected 'Super'/'Neuschnee' single. On 'Super 16', the track is slowed down to a dolorous, determined plod. 'Neuschnee 78' is, as the title implies, a sped-up version of the original, as if Rother and Dinger have been replaced with Pinky and Perky. 'Cassetto' and 'Hallo Excentrico' feature further distortions and elastications. The technology is crude, of course, but the practice of remixing is demonstrated to be one of immense, transformative potential. It's an inspired moment of cheek, whose implications were profound. The critics of the day, however, who were no more conscious of a future remix culture than they were of the coming of the internet, were derisive.

'It was out of desperation really,' laughs Michael Rother. 'We left the record company completely out of the picture. We paid the production costs out of our own pocket. That was always important to us, to prevent anyone from meddling with our idea. But we were poor and we spent too much time on the sixteen-track recording of the first side. So we didn't have a complete album. Also, it's true that the record company didn't do a good job of promoting the single. But we wanted it on the album. It wasn't preconceived, it was made on the spot in the studio.

'I remember at the time the critics hated us for the second side, and many fans in Germany thought we had gone completely crazy. The idea of treating recorded music in an unusual way simply wasn't understood.

'In the seventies, there wasn't much of a German music media that paid attention to us. There were maybe two and a half journalists in all of Germany who were interested in what we were doing. The rest of them wrote about the Bay City Rollers and Abba. So it's not that they didn't take us seriously – they completely ignored us.'

There were further problems when Neu! attempted to realise their musical vision on the road. They tried in 1972, but it simply didn't work. One drummer, one guitarist was simply half a band as far as audiences and promoters were concerned. Rother tried to introduce a tape machine onstage, but this was regarded as inauthentic, as cheating. Live meant live – machines, in 1972, were the enemy of liveness. They tried to take on Uli Trepte of

Guru Guru and Eberhard Kranemann, who had been in early incarnations of Kraftwerk, but that didn't work out. 'Uli Trepte was a nice guy but also somehow with no ideas, like playing notes like the blue from the sky, as we say in Germany,' recalled Dinger. 'Not so much sense, which you quite often find with musicians. So what came out of this was totally not what we wanted.'

Rother took his leave of Neu!, went to Forst and, in the spring of 1973, hooked up with Hans-Joachim Roedelius of Cluster. 'He played on the piano and I played on my guitar and it was beauty on the spot, it was amazing, it was something I hadn't experienced in that intensity before, except in combination with Klaus on drums,' Rother said. 'But to play melodies and sounds and the special way Roedelius worked the distortion and delay, that impressed me. Just the piano and my guitar sounded really beautiful. So that was why I decided to stop Neu! and start Harmonia instead.'

Dinger, too, felt he had reached a hiatus with Neu!. 'During the recording of *Neu! 2* I realised that I had done everything that I could do with drumming,' he told Michael Dee. 'I spent a lot of time trying to make the music more melodious and I also began to write lyrics. It was a conscious decision on my part. I wanted to be more concrete and to reach more people.'

The divergent characters of Rother and Dinger were revealed as they temporarily went their separate ways – Rother happy to recede into the joys and exploration of music for its own sake, as a going concern, naturally, but no more. The more combative Dinger, meanwhile, wasn't content to languish in the backwaters of the music industry, or to listen to the wind ruffling the leaves out in the forest. He wanted the city – he moved to Düsseldorf, which he loved, especially the Altstadt. He wanted to break through. Moreover, he baulked at the commune-based, egalitarian principle that underpinned the Krautrock ethos. He was fed up of the restrictive role of holding down the backseat at the drum kit alone. He yearned to be a frontman. He took up lessons in guitar, melody and composition.

With Rother away with Harmonia, Dinger set up his own Dingerland label, visited London with his brother Thomas to meet with John Peel, produced an album by the group Lilac Angels (named after the *Neu! 2* track) and put on free concerts in Düsseldorf, all off his own initiative and all to no avail. He ended up some 50,000 marks out of pocket. Rother, meanwhile, was dismayed to find himself the most commercially ambitious member of the Harmonia collective while they resisted his efforts to drag them in a more pop-oriented direction.

Rother duly reconvened with Dinger, now in tandem with his brother Thomas and Hans Lampe, back in Düsseldorf. YouTube yields a sub-two-minute fragment of the four of them playing an early live version of 'Hero' which is thoroughly telling. Amid a swirl of bubbles and dry ice, sporting a baggy pair of white dungarees and a silvery guitar sling, Dinger, hair relatively short for 1974, stomps about brandishing his guitar and flailing at it with semi-tutored abandon, revelling in the attention. His swaggering would be more risible were it not for its uncanny anticipation of punk – his gum-chewing, angular features contorted with a sort of self-satisfied insolence. Rother, meanwhile, can be spotted skulking passive-aggressively in the background behind a large tape machine, his long hair like semi-drawn curtains across his countenance as he glowers at his partner in a manner not dissimilar to Russell Mael at his brother Ron in Sparks – only Rother looks like he means it.

When it came to making *Neu! 75*, the third album of their contractual obligation, the pair agreed that in reflection of their divergence, they would take a side each. Side one would belong to Rother, with Dinger supplying percussion, side two to Dinger. Side yin and side yang.

Neu! 75 represents a high point of accomplishment, in terms of execution and production (Conny Plank, take yet another bow).

Opener 'Isi' sets out full of the sunny spirits of 'Hallogallo' and 'Für Immer' before it. Only Cluster and Eno elsewhere in the world at this time were making music with this gleaming sensibility, so clean and mobile, so bluesless, so deceptively bland yet keenly intelligent in its contours, colour and direction. Then, however, comes 'Seeland', on which once again the pace drops and an uneasy, beautiful calm descends. Once more, the feeling is of an artistic instinct that has travelled far and now finds itself alone, wondering what, if anything else, lies ahead and where everybody else is, and will they ever arrive here in numbers too. Waters lap, guitars wheel like lonely shooting stars and a premature afternoon darkness seems to fall.

Finally, with the melancholy of 'Leb' Wohl' ('Farewell') and its spare, ambling piano, mortality seems at hand. The waters have all but ceased to lap, and the image that comes to mind is that of Arnold Böcklin's portrait *Die Toteninsel* ('The Island of Death'). Rother's vocals are weak emissions, like a dying man trying to muster breath for a last testimony. It's as if, over the course of twenty minutes, we have gone through the three ages of a life.

All of this is purely interpretation on the author's part – finding unintended significance in Rorschach instrumental inkblots, perhaps. In common with many of their contemporaries, Neu! did not enter the studio with a blueprint or prepared material. What happened instrumentally happened, and was not strategic. Says Rother, 'How the people understand and interpret the music has always been a big question mark for me, and often it surprises me what they find in it. But that's fine, and how I would like it to be. It comes down to the individual background of the listener, as well as their investment in it – if you just engage with the surface, you will get less.' However, and despite being Rother's own compositions, it's quite uncanny the way *Neu! 75* follows such a similar trajectory to that of both opening sides of *Neu!* and *Neu! 2*. The pattern repeats itself. They shared with Kraftwerk a certain machine unflappability, but in their continued probings Neu! investigate what space and darkness lies beyond these structures.

Side two belongs to Dinger. 'Hero' is one of the foundation stones of the Neu! legend, the track some regard Bowie as obliquely referencing on his own, much more famous 'Heroes', but whose influence can really be heard, in its lowing despair, on 'Theme' by Public Image Ltd, as sung by avowed Krautrock fanatic John Lydon. 'Just another hero, riding through the night!' screeches Dinger, sarcastic and distraught, as if decrying the futility of Neu!'s *motorik* drive nowhere. Meanwhile, as he directly states, his girlfriend Anita has left him, returned to Norway, he suspects at the behest of that most loathed of family symbols to one of his generation, the father. An eminent businessman, Anita's father had been against his daughter consorting with a delinquent-looking sort like Dinger and had duly sabotaged the relationship, so far as the drummer was concerned. 'Fuck your business, fuck the press/ Fuck the bourgeoisie, fuck the bourgeoisie!' he rages to the skies. 'Your only friend is money.' Devastation at losing the love of his life is compounded by his recent bankruptcy woes. Business has done for him both financially and emotionally.

And yet, as this flailing gobbet of pre-punk fury fades ungently into the night, swept up in the indifferent whistle of an apocalyptic wind, it's followed by Neu!'s most aggressively affirmative moment to date, in which all Dinger's negative energy is channelled like a Delta racing car speeding across a blackened desert. 'E-Musik' is a reference neither to tuning nor to the drug but to *ernste Musik*, or 'serious' music, mocking Germany's inbuilt high–low cultural distinction (how dare a rock group, academic outsiders, claim for themselves such elevation?), while also making a statement of intent. To misquote Beckett, out of the depths of despair, Dinger declares, 'I'll go on. I'll go on. I'll go on.' Reverse is no option. Forward is the only place left to go.

Dinger is on guitar and vocals and plays no drums; percussive duties are taken up by brother Thomas and Hans Lampe. Despite his traumas and frustrations, Dinger ends his half of *Neu! 75* on an almost triumphant note, with 'After Eight' roaring into the sunset with a raucous vivacity that contrasts starkly with Rother's 'Leb' Wohl'. The whole side is a rev-up, a dry run for his career with La Düsseldorf, whose rockier, more commercial fare would see them exceed sales of a million, far in excess of Neu! – David Bowie would even describe them putatively as the 'soundtrack of the eighties'.

'Somehow, I wanted to get [Thomas and Hans] involved in this last or third Neu! record, and appeared with them in Conny's studio,' Dinger told Chris Bohn. 'But nobody really liked this idea, really. Conny was also not so enthusiastic about it, so we made this sort of deal that I should at least play drums on one side of the album. Also mentally I decided that on *Neu! 2* somehow I always had the feeling that what I did drumming-wise, I couldn't achieve anything better or more. That was a difficult situation, so I decided, okay, I'll go back to drums again once more on the first side of *Neu! 75* and that was it then really. On La Düsseldorf I didn't do a single drum hit, totally not, I did all the rest, but not that any more.'

Neu! went their separate ways. Michael Rother rejoined Harmonia, hastily re-formed after Brian Eno had expressed an interest in working with them, having seen them in Hamburg in 1974 following a tip-off from a journalist. He eventually collaborated on 1976's *Tracks and Traces*, a series of 'sketches' recorded onto Rother's four-track machine that was first released in 1997 and reissued in 2012. In 1977, Rother was apocryphally supposed to have refused to work with David Bowie, who had been convinced partly by *Neu! 75* that West Germany, not America, was now the place and was living out a sort of Isherwood-inspired fantasy/reality of a neo-Weimar Modern Young Artist in Berlin. However, as Rother has repeatedly insisted, the reason the collaboration never happened was down to 'trickery' on the part of someone in Bowie's camp. Discussions between Bowie and Rother had got to quite a detailed point before the phone went silent. For years, Rother had assumed that a fickle Bowie had simply lost interest in the project, after he received a call from a third party informing him that his services would not be required in Berlin after all. Only when Rother read an interview some years later in which Bowie believed Rother to have turned *him* down did the guitarist suspect skulduggery.

'My guess at what happened is that people in his team were a bit anxious – sales were going down because his experimental approach to music wasn't commercial enough, his fans wanted a continuation of the Ziggy Stardust era,' Rother would reflect. 'It's so strange to me that twenty or thirty years later his three Berlin albums are considered to be his best by many fans and critics. But at the time it was different. The sales were dropping considerably and maybe it was decided that David Bowie would make better pop music without another German guy as inspiration on his team. It was strange twenty-something years later to hear him tell a very different story. But it's no use now crying about the fact that *Heroes* was made without my guitar and without my input. But who knows, maybe I would've destroyed the album.'

None of this was any great tragedy. It is unlikely that Rother would have deflected Bowie from his grand pop musical intentions, merely figuring as a credited musician. As it was, he was now working with Can's Jaki Liebezeit on a series of watercolour solo albums, commencing with 1977's *Flammende Herzen*, whose musings, like those of the Durutti Column, were of sufficient intensity and beauty to flutter on just the right side of New Age.

As for Dinger, he regretted the demise of Neu! but had never felt altogether personally compatible with Rother, not least on the issue of drug consumption. As chieftain of La Düsseldorf, he was more in his element, although their albums seem to fall somewhere between the stools of Neu! and conventional proto-punk, too removed from the avant-garde to be considered as central to the Krautrock canon, not quite thoroughgoing and defined enough, particularly in the vocal department, to really stand out among the well-drawn characters of eighties rock. La Düsseldorf may have sold many more albums than Neu!, but it is Neu! who have the present-day cachet.

Unfortunately, the Dinger history of combative situations would continue as he, brother Thomas and Hans Lampe fell out over the issue of division of incoming monies from La Düsseldorf. The problem was 'too much, too fast', Dinger would later ruefully reflect. 'Big money was coming in and we had no one to advise us on how to handle it. How to handle big money had never been a problem in our family. The dispute between me and my brother became a family tragedy. It killed my father. I made up with Thomas but sadly not with Hans.'

Meanwhile, the Neu! legend continued to grow. In the *NME* in 1981, Andy Gill urged readers to go through 'hell and high water' to obtain a copy of *Neu! 75*; I acquired my own vinyl edition from a fellow student for a princely £2 that same year. Over the next twenty years, however, while retrospective interest in 1970s German music grew in wave after wave, no agreement to reissue the *Neu!* albums could be reached to satisfy Rother, Conny Plank's heir Christa and the ever-querulous Dinger, who angrily took to the courts to block an attempt by Polygram to re-release them. Meanwhile, cassette editions and bootlegs were hipsters' only access to these legendary but elusive Krautrock milestones. Dinger tried to track down those responsible for these unofficial, unsanctioned releases but found that the trail went cold at a PO box in Luxembourg. He even declined interviews on the grounds that they would effectively act as promotion for the bootleggers. Two 'official' CDs did appear, strictly collectors' fare which their makers had never intended to see the light of day, as well as what was grandly bandied about as *Neu! 4*, recordings made in 1985 and 1986 by Rother and Dinger together which don't really deserve to be bracketed alongside the first three.

'Neu! vanished from the stores in the early eighties – and Harmonia never existed!' recalls Rother. 'It was only my solo stuff which made me survive in the eighties. It started returning with Julian Cope and the *Krautrocksampler*. When that came out, very slowly people started asking about Neu! – even German journalists, which was very surprising.

'In the nineties there were quite a few companies who wanted to release the *Neu!* albums, like Mute Records. It was all very frustrating – for me it was frustrating because of Klaus, and for Klaus it was frustrating because of me! He wasn't happy with my approach, which I think was more practical. He had very high, very unrealistic expectations – he wanted a "million-dollar bash", in his words, a solution to all his financial problems with the Neu! deal. My girlfriend said, "If you think you will reach an agreement with Klaus, then you're just as crazy as he is." But I had no choice. Anyway, he alienated everyone in the companies with his attitude, his behaviour. That was the dark decade.'

It was, however, the decade in which Neu! accumulated kudos as an underground buzzword. Sonic Youth were one gateway, in their guise as Ciccone Youth on 'Two Cool Rock Chicks Listening to Neu' from 1988's *The Whitey* album (Maria Minerva later referenced this reference with her own 'Ten Little Rock Chix Listening to Neu' in 2011). Ironies abounded – although the name Neu! was intended to lampoon the inane, in-your-face brashness of advertising methods, it was also a highly effective, modernist and direct brand name, as opposed to, say, Amon Düül. What's more, the fact that their albums were so hard to get hold of, exchanged on old vinyl or cassette copies, lent them a distinctive, hip exclusivity.

'Yeah, you're probably right about that,' sighs Rother. 'But it was a pain. It was very, very difficult. But that's behind me, fortunately, and whether we deserved it or not, Grönemeyer came along.'

Born in 1956, Herbert Grönemeyer is one of the most successful but improbable figures in German popular culture. A TV and film actor who appeared in Wolfgang Petersen's *Das Boot* (1981) as Lieutenant Werner, he also enjoys the distinction of having recorded the best selling German-language albums of all time, including 1984's *4630 Bochum*, with which he first made his mark. A highly accomplished performer, he is not commended to Krautrock purists. His *après-garde* populism is antithetical to the innovative spirit of Neu! and their contemporaries, as is his strong emphasis on vocal performance and lyrical composition. His piano stylings and full-throated vocals designed to bring the plaster falling from the ceiling of large venues are very much in a tradition of big, indisputably sincere epic pop that includes Peter Gabriel and Elton John. Having numerous artists like that of their own, the UK and US did not embrace Grönemeyer when he attempted to make a transition into the English-speaking market, despite the assistance of XTC's Andy Partridge and Peter Hamill of Van Der Graaf Generator; indeed, they struggled to get any sort of release at all. He is not entirely beloved in his own country – one eminent German critic drew a parallel between his success and that of the Wombles in the UK.

However, Grönemeyer, though hardly a Scott Walker, was never a mere Schlager merchant. Politically, he was always outspoken and on the side of the angels, campaigning for green issues and against poverty, and taking a series of German chancellors, including Angela Merkel, to task for their political failings rather than observing a bland celebrity neutrality. Furthermore, in 2000, he put the combative, idealistic side of his artistic nature to the fore when he founded Groenland Records, following the success of an EMI-commissioned CD box set entitled *50 Jahre Popmusik und Jugendkultur in Deutschland* ('50 Years of Pop Music and Youth Culture in Germany'). His very first release was the long-overdue reissue of Neu!'s back catalogue, at last on terms agreeable to all parties. It was released in the UK but not in Germany, where journalists were bewildered at a star like Grönemeyer taking such an interest in this obscure duo, not so much has-beens as never-weres as far as German audiences were concerned.

'He had a tragic personal history at the time,' says Rother. 'His wife had died, his brother died [of cancer, both within three days], and that made him want to do something with his energy because he couldn't make music or perform. It's strange for me to think it took something like this to happen for the records to come out . . .'

Speaking in 2012 to Wyndham Wallace of *The Quietus*, Grönemeyer had his own thoughts on why he had succeeded where other labels had failed. 'With my knowledge I know the dangers you can have with a label. You know the dangers an artist can have. And maybe in the end it was a part of what Neu! liked about me. It was the same shock for them: he's a mainstream artist and he comes across suddenly with these kinds of ideas that you don't expect from these kinds of artists. You think, maybe, "Here comes this idiot around the corner." But I like that. I think music is an art form.'

Like many musicians of his generation, Klaus Dinger found the retrospective appreciation of younger artists gratifying but a little hard to take on board. 'I can't say that I mind, as long as people mention where they borrowed their ideas. I haven't heard Stereolab. People often send me CDs and cassettes, but quite frankly I don't listen to them. It seems I am always busy with my own projects. I prefer to listen into myself, which is quite difficult in an extremely stressed, tense and chaotic life.'

'Klaus sounds like he was quite a difficult character,' says Tim Gane. 'Once, Stereolab played in Düsseldorf and he really hated us, he was very angry with us. He was convinced we were ripping him off. But friends of his were saying, "No, no, it's not like that, you should check them out." So he came down, got to the door but he wouldn't come in – the fact that there were so many people at the gig just made him angry again, so he stormed off. But I think that's strange, the attitude of thinking you're ripping off an element of someone's sound but not seeing it as having come from a passion. But he seems to have had this problem with a few other people too.'

Dinger died in 2008, just short of his sixty-second birthday, of heart failure. He and Rother were never absolutely reconciled. Rother had objected to Dinger's fronting a project called La! Neu? on the Captain Trip label, which had released the *Neu! 72 Live* and *Neu! 4* albums, of which he had heartily disapproved, in their original form at any rate. Dinger, in turn, had been openly contemptuous of some of Rother's post-Neu! musical methods, particularly his recourse to the synthesizer. It's possible that the differences between their characters were more complex than sometimes presented – Rother was quite capable of being very stubborn himself on a point of principle, while it seems that Dinger was always the more anxious for the pair to be reconciled and work together. Today, Dinger's memory is preserved by his partner Miki Yui. In 2012, she published *Ihr Könnt Mich Mal am Arsch Lecken* (*Lick My Ass If You Can*), a typically combatively titled volume of photos, artwork and essays devoted to Dinger, who never quite became the memorable face, the searing rock icon he often seemed to desire to be.

Yui agrees that Dinger did indeed harbour grand, probably unrealistic ideas of rock superstardom, all of which were undermined by his warring nature. 'He was a real rock-star kind. He didn't put on brakes. He wasn't moderate. He didn't care about health, he did what he wanted. So yes, I think he did want that kind of success, but being a punk means not being able to get along easily, socially and financially. He sometimes asked for too much, his ideas were too big. His dream for La Düsseldorf was to have more and more success, to tour more, but after the success of the second album, *Viva*, the third album was a bit in its shadow. After that, it was too late because the other band members went against him, he was in this court procedure for quite a long time, and so he was in dispute over various rights. Not being the industry's darling, doing whatever they wished, it was so difficult for him to break through. More important to him was to be true to himself. He chose to fight against the music business rather than get along with it, which I find remarkable. Not many people could do that.'

Happily, Dinger was not so volcanic in his domestic life. 'Maybe I came to him at a good time – maybe my own Japanese influence, not fighting too much – I didn't experience that in our personal life. He was aware of what he did in his history – and while he is not the kind of person to say sorry, he did say that he did certain things wrong. He was also a big fighter against the industry, always proudly on the side of the freedom and the rights of artists. Proper acknowledgements, proper payments. He said about himself, "I am arrogant! That's me. That's Düsseldorf. Look at Kraftwerk. They're arrogant too. That's because they're also from Düsseldorf."'

Dinger was, as he put it, the 'total artist', working without management or lawyers or tax consultants, or anyone who might impede his self-created self-image or taint its originality for the sake of commercial interests. He was a one-man rage against the machine, riding through the night, a pure, whirlwind creative force. As Yui puts it, 'He always talked about quantum leaps. He was first of all an *enfant terrible* – but he had a respect for a certain part of the culture in which he grew up. He was never religious but had a respect for the religion he grew up with. He was very conscious of his roots. In order to make a quantum leap you have to know very well the place from which you are leaping – as well as have a vision of where you are going.'

In the first decade of the twenty-first century, Dinger's next leap was Japandorf, involving artists from the Japanese community in Düsseldorf, which had grown significantly since companies from Japan were first drawn to the city because of the Ruhrgebeit – both its industry and culture. According to Yui, he had been impressed, in working with Captain Trip, by what he saw as the Japanese attention to detail, which matched his own. Through the sculptor Masaki Nakao, Dinger began recording sessions in which he encouraged the non-musical artists in particular to sing, play and express themselves. Japandorf existed over the course of several years, and was as much about the artists communing, camping and talking together as the studio sessions, which only saw the light of day in 2012. Dinger himself was working on these sessions, his creative sparks flying upwards, right up until his death. He and Rother were only in irregular communication; disagreements about the future direction of Neu!'s affairs still lingered and the shocking suddenness of Dinger's demise precluded any last meeting and reconciliation. Said Rother, 'In a way I have made peace with Klaus on my own, and maybe he's aware of it.'

In 2010, Rother toured with Sonic Youth's Steve Shelley and Aaron Mullan, guitarist and vocalist with the Tall Firs and also Sonic Youth's sound engineer, playing the music of Neu! under the name of Hallogallo. 'It was a situation of Michael being able to travel and play music of Harmonia, Neu! and from his solo recordings with bass and drums,' Steve Shelley tells me. 'So, of course, I wasn't attempting to take the place of the legendary Klaus Dinger but trying to serve the music that was presented nightly in concert by Hallogallo 2010.

'Neu! music has been such an inspiration and influence on my drumming and in general to the music of Sonic Youth that I didn't feel I needed to channel Klaus but more serve the songs as best as I could. I think in the end we only presented two Neu! pieces nightly at our concerts – but even so, Klaus Dinger was a big part of the audience's enjoyment of the music we played and the groove we presented on a nightly basis. There's a lot of love and respect out there for Klaus Dinger's musical contributions.'

This was undoubtedly so. Watching the trio play at the Barbican in 2010 was neither chilling nor blistering, not a chainsaw assault on the fabric of complacent expectations, nor a dull, retro plod up old, predictable alleys, but a tremendously warm, rewarding experience. The packed venue hummed with a quiet and educated appreciation of Neu!. For a duo with such a limited catalogue, such narrow appeal in their own time and relatively minimal approach to soundmaking, they have had a key bearing on punk, ambient, David Bowie, the post-punk Europhile tendency, post-rock and who-knows-what that is yet to come.

'Could Neu! have come from anywhere but Germany?' the filmmaker Stefan Morawietz asked Klaus Dinger in 2006. Dinger was quite definite. It was no coincidence that Neu!, like so many other groups, came from Germany, he replied – and further, no coincidence that Neu! had come from Düsseldorf, emerging from the unique friction between that town's fine art scene and plethora of advertising agencies.

Rock music does not change the world but the world changes rock music, and so it was with Neu!. Despite the absolute novelty and originality for which they successfully strived, Neu! were paradoxically, inescapably related to Germany's past, on both a historical and a personal level. Referring to him as she habitually does in the present tense, Miki Yui says, 'I think Klaus is against war but is also very conscious about what Germany and the world went through. In *Neu! 75*, you'll see that a picture is hanging behind him, a black-and-white photo of his grandfather and his great-uncle from World War I. For him, when he called the group Neu! he did not just mean it in a cultural sense but in a historical sense.' The Dingerbeat propels us from a dark and sunlit past on and on through the nocturnal uncertainty of our own times in search of a new dawn. Not a joy ride, but a necessary one.

6 the Berlin School

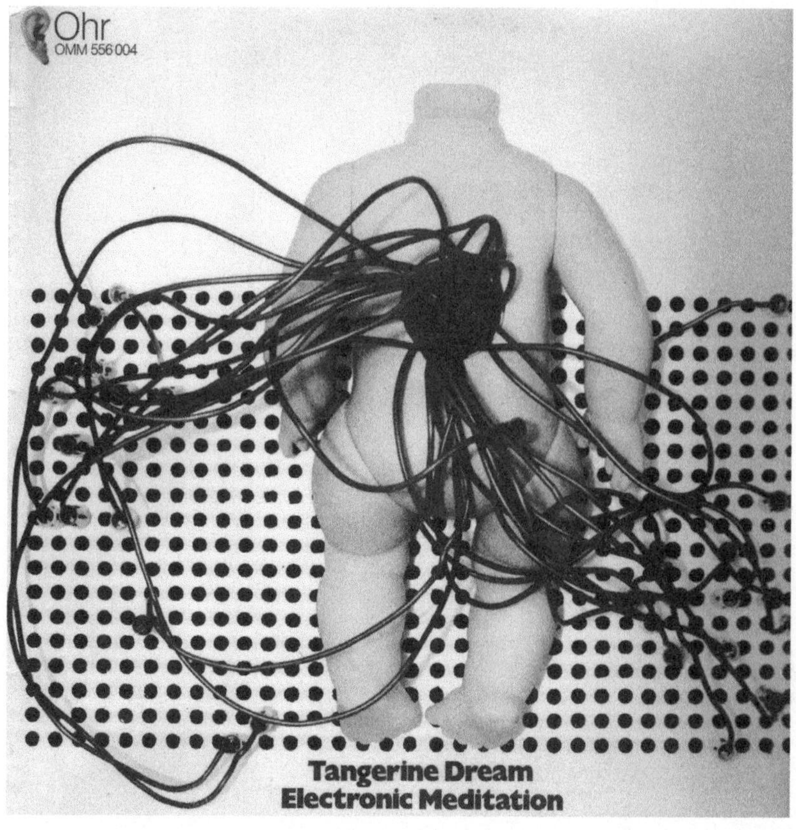

In 1995, I came to Berlin to visit the Reichstag, which, four years prior to its reopening as the seat of parliament, was trussed and wrapped in heavy, silvery fabric by the environmental artists Christo and Jeanne-Claude. In Britain, the happening was mischievously reported as having been a damp squib, if it was reported at all – another folly of modern art ignored by a robustly sensible populace. In fact, on arrival in the city in that blazing blue summer, it was clear that the event was a triumph. Thousands, millions eventually flocked to the lawns surrounding the Reichstag each day as if it were a rock festival, picnicking, music-making, basking in the extended moment. The fabric, immaculately draped (some of Christo's earliest attempts at wrapping large outdoor physical objects were less technically successful), reflected the changing hues and stages of morning till dusk, in a way reminiscent of Monet's series of paintings of Notre-Dame.

The spectacle was both shimmering and resonant. It was a tribute to the German authorities that they had permitted this event – is it conceivable that the city of London would ever, under any circumstances, have been sporting enough to have tolerated a similar treatment of the Houses of Parliament? The very gesture, made while Germany was still in the early throes of reunification, seemed to confirm that in restoring Berlin as the national seat of government, away from drab, functional little Bonn, Germany had effectively restored its soul. The silver coating rendered the Reichstag ghostlike – to look upon it, veiled thus, was to contemplate its past, at the very centre of the turbulent German twentieth century. It was built in 1894, and from one of its balconies in 1918 Philipp Scheidemann declared the German monarchy dead and a new republic born, if only to try to forestall the 'workers' republic', which temporarily held sway in Berlin, being declared at the same time by the communist Karl Liebknecht.

It was the seat of government for the Weimar Republic until, in 1933, it was burned down in a fire for which a mentally disturbed Dutchman, Marinus van der Lubbe, was blamed and executed, though many suspected it was the work of the Nazis themselves, a 'false flag' operation. Certainly, they used it as a pretext to suspend civil rights in the name of national security. The building sat in helpless disuse during the Third Reich, but by 1945 was a symbol of the ruins of Berlin, the sort of photographic image without which no retrospective of German postwar culture and art is complete. It was in such disrepair after the war that there was debate as to whether or not it should be torn down. However, it was restored in the early 1960s, thereafter biding its time, as it had done for much of the century, bearing central and silent witness to the most turbulent events of modern times, until in 1990 it was the backdrop to celebrations following the collapse of the Berlin Wall.

The silver wrapping also had the connotations of a gift – a present to the future.

No great city, not London, not New York, not Paris, not even Moscow, wears the scars of twentieth-century trauma the way Berlin does. Many of its streets and tenements are still riddled and strafed with bullet holes, a legacy of the Soviet advance on the city. Even today, with the remnants of Checkpoint Charlie cleared to make way for a vast business centre, the city is dotted with reminders and memorials of the Second World War, from the bleakly understated 'Topography of Terror', former site of the SS and the Gestapo in Niederkirchnerstrasse, to Peter Eisenman and Buro Happold's Holocaust Memorial near to the Brandenburg Gate, whose sloping, undulating series of concrete slabs seeks to speak volumes about the unspeakable, in abstract form. Berlin is not exactly a 'pretty' city, in the cosy, old town, nostalgic sense. It is harsh, brusque in its modernity and its juxtapositions, though in unexpected spaces it throws up glimpses of the surreal. Just 250 metres from the formidable new Hauptbahnhof and a gigantic hoarding for a new Apple store, I chanced on, and photographed, a scenario that could have come straight from a Giorgio de Chirico painting – a tall, thin tower belching a weak plume of smoke, a slanted grassland with two silhouetted passers-by, a distant green belltower atop a red slated roof. Berlin's face is set three ways – yesterday, today, tomorrow. It seems to be in a state of perpetual deconstruction and reconstruction – cranes crowd on the skyline in their dozens at any time. It's not hard to understand why Einstürzende Neubauten were conceived in Berlin. And, despite its unfortunate timing in being released a year before the Wall fell, an event scarcely anticipated in the film, Wim Wenders's *Wings of Desire* nonetheless captures something of the supernatural air of the city, a palpable, invisible sense that seems to lay its hand on your shoulder on every corner like the ghost of a stranger. Perpetually half built, crumbling on the brink of bankruptcy, yet constantly renewed by the international flood of designers, writers, musicians and DJs attracted by its still-cheap rents as the city's artistic quarters stave off, for the time being, the deathly prospect of gentrification.

In the first half of the twentieth century, Berlin feasted artistically on its own decay and ruin. Its very aesthetic sense of itself is celebrated in Walter Ruttmann's 1927 film *Berlin: Symphony of a Great City*. It was in Berlin's Choralion-Saal in 1912 that Arnold Schoenberg's *Pierrot Lunaire* was premiered, which, in its intoxicating and gloomy way, heralded the end of the gilded era of nineteenth-century German romanticism. Dada had a very active chapter in Berlin following the end of the war, a hub for the activities of the artist George Grosz and his caricatures of the surly, bull-necked German bourgeoisie; John Heartfield, whose bitterly satirical photomontages tracked the rise of the Nazis; and the writer Walter Mehring. Club Dada meetings abounded, as well as periodicals such as *Jedermann sein eigner Fussball* ('Every Man His Own Football'), while activists like Johannes Baader committed Dadaist outrages – for instance, bursting into Berlin Cathedral during the Court Chaplin's sermon and bellowing from high in the choir, 'To hell with Christ!' Thomas Mann wrote of the 'dreadful euphoria' of the 1920s, in which a cabaret scene thrived as runaway inflation wrought catastrophe. Brecht wrote *The Threepenny Opera*, and by 1930, Oskar Sala had composed his *Elektronische Impression*, employing the Trautonium, a prototype electronic instrument. Meanwhile, long in advance of Neu!, the word '*motorik*' was applied to the work of Paul Hindemith and his search for more precise, machine-like rhythms. Composers like Hindemith sought as best they could for a music that reflected the functionalist aesthetic of the Bauhaus movement.

Following the rise of Hitler, such activities were heaped with public derision, consigned to the Degenerate Art and Degenerate Music exhibitions. After the war, the import of rock 'n' roll and, later, sixties British beat music drowned out any tentative attempts to revive the homegrown traditions of Weimar or pick up the thread tentatively laid down by Sala and Hindemith. The old world stood in the shadows of the Coca-Cola headquarters depicted in Billy Wilder's *One, Two, Three*, starring James Cagney and filmed in the city. Only in the late 1960s would decades of relative silence be broken, first by the atonal European riposte to American free jazz headed by the leviathan Peter Brötzmann and Alexander von Schlippenbach, and later by the still less hinged sound experiments of the Zodiak Free Arts Lab.

One of the seemingly less consequential Berlin landmarks is in Hallesches Ufer, along the north bank of the Landwehr canal, which chugs inconsequentially through the Kreuzberg district, as if part of the city's drainage system, flanked by some rusty, heavily graffiti-tagged barriers. Squashed as if to fill in an unsightly gap between two differently styled grey apartment blocks, its front looks like a series of large stacked tiles which falls short of both its neighbours. Over the entrance, a desultory blue neon sign indicates that this is HAU 2, the poor relation of HAU 1, housed rather more elegantly around the corner, two venues which supplement the city's Hebbel Theater. It has always been a theatre house – between 1962 and 1981 it was home to the Schaubühne am Halleschen Ufer, a political theatre company. However, for a few brief, crucial, legendary months in late 1968, it was also a live-music venue.

The Zodiak Free Arts Lab was founded by Boris Schaak, Hans-Joachim Roedelius and Conrad Schnitzler. Roedelius is the only survivor of the trio – Schaak died in 2012, Schnitzler in 2011. Although not Berlin-born, Schnitzler epitomised something of the concrete quality of the city. He was a key figure in Krautrock, yet in spirit belonged to movements from decades to come, such as punk, industrial and techno. Resolutely short-haired even in the sixties and seventies, he hated hippiedom, was practically amusical and ultimately preferred working solo rather than in groups, where he proved to be too difficult even for his closest colleagues. 'He was a good but downright difficult friend, and when it came to art, he was relentlessly eccentric,' commented Roedelius in an affectionate tribute to him on his death.

I never met Schnitzler, though we did both take part in a documentary about Kraftwerk and the German musical legacy for Prism films in 2008. 'All these people making music with the drums and flutes, I hated it – and melodies that were like worms in your head,' he said, shuddering at the spirit of the age in which he came of age. 'All day long, rattling in your head. I wanted something that was in – and then you lost it already. Only if you can't play instruments can you really make free sounds. And I wanted to have noise/sounds composed together – a steam hammer here, a bird piping there, a car goes by . . . and be like the director of all this. As an artist, you have to create something new.'

He was the anti-Krautrocker. 'I hate people,' he told *The Wire*'s David Keenan in 2006. 'Seriously. I'm not a flower power guy. I'm not soft eyes. I'm eyes with bananas in. I have Xs in my eyes.' Nonetheless, he was right there at the root of the movement, like a stone propping up a fledgling plant.

He was born Konrad Schnitzler in 1937, to a German father and an Italian mother, and wondered often in life if these dual nationalities and their supposed temperamental differences were at war inside him. He grew up in Düsseldorf, his childhood memories resounding with the metal-on-metal chaos of war and its ruinous consequences. He vividly recalled the bombs, the screaming terror of the populace, the window panes which revealed not domestic interiors but the light of raging fires. Although his father was a trained musician, Schnitzler stubbornly resisted his efforts to make him learn an instrument, as if to do so would have meant kowtowing to authority and conformity and a staid, oppressive Germanic notion of *Kultur*. He took labouring jobs, including one in a textile factory, where he once again found himself assailed by modern industrial cacophony, the great rooms resounding to the communal din of machinery, and another as a sailor, fixing the engines of ships. Noise was his element, and rather than seek out respite in tranquillity after his day's labours, he subjected himself to the great extremists of the mid-century – Stockhausen, Nono, Cage, Charlie Parker, free jazz, broadcast on late-night radio.

In 1961, he began to study art under the tutelage of Joseph Beuys at the Düsseldorf Staatliche Kunstakademie. At this point, the Fluxus movement was at its height, and all its concomitant, neo-Dadaist notions of blurring the distinctions between different media, artist and audience, art and life, the *Hoch* and the low, all the stuffy insistences that impeded the absolute democratisation of art.

Schnitzler's first artistic forays were in metal sculpture, and then in films, though he later decided to bequeath his camera to his son Gregor, who went on to become a successful filmmaker. With the instruments of musique concrète now more widely available, however, particularly tape machines, he began to look at the possibilities of sound itself as an artistic medium, rather than the stuff of which music and melody were made. He engineered his first sounds by scratching and violating the films on his projector. His very first music project, with Hans-Joachim Roedelius, was called Geräusche ('Noises'), in which Schnitzler achieved sounds with pots and spoons using contact mikes, or amplified conventional acoustic instruments such as the violin to create discordant effects more in keeping with the harsh reality of industrial life which he felt it necessary to impress on his audiences – down with art as a dippy, bucolic refuge from reality. By now it was the late 1960s, and in Berlin as much as anywhere, Geräusche chimed in with the discordancy of student fomentation.

Hence the Arts Lab, which was founded on the same basis as the deal struck by Hugo Ball and co. when they opened the Cabaret Voltaire in 1916 – they promised to fill the place with customers who would buy beer and food, as well as take in the challenging bill of fare. (The artists themselves would help prepare the food in the kitchens before the shows.) Indulged by the radical theatre producer Peter Stein, they were able to rent from him a basement space in the building, two large rooms, one painted all in black, the other in white, at Schnitzler's insistence – he wanted to purge the place of any rainbow connotations of hippie nonsense. The idea was to create a sensory-deprived space in which you had to actively create your own sensations, in which anything could happen, in which anyone, theoretically, could join in. He staged happenings, including one of his own which simply consisted of the sound of paper being crumpled. Schnitzler's advertising techniques were remarkably similar to this artistic endeavour – he would simply strew fliers containing basic information about the venue and its events in the streets, with gigs challengingly announced as 'noises', melody being considered tainted, as if by association with the 'Horst Wessel Lied'.

Schnitzler explained his philosophy as follows: 'If lots of people make noises, it becomes an orchestra . . . If you do it alone – for example the sound of a stone on linoleum – that's a solo track. If you play these sounds and record them onto different tracks, it becomes a composition . . . Make horrible noises with instruments and microphones and echo-machines. Just do it and produce as much noise as you want. If you organise this noise it's not just pure chaos . . . it can grow into music. This noise-making was meant as a way to express and explore your inner self. It wasn't meant to create music in a traditional way at all. Basically, the idea was to create sounds for communication, to let others experience your own philosophy.'

It was chaos – bands would play on the same stage simultaneously, sets would last for several hallucinogenic hours (the club was not allowed to open until late in the evening, after patrons of the theatre had safely left the venue), pinball machines and radios would resound in tandem. No chink of luminary respite was allowed – Schnitzler had painted both neon lights and windows black.

Nonetheless, and despite the frequent attentions of the local police, who assumed the place to be a den of drugs and delinquency, as well as political agitation (the Umherschweifende Haschrebellen, or 'Roaming Hashish Rebels', planned outrages against President Nixon at the venue), the Zodiak Free Arts Lab was a success, tracking the movement of German underground music from conventional guitar-based rock, such as agit-troupe Ton Steine Scherben, and free jazz to the incubation of something quite original. Peter Brötzmann and Alexander von Schlippenbach played there, but so later did Ash Ra Tempel and Tangerine Dream in their earliest incarnations, as well as Klaus Schulze.

Following the demise of the Arts Lab, Schnitzler was invited to join the very first incarnation of Tangerine Dream, despite his being unable to play any instrument as such. With Klaus Schulze on drums, Schnitzler would play the role of 'outsider'. Edgar Froese, the founder and constant member, felt that the trio needed an amusical element to make proceedings more interesting. 'I said to Edgar, "You know I cannot play?" He said, "That's good,"' Schnitzler told David Keenan. 'This was when Froese and Klaus Schulze were playing together. They played rock music and I was there to break the rock music, to make it kaput. I did everything against it, putting as much noise in as possible.'

Tangerine Dream would record their debut, *Electronic Meditation*, in late 1969, in a factory in Berlin, onto a two-track tape machine, with Froese wrenching heavy sounds from a Marshall amp and the industrial setting practically functioning as a musical instrument in itself. The 'electronic' element was limited to tapes and modulators. Even the 'addiator' used by Schnitzler, an ancient form of calculator that had been available since 1920, was pre-electronic, consisting of sheet-metal sliders. Synthesizers were at this stage beyond the wherewithal of the trio. Froese played six- and twelve-string guitar and piano, Schnitzler cello and violin, while Jimmy Jackson and Thomaș Keyserling made uncredited contributions on organ and flute respectively. *Electronic Meditation* is galaxies away from Tangerine Dream as they later came to be known and revered – and for some, that is a very good thing indeed.

The portentously titled 'Genesis' lives up to its birth-of-a-universe billing, amorphous, convulsive, a flurry of flute marking the pangs of Creation, as Schnitzler's cello saws remorselessly through the middle of the piece. 'Journey through a Burning Brain' maps out new regions in space, an organ rolling gaseously through the mix, but it's Schnitzler's strange series of clicks, like a vinyl malfunction, rather than Froese's nascent, tentatively melodic guitar runs, which subtly hints at the harsh, empty indifference of space, with Schulze's tumultuous drumming impacting like a meteor shower. Again, on 'Cold Smoke' and 'Ashes to Ashes' it seems to be Schnitzler's periodic job to prevent the music from falling into a pleasant, science-fictional reverie. Atmospheres build, but they're jagged, halting, catastrophe-prone. The album concludes with 'Resurrection', with its backwards recitation from Froese, as if the Creator is issuing a coded message from the heavens. (In fact, he is reading the terms and conditions on the back of a ferry ticket.)

'We didn't like the existing music at all and didn't want to copy English/American music,' said Klaus Schulze. 'Today, when I listen to it, if I dare to, it's rubbish – but it's important because we tried at least . . . what would take off later, none of us knew. But to break through, it was very important, this album, and inspiring for other musicians – even if they don't do this, at least go in another direction.'

As a blueprint for future electronic/ambient/free-rock strategies, *Electronic Meditation* is invaluable, one of the great, stony relics of rock futurism. It would have been fascinating to see and hear how this trio might have developed working together, but it was always going to be difficult to pen in three such burgeoning talents. The young Schulze felt fazed and hobbled by the presence of Schnitzler, yearning to break out, uninterrupted in his own right, and see where the music flowed. Schnitzler himself, meanwhile, focused his energies on Kluster, the experimental trio he formed with fellow Zodiak denizens Hans-Joachim Roedelius and Dieter Moebius (who would later, as a duo, form the gradually more peaceable Cluster), with whom he worked simultaneously in 1969.

The opportunity for Kluster to record their debut album presented itself when Oskar Gottlieb Blarr, a forward-looking cantor and church organist with a penchant for such religious avant-garde composers as Olivier Messiaen, decided that Kluster had the potential to disseminate the word of God. On 21 December 1969, he arranged for the Kluster trio to be spirited into a Cologne studio owned by the church label Schwann-Verlag, who would release the album. There, in practically real time, they recorded the two sides that make up *Klopfzeichen* (*Knocking*). Conny Plank was at the mixing desk, and his experience as a studio assistant at the Westdeutscher Rundfunk, plus the high-quality acoustics, lends the first Kluster album a level of high definition that makes it feel as if it were recorded the day after tomorrow, rather than over forty years ago. The contrast between *Klopfzeichen* and *Electronic Meditation* is like the difference between scratchy Super 8 footage and video tape. Schnitzler's drones, which drag ominously throughout, are distinctive enough, but the clanking, recurring, overlapping echoes maintained by Moebius and Roedelius and mixed by Plank are much less easy to trace to their instrumental origins (a single, reverberating note plucked on a cello). This is not so much music as the artful, purposeful interplay of sounds, liberated from scale, metre, melody, mobile sculptures floating in a zone somewhere between free rock and musique concrète that was neither 'high' nor 'low' but way out there. It's deeply prophetic – one thinks of the likes of Throbbing Gristle and Nurse with Wound, who were themselves considered to have emerged from a nowhere place of cultural ruin in their own times.

Following the recording, there was an additional vocal overdub by Christa Runge, in which she read out lines, in German, full of exhortations and declamations of the morally sunken West German state. These certainly lend the piece a countercultural stamp, a rare, polemical dimension to a music that generally fought shy of direct reference and lyrical confrontation. Kluster merely agreed to this overdub, however, at Blarr's insistence – it was nothing to do with them.

Side two was purely instrumental. Again, the cello clanking of side one ghosts throughout the track, while Moebius chimes in with selected notes on a car battery amid sporadic, Gothic vocal murmurs, as guitar distortion builds to near suffocating levels marked by a squeal of feedback before receding, then peeling away into a series of anti-solos, as if instruments are being spanked, rather than played. For Schnitzler it could theoretically be a revolt against the tutored classical world, with all its grandiose pretences and false resolutions. It parallels cultural processes of disintegration and beginning again, but despite the speed with which it was laid down, its improvised processes and the intensity of its impact, this is not a wig-out or primal roar of discontent. Each element, each juxtaposition is applied by the trio with the meticulous, meditated cool of an artist at the easel, with a sort of furious patience – this was the unrequited noise of the times.

Kluster toured extensively, playing primarily in gallery and museum spaces, often for hours at a time, with their arsenal of conventional instruments subject to ring modulators, reverb units and tape delays. They recorded a second album, *Zwei-Osterei* (*Two Easter Eggs*), in February 1970, with vocal overdubs again added at the behest of Schwann. Side one, 'Electric Music and Text', is superb, with its sawing strings and biblical torrent of mutant instrumentation and tortured feedback, so far ahead of its time you wonder if its time has even come. The added text, this time read by Manfred Paethe and religious in nature, was written by a clique of radical young poets assembled by Blarr. Schnitzler in particular winced at the spoken-word text, included as a condition of the album's limited-edition release, later stating in an interview that it was as well not to know what the words meant, merely to take them as a textural layer, an obscure, Teutonic incantation. 'If you know what it means, it's terrible,' said Schnitzler.

The anti-beauty of Kluster was in the way Schnitzler rubbed up the wrong way against the music, undermining the lie of musical tonality. However, Schnitzler also had a tendency to rub his fellow musicians up the wrong way. After one further album, *Eruption* (1971), Kluster split up, with Moebius and Roedelius recording together as a duo, pointedly softening their name to Cluster. As

Roedelius delicately put it years later, following Schnitzler's death, 'After a while, Moebius and I no longer agreed with the direction Conrad wanted to take with the project, nor he with our artistic input. And so, as one says in the language of musicians, we separated amicably.' Schnitzler spoke kindly of his ex-colleagues too – he would later reunite with Roedelius – but also described both Cluster and Tangerine Dream as 'soft music'. A harsh judgement, but then Schnitzler was, by his own admission, a 'harsh guy' who regarded anything approaching melody, or any musical form that might be remotely commercially viable, as a capitulation.

Confusingly, at the same time as Schnitzler was recording the *Eruption* album, he was also working with a trio by the name of Eruption, whose other members were recording engineer Klaus Freudigmann and Wolfgang Seidel, drummer for Ton Steine Scherben, who was sympathetic to Schnitzler's noisenik ambitions. 'The goal [of Eruption] was to create music without hierarchy – no division of labour, i.e. rhythm section and soloist,' explained Seidel to journalist Tiago Jeronimo. 'And it meant the right relation of sounds. There were no "right" or "wrong" notes and no division between musical notes and noise. Every sound that could be organised in a context could become music. And we did not care about compositional rules that imprint a predictable order on the music.' Erstwhile compadre Edgar Froese was able to afford state-of-the-art synthesizers – Schnitzler and co. looked on at them and the price tags on their equipment with waspish disdain, if not a little envy. They themselves were proudly making do with oscillators and conventional instruments modified with contact mikes glued to them or abused with sticks. At any point, Eruption might mean as many as ten musicians playing together onstage, among them Manuel Göttsching and Klaus Schulze, a loose, fluid collective whose very number defied fixed, foursquare notions of the rock group.

Even so, however, it was only when Schnitzler himself acquired a synthesizer – the portable EMS Synthi A – that he was able to realise what had been his hitherto impossible dream all along: to make music alone, on his own terms without the need for other human collaborators, however compliant. Although he had been co-responsible for an impressive discography, he simply was not a natural collaborator, a team player. From 1973 onwards he flew solo, a prolific human sound machine with a fine disregard for the commercial folly of flooding the market.

Whereas the old Moog routed signals using patch cables, the EMS Synthi A used a patch matrix with reconfigurable resistive pins. That would appear to mean that Schnitzler was able to tweak more range, colour and variance in sounds from the machine. (The Synthi A played a significant cameo role on Pink Floyd's *The Dark Side of the Moon*, the album that marked that band's complete transition from psychedelia to shagpile mega-rock.) 1973's *Rot* ('Red') was released in a limited edition of one thousand, part of a 'colour' series that also included the early *Schwarz* ('Black'). Opener 'Meditation' sees Schnitzler tour inquisitively around the outer capabilities of his new toy, sustaining a laboratory drone, as he unleashes an arcing, plunging series of increasingly distorted metallic notes like missiles, each one leaving its individual dent on the skull. 'Meditation' is a wonderfully inapt title, as this music is wholly inappropriate for the mental solipsism of uninterrupted reflection. On the equally inappropriately titled 'Krautrock' on side two, notes descend in accelerating, alien swarms. There are few points of comparison – the joyful noise of Sun Ra, perhaps, or Metamono, a group led by Irmin Schmidt's son-in-law Jono Podmore, who undertake twenty-first-century adventures in antique analogue.

Challenging as it is for the average, lazy, sweet-toothed listener, *Rot* is *Tubular Bells* compared to its predecessor, *Con '72*, recorded at the German Institute in London that year and eventually reissued by Qbico in 2002. This is assault music without aesthetic concessions of any sort. Initially, those watching and listening might have taken Schnitzler for a man who had no formal training and was simply wreaking violent, mischievous havoc with the knobs and phasers on his equipment, like Bart Simpson let loose in the Radiophonic Workshop, seeing how far the buttons could go without breaking off, what maximum abrasion to the eardrums might be achieved. Perhaps they would not be far wrong. It's a music of violent, hectic ascents and crash-landing descents. It's the very antithesis of Kraftwerk and Tangerine Dream. It posits not the functional harmony of the man–machine relationship but the chaos that could occur if machines fell into the 'wrong' hands or were simply allowed to run amok. Klaus Schulze spoke of the EMS Synthi A as a machine he could use for 'typical effects like water, wind, twittering and thunder', but there is none of that pretty stuff for Schnitzler. On *Con '72*, he doesn't use synthesizers to paint pictures of the cosmology but repeatedly punches you in the face with the reality of the here and now – here is a man, on a stage, and this is a machine and this is noise. There is no attempt at sentiment, transportation to other places, or pleasant colouration. After a while, you submit to the experience, to its punitive, necessary validity.

Hereafter, Schnitzler produced an abundance of material in various formats, always on his own terms, his core audience probably never exceeding a couple of hundred people. These were often perfunctorily titled, with the air of a man who considered his output done with in his own mind, once it was released. There were further additions to the *Con* series, the *Red* and *Black* cassette releases, an overall attitude to recording and releasing material that prefigured the (post-) punk DIY aesthetic by years. No polishing or greasing, no commodification. He also anticipated techno – *Ballet Statique*, originally released as *Con* in 1978 but re-released in 1992, is elegant prototype electropop which opens up spaces and opportunities later exploited in full by admirers and beatmakers like Mixmaster Morris, and which is surprisingly pleasing to the ear. It was as near as he came to some sort of commercial success. However, when he landed a deal to record a twelve-inch two years later, he refused to sign any sort of contract with the record company, meaning that he made no money from the venture. Although always stamped with his obdurate character, Schnitzler's body of work encompassed a vast range of techniques and implements, from minimal to maximal, all the colours in between and every harsh shade of grey.

Ultimately, however, the very process whereby he released his work was, in a sense, a work of art. His fifty-hour Cassette Concert, which took place under the auspices of the René Block Gallery in Berlin, was an example of his interest in John Cage's idea of indeterminacy, as well as the absolute democratisation of art – the 'artist' was no longer king, displaced from his centrality in the production of the work. The 'concert' overseen by Schnitzler consisted of various cassettes playing pure electronics and found sounds, which audience members could interfere with, synchronise or remix at will, the materials having been put at their disposal.

That said, there was clearly something of the brazen attention-seeker about Schnitzler. How else could you describe a man who ostentatiously stood literally in the middle of fields to make his field recordings, microphone in hand like some avant-garde scarecrow, or in the streets atop stepladders, or dressed from head to toe in white leather, carrying aloft a Dada-style mannequin's head on a pole, distributing cassettes to bewildered pedestrians or haranguing them in a robot voice through a loudspeaker attached to a crash helmet? Not so much a one-man band as a one-man happening. Schnitzler may have wished to efface the artist from the customary process of artistic production, but this was not exactly self-effacing behaviour. He rejected commercialism, but a small part of him craved superstardom. Towards the end of his life, when asked by *The Wire*'s David Keenan about his favourite groups, he chose Hawkwind. 'They had a Synthi A in the frontline! That could have been me!' he reflected, wistfully. 'This was my part! I never found that part though. Nobody has ever approached me since and asked me to join a group with them. No one has asked me to sing with them either, because I can do that too.'

Schnitzler opted not to take the path of commercial music-making. However, as someone who trained as an artist, whose work was conceptual in nature and often showcased in galleries, one wonders how much money and prestige he might have accrued if he had been working in the visual arts, been more sparing in his output, enjoyed some sort of corporate patronage, with his exhibited work accompanied by catalogues or small plaques written up in the accepted arthouse vernacular of critical validation. As it was, the struggle to maintain money was a lifelong and voluble concern of Schnitzler's, and helped account for his prolific activity. The question of money, he once said, was 'surely the most existential question for an artist'. He confessed that it was only with the assistance of his wife Gil that he could buy a house on the edge of Berlin in a dreary but quiet suburb so that he could be left alone, in peace to disturb the peace artistically.

It is tempting to place a psychological interpretation on Schnitzler's almost incontinent need to expel noise into the public sphere, in what amounted to a lifelong Campaign Against Real Music, constantly emitting signals designed to jam up the well-oiled systems of the commercial sounds machine whose output governs, comforts and consoles our lives, a would-be gallstone in the works of the body pop. Was it some attempt to expel the earliest, brutally traumatic experiences of his childhood, in which he was denied by the clamour of war the usual shelter and cosy, enabling fictions of our earliest years?

He himself was hostile to the idea that his music was in any way autobiographical. 'It is pure sound that I make,' he told David Keenan. 'And I'm not expressing myself in any way when I'm making it. If anything, I express myself more when I listen back to it, when I go upstairs and listen to it and have one hour of joy. But I have to tell you I am not making sounds for pictures, not even pictures in your brain, not even for memories.' Maybe he protested too much. His compulsion to produce art music, as well as texts and film, at such a fantastic, continual rate could not have come from a mere interest in formalism alone, but a raging, perpetual inner motion (as well, perhaps, as an emergency need to pay the rent). He continued to record, unabated, right up to his death aged seventy-four, cutting the figure of a man twenty years younger. His bloodyminded sense of integrity, his total refusal to make even the most sensible compromises or to settle in any sort of comfort zone or to retire into retrospection, his visionary rejection of the prevailing, hippie dream of his own day put even Krautrock to shame – yet he remains, then, now and tomorrow, a cornerstone of modern music, Krautrock *in extremis*.

*

Klaus Schulze, on the face of it, has certain things in common with Conrad Schnitzler, briefly his colleague in Tangerine Dream. Like Schnitzler, he went through various combos only to discover he felt comfiest determining his own vision as a solo artist, and, as with Schnitzler again, it was the synthesizer that enabled him to do this. Schulze, too, is a compulsive creator. 'I produce more music than a record label can release. After all, I do nothing other than working – playing and recording – in my studio.' His working hours, by his own estimation, vary between eighty and 120 a week, and, as was the case with Schnitzler, he has had to retreat from Berlin in order to work undisturbed. 'I have lived at my house here in the forest for thirty-seven years now, which is the greater part of my life and much longer than I have ever lived in Berlin,' he tells me. 'I moved from the city to a village in the western part of Germany already in 1975. I am the one who produces a lot of music every night. First, it was my retired parents who had moved to the West German countryside, and shortly after I just followed them for private reasons, and bought an old house not far away from them. I liked the idea of having my own house and being able to build my own studio in it.' In terms of music, however, he eschewed the reverie-busting brutalism of Schnitzler. 'I prefer beauty,' he says.

Genial and polite, Schulze nonetheless has a slightly passive-aggressive attitude towards journalists and their enquiries – it may be that a journalist once ran over one of his ring modulators, or a scepticism towards the regular writer's idea of the relationship between music and meaning. Certainly, his interviews are dotted with swipes at the fatuity of writers and their hope that he will say something sensational, which he is at pains to dash.

'"Music is just notes. What you speculate beyond that is pure nonsense." That's from Igor Stravinsky, and even if it's not always true, it has some great meaning,' he says. 'Because, indeed, people often tend to put too much into music. They seem to like this game much more than to learn some rules about music. It's easier. If it's good or bad, I won't judge.'

A tentative enquiry about whether the political consciousness of the late 1960s in Germany had any effect on him as a musician is met with a curt, and final, 'No.' The major events of the period do not appear to have impinged on him creatively the way they did on so many of his peers. 'All young men have the same fun and the same problems, they don't care much which country they live in. They care much more for the girls.'

If not drawn towards the barricades, Schulze was drawn towards the musical vanguard. Having started musical life with a free-rock-oriented trio called Psy Free, who confined their activities to playing clubs in Berlin, he studied with the Swiss-born composer Thomas Kessler, who initiated Schulze and others, 'just like in school', into the world of filters and electronics, as well as making facilities and rehearsal space available to young musicians who otherwise would not have been able to practise. However, when I ask if, as for Can and Kraftwerk, Karlheinz Stockhausen loomed as a forebear to Schulze, he scoffs as if I had cited James Last or Jean-Michel Jarre. 'Are you joking? Have you checked how much "electronics" Mr Stockhausen had used and published during his life? Just out of interest, in the late seventies someone counted his compositions, because every "serious" journalist asked me about Stockhausen. At this time there were about eighty Stockhausen compositions available on LPs, but only three or four used (mostly just partly) "electronics", and then just very simple tools. Stockhausen has published two books and I have read them very early, during my student era; and I liked his theories. Interesting. But what I heard from him, both his music and interviews, had no influence on me or on my music.'

Stockhausen, asserts Schulze, did not really engage with synthesizers, as opposed to basic modifying devices, until relatively late on – not until the mid-1980s, long after Schulze himself had explored their possibilities. 'A close friend and fellow musician of Stockhausen gave (long after his death) a long interview and he told openly that dear Karlheinz was not such a huge friend of electronics and far from being an expert in it. He had to ask others if he wanted to use a synthesizer. Or a mixer. Stockhausen is mostly a myth. How many journalists have indeed checked and heard his music?'

All of which might seem like a pedantic, musicianly adherence to technical truth which disregards the sound regions Stockhausen opened up to the future imagination with works like *Kontakte* and *Hymnen*. However, Schulze's own take-up of electronics was undoubtedly thoroughgoing and lifelong, and he himself would build gateways, perhaps less remote ones than Karlheinz, through which others followed.

Although his accredited role was as drummer on the very first Tangerine Dream album, a position he occupied for eight months, he did try to introduce some homespun electronics ideas of his own, which Edgar Froese knocked back. 'I had "silly" ideas at the time with Tangerine Dream. I had no expensive instruments at this time, if indeed such things existed yet at all, so I tried to create my new sounds with a tape recorder, with a cheap echo machine, with a cheap little electric organ, with a broken guitar amplifier. And with an electric guitar that I used in connection with the echo machine as rhythm, or to create some string effects with a metallic bottleneck, also by using a good deal of echo. At one Tangerine Dream gig I tried to use backwards tapes of my home-recorded organ playing, but Edgar didn't like that, or my other "experiments". So he told me, "Either you stick to the drums alone, or you go." So I left Tangerine Dream. About thirty years later a fan told me that he had read in Wikipedia that "Klaus Schulze had learned electronics from Edgar Froese" – and I had a big laugh!'

As a percussionist, Schulze's forceful, regular playing had what some described as a 'machine-like' quality to it, if not quite as thought through as that of Can's Jaki Liebezeit. It did, however, reflect a desire to move on from the sixties blues/beat models being aped to death elsewhere. 'My interest in pop music was not the usual preference for blues rock with its 4/4 beat and the accentuation on a certain beat. I liked more the groups with a new sound. At this time this was mostly created by guitar bands: the Spotnicks, the Shadows, Duane Eddy, the Ventures. I liked them. They didn't have the down-to-earth blues background which most German bands tried to copy. But maybe it was my older brother, who was a jazz fan and a drummer and he liked Buddy Rich, and his records had maybe an influence on my drumming style. I don't know. It was just the way I was playing, like clockwork, without much thinking about it.'

Schulze joined, then left, Ash Ra Tempel. As he told *Eurock*'s Dave Kirby in 2000, the scene in Berlin was far more fluid and informal than it might seem from the perspective of rock historians.

'Many bands at that time were founded, closed down, and many musicians wandered from one band to another . . . I'm no rock-band musician looking for the warmth and comfort of a band and I'm no orchestra member who urgently needs a conductor.'

For his 1972 debut album, *Irrlicht*, a word which roughly translates as 'Ghost Light' or 'Friar's Lantern', Schulze created his own symphonic feel by using a recording of an orchestra played backward, a malfunctioning amplifier whose brokenness added an interesting filtering effect to the sounds he committed to tape, and a modified organ. The resultant awning of sounds, arrived at through a process of slow improvisation rather than composition, is perhaps the most radical and unearthly he ever generated – dirty, yellow, toxic noise cascades and twists from the rafters, the organ sounds like the manic playing of a headless spectre. It's at once static and frantic, evocative and absolutely peculiar. On YouTube, someone has downloaded the whole album and projected onto it 'visions of apocalypse' – sci-fi imagery, desolate artworks, photography of the cosmos, Dalínian imagery – but these are just that, projections. In reality, it defies pat, imagistic comparisons.

He describes the album as relating to musique concrète (although it is generally more tonal than the works of Varèse, Ligeti or Stockhausen), but while it plays lingeringly on the mind's ear, it resists referentiality. Again, as with Schnitzler, you begin to understand what he means when he says that his music is quite separate from any verbally expressible themes, messages or ideas. Although well acquainted with the writings of Georg Trakl and Friedrich Nietzsche, and with Russian literature, Schulze does not try to transcribe their thoughts into sound. 'Writing and making music are completely different ways of expression,' he believes. Hence, perhaps, his wariness with journalists and their desire to attach meanings to his work that he himself never intended. Nor was any spiritual dimension implied in the fact that Schulze often presented his work in churches – they were simply cheaper to rent than conventional concert halls, that was all. Nihilism, however, this isn't – *Irrlicht* is something, the faint dawn of a new, expansive, modified approach to music-making and something unheard in the Anglo-American rock canon of the early seventies.

1973's *Cyborg* followed, and hangs similarly to its predecessor across its ninety-seven minutes, except that now Schulze has acquired a synthesizer, and with it a rich, platinum but slightly more conventional addition to the mix. Even so, sections still buzz like malfunctioning striplights and the feel remains of the analogue, improvised, half-lit pre-dawn of electronic music that some in the twenty-first century wish could somehow have been preserved right through.

As the decades progress, and Schulze invests in new equipment and diversifies with extra instrumentation and even somewhat liturgical vocals, it has the effect not of enabling him to travel further into synthspace but of pulling him back closer to the orbit of conventional progressive rock. *Blackdance* is perfectly decent, with its muezzin keyboard soloing, brisk percussion and swirling synths. *Picture Music* and 1976's *Moondawn*, on which the Moog makes its first appearance and with which he achieved a measure of commercial success, are still further fallen to earth. This musical style would become codified as the 'Berlin School'. However, when it came to the use of electronic instruments, Schulze was still relatively far ahead of the curve, as he found when he worked with British engineers in the mid-seventies. 'I was astonished and a bit appalled about the British way of working in the studio,' he tells me. 'It was so very normal and uninspired. Synthesizers and the work with these instruments seemed to be totally unknown to the engineers; to explain to them the imaginative and rhythmic use of "echo" and "repeat" took some of my time and patience. But gladly, I had enough of that.'

With a commercial demand having developed for long-form electronic music, Schulze was able to make a good living in the

1970s – at this point, he became notable as an evangelist for synthesizers at a time when technophobia, or plain befuddlement at the equipment, was the default attitude in rock. His albums were much closer to New Age than the golden era of sixties and seventies underground experimentalism – clean, accessible, and now digital. The very title of 1981's *Trancefer* bodes a little ill. In his excellent *Berlin Sampler*, the writer Théo Lessour unkindly says of Schulze that ultimately he 'got bogged down in endlessly churning out albums which demand extraordinary courage to sit through'. He singles out the 'astonishingly windy proto-funk' of 1977's *Body Love*, 'actually composed as the soundtrack to a porn film'. And yet such are the dialectical twists and turns of pop history that the very sleazy connotations of the *Body Love* soundtrack, and its snaking, sequencer gloss, sound rather good to jaded/sophisticated postmodern ears; you can see why the late Pete Namlook would have considered it worth his while to collaborate with Schulze on the *Dark Side of the Moog* series.

*

Although the number of albums released under the group's name runs into triple figures, despite the group's constant and main man Edgar Froese having been active for approaching half a century and achieving the sort of worldwide success denied to his German contemporaries, Tangerine Dream intersect only briefly with the Krautrock narrative. Edgar Froese followed a similar trajectory to many of his more musically inquisitive peers. He was born in Tilsit, East Prussia, which was renamed Sovetsk after the area was annexed by the Russians in 1945, when Froese was just one year old, with all Germans expelled from the town and replaced by Soviet citizens. 'I was a so-called cosmopolitical person from day one,' Froese later said, in reference to this upheaval and its attendant privations. He was tutored in guitar and piano in his teens, and his first gigs were at servicemen's clubs in the mid-1960s.

Parallel to his musical development, however, was an interest in and aptitude for the fine arts – he would study sculpture at art school, and there would be a lifelong visual dimension to Tangerine Dream, with Froese painting as a means of working up inspiration for his compositions, and light shows being an indispensable component of Tangerine Dream's live appearances. His would be the kind of music you 'saw' as well as heard – he would be assisted in this epiphany by the Technicolor explosion of British psychedelia in the late 1960s, including the Beatles, who would provide the inspiration for the group's name, and the cloudbreaking achievements of Pink Floyd, to whom Froese would pay frequent homage in titles like *Madcap's Flaming Duty*, a loving reference to early Floyd frontman Syd Barrett. 'When Tangerine Dream was playing clubs in the late sixties in Germany, we used to love *Piper at the Gates of Dawn* and we played "Interstellar Overdrive" just about every night. The early Floyd stuff was so strange and so different from everything at the time.'

Earlier than that, however, while fronting a short-lived combo called the Ones, Froese experienced a significant eye-opener when his group were invited to play at Salvador Dalí's villa in Cadaqués. Proximity to the extravagant Surrealist genius in the midst of his opulence jolted Froese into a more experimental direction, finding ways in which the radical, formalist movements of twentieth-century art might similarly open up new horizons for the relatively stunted little animal that was mid-sixties beat music. 'Everything is possible in art,' the twenty-two-year-old decided. In 2005, Froese would pay tribute to Dalí with his solo album *Dalinetopia*, whose gruesome cover beggars the powers of description, featuring as it does a garish, overcrowded, would-be Dalínian dreamscape containing, among other detritus washed up on a distant New Age shore, a golden globe, an eagle's head, a blue planet and a dog in a jacket, as well as the masters Froese and Dalí sitting in conference. By this point, however, Froese had ascended to another place.

In the late 1960s, as a fixture at the early Essener Songtage festivals and a regular at the Zodiak Free Arts Lab, Edgar Froese was among the first generation of German musicians to seek out and find ways of breaking the bounds of the overseas occupation of rock music and developing a new language that drew on a wider, academic training rather than simply looking to hone iconic postures of rock attitude. *Electronic Meditation* saw him pull together Conrad Schnitzler and Klaus Schulze, but ultimately neither was prepared to play second or third fiddle to Froese, who always retained the captain's chair.

For 1971's *Alpha Centauri*, the second album in what would later be termed Tangerine Dream's 'pink years', in tribute to the colour of the distinctive ear on the Ohr label logo, Froese introduced a synthesizer, operated by one Roland Paulyck. However, the group mostly relied on traditional instruments such as organ, guitar and flute, but filtered and treated to create cosmic soundstrokes. His main collaborator in the group was Christoph Franke, who had been drummer with Agitation Free and would help develop the sequencer as a live instrument, the crucial, outboard motor the group would use to navigate through their live improvisations.

Opener 'Sunrise in the Third System', though still marinated in lo-fi hiss, announces itself as a *kosmische* proposition, as a sustained organ chord orbits and a theremin-style wail dances overhead like the aurora borealis. None of the harsh abstractions of *Electronic Meditation* – it's near impossible not to think of the night sky. 'Fly and Collision of Comas Sola' sees flocks of starlings swoop like the treated soundtrack to Hitchcock's *The Birds*. Solemn, lightly mundane organ undulations and trilling flute are threatened sporadically by a precipitation of laser-attack sequences which build to an intensity marked by Franke's percussion, so furious it's as if he is systematically smashing his kit to pieces. As with Klaus Schulze,

Tangerine Dream are already delving into a dark side beyond the *Dark Side of the Moon*, into speculative realms uncharted by the mainstream sound astronomers of the day.

With its discreet synth underlay, the title track is a foretaste of the sort of soundtrack work which would eventually make the members of Tangerine Dream their careers and fortunes, but the asymmetrical way in which the various sound elements war and overlap suggests a group who are thankfully still very far from settling into familiar electronic patterns. On 'Ultima Thule' (Parts 1 and 2), meanwhile, Froese's full-throttle guitar wash demonstrates the unique influence of Jimi Hendrix, not so much as a fretboard virtuoso but as a man who used his guitar the way a modern-day action painter might use a spray can – a futuristic sound artist.

For 1972's formidable *Zeit*, the line-up was augmented by Peter Baumann, with a guest appearance from Florian Fricke of Popol Vuh, who brought with him to the sessions his Moog synthesizer. A Cologne cello quartet also features on the opening track. A few short years down the line, ardent punks would gob with contempt at Tangerine Dream and *Zeit*, whose titles alone – 'Birth of Liquid Plejades' and 'Nebulous Dawn' – were proof sufficient that this was an album footling around distant galaxies of faraway irrelevance. However, *Zeit*, one of Tangerine Dream's very greatest works, would foreshadow like a dark star the likes of Fripp and Eno on 'An Index of Metals', as well as Paul Schutze and his fellow dark ambient travellers, to say nothing of the minimal solemnity of composers like Henryk Górecki, who enjoyed a moment of popularity in the 1990s with his Third Symphony. This is particularly evident on 'Birth of Liquid Plejades', which bears out the concept underpinning the album – that the notion of time going forward is illusory, that time is, in fact, motionless. This, in every sense, negates the idea of 'progressive rock', in which category Tangerine Dream were sometimes bracketed, a genre which itself fell victim to the vagaries of fashion it felt itself to be above.

'Nebulous Dawn' is all shadowy, shifting abstractions at wrong angles, their provenance and precise outline unclear. An occasional bass saws into the foreground, synths bubble busily on the periphery. This is a music that fails to settle into any sort of rhythm, or easy pictorial representation – it vaguely conveys the remote workings of a universe utterly indifferent to human beings and their own little timelines. As Froese himself put it, when asked about the fate of the planet in 1982, 'the earth will recede as the waters rise. The painful thing is that people think it's being done to them, personally – they have sixty, seventy, eighty years of life which are so important to them and cannot see why nature would do this terrible thing "to me". They are only lost, however, in cycles that span hundreds and thousands of years.'

It's an idea that reminds one of Stockhausen, who also anticipated cataclysmic events 'at the end of this century and the beginning of the next. There is no other way.' In his own immense compositions, the 'backdrop' is all – the traditional, subjective, egocentric human narrative drama is cast into yawning insignificance.

'Origin of Supernatural Probabilities' and the title track are similarly disquieting, hanging there like some vast, unstirred cosmological fact, their slow, worming drones and wheeling arcs going beautifully and obliviously about their business. There is no Brian Cox-style smiling mediator to console the listener, nor any daft simulation of alien invaders or meteor attacks. Just an immense suspension of light and sound, not cool, not cold, not warm. Their very relationship to time and place, their evocation of those distant corners of space that always existed and always will, irreducible to melody or narrative, accounts for their timelessness.

Great as *Zeit* was, it was also music guided by an artist indifferent to the workings of his German musical contemporaries such as Faust, whom Froese said he had never heard of. His driving concern was to explore increasingly advanced technology to take him further and further away from a cultural landscape with which he felt no great kinship. 'There isn't much music created in my home country I could feel sympathetic with,' he said in 2010. 'It's partly my musical taste as well as my passion for experimental journeys in various directions. So, my fellow people are far too conservative to follow new ideas and structures in music. The only exception is the field of classical music – but that's mostly historic and has nothing to do with contemporary movements.' So much for, well, so much.

1973's *Atem* would be Tangerine Dream's last for the Ohr label, with whom Froese was increasingly dissatisfied, and therefore the last of the 'pink' period. The Moog was dispensed with, but now Froese had a Mellotron, much beloved by groups like Genesis and the Moody Blues at this time, and his extensive use of an instrument whose characteristic faux-orchestral strains mean that it tends rather to sound like itself, regardless of who is playing it, does tie *Atem* a little more to its period. The very use of the title *Atem*, which Kraftwerk had used a year earlier, slightly negated the idea that Tangerine Dream were navigating entirely unexplored territory. Still, its remote, Hubble telescope visions, accompanied by the discreet put-putting of a sequencer, were sufficiently unlike anything else being recorded in the UK at that point for John Peel to declare *Atem* his Album of the Year in 1973. A young Richard Branson duly pricked up his ears and Tangerine Dream departed Ohr and their German base to embark upon the remainder of what would be a highly successful career as expatriates. Branson had started Virgin Records as a mail-order company specialising in import LPs, including European ones, so was in a position to see which of the new German groups were doing business commercially.

The scampering sequencers that dominated *Phaedra* in 1974 were an indication that Tangerine Dream were now voyaging in one direction, never looking back to the nebulous futures they would prefigure on *Zeit*. It's a decent album but listening to it following *Zeit* and *Atem* can only be compared to the experience of being in a darkened room and your eyes accustoming themselves to what had seemed like enigmatic shapes, now revealed as ordinary household objects, or the experience of a distant, unidentified light in the night sky eventually revealing itself as a jumbo jet coming in to land. As the years went on, the more they availed themselves of the latest and most expensive equipment, the more Tangerine Dream would sound retrospectively dated, far more so than in the days when Edgar Froese constructed, modified or custom-made his instruments, resorting to his imagination rather than record-company revenues. Eventually, they would move into the lucrative world of soundtracks, the music subordinate to often banal, commercial narratives. 'The best move I made in terms of music and the business was to bring my music to the UK and team up with Virgin Records,' Froese would later say. 'So one step led to another and it is really about following your inner self, being part of the art form and creating the music rather than consciously thinking about being in the forefront of electronic music.'

That said, the mid-seventies would have been a good time to catch Tangerine Dream live. Unlike Kraftwerk, they did not present some potentially mockable or disconcerting spectacle of cold, Teutonic effeteness. Some of their overseas concerts had an ironic but perhaps reconciliatory air about them, such as a concert at the cathedral in the city of Coventry, following the release of *Phaedra*, their first great international success. As Froese quipped, 'Forty years ago they came to bomb the place, today they come with synthesizers.' In the mid-seventies, their equipment was a formidable spectacle – banks of knobs, leads, keyboards, speakers and gigantic tape reels gave the impression that they were marshalling vast technological resources, though what they generated then would today be achievable on a single laptop. Initially, their concerts were dimly lit affairs, extremely so in the case of York Minster, where they performed in near total darkness. However, by the time they made their concert debut in 1977 in the USA (in

Milwaukee of all places, that hotbed of Germanic futurist electronica), they had developed a formidable light show, a veritable laserium.

From Sheffield to Spain, from Bilbao back to Berlin, their music still represented a singular challenge, improvised and billowing like dry-ice sculpture. However, live in particular, in grand settings, it represented an experience – what some might call *Gesamtkunstwerk*, others mere son et lumière – to audiences embracing the supersonics of Donna Summer and the new sci-fi dimensions of *Star Wars*. For many, Tangerine Dream were synonymous with synthesizers but, despite their popularity, they were still as remote a prospect to the average young punter as foreign travel, given the mortgage applications required to buy double albums at the time and their lack of TV exposure.

*

The amorphous electronic explorations of Tangerine Dream and Klaus Schulze may have been dubbed the 'Berlin School' but unlike other music that came from that city, be it the cabaret of the 1920s or the fractured post-punk of the 1980s, it did not seem to have the imprint of the city running through it. When Bowie alighted on Berlin in 1976, the place was culturally a ghost town in many ways. Once the capital city, it was now a detached island fragment of a damaged past, doomed permanently to be split in two, occupied by fading memories of the Weimar Republic and Isherwood and the silent but visibly unresolved agony of the Second World War. The Zodiak Free Arts Lab was long defunct, the music to which it gave rise having long since floated far and wide, to concert halls and cathedrals across Europe (though not, in Klaus Schulze's case, America – he always refused to play concerts in the USA), or into the ethereal reaches of the New Age bracket, whether the musicians considered their music 'new age' or not.

When he descended on Berlin, David Bowie reactivated the sense of the city as a pop-cultural locus, restored its connections with its past. Since the late 1970s, the city has been a permanent hub of activity, in which the very sense and feel and tradition of the place feeds psychogeographically into what happens there, from Einstürzende Neubauten to the Love Parade.

And yet Klaus Schulze was a part of that restoration, too. Though he did not offer as obvious a template for the electrification of pop music as Kraftwerk, he could justifiably claim to have anticipated the trends of the 1980s and 1990s, when the influence of electronics fanned out across a range of styles, from dance to trance, ambient to techno. It was he in 1979 who had established a label, Innovative Communication, that helped make the use of synthesizers a real prospect for young musicians, the way Thomas Kessler had showed him the ropes a decade earlier.

As he himself put it in 1994: 'It was Edgar [Froese] and me who fought hard, who starved, who put our souls into electronic music in 1971, 1972, 1973, 1974, 1975, 1976, 1977, 1978. It was Edgar and me who made hundreds of concerts for twenty-five years, who gave literally thousands of interviews, showing and explaining to the world about this crazy new music, the music of today and tomorrow. Our music is now accepted by a new generation who does not have the prejudice of their parents; these kids grew up with electronic music of all kinds. That these people, listeners, artists, or journalists look for the beginnings of this music, is normal. And what do they see? Kraftwerk, Tangerine Dream, and me – against a lot of opposition and laughter, but with no compromise. Today, electronic music is a normal thing. We have won, if I may say so.'

7 Fellow Travellers

The 'Krautrock movement', implying as it does a single bloc of musicians moving simultaneously in one direction, voluntarily under the same banner, is a phrase that requires lots of qualification. Many groups were defunct before others had even started up, their failure not always undeserved – 'experimental' music carries with it the implication and reality that some experiments fail. Others carried on ploughing their own, divergent furrows, obscure but remarkably persistent. Who was to know which way the chips would fall in 1969? Which acts would manage to cling to the spinning top of neo-psychedelia and experimentation as German music, so long content to provide cover versions and docile imitations of Anglo-American pop, whirred strangely out of control? In which direction would things go? The Ohr label in particular provided an outlet to some of those groups who might have been, who appeared plausibly to be blazing a trail that would light up the seventies. They're at least testimony to the diverse tributaries which trickled towards the great torrent of new German music, even if some of them dried up altogether en route.

Xhol Caravan's moniker went through various changes. They started life as Soul Caravan, dropped the 'Soul' in favour of 'Xhol' to mark their shift in sound following Germany's exposure to Zappa and Pink Floyd at the Essener Songtage festivals, and then dropped the 'Caravan' so as not to be confused with the English group of the same name.

Soul Caravan were born out of exposure to the Motown Sound. Its co-founders, saxophonists Tim Belbe and Hansi Fischer, were born in Wiesbaden and Bad Schwalbach respectively, both in the US-occupied zone where GIs were apt to party to the Sound of Young America. It made sense to pander to this captive audience, and so, in 1967, Soul Caravan were born, playing Tamla Motown covers. They played the Essener Kabarett, the precursor to the Essen Festival at which so much of the new German music was birthed the following year. They were fronted by two American singers, James Rhodes and Ronny Swinson, and their debut album, *Get in High*, is standard-issue R&B, though inflected with some of the more colourful, psychedelic elements that were already beginning to tinge the Motown output back in Detroit, to Berry Gordy's mild consternation. The album also showed chinks of awareness of the free jazz blazing from the edges. It's a fascinating snapshot of a period in transition for German music, from mere service industry to the occupying forces and a Coca-Cola-sated populace, to something more assertive and freely expressive.

After some personnel changes, Xhol Caravan released the single 'Planet Earth'/'So Down', the B-side in particular featuring a towering vocal performance from James Rhodes, dripping with honeyed melancholy that captures a feeling, shared by the Doors, of the sunshine blaze of hippie idealism giving way to a premature dusk. It's indisputably of its time – well-appointed, trippy soul with a typically echo-laden sixties production that would undoubtedly sit well with Gilles Peterson or any period revivalist. For Xhol Caravan, however, it was another signpost on their descent into the new.

Next came the album *Electrip*, which opens with the sound of a flushing toilet, as if to say, 'Out with the old shit,' or as a more blunt, satirical representation of the sentiments expressed on 'So Down'. 'Electric Fun Fair' is a caustic, 'roll up, roll up' instrumental depiction of the circus of late-sixties pop, which Xhol Caravan are now more sceptical commentators upon than participants within, though its funky chops and changes do raise the counterfactual question – suppose Krautrock had proceeded in a more neo-Motown direction, retained more of the funk rather than going back to the basics of metal, electric and concrete? 'Pop Games' opens with sped-up chatter, overexcited babble, then a jazz-rock passage stooped with gravitas, as if frowning on the frivolity of the hedonism of the whole love 'n' peace 'n' drugs cavalcade, before descending into a miasma of phased soloing, teetering on the edge of something like cacophony – an instrumental cautionary tale against the perils of excess hedonism, maybe, but also hinting at a further evolutionary stage of their funk/psychedelia fusion to come.

A period of heavy gigging followed, some of which formed the basis for live-album releases that saw Xhol increasingly lost to oceanic jamming, the organ sounds of Ocki Brevern playing a more dominant role – his treated keyboard interventions bordered on abstraction at times, à la Pere Ubu's Allen Ravenstine. His apotheosis came with *Motherfuckers GmbH & Co. KG*, whose title alone is an indication of how seriously Xhol were taking their commercial prospects at this stage. With the group at loggerheads with Ohr label boss Rolf-Ulrich Kaiser, the album, though recorded in 1970, was not released until 1972. Its cover could not be more perfunctory or ostentatiously indifferent – just a scrawled tracklisting and the words '2 Years Old' graffitied as if in protest over the top. By this point, they had ventured many miles from the pop citadel into the remote terrain of academic minimalism. The nine-minute 'Orgelsolo' ('Organ Solo') is an arresting, elongated snapshot of the group at what would turn out to be their terminal stage – devoid of funk, the solo is practically a flatline, looming, twisting, burning and glowing, like a long, thin, wiry strand of absolute electric Krautrock essence – this is what they had burned down to, victims of their own curiosity and disaffection.

*

When I asked Krautrock historian and filmmaker Stefan Morawietz if there was some truly lost band of extremists I had neglected, he frowned for a moment, like some Orkneys resident asked if there existed a more obscure, even more northerly island that could still be considered part of the British Isles. 'A band called Limbus on Ohr,' he said. 'Limbus. Very, very obscure. Compared to them, even Faust sounds commercial.'

In the pantheon of Krautrock, Limbus are thrown down like a gauntlet. When Nurse with Wound cited them on a list they drew up of their influences, it was as if to suggest that there is more Krautrock in heaven and earth than is dreamt of in your philosophy, Average Music Fan. You may think you know Krautrock, but while there lies a Limbus awaiting your discovery, your journey is far from complete. The Limbus test is the ultimate test. Venture to Limbus and you can truly claim the right to hoist your freak flag high on their neglected outcrop.

Limbus were founded in the student hotbed of Heidelberg in 1968 and consisted of Odysseus Artnern, Bernd Henninger and Gerd Kraus, who swapped around an array of conventional acoustic instruments which they put to unconventional use, like terrorists sadistically making playthings of their hostages from the high-ranking bourgeoisie. Their debut album, released on the Atlantis label, was entitled *Cosmic Music Experience*. To some, that might represent a challenge, but in Limbus's case the title was a travel-brochure blandishment compared to what actually lurked in its grooves. 'Valiha' commences with a flurry of wind chimes, bells, strings and cymbals, before tom-toms strike up, a quiet communion of neo-folk improv. 'Breughel's Hochzeitstanz' features some electronic bowing, followed by the gentle sounds of what resembles kitten evisceration, to an accompaniment akin to an untutored child having a go at the recorder. The feeling isn't so much of a cosmic revolution in your head as having been locked in a basement with a group of acoustic maniacs. There are no overdubs, no retrospective correction in the studio – this is happening in real time, in a confined space.

For their next album, *Mandalas*, Limbus (now Limbus 4) did enter the studio, armed with additional, weightier instruments. Cellos and organs create a rolling seabed, over which proceeds a submarine detritus of rusted, scraping fragments of instrumentation. What dominates, however, from above the water level, is the ritual skirling of a kazoo-like instrument. Unlike *Cosmic Music Experience*, there is a feeling of mental transportation that arises from *Mandalas* – to a prehistory, to the founding of the City of Ur, perhaps, as high priests ritually consecrate a place of communal worship, central to the new society dawning. However, the abrasive, dissonant edges of the music keep puncturing the fourth wall, dissolving the dreamcloud and laying bare to your mind's eye the less beguiling sight of longhairs picking up instruments and messing about with them in the vague hope that from their random parpings, cello sandpaperings, drones and bongo pattering, some alchemy or transcendence might be achieved. With others it would, but Limbus were the seed that did not take, cast onto their own creative barrenness. Others have taken the Limbus test and succeeded. They find in them a more daring prototype to Can's 'Ethnological Forgeries' series, a music that in its total rejection of preset cultural patterns floats free from earthly conventions and shows how, free of habit and inhibition, you can inscribe something altogether new in the skies. That Limbus themselves failed to garner even the modest success enjoyed by some of their experimental contemporaries suggests either that they went too far, or simply that they weren't all that good.

In 1970, a documentary was made entitled *Sex Freedom in Germany*, which is well worth seeking out. Boasting the high production gloss and editing skills that have enabled Pearl and Dean cinema adverts to stand the test of time, it purports to examine, in the pure spirit of research, the sexual revolution that has apparently transformed life in Germany. It's essentially designed as a peephole for the vast majority of Germans, for whom sexual revolution was in reality as distant a prospect as invasion by Martians. It canvasses the opinions of members of the public, almost exclusively young and male, who tend to be overwhelmingly positive about the prospect of free sex with available and uninhibited women, except for one young man who frowns that the new 'sex wave' is being 'agitated from behind the Iron Curtain – it's a theory I came up with, by myself'. Another slightly older man of Luciferian aspect pledges that in 1973 he will run for parliament under the banner of the German Sex Party.

Amid the hazy scenes of longhairs wigging out stiffly to beat music and rings of pleasured 'porn star' types slouched in circles is footage of a group called Anima, who comprised the husband-and-wife duo of Paul and Limpe Fuchs. Their appearance is even more unfortunate than their surname. Limpe is shown swaying to a soundtrack, naked but bodypainted in jet black. This could pass for a pertinent comment on the 'absence' of women from the new sexual discourse, silhouetted out of existence by a patriarchal, sexist oppression masquerading as liberation. However, the effect comes across more like a sort of inadvertent porno blackface. Husband Paul also appears, his hair shooting up in all kinds of novel directions, his pudgy, toothy leer giving the indication that he may have over-relaxed in preparation for the ordeal of being interviewed on camera. In their performance together, it appears that they equate nakedness, or specifically the nakedness of Limpe (Paul's body we are spared), with some overall societal breakthrough. We see her hammering at a drum kit, in a series of edits in which she is alternately naked and clothed. Paul, meanwhile, trumpets away on a self-made instrument, an elaborate length of metal hose, or crashes a pair of cymbals together as the pair chant wordlessly, as if to summon from on high the ancient spirits that will unchain the uptight German masses from their bourgeois bondage.

If the filmmakers had actively intended to cast them in the most risible possible light, they couldn't have done a better job. As a group who set out to channel into music the latent energies that bellowed through the late-sixties counterculture, Anima probably deserve better than this fragment of a legacy. Their self-made instruments were in the honourable tradition of composers like Harry Partch, even if they didn't match his compositional heights. They set themselves outside the commercial culture, bidding audiences to shed their conformity if they wished to embrace them. Their idealism, certainly, was unsurpassed. Music for All was the idea – seize the instruments, bend them as you will, construct your own. In all of these respects, they were, in principle, a part of the early Krautrock ancestry, albeit an eccentric branch that didn't yield offspring (metaphorically speaking – Paul and Limpe did have a son, Zoro, who actually joined the later line-up of the group). Anima proved a surprisingly enduring proposition. They made two records with the Austrian composer Friedrich Gulda, whose high-academic background did not render him averse to trends in new music, while Limpe continued to perform as a solo artist, her zest unabated, well into the 1980s.

Frank Zappa and the Mothers of Invention's impact on German music was immense, albeit as a general encouragement to think along different lines and to reject the idea of rock 'n' roll as what the writer Simon Frith would later term 'fascination with America'. Key to the Mothers of Invention was puncturing, satirical commentary, not just on the authorities but also on the often ineffectual opposition of the counterculture. In the main Krautrock tended not to address such issues directly, expressing itself instrumentally, subliminally. There were, however, exceptions. Floh de Cologne, formed in 1966, were one example. Their roots were in political theatre, and this they never really abandoned. Rock music was merely a vehicle for their scathing, dissenting texts – eventually, they would embrace multimedia strategies, incorporating visual elements to bludgeon home their message. They were highly pertinent, but not immersive. Their scorn for rock 'excess' left them standing on the side of the pool. Titles such as *Profitgeier* ('Profit Vultures', one of the albums they released on Ohr in the early 1970s) and songs like 'Die Luft gehört denen die sie atmen' ('The Air Belongs to All Those Who Breathe It') were unashamedly polemical. As is often the case with such polemicists, musical experimentation is considered profligate, decadent and a distraction from the most important element, the lyric and its message. Hence, 'Die Luft gehört . . .' is delivered in a deadpan manner across a spindly, functional, organ-dominated late-sixties beat-music backdrop.

Humour travels poorly across time and land, and it is not possible to do justice to the full impact of Floh de Cologne, certainly not through translation. On the strength of their music alone, they could never take a place in the first rank alongside Can, Neu!, Faust, Kraftwerk. However, in every countercultural scene it is necessary for certain groups to carry the can of explicitness for other fellow travellers, so that a stance of political dissent by association can be taken for granted across the scene (even when such groups have to endure being teased for their overtly political outlook by those who shy away musically from such 'obviousness'). Floh de Cologne did the dirty work of rock in opposition and deservedly endured.

Guru Guru were formed in 1968 by Mani Neumeier, drummer and dominant permanent presence in the group, with Uli Trepte, later of Faust. Born in Munich in 1941, Neumeier grew up steeped in the music of Louis Armstrong, Miles Davis and John Coltrane, all of whom would prove foundational to his sensibilities. He joined the Irène Schweizer Trio and, as his take on jazz became freer, intersected with future Can drummer Jaki Liebezeit while working with the Globe Unity Orchestra.

Life was tough initially for Guru Guru, living aboard their

tour bus on a diet of jam sandwiches, before conditions improved and they took up communal life and all its economic advantages. Their performances were confrontational – no hiding behind their shrouds of long hair or amid banks of equipment. They termed what they were doing 'action music'. They took drugs specifically to jolt themselves from what they termed 'the A–B–A of music as well as our lives', and sought to do the same to their audiences. They used various props, including masks and even chickens, to illustrate their song lyrics, and once had a performance in Heidelberg shut down by police.

Their first album, *UFO*, did not appear until 1971. Judged as a purely musical proposition, Guru Guru are heavy work indeed at this stage, moving up and down the registers like giant industrial hoists. Parts of it make Throbbing Gristle sound like Depeche Mode. Fragments of wah-wah are lost, indistinct noises muffled in heaping mounds of gravel. At one point, we're wading waist deep in rusty water. This is raw, barely treated rock noise, subjected to the same annihilation by abstraction as had been visited on jazz in its historically terminal 'free' phase, rising in ear-splitting crescendos to a brutal confrontation with the rubble of newly dynamited preconceptions about the shape, direction and origin of rock music. Hard to speak of an album that's so in pieces as a 'cornerstone' of German music, but as a founding statement of intensity it's matched only by Kluster/early Cluster. 'Der LSD-March' is conducted at a sombre, slow pace, almost a matter of (heavy) duty, a stern acid test. Flutes flurry like small snakes fleeing and being trampled underfoot, guitars clang out single notes, drone, shred and wail (but rarely squeal) as Neumeier's drumming surfs its own cymbal waves. Only in recent years has metal, in its late, mature phase and even then only on its outer fringes, come around to this way of playing, this sort of vice-like intensity and density.

Already, however, with 1971's *Hinten*, Guru Guru – the trio of Neumeier, Uli Trepte and Ax Genrich on guitar – are beginning to lighten up a little. The smoke and sludge are clearing, and at times this almost resembles recognisable rock jamming of some sort. This is partly down to the influence of Conny Plank on engineering duty. There are vocals, groaning amid the weight of the playing, the guitar feedback, contact microphones and percussion that brings chunks of girder falling from the rafters. It's often self-descriptive – 'Electric Junk' is just that, rock as avenging noise pollution, retaliating against a consumerist society imposing itself onto the heads of the young. The trio dirty every last atom of space with their noise, and even the quieter sections only make room for muddied, distorted 'vocal' statements. It's music that's intended to mess with the cerebellum, to sow confusion, not to contaminate innocent minds but to reveal the state of the world.

By the time of 1972's *Känguru*, considered by many to be their finest album, Guru Guru have migrated further centreward from their free-form origins towards something more resembling a lengthy homage to late Jimi Hendrix. On 'Oxymoron' Ax Genrich eventually breaks off from teasing strokes of tonal colour from his guitar and, in a strained, untreated gurgle possibly intended as a joke, relates, 'Yesterday, I took a trip.' It's hard not to feel that a spell has been broken and that given the criticism that vocals are the weak link in Krautrock, it might have been better for them to have kept their mouths shut rather than remove all doubt. 'Immer Lustig''s circus parade-style opening is a reminder of their satirical origins, but overall you suspect that over the years of playing live, they had learned what worked with crowds and what left them cold and, consciously or subconsciously, stuck to what worked, shedding the freakier, freer stuff. From here on in, Guru Guru's long progress was along the much-travelled corridor of conventional heavy rock. They're still travelling today, with Mani Neumeier the remaining, constant member of the group.

'Kraan should be right up there beside Can, Kraftwerk and Tangerine Dream in the list of Germany's finest,' enthused the writer Gregory Shepard in 1976, as the group were heading to the USA. Formed around 1970–1, they were one of a number of groups who began gigging around Berlin before falling in with one of those benefactors who dot the Krautrock story, one Count Metternich, an arts philanthropist who loaned them the use of a farmhouse of his in the Teutoburger Forest, in which spectacular, pretty and secluded setting the group lived communally for some years, using the farmhouse as a base to tour West Germany. Still in existence to this day, their core members are guitarist Peter Wolbrandt and bassist Hellmut Hattler. Alto saxophonist Johannes Pappert was also in their line-up for their first several years, and they were later joined by Ingo Bischof on keyboards.

Their self-titled debut album was released in 1972. Tracks like 'Kraan Arabia' set off at a promising rhythmical pace, before the guitar and sax exchange imitative Arabic phrases that feel more like touristic flourishes than a genuine effort to recast the rock format. After a few minutes, this is fast-paced rock jamming with the Eastern influence reduced to a hint of saffron. You could describe them as 'fusion', with the element of jazz afforded by the sax phrasing and their meandering changes and solos, but Kraan wear their outside influences like hats, rather than allowing them to really get in among their essentially orthodox approach. The mouldy whiff of the early seventies is ever present, *Whistle Test* rock, all chugging riffs and dangling long hair. 'Mind Quake' from *Wintrup*, recorded the same year, is fitfully interesting, particularly a section five minutes from the end in which a guitar solo is overlaid with the slurping, clinking sounds of what is apparently the rest of the members taking a tea break. The declarative vocals and pensive lyrics only add to the feeling of a band who are requesting our attention on Anglo-American rock terms. *Andy Nogger*, their last album featuring the original line-up, is likeable enough, but despite some interesting flourishes, it only confirms that for all their popularity and occasional eccentricity,

Kraan never really belonged anywhere near the top drawer of 1970s German music.

Nektar are another group often filed under Krautrock, if that term simply means 'rock that was undertaken on German soil'. Their main man, Roye Albrighton, was, as his name suggested, a British expat, and they were sufficiently in keeping with the mores of the late 1960s for an American producer to fly them out to Boston for a recording session. Their stay lasted just a few weeks, however, and they returned to West Germany, settling in Seeheim and signing to Bacillus Records. A sense of exile and a determination to prove themselves overhangs their subsequent busy career, in which they attempted a series of Major Rock Statements over the course of double-disc albums and extended, ruminative pieces. On *A Tab in the Ocean* (1972) they explored the dichotomy of inner/outer space, a typical Can/*kosmische* theme, but did so lyrically, with standard-issue, angst-ridden, breast-beating rock harmonies, rather than through their instrumentation, whose spatial sensibility isn't that much different from Deep Purple's.

They made concept albums. *Remember the Future* (1973), considered to be their masterpiece, is about a blind boy who makes contact with an extraterrestrial being. Again, however, there's no great musical sense of the unearthly or uncanny intuitive. With its portentous opening, austere Hammond organ phrasing and silvery winged vocals serenading a forthcoming Revolution of some description, *Remember the Future* sits somewhere between Yes and the *Jesus Christ Superstar* soundtrack. Their subsequent career saw them take on an increasingly chromium-plated, US-radio-friendly hue, as if fighting a battle for recognition for German-based rock, but on the other side's prog terms. Although rather more popular in Germany, as well as abroad, than most of the canon of experimentalists, ultimately Nektar didn't change the shape of anything much at all, except themselves – over the years, they've been through a series of line-up changes but have carried on trucking to this day, according to their own lights. In 2013, they came back with the album *Time Machine*, recorded with an immaculate disregard for every major popular musical development of the preceding forty years.

*

> 'Studying music in the 1960s, our professor had informed us in a lecture that Africans had thicker skulls and smaller brains. He said this in a lecture! . . . That was still Nazi thinking.'
>
> Christian Burchard

Embryo were founded by drummers Christian Burchard and Dieter Serfas, and initially grew out of the burgeoning Munich scene – Chris Karrer of Amon Düül was for a while among their number, as was Mal Waldron, whose pedigree included a stint working with Billie Holiday. Their first album, *Opal*, was released in 1970 and stands up well, with its almost Beefheartian, angular arrangements, and violins, courtesy of Edgar Hoffman, which cut across the soundboard like chalk. Its most intriguing number is 'End of Soul', in which the last rites of the genre are read out in deadpan manner – 'The fact remains that soul is dead/And the hopes of many of its followers will be carried to the grave with it.' Whether this is a lamentation, or similar to Hendrix's burial of surf music on 'Third Stone from the Sun', or a reflection on the way that even groups like the Temptations were putting old-style sixties showbiz-friendly soul to the psychedelic sword, soul certainly was not dead in 1970 – in fact, like German music, it was on the point of entering one of its most fertile, liberated and electrically charged phases.

Certainly, Embryo were the very antithesis of white-rock triumphalists. From this point, they would rove across a truly global brief, taking in jazz and pan-continental musics. They had the impulse to explore other musics, other cultures, which operated to varying degrees across the spectrum of German arts at the time, to such a creditable extent that it removed them altogether from the concerns of their experimental peers, who were more about self-invention. Embryo were about absorption, recruiting the likes of multi-instrumentalist Trilok Gurtu, among others. The cover to their 1973 album *We Keep On*, featuring the late US expat saxophonist Charlie Mariano, is especially striking, its image of a cracked cosmic egg on a cloudy skyline providing one of the central images of Krautrock literature. Benefiting from a study trip the group made to Africa and India, with its shrieking, vivacious electric flurries and shockwaves of pan-ethnic elements, sewn at breakneck speed through a fast-cut mix of electric keyboards and jazz rhythms, it's commended to fans of the more fiery funk and rock-jazz fusion of the era, be it Herbie Hancock's *Sextant* or Miles Davis's *Bitches Brew*. 1973 was the high point for such explorations generally, and although they've carried on recording, touring and globetrotting over the decades, Embryo never quite caught the electric eel by the tail the way they did on *We Keep On*.

Günter Schickert was born in Berlin in 1949, a stone's throw from the Kaufhaus des Westens, a vast department store in the centre of the old western half of the capital. As a child, Schickert toured its multiple sales floors, including a large record department where he first heard the music of Chet Baker and took up the trumpet. In the late sixties, like many of his generation, he developed a love for the Rolling Stones and decided to play guitar. He was among those irradiated and influenced by the happenings at the Zodiak Free Arts Lab, where he met, among others, Klaus Schulze, with whom he would later play. It was 1974, however, before he made his first album on the Brain label, recorded while he was holding down an office day job and released in 1975, having experimented for a year or so on playing echo guitar, similar to that used by Manuel Göttsching of Ash Ra Tempel.

The title of *Samtvogel* ('Velvet Bird') implies luxury and free flight, and so the album does, in a way. Opener 'Apricot Brandy' is mazy and jazzy enough initially, before it undergoes a series of mutations. However, its centrepiece is one of Krautrock's most infernal, cascading, extended works. 'Kriegsmaschinen, fahrt zur Hölle' ('War Machines, Go to Hell') uses a Dynacord guitar amplifier, a Fender Jazzmaster, a Dynacord Echochord S-75, a microphone, a Marshall Fuzz Face and a Crybaby wah-wah pedal: actually quite a modest arsenal of soundmaking equipment considering what he achieves over the course of the track's seventeen minutes. Without the anchor of a beat or any accompanying bassline or melody to plot its course, 'Kriegsmaschinen, fahrt zur Hölle' is a dark, sustained acid bath, a thick forest of timbres, whose remorseless bombardment of seething drones is more black-hole rock than space rock, burying the listener alive, layer by layer, with Schickert's sporadic vocals like the cries from inside a coffin. Bombardment is the word. The pacifism of the track's title is clear enough and universally applicable, but it functions as a simulated trauma, an endless firestorm reimagined. Schickert still plays the piece live and its strength, if anything, is reinforced nowadays, thanks to the heavier technology and equipment available to him. Like Sunn O))) live, it's a ritual, purgative experience the like of which every music fan ought to experience at least once in their life, like a trip to Mecca. Its eddying wash of echo also makes it a strangely exhilarating, even cleansing experience, like sweating toxic mercury out of your pores. Schickert had to wait five years before he recorded his second album, 1979's *Überfällig*, which maintains both the approach and the high standard of its predecessor and, lost in its own time, deserves revisiting.

Considering how hard even those who are considered the major players of the era had sometimes to struggle to attain studio time, get concerts and maintain their own dedication as musicians in the face of public apathy and lack of funds, it's unsurprising that many others lost their precarious footholds and dropped away. It's probable that there are other minor treasures buried beneath the layers of history that have accrued since the 1970s, which Krautrock students of today and tomorrow will joyfully unearth. One has to be wary, however, of the tendency of obsessives to equate the 'newly discovered' with the 'actually worth a listen'. It's most likely that most of what is worth hearing has already come to light. Most – but maybe not all. Certainly, the Krautrock journey is an incomplete and a poorer one without these fellow travellers.

8 A Raging Peace: Cluster, Harmonia and Eno

Six years older than the eldest Beatle, born just a few months before Elvis Presley, only eight years junior to Karlheinz Stockhausen, Hans-Joachim Roedelius is still active on the verge of his ninth decade, as his Facebook page attests. Born in October 1934 in Berlin, one of the co-founders of the Zodiak Free Arts Lab, he had several years on most of his contemporaries in the burgeoning Krautrock scene. The son of a dentist, many of whose clients worked at Berlin's prestigious UFA film studios, he was invited when just six years old to co-star in a film alongside Nazi pin-up blonde Ilse Werner in the 1941 propaganda film *Reitet für Deutschland* ('Ride for Germany'). Although he barely understood the demands of his profession, fell off the horse on which he was supposed to be riding for Germany and could only be induced to persist at the studios with the promise of chocolate and electric trains, Roedelius starred in several movies as a child, even making the cover of *Deutsche Illustrierte*, looking suitably Aryan and soulful as he nestles against the bosom of actress Brigitte Horney.

The war, however, put an abrupt halt to his gilded childhood. His father was barred from active service having worked for the Red Cross in the 1914–18 war, and Hans and his mother Gertrud were evacuated from Berlin as the Allied bombing intensified, to a small hamlet in East Prussia whose unspoiled, bucolic pleasures struck a stark contrast with the incendiary trauma and chaos of Berlin under siege. Roedelius played truant from school, instead wandering the fields, seeking out the company of frogs and wild geese, until he was conscripted to the Hitlerjugend in the last, crazed days of the Reich, in which children were expected to offer the last line of resistance against the advancing Allies. 'Fortunately, the war ended before we had to fight,' recalled Roedelius, who at eleven would have had no choice either way.

The aftermath of war was most difficult for the Roedelius family, as poverty and disease ravaged the people eking out an existence as best they could in the ruins. Roedelius's father died in 1948. With the household income amounting to 'not enough to live on and just a bit too much to die on', Roedelius, barely into his teens, was forced to forage to provide basic subsistence for the family, going into the forest to cut down firewood, working for local farmers in exchange for food, or, if food was not at hand, scrumping apples from the orchards. While West Germany enjoyed the benefits of the Marshall Plan and the patronage of the Americans, Roedelius was caught on the eastern side of the border, and once again he found himself conscripted, this time into the ranks of the Kasernierte Volkspolizei, a de facto East German army.

Taking advantage of his job as barracks postman, Roedelius deserted and then defected to West Germany, only to find himself wintering in a damp, dismal hostel. He returned to East Germany and was instantly arrested by the Stasi, who accused him of being a spy sent by the West. Embittered by his experience and defiant of his captors, Roedelius was imprisoned for five years at Bautzen. There he realised that only a counterfeit display of conformism could guarantee his release, so he wrote reams of doggerel in praise of the DDR's leader, Walter Ulbricht, dripping with penance for his desertion and denouncing capitalism. He must have drawn on all of his childhood acting experience, for he was held up by the authorities as a model prisoner and secured early release two years into his sentence. Biding his time, he took up work as a masseur, before managing to slip over the border into West Berlin in 1961, just prior to the building of the Wall.

This time, West Germany was booming economically and

Roedelius was able to take various menial jobs, from garbage man to waiter, before falling back on his training as a masseur. Having for so many years concerned himself purely with the business of survival, Roedelius could at last look up and about and contemplate a Germany that remained spiritually and morally ruined, despite its superficial, material success. He took inspiration from the arts, from the exiled American Living Theatre group of Judith Malina and Julian Beck, as well as the APO protests led by the ill-fated Rudi Dutschke. It was high time, he realised, for people like himself to act, to begin rebuilding a society that mistakenly considered itself to have been fully rebuilt under Adenauer and the Americans. He gave up his day job – it was time to take matters into his own hands, rather than use those hands to soothe the flaccid muscles of West German businessmen.

Roedelius drifted into the bohemian underworld, hooked up with Conrad Schnitzler and, inspired by his outsider attitude, joined him in two successive noise ensembles, Geräusche and Plus/Minus, whose live work consisted of blasting out atonal sounds at ear-splitting volume using pieces of metal tubing. Following the break-up of these ensembles, their demise unmourned by the German public, Roedelius and Schnitzler took a brief sabbatical in Corsica at a nudist colony, where Roedelius again showed his practical and versatile manual skills by working as a roof tiler and indulging in impromptu, all-night improv sessions on found metal objects, to the consternation of his naked onlookers. Back in Berlin, Roedelius then co-formed a musical collective, Human Being, whose members included his girlfriend Beatrix Rief and future artist Elke Lixfeld. They chipped in from their day jobs and bought a collection of traditional instruments, including flute, violin and a cello, which was sawed with almost malicious vigour throughout their sole recording, *Live at the Zodiak*, made in Berlin in 1968 in the early days of the club, and a precious taster of the absolutely free improv with which the minds of the club patrons were opened, forcibly or otherwise.

The highly trained British free-music collective AMM had declared that their own brand of improvised music was not a free-for-all – they once had to upbraid a group of hippies who had tried to join in with one of their gigs, assuming it was some sort of jamboree for talentless exhibitionists who thought anyone could and should piss in the general pool of 'self-expression'. On the contrary, said AMM – hardly anyone can do it, they insisted. Much as splashing a few buckets of paint on the floor did not make you Jackson Pollock, so was AMM music impossible without a rigorous underpinning. You had to think, train your way to this place, exercising discipline all the while.

Human Being are a partial retort to that. Said Roedelius, 'Human Being wasn't bound to any style, genre or mode. We just fiddled around with feedback, echo machines, prepared tape and loops. None of us were academically trained. We had big meetings to talk about our methods, but nothing was written down . . . the audiences, high on dope, were wildly enthusiastic.' What remained true was that this was not the sort of music you could make, and carry on making, on a whim. Preparation was required. Roedelius, like Schnitzler, was untutored – he had not 'learned' the way to this point through rigorous training. Rather, ensembles like Human Being were an implicit reproach to the *Hoch* academies whose standards were imposed on young Germans as a matter of cultural course, as if musical training was a way of being bound to the state at the highest level, rather than a means of individual expression. This was their own route to the valley of 'noise', and it was important that they take it.

Live at the Zodiak suffers inevitably from the low quality of its recording, but that also lends it a certain antique mustiness, the feeling of a dusty relic uncovered from the very dawn of Krautrock. Its opening feedback drones, punctuated by the irregular but insistent plucking of a cello, are like the slow awakening of a slumbering beast, a new noise stirring, old engines lighting up and rebooting after a long, long lay-off. There's a ritual solemnity about these repetitions, as they're increasingly flanked by other scrapings and sawings of obscure origin. The playing is not virtuoso but there is a guiding hand, a sense of logic and drama as the sound burgeons and unfolds, that will not be denied. The constant presence of cellos adds an underpinning of gravitas to proceedings, a seriousness of purpose, warding off shirkers. There's no reference to any style or genre – not classical, not jazz, not rock – no technique or received pattern. The effect is of all sluices opening, of gradual, tonal immersion, like the water level building up in a canal lock. Gradually, new patterns and rhythm swim into play, as human voices join in with obscure incantations, like a distant procession headed by a high priest swinging incense heading slowly your way. Motors begin to rumble and sputter, the rhythms begin to thump more heavily, the chants, in some invented foreign tongue, grow more violent, as if a blood sacrifice is imminent. A chaotic, clangorous passage follows, a mammoth struggle, before a single electric guitar picks out the glint of a pastoral vista amid the ash and gloom. *Live at the Zodiak* is hardly a 'finished' work, but as a harbinger for all that was to follow over the next several years it's prescient and invaluable. And although *Live at the Zodiak* exposes Roedelius's lack of tuition, it also demonstrates his superb intuition, an inner drive which has seen him record consistently and prolifically for well over forty years, during which he has journeyed autobiographically back and forth from the trauma of noise to the pastoral idyll, the one informing the other. For, as the writer and Roedelius biographer Stephen Iliffe puts it, 'Only someone who has known sustained darkness can appreciate the strangeness of the light.'

Like Roedelius, Dieter Moebius is as busy as ever, over four decades since he first began making noise that became music. 'Too busy!' he reflects from Andalucia, where he spends half his time when not on the road. He must know he has many years ahead of him. When I speak to him, he is preparing to tour a live soundtrack of Fritz Lang's *Metropolis*, a decision described by one reviewer as 'inspired', as his own performance, generating whirling, mobile inventions of rhythms, basslines and loops, makes him the perfect accompanist to the mad science generated by the inventor Rotwang in the movie. He and Roedelius last worked together as Cluster on 2009's *Qua*, a quite excellent album of elusive, irregular sound capsules, the heavily modified fruit of forty years of collaboration. More recently, he could be seen onstage with Michael Rother and Camera, the young Berlin-based troupe creating a twenty-first-century rhythmical assault from Krautrock's old bones.

Moebius and Roedelius – it's as if they were destined to be musically twinned since the ancient classical era. Moebius frequented Zodiak Free Arts Lab, where he describes himself as 'a listener' rather than a player. Born in Switzerland in 1944, where his family had sought refuge during the war, he took his studies in art, first in Brussels and then in Berlin at the Akademie für Grafik, Druck und Werbung. But like many of his generation, he had a political as well as an aesthetic consciousness, demonstrating against the Altnazis and hate figures like Axel Springer. 'We were a lot of times on the streets instead of studying,' he remembers. 'As young people we were not very proud to be German. The reason why this movement of "Krautrock" was born was because we were all tired of listening to bad German music and imitations of American music – something had to happen.' When not in the Arts Lab, he was generally to be found propping up one of the many bars in Charlottenburg. It was on one such night that he ran into Schnitzler and Roedelius, who asked him if he'd like to join their group. Moebius, whose mother played classical piano, had had a little musical training as a child before having his head turned by jazz and rock 'n' roll, the stranger the better. The next day, they began rehearsals, and shortly after that, the trio, known as

Kluster, played a twelve-hour concert in Berlin's Galerie Hammer.

Despite making such an incisive impact on Berlin's modern musical tapestry, Moebius was not long in the city. 'When we formed Kluster, we left Berlin almost immediately, forever!' he tells me. 'We toured Europe. Berlin was like a village at this time, surrounded by the East. To be successful you had to go to West Europe, and each time you had to cross the East German border – and it was a big, big drag. Having so many instruments with you meant that you were always getting searched. And so it was much easier to go to West Germany.

'Of course, as a young guy of twenty years, there was an advantage in going to West Berlin: it was that you didn't have to do your military service. I was Swiss-born but I am German – if I had been in West Germany, I would have had to do my military service. I was born in Switzerland because of the war – I am as old as that.'

Moebius and Roedelius first encountered Conny Plank at the Rhenus Studio in Cologne, when he was at the controls for the recording of the two Kluster albums, in a single session on the same night, along with Conrad Schnitzler. Plank seemed capable enough, but at this stage they didn't fully apprehend just what this tall, kindly, slightly ursine young man was capable of.

The ever-maverick Schnitzler broke away, and Kluster became the serendipitous duo Cluster. Like Neu!, they represented a perfectly functioning marriage of contrasts – 'romantic Roedelius and chaotic Moebius', as the latter puts it, amateur artists devising new geometry and colour schemes on the fresh slate of new German music, making the best of whatever sound kit was available to them. However, on their debut, self-titled album, there is none of the almost eerily picturesque garden prettiness that characterises some of their later work. With the assistance of Conny Plank, Cluster had managed to bag a contract with Philips, one of a number of labels, including Polydor, who imagined there to be commercial potential in the new German music wave, following the relative success of groups like Can at Liberty/UA, and were making blind signings as a result. Their accounts department would eventually write off Cluster as a folly – the label released a masterpiece by mistake. How it was waved through in the first place remains a mystery.

Cluster was recorded in Hamburg, with Conny Plank at the controls, who, as was his wont, enabled Moebius and Roedelius to add colour, depth, focus, vividness and even a sense of structure to their output. 'His studio was previously used to house farm animals, pigs,' recalls Moebius of working with Plank. 'It was a long, long building, just one floor – you could have a length of recording tape sixty metres long. We set up the machines and round and round it would go. I'm not such a good technician! I know he had a camera on top of the mixing console so that he could take a picture and know how to set up all the equipment the next day.

'He had a big part in our group, because at this time Cluster had no money – he would work with us for free. He would always have the latest gear from the UK, from Japan, and he knew how to handle the equipment, some of which was so complicated at the time we had no idea how to use it. He would explain to us how it worked and then we could use it. So it was a symbiosis between him and us.

'At this time, he worked with groups when they were nothing, had no fame at all and no idea if they would have any sort of hit. That was the case with the whole scene. Now, there has been a revival, but back in the 1970s, even the 1980s, this music was simply not well known. These "Kraut" groups as you know them now – even Tangerine Dream, Can – they were famous in France and the UK but not in Germany! That was a little bit the same with us, but we were totally uncommercial, so it's quite normal that we didn't earn a lot of money.'

The album, however, still has the impact of a meteorite decades after its release. Its cover, depicting a yellow and orange triangle and a set of blades, teeth interlocking and pointing north-east, barely hints at the abstract carnage within. Its three tracks are untitled, referred to only by their duration. It's real end of the world, beginning of the universe stuff. Opener '15'33"' half refers to John Cage's '4'33"' but is among the ten least quiet tracks ever laid down. Bubbling apocalyptically from the outset, its treated effects belch pluming arcs of pure sulphur from all angles – à la Stockhausen's *Kontakte*, in a sense, but less academic, more heated and tonal in its multiple eruptions. It sounds as if it were generated by forty-feet-high banks of synthesizers in some vast, sub-volcanic hideaway leased from a Bond villain. In fact, these chugging, molten noises are achieved on conventional instruments, as well as audio generators and amplifiers. As with Faust, however, there is a determination to mask the origins of the music – all must be new, blasted in the furnace of the moment.

'The first set-up of Cluster was interesting,' recalled Conny Plank in 1987. 'We had five oscillators, a few tube distortion units where we sent the sound through the tube and could adjust the amount of distortion. We had echoes where you could change the speed of the echo in real time. We used normal organs and Hawaiian guitar; when you treat a Hawaiian guitar really heavy it sounds like electronic music. We used tape loops. We had a quite complex set-up of all these things that were mixed. Sometimes we worked with a drummer, sometimes with cheap Italian machines.'

'7'38"' and '21'17"' are marginally more subdued in their radioactive afterthrob, enabling the surviving listener to home in on their details, their dimensions – half-hidden amid its overlap and overmatter are the sort of girder-melting, post-industrial sounds which would course through post-punk, Cabaret Voltaire, 23 Skidoo, Throbbing Gristle, with all their intimations of annihilation. But the sounds of Cluster are birth pangs, the smelting and reshaping of the metal elements of rock. This is not ambient – this is a cranial enema.

For Philips executives who attended any playback session for Cluster, it must have been as congenial as watching their own headquarters being burned to the ground. Cluster were dropped like a cinder. However, they quickly found a home at Brain Records, founded by Günter Körber, a former employee at the Ohr label. With its propeller drones, autogenerated systems noise and refusal to settle into preset, humanly recognised patterns of any sort, *Cluster II* is similar in its overt, mechanical assault to its predecessor, only divided into individual tracks, its sole concession to normality.

When they took to the stage to present their work, at exhibitions, or as support at festivals such as Fehmarn, in West Germany, where Jimi Hendrix headlined less than a fortnight before he died, or supporting Kraftwerk, Cluster were too much even for audiences whose preconceptions had dissolved in a haze of dope. Roedelius's future wife described one of their concerts as 'an act of noise terrorism'. Dieter Moebius agrees that their gigs did not always go down a storm.

'Oh, they didn't like it a lot of the time,' he laughs. 'We were very loud and very chaotic. People were very hostile. They wanted to beat us up. They threw things. Tomatoes. I remember one time a young girl coming up to stage, crying her eyes out and shouting at us, "Why are you doing this?"'

Cluster could have carried on in this gruelling mode, cutting through the hippie sensibilities of the day like a runaway combine harvester through a wheatfield. However, the toll of constant touring was having an effect on their health, Roedelius in particular. Their noisenik days ground to a halt. Moebius denies, however, that their sheer lack of money or commercial fortune influenced their subsequent turn towards musicality.

'No, it's not that – it's that we were autodidacts as musicians. It wasn't that we said, "Now we have to be commercial, to make money." We were just slowly learning about things like harmony and structure.' A change of environment was urgently required, and this presented itself when a large farmhouse became available in the rural depths of Lower Saxony, in Forst, close to the River Weser and utterly remote from the distractions, comforts, stresses and amenities of the big city. It sounded idyllic, spoke to a desire, common to German musicians of the era, for pastoral retreat – but when the Cluster duo drove up to the 'Weserhof' in their tour van, Moebius was initially all for turning right round again.

'I only remember that we went there to look at it, because an antiques dealer invited us to come and live with him,' he told journalist Geeta Dayal. 'He got it by telling the government guy that he will make a cultural centre. So he needed some artists to live there. When I saw it for the first time, I didn't even want to leave the truck! I said, "I'm never going to live in this place." There were no windows, it was all muddy . . . it was all really fucked up. You had to be very optimistic to imagine that you could live there. There was only one water place, one tap for three houses. There were no toilets, no electricity.'

It was, however, a large and absurdly cheap property, with Tudor-style features to the exterior, set over two storeys, a former storage facility for beer and corn that had also doubled up as a courthouse. Roedelius, with his rural hankerings, took quickly to the place, which the duo made habitable by throwing rugs and whatever bits of cheap furniture they could salvage about the spacious premises, along with their make-do-and-mend array of equipment.

Among the first visitors to Forst was Neu!'s Michel Rother, who had met the group in 1971 and, with Klaus Dinger, been sufficiently impressed with them to consider merging into a four-piece. With Neu! currently in hiatus, Rother rolled up at Forst for a jam session, bringing with him his own instruments, including a primitive sequencer. The sequencer was an instrument that when it became too well-developed was the artistic undoing of *kosmische* music, but for now provided an intriguing, bellows-like pulse. Forst answered a similar yearning in Michael Rother's soul to that in Roedelius's (Klaus Dinger was far less enamoured of the place) and he decided to stick around. The trio would work together under the name of Harmonia, an amalgam of 'Harmony' and 'Ammonia', as wittily depicted on the Moebius-designed cover art of their debut album, recorded during the second half of 1973 and released by Brain Records. It featured what looked like a garish advert for an imaginary detergent, the brightest thing to hit the market in years.

In some comic-book parallel 1970s Germany, *Musik von Harmonia* should have been one of the albums that drew the nation's youth like moths to a giant electric lamp, pouring out of the cities and deep into the forest, eyes upturned, mesmerised and awestruck by its quietly dissident, slowly vibrating beauty. 'Watussi' opens briskly, on Rother's sign, sitting in relation to the brief sixties dance craze the way Kraftwerk's 'Autobahn' does to the Beach Boys' 'Fun, Fun, Fun', exuberant but also elaborate and filtered in its cerebral, clockwork interplay of rhythms, looped electric emissions and reverberating guitars, as if to signify the distance between the irresistible surface thrills of American teen pop and the more austere, contemplative recesses of seventies German music.

'Sehr Kosmisch' is that most pearl-like of things, a German pun – I am not alone in having in the past fallen into its little trap and spelt it as 'Sehr Komisch' ('Very Funny'). Here, it's Moebius and Roedelius who dictate the sombre, measured pace. It's all backdrop, a vast yet somehow compact tableau of infinite drones and sparing but telling droplets of keyboard into the dark pools of the near-starless cosmos. Somewhere in the background, a chugging rhythm labours at low wattage, deliberately subordinate in the mix, putting human activity in its place in the universe. 'Sehr Kosmisch' slowly hoves into view and still more slowly fades out, gigantic and stately in its process. 'Ohrwurm' ('Earworm') is a slight return for the Cluster duo to their world of unfettered, adulterated sound, albeit with its abrasive edges planed away as they continue to learn their craft.

However, as 'Sonnenschein' ('Sunshine'), with its exuberant, asymmetrical pulse, further attests, this is no longer the noisenik Cluster of old – here, with Rother as their youthful guide, they are finding their way around the world of warm pop tones, tape loops and inventive rhythms, experiencing new kinds of joy. 'Dino' is Neu!-style *motorik*, admiringly shadowed by Moebius and Roedelius.

'Ahoi', in its deceptively simple and limpid piano and guitar phrases, prefigures Eno's ambient period, dying away and then resurging, shiny and anew, like a leaf immortalised in silver. Small wonder that Eno, fresh out of Roxy Music, would claim that Harmonia were 'the most important band in the world'. Here was a group who had already alighted on a prototype version of the strategies he would develop into his own. 'That's very exaggerated!' laughs Moebius, at what he regards as Eno's extravagantly generous praise.

Maybe Eno was not exaggerating. 'Veterano' and 'Hausmusik' are perfect, notional pop miniatures, the latter a speculative, charcoal piano sketch overlaid by a swell of raw electronics. It's entirely coincidence that a genre, house music, did indeed come to be born some fifteen years after this release, bearing no relation to this track – yet it illustrates how Harmonia were envisaging multiple, imaginary pathways for new music.

In the actual world, Harmonia's importance was lost on the pop-loving populace. They were lucky to muster audiences of fifty people, even in a hip vortex like Amsterdam's Paradiso club. As Michael Rother recalls, 'It was nothing less than a complete commercial disaster in the 1970s. I remember driving three hundred kilometres to a discotheque and playing to three people. The record sales were terrible. It made me so happy, thirty-five, forty years later to see it become accepted. Because I always believed in Harmonia as much as I did Neu!. I can't imagine how my development would have been without having lived and played with Harmonia.'

And yet, as the album *Live 1974*, eventually released in 2007, shows, those who were lucky and indeed compos mentis enough to experience Harmonia live were witness to a music decades ahead of its time, spontaneously created before their very eyes. The concert took place at Penny Station in Griessem and acts as a close companion to the debut album, containing all-new, improvised material.

Michael Rother has special reason to recall the gig. 'I remember it very clearly,' he tells me. 'I met the girl who would be my partner for the next twenty-five years that night. We had played with Kraftwerk there earlier. We were sure that was one of the best ever Harmonia concerts. It was a converted railway station, the venue, with maybe just thirty or fifty people attending and mainly talking all the way through. We were a bit shy at the time – it was quite early in the Harmonia career. We played very improvised music – the idea was that one of us would start with an idea, some percussion, a piano pattern, and the rest would join in. We would fade out tracks but sometimes the fadeouts are longer than the tracks – because we didn't know how to bring things to a stop. You hear the people talking more loudly during these fadeouts.

'But we all agreed that that was a great concert, which is why we didn't erase it. The kind of tape we used, Revox tape with the big reels, was incredibly expensive, so we had to erase over it mostly – but not this one. I kept it, it was always on my shelf and at the back of my mind – I was totally happy to see that that document was finally made available. It got some wonderful reviews.'

'Document' is the word. With its strange, premature fadeouts, as described by Rother, and the slightly fuzzy tones of the lo-fi, tape-recorded sound intermingling with the desultory chat of audience members, on *Live 1974* you get a vivid sense of both the intimacy between players and audience and also an element of befuddlement, as Harmonia feel their way through these pieces. It's superb, however, a Krautrock relic of genuine value. 'Schaumburg' ticks and tocks remorselessly as Rother's guitar scratches and surfs over the keyboards; the speedboat celerity of 'Veteranissimo' is like tracking back from an overhead ocean shot to see the group get smaller and smaller as the sea gets bigger and bigger, to the point where they're a dancing black speck. Best of all is 'Holta Polta', whose title is an onomatopoeic reference to the track's chuckling rhythm but which is dominated by a recurring, bassy twang whose closest relative in the world of sound is the clonking noise made by the swinging doors of the dining room in Jacques Tati's *Monsieur Hulot's Holiday*.

Harmonia would record a further album, *Deluxe*, released in 1975. However, by comparison with the first album it feels just a little too light, lacking the gravitational pull of Moebius and Roedelius's influence; they feel like guests on what is more of a Michael Rother album – a fine one, for sure, but as Moebius today admits, the hearts of the Cluster duo were in it less and less. 'Of course, Harmonia was an attempt to be commercial but in the end, Achim [Roedelius] and I weren't very happy with it. The first Harmonia album has a lot of the feel of Cluster the way we play it, but the second is more Michael Rother . . . and so we stopped with that and went back to Cluster – we were happy not to rehearse any more.'

'It could be really beautiful,' recalls Rother of Harmonia. 'If we look back at the development of Harmonia between 1973 and summer 1976, we improvised entirely, without structure. At the time Roedelius and Moebius weren't so interested in my idea of having more structure – because we had these great problems when we played live. Later, we changed hats – Roedelius nowadays is more into the 1975 stuff, not the earlier, 1974 stuff.'

Anyone following the Cluster discography album by album would be confused by *Zuckerzeit* ('Sugar Time'), their third LP, and the apparent quantum leap it represents from noise to avant-pop, but it makes perfect sequential sense, given that it was recorded in the immediate aftermath of *Musik von Harmonia*, in early 1974, as Michael Rother returned to resume his contractual obligations with Neu!. Rother is credited as co-producer but his contribution was simply to leave behind his stash of Farfisa instruments, four-track and stereo master machine. Moebius and Roedelius enjoyed playing with the Elka drum machine, seeing what strange rhythmic hybrids you could get if you mixed up the presets, pushing the tango and cha-cha buttons at the same time.

Without the tidal force of Rother's playing towing them in a melodic direction towards pop shores, Moebius and Roedelius experiment freely, rolling out track by track small, metal, mobile models for an imminent electropop future. Each track is a solo composition – the pair were developing separate lives, united by an artistic understanding but not joined at the hip. For this album, they recorded in separate rooms on different days. This gives some sense of the differing characters of the duo, Roedelius with his propensity towards miniaturist lyricism and the odd oriental flourish, Moebius fonder of metallic abstractions. So 'James', by Moebius, is a grinding, Meccano-assembled, robotic parody of the blues, while 'Marzipan', by Roedelius, is all glowing curlicues, chirruping with avian beauty. Both, however, are meta-metallic versions of 'real' pop, gleaming, homemade paradigms, imaginary, alternative takes on the real, big, neon-lit thing, throbbing banally away in the big cities.

There are hints also of Eno's forthcoming *Another Green World*, in the shantyish gait of tracks like 'Hollywood' or the woodblock-like drum-machine effects of 'Rosa'. Eno made no secret of how impressed he was by the Cluster axis. Like Michael Rother, he admired their ethos, the way they situated themselves physically quite outside the music business, their self-sufficiency. He liked the way that they seemed to live as they worked, the pace and values of life at Forst. He first met them in 1974, having lauded *Musik von Harmonia*. When he eventually came to stay at their commune, he joined them in going to the forests to collect wood, babysitting, cooking, eating, talking together, from which the music, when they repaired to another room to prepare it, arose as naturally as smoke from a fire.

Cluster were a palpable influence on Eno. He reciprocated by raising the profile of the pair by association with him when they subsequently worked together, and also helped to tighten up their material. For such a cerebral artist, one of Eno's greatest strengths has always been his uncanny, untutored and unerring sense of what simply works, of where and when to place the notes. He also knew, both instinctively and strategically, where to place himself in relation to what was essentially going on, as opposed to what was fashionable or what hirsute rock god was currently being trumpeted by the music press. He identified the Dingerbeat as one of the vital motors of the seventies – and now, when he heard that Cluster were playing in Hamburg at the Fabrik, he placed himself at the front of the crowd and joined them onstage for a jam session. 'There were a lot of guitars, organs, machines, it was easy for him to interfere,' recalled Roedelius of the occasion. A musical conversation was struck up there and then.

'After Roxy Music he was searching for a new way, and in Germany he found something,' says Moebius. 'But we learned from him too – I was always a fan of Roxy Music, also David Bowie from that era, before that the monotones of the Velvet Underground, many others, so many. I'm sure we learned things from Brian as well, and when we worked together on *Before and After Science* in 1977.'

Brian Peter George St John le Baptiste de la Salle Eno was born in Woodbridge, Sussex, in 1948, and sent to a Catholic school from which he decamped at sixteen to study art at Ipswich Art School. From then on, his eventual involvement in rock music had far more in common with his overseas German contemporaries than the English. Sure, a number of English rockers had gone to art school, but this was more out of an attraction to the bohemian lifestyle and laxity of the institutions, rather than any avant-garde impulse towards new forms and methods. Exposure to art school didn't stop John Lennon from famously sneering that 'avant-garde' was the French for 'bullshit'.

For Eno, it was quite different. He had gone to art school not merely to smoke pot but also with ideas of becoming a painter, taking an active role in the plastic arts. He was fortunate to come under the tutelage of Roy Ascott, an enthusiast, as Eno later would be, for cybernetics who, through a series of exercises, encouraged his pupils to expunge from their minds the idea of the artist as someone who sat in front of an easel with a beret dabbing into a palette of watercolours and staring at fruit bowls. He also introduced Eno to John Cage, the key twentieth-century bridge-builder between contemporary music and the visual arts. Developing an interest in sound machinery and recording techniques, Eno came to realise that sound could be a medium for artistic strategy.

Eno had no plans to join a rock band until persuaded to do so by his friend Andy MacKay, saxophonist with Roxy Music. Eno agreed, but his role within the group would mirror that of the great young German practitioners, who approached rock from an arts background, aware of a twentieth-century academic tradition that was, in formal terms at least, far more radical than rock 'n' roll. He was into sound manipulation, and his original role in Roxy Music was to lurk at the back of the stage behind wood-panelled banks of recording equipment, twiddling knobs, processing their output. In 1971, this sort of thing was a given in, say, the Wümme studios of Faust, where each group member had the means to distort and mess with their colleagues' instrumental work via their 'black boxes' as they played. This was their modus operandi. For a guitarist like Phil Manzanera, however, it was quite a new and fazing experience to crash out a chord on his guitar and then for a ten-second delay to follow before it emerged from the speakers.

Roxy Music, founded and led by Bryan Ferry, were certainly no slouches in the novelty stakes. To look at them, it was as if there had been no Elvis, no Beatles, that these were the late 1940s and that they were proponents of an altogether new form of popular music, arisen from the greased-back, stylish loucheness of the times. They felt like an imaginary throwback, but the supersonic element provided by Eno and his EMS VCS3 synthesizer was like a zap from the future.

This was exacerbated as Eno threw himself into the visual aspect of his role with an outrageous flamboyance that outdid any of his glam peers. Sweet had nothing on him. He was more Bowie than Bowie. Pouting and apparently scornful of rock 'n' roll norms and their required craftsmanship, he described himself as a non-musician, yet there he was, shamelessly flaunting himself onstage, on TV, while more obscure but honest toilers worked their chops in guitar shops. He was as much a provocation as was the spangly, aggressively effeminate Adrian Street in the world of British wrestling. He wore giant feathers and apricot lipstick, and as his hands coursed across the synthesizer keyboard, they were clad in spangly silver gloves. The man who would later make *Discreet Music* had no intention of shying away onstage or of not making a show of his role within the group – instead he would cut through the leopard-print fabric of Ferry's suave pop stylings with laser electronic interventions, most dazzlingly on 'Virginia Plain' and 'Ladytron'. Indeed, Roxy Music could be said to have been one of the first major groups to be influenced, whether they quite knew it or not, by Krautrock, as by the time of *For Your Pleasure* Eno had fully absorbed the rhythms and methods of groups like Can and was using his technical wherewithal in the studio to bend the Roxy sound accordingly.

Trouble was, he was beginning to overshadow Bryan Ferry, who was in danger of playing straight man to Eno's star turn. Offstage, too, Eno cut quite a dash. He was a bright and garrulous interviewee, and, despite his elfin, almost startlingly androgynous appearance, he was, to use the old parlance, a rampant and prolific cocksman on a scale that bore comparison with the likes of Kiss's Gene Simmons.

Eventually, all of this began to rankle with Ferry. This was his group. Finally, in a demonstration of alpha-male dominance, he shot up from behind his keyboards and took centre stage at the mike, hurling shapes as if to show one particular member of the backline who was top dog. Tensions rose, but it was Eno who backed down. It wasn't just Ferry he was up against but the orthodoxy of the British pop and rock establishment, who in 1972 simply weren't ready for the sort of foreign-derived reconfigurations Eno might have had in mind, certainly not at *Top of the Pops* level. Eno quit the group, famously dancing down the King's Road with relief as he did so. Roxy continued their career, producing a series of immaculate singles and albums, well tailored but always tailored for popular, if discerning appeal.

Eno found himself in a quandary, post-Roxy. He remained frantically busy, working with artists like John Cale, Robert Wyatt and Peter Schmidt, with whom he conceived the Oblique Strategies oracle-card series, another John Cage-inspired, aleatoric practice in which musicians struck by a creative block could pick a card and follow one of its aphorisms ('repetition is a form of change'). He recorded *No Pussyfooting* with Robert Fripp, providing an undulating bed of drones over which Fripp's guitar journeyed and cascaded, the overall effect similar to that of Ash Ra Tempel across the water. He would go on to found the Obscure label, which ushered infield British artists such as David Toop, the Penguin Cafe Orchestra, Michael Nyman and Gavin Bryars, who would now find themselves as outlying reference points in the rock-music press. I, for one, only became aware of these musicians thanks to their single degree of separation from Eno. He would introduce the concept of ambient music, which, despite its lush, romantic sunset evocations, was a systems music, practically mathematical.

There's little doubt that Cluster's ideas helped crystallise Eno's own. It helped that they had arrived at their present pass from a different cultural route and historical background. Eno was not driven to make music by the pains, identity crises and upheavals that resulted from wartime. That aspect of his upbringing was comfortable and settled. Sheer innate curiosity drove him – but not the same burning imperative for untrammelled self-expression that drove the Krautrock generation. They were unlikely to find creative satisfaction in a music, as Eno did, that could be reduced to a diagram on the back of an LP sleeve. They met from opposite sides.

Their first album released together was 1977's magnificent *Cluster & Eno*, but prior to that came *Tracks and Traces*, a September 1976 collaboration between Eno, Roedelius, Moebius and Michael Rother (who had returned to Forst following the demise of Neu!), which was not itself released until 1997. It's quite extraordinary that these recordings were considered by all concerned to be essentially recreational at the time, not worthy of release – but then, all of these artists were busy enough: Cluster with *Sowieso*, their follow-up to *Zuckerzeit*, recorded in just two days after these sessions; Rother about to embark on his solo career; and Eno with his fingers in as many pies as ever. That *Tracks and Traces* was considered surplus at the time just shows what a staggeringly fecund time the late seventies were for this particular axis.

The thrashing, serpentine rhythm and bass of 'Vamos Compañeros' suggest at once the Eno influence, a foreshadowing of the sort of itchy 'Fourth World' funk he'd develop in tandem with the likes of Jon Hassell and David Byrne. 'By the Riverside' is an electric watercolour sketch of the Forst location, its arresting simplicity a deceptively challenging proposition, especially in the mid-1970s, when mainstream rock fans confronted with this sort of work scratched their heads at its supposed inactivity and lack of meaty substance. It's a paradox – music so unassuming it seems intended to evaporate thirty seconds after listening, but which has endured the ages while so much Anglo-American music of its era lies mouldering in the attics of irrelevance.

'Lüneberg Heath' is again Eno-driven, given compositional focus by the fixed geographical point of its album title, a nature reserve in Lower Saxony. 'Don't get lost on Lüneberg Heath,' Eno intones, but the fog of blurry guitar and keyboards issued by the Harmonia members feels like an invitation to do so – to envelop yourself in the new German Other.

'Sometimes in Autumn' prefigures some of Eno's longer-form works like *Thursday Afternoon* – the ambient broth stirred here, with its fifty sublime shades of grey, would sustain all the chefs involved, as a collective experience of making music derived from the season and place in which it was made, as well as allowing a piece simply to breathe and be in its own time. Commonplace today, such musical exercise was audaciously minimal and rare in 1976. 'Weird Dream' again sees Eno knitting together the texture and material naturally unfurled by his German compadres, giving figurative shape to what might otherwise have been pure abstract expression. The almost drunkenly sprightly 'Les Demoiselles' could be a reference to Picasso's *Les Demoiselles d'Avignon*, the cubist painting which effectively inaugurated non-figurative modern art. Cluster and Eno are unassumingly revolutionary themselves, quietly helping establish a new pop which is not blues or verse and chorus-based but more of a sketchbook, in which ideas are visualised in line and colour. The very titles of 'When Shade Was Born' and 'Trace', sub-two-minute morceaux added as afterthoughts, seem to affirm that *Tracks and Traces* is music about the very idea of making music, albeit made in the most relaxed, communal and natural of surroundings.

Tracks and Traces, as retrospectively titled, was self-produced. For the album *Cluster & Eno*, however, released on the Sky label, the trio, minus Rother, decamped to Conny Plank's studio. His touch is immediately evident in the spatial depth and as-if-recorded-an-hour-ago clarity of opener 'Ho Renomo'; in fact, so immaculate is his treatment that you almost have to squint to attend to the deceptive oddities of the track – Roedelius's tinkling piano runs, like water pouring endlessly from a jug, the lagging, flangey effects hovering incongruously in the background, the looped, insistent bass motif supplied by Can's Holger Czukay refusing to be dismissed from the grand chamber of activity despite its lowly status in the sound scheme.

With 'Steinsame', the decades collapse as if viewing high-resolution early colour photography, as you refuse to believe this music is almost forty years old. 'Wehrmut' alludes to a coinage by Wittgenstein in which he intoxicatingly combines *Wermut* (Vermouth) with *Wehmut* (melancholy). With its solemn plumes of electronic smoke winging off one by one at strange tangents, is another case of 'less is more beautiful', though by now you begin to wonder if Eno's immaculate, romantic, systemic sense of where everything should best be placed is achieved at the expense of trammelling the wilder aspects of Cluster's spontaneous, untutored nature. But then, as 'Mit Simaen', a solo piece by Roedelius, suggests, the senior member of Cluster himself was gravitating towards a restrained classical style, simple evocations of nature in its undisturbed, continuing stillness. This is in keeping with the album's sleeve, in which a microphone is held up to a backdrop of skies and passing clouds.

The Catholic Roedelius's embrace of such relatively straightforward fare recalls the similarly devout Hugo Ball, early leader of the Dadaists, who later abandoned the movement, stating that he could never bid chaos welcome. Further collaborations with Eno on the track 'By This River' on *Before and After Science* and the

1978 album *After the Heat* suggested that Cluster were content to stand at Eno's shoulder, casting shadows of Germanic gravitas over his undertakings, that their noisenik days were a folly of the dead, forgotten past.

It would be more complex than that, however. Roedelius may describe himself and his junior compadre as 'like two old chaps who communicate better through sounds than words', but despite their benign appearance and natures they have continued to record prolifically, well into middle age and beyond, with an energy that suggests no surrender to the lukewarm spas of mediocrity. Since 1978, Roedelius has released over fifty further albums, taking in a range of styles from neu-Krautrock noise to horticultural electronic chamber music, to high BPM funk, to exercises in orientalism and looped atmospherics, a sustained level of activity that has kept pace with each new wave of curiosity about seventies German music. Moebius has been busy too, with or without Roedelius, making music that, as he says, 'comes from the stomach and not from the brain. When I am in my own small studio in Berlin with my eight-track, it's the same way. The first take is the last.' With no great frantic effort on their part to make a big push, they have acquired an international following. As Moebius muses, 'It's funny. Over the years, Achim [Roedelius] and me lived in Munich, Hamburg, Cologne, Düsseldorf – yet we are still even nowadays better known in the UK, France, Japan, USA than in Germany.'

9 Popol Vuh and Herzog

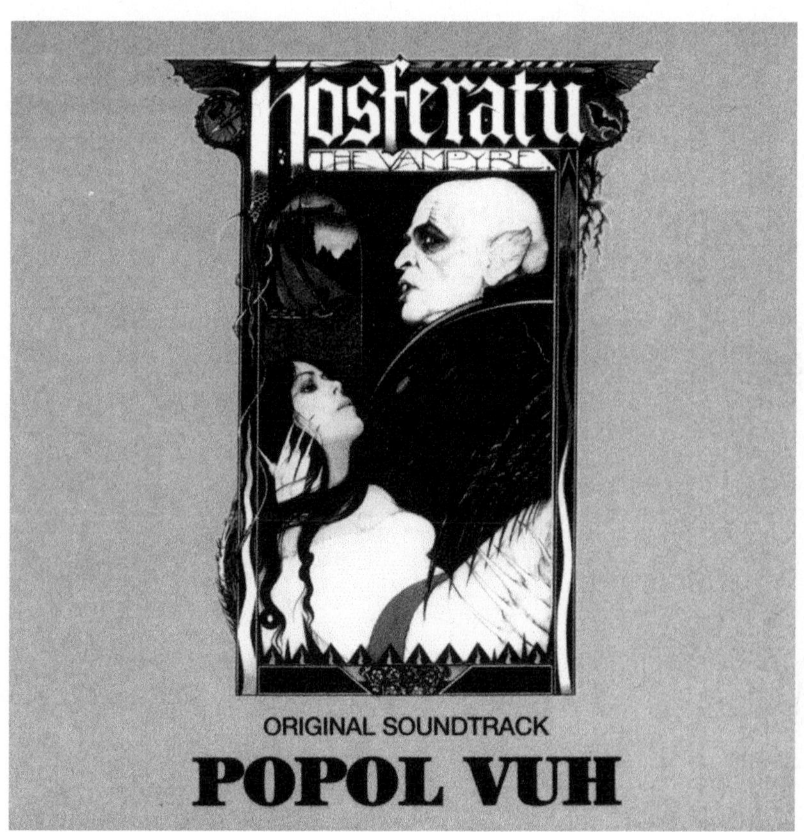

Formed in 1969, and with their leader Florian Fricke having managed to obtain a Moog synthesizer long before such instruments were available to his peers, Popol Vuh are understandably considered to be foundational to the Krautrock phenomenon. Fricke's credentials were impeccable. Born in the Bavarian island town of Lindau in 1944, he was introduced to the piano as a child. 'I began to make music when I was eleven,' he told Sandy Robertson of UK magazine *Sounds* in 1981. 'Classical piano. I went to a special high school for music when I was fifteen, though people usually go there when they're twenty or so. But my father convinced the authorities of the school that I was ready.' He continued his studies at Freiburg and later Munich, airily claiming his life's work to be in the tradition of Mozart and early polyphonic music. Among his tutors was the brother of the great twentieth-century composer Paul Hindemith. He would discover free jazz – throughout his life he would claim a spiritual kinship with John Coltrane's contemporary Pharoah Sanders. He would also briefly hook up with Manfred Eicher, who later founded the ECM label, in a jazz-fusion combo. His head was further turned from his studies by his interest in film, which was producing a radical new crop of auteurs – Krautfilm, so to speak, though no one ever had the poor taste to coin such a phrase. One of his first paying jobs was as a film critic for *Der Spiegel*, among others. He was also, inevitably, touched by the insurrectionary spirit of the era, but it was one aspect of that time in particular that affected him, as radical young Germans turned against their economic benefactors the Americans, revealed as imperialists by their involvement in Vietnam. As he told his friend Gerhard Augustin, to whom he granted a rare interview in 1996, 'There was also a spiritual revolution. We have discovered the Eastern part of this globe.'

There was certainly an interest in Eastern culture among the more hirsute wing of 1960s German youth, for various reasons: as a riposte to the hegemony of the West, as an exotic alternative, for its cultures whose mantras and drones provided a perfect accompaniment to the ingestion of drugs, or simply to follow the path taken by the Beatles, much as so many young German people had done in the earlier part of the sixties and the beat-music era. Fricke, however, wanted to look further and go deeper. The epiphany he experienced when he came across the old Mayan book *Popol Vuh* ('Book of the Community', though the name was handpicked for the difficulty of translating it precisely) hit home 'like a thunderstorm', he said. If Krautrock was about beginning again, Fricke was resolved to cast back his mind to the very beginning of Creation, fired up by the beautiful founding myths of this lost South American people. He didn't fixate exclusively on the *Popol Vuh*, however – he found inspiration also in the Bible and the Bhagavad Gita, the 700-verse Hindu scripture in which Krishna imparts the doctrine of the path to devotion.

Fricke was one of those for whom religious belief is spiritual rather than dogmatic in nature, fed by the multiple revelations of God to ancient cultures across the globe but subscribing exclusively to none of them. 'A conscious reflection upon religious origin is included in this music, but not in particular to any religious groups,' he said of his 1972 album *Hosianna Mantra*, a 'musical mass' whose title clearly implies a fusion of Eastern and Western religious mores. His sometime producer Gerhard Augustin described him as 'a sincere, very religious person – but not so much a Christian believer – more a universal believer in different directions'.

There is no greater assistance to those seeking to dedicate themselves to the spiritual life than considerable family wealth. Fricke was fortunate in this respect, enabling him to buy the then ruinously expensive Moog synthesizer, valued at 800,000 Deutschmarks at the time. He was one of only two people who owned a Moog in Germany at the time – the other was the composer Eberhard Schoener, who introduced it to Fricke. It was a prized possession and he generously lent it out to fellow musicians whose adventures in sound left them impecunious and forced to create effects through the modification of cheap or second-hand instruments. These included Tangerine Dream in their earliest days – Fricke himself would play the Moog on *Zeit*, though on a personal level his disposition for soft drugs and hazy contemplation while recumbent on Persian carpets did not commend him to the abstemious and straight-edged Froese.

Fricke described such vices as 'minor excitement'; on record, he would cut a spiritually remote figure, relying on his fellow players to provide a necessary earthiness as a counterpoint to his explorations of the Moog, whose ability to pump out proto-sequencer-style bass drones, like a pair of bellows, made it suitable for his exploration of his 'inner consciousness', fired up with visions of the ancient Orient and ninth-century Mayan ritual. Not just his imagination, mind: Fricke had the wherewithal and opportunity to travel extensively and witness at first hand life in other parts of the globe – Africa, the Himalayas.

Popol Vuh's debut album, *Affenstunde*, which means something like 'Monkey Hour', was released in 1970. Its cover is, on the face of it, a quintessential hippie tableau. It sees Fricke, in sleeveless sheepskin top, attending to his Moog like a radio ham, as percussionist Holger Trülzsch sits swaddled in Afghan coating astride his drumskins, while Bettina Fricke, Florian's wife, who co-produced the album and designed the cover, attends to her tabla. However, as the three parts of 'Ich mache einen Spiegel' attest, these were sounds quite unlike anything else proceeding from the primitive circles of the early Krautrock communes. Beginning with a simulation of birdsong, we are immediately plunged, as if through a black hole, into the outer reaches of uncharted space. It's as if Fricke is still in the process of exploring the Moog and its possibilities, and in so doing channelling the frequencies of the cosmos, the continued, unreceived transmissions of the Big Bang, burbling back and forth in regular patterns from one end of the universe to the other. Even today, it sounds otherworldly, beguiling, perhaps precisely because of its 'datedness', its raw technological naïveté a rarity in today's world of ubiquitous, incidental electronic blare. A film student, Fricke would doubtless have recently seen Kubrick's *2001: A Space Odyssey*. He spoke of *Affenstunde* as looking to 'capture the moment when a human being becomes a human being and is no longer an ape'. There are reminders, as his Moog rears up from the mix, of the moment early on in the film in which the primates throw a bone in the air, only for a jump-cut to transform it into an orbiting spacecraft centuries hence.

The title track, featuring the clatter and pounding of Trülzsch's percussion fading in and out of the mix, also reflects this dichotomy of the primitive and technological advancement, suggestive of mankind's great evolutionary span but hinting at the dangers of becoming disconnected from a knowledge of the ancient past. It then gives way to an extended passage of drones, broken up with excitable flurries, faintly reminiscent of Terry Riley's *A Rainbow in Curved Air* but not so systematic. Indeed, if anything, Fricke, despite the discipline of his classical training, has a tendency to doodle superfluously at times.

Fricke was not oblivious to the fact that this music would have a somewhat druggy appeal, and was aware that it was listened to by potheads not necessarily embarking on a lengthy inner voyage to enlightenment. 'My music was especially geared to this clientele – I did not make music for classical-music lovers.' He might have seen this at first hand in live situations, but Fricke was, throughout his career, as shy as a badger when it came to playing concerts, venturing out only infrequently. His personal circumstances meant that there was no need to raise vital pfennigs by getting bums on seats, or in this instance, bums on floors, to boost his income stream.

For 1971's *In den Gärten Pharaos* ('In the Garden of Pharaohs'), Fricke and co. decamped to the Pilz label, set up that year by the notorious Krautrock entrepreneur Rolf-Ulrich Kaiser. It consisted of just two side-long tracks, with Fricke's Moog again to the fore, supplemented by organ and piano. The opening title track commences in similar vein to *Affenstunde* – the distant sounds of birdsong and the lapping waters of a simulated landscape supplanted by the dark, billowing tones of synth, throbbing ghoulishly from every corner of the mix, ascending, descending, probing and overlapping. Fricke has mastered his instrument, overcome some of its wobblier, patchier tendencies that were still entertainingly evident on the debut, while Trülzsch's percussion is now rhythmically plundered from African and Turkish traditions, doing battle with the starry lights and meteoric runs of the Moog. It's an absorbing soundclash, in which the ancient and future coexist once more and space and time are collapsed – even if it doesn't represent that significant an advance on the debut album. Theremin-style wails hove into earshot, before a concluding passage of melodic, orthodox electric-keyboard beauty emerges like a smile from the gods, in one of the most benignly joyful sections in all of Popol Vuh's canon.

'Vuh', by contrast, recorded in the ecclesiastic setting of a church, is immediately a sterner proposition, as Fricke strikes up on an organ from high in the rafters, amid the theatrical shimmer of cymbals. A series of downbeat keyboard phrases is repeated liturgically, joined by a simulated choir, as if to announce that this will be no easy ride and those here for pleasure alone might do well to get up and leave. The organ tones hang like a Gothic awning for several minutes with cathedral permanence, announcing themselves over and over rather than embarking on the narrative of a solo, as percussion breaks out in rebellion now and again at the admonishing air of the track, before relapsing. In some ways, it prefigures the likes of Sun O))), whose metal is formally arranged into a ritual almost for ritual's sake. 'Vuh' is a black mass of sorts, but containing no text, injunctions or dogma, merely structure and gravitas. 'A mass for your own heart' is how Fricke himself would describe it.

The additional tracks on the 2004 SPV reissue really enhance the album; had it been released in the CD age, with the increased time span of albums, they would surely have been included. 'Kha-White Structures – 1' feels in keeping with the Egyptological air of the album's title – here we are on flat, horizonless, sandy North African plains, dominated by the magisterial, piping trump of a wailing Moog. 'Kha-White Structures – 2' maintains a high-pitched electronic peal around which the Moog coils its oblique variations. For the less tolerant it will resemble an uninvestigated car alarm; for the hardier listener it is like the doors of sonic perception jammed wide open.

It was at this point, however, that Fricke made the decision to abandon his synthesizer altogether. He sold it on to Klaus Schulze, for whom the machine would become the centrepiece of his sonic arsenal as he voyaged solo through the 1970s. Fricke was quite honest about the decision. 'I'm a conservative artist,' he said. 'I'm not interested in just pressing buttons, so I went back to piano. Sometimes the power would vary so you couldn't always get the same sound on the synthesizer. It's too dependent on the machinery. It's nothing human. The piano is more direct. That's when I realised that I'd probably be happier if I lived my life with music that had acoustic instruments.' He added that he was uncomfortable about using synthesizers for music with Christian, religious connotations.

It's for this reason that Popol Vuh's first two albums are considered as separate from the rest of their canon. After that there is a cut-off point beyond which many do not proceed. They are no longer 'proper' Krautrock, for the purists. Electronics were *de rigueur* for new German music, a key tool in its process of self-reinvention and rejection of passéist, blues, verse-and-chorus-based forms.

And, in a sense, the purists have a point, precisely because of the purity to which Fricke aspired. It was more than a matter of Krautrock = electronics; it was the spirit in which they were used that mattered also. Early Krautrock was a matter of improvising and modifying what you had at your disposal – whether in the studio, via the ingenious wiles of Conny Plank, or by the way you treated your instruments, not only to wrest original, customised sounds from them but also to tear up the tracks and traditions of the old worlds of classical and rock.

Despite being one of the very first people in German music to make extensive use of the Moog, and, moreover, in sound settings which departed from previously known earthly norms, you sense that Fricke is working within the preset limits of his expensive instrument, rather than really testing its potential or attempting to modify it in any way. His playing of the Moog is 'pure' Moog, no filters, no add-ons as such. Given its expansive range as well as its price tag, that's understandable, but it does mean that for him, playing the synthesizer was merely a matter of 'pressing buttons' – he felt at the mercy of its whims, its volatility and unreliability, whereas with a piano, and the benefit of years of training, he knew precisely what to expect when his tutored fingers hit the keys. Klaus Schulze, the grateful recipient of his Moog, said that Fricke 'chose electronic music and his big Moog to free himself from the restraints of traditional music, but soon discovered that he didn't get a lot out of it and opted for the acoustic path instead. Here, he went on to create a new world, which Werner Herzog loves so much, transforming the thought patterns of electronic music into the language of acoustic ethno-music.'

For *Hosianna Mantra*, in 1972, there were wholesale changes. In came Conny Veit on electric and twelve-string guitar, Robert Eliscu on oboe, Klaus Wiese on tamboura and Fritz Sonnleitner on violin, while the Korean Djong Yun, daughter of a composer, took up vocals. Fricke himself played piano and harpsichord.

For Popol Vuh fans, *Hosianna Mantra* is Fricke's Everest, a masterpiece of quasi-religiosity in which East and West are straddled, as implied in the album's title. 'A high point in the history of music,' insisted writer and Vuh-head Gary Bearman in 2008. It's certainly strong in many respects, according to its own lights – you can see how and why Kate Bush was a fan of the album, what ideas it lit up in her. But for those more accustomed to the tactics of other seventies German music, it feels like a departure from the movement.

Opener 'Ah!', with its harpsichords and the bright planes of Veit's guitar, is impressive but a touch sepulchral. It seems to speak too much to the opulent, stately-home ornateness of the cover image. There's a promising moment when Fricke cuts loose and runs down the course, right to left, of the keyboard – but then he simply repeats the motion, before running up in reverse, from left to right over and over, just so. It's hardly the most formidable demonstration of his training, nor of the possibilities of the piano as a chamber instrument in a new, expanded form of rock music, certainly not compared to, say, Keith Tippett's jazz adventures on King Crimson's 'Cat Food'.

On 'Kyrie', Veit's guitars come fluting to the fore, exceptionally pretty and luminous, a little higher in the mix than Djong Yun's vocals, but for all the elaborateness of the arrangement, it's strikingly chaste, if certainly not anodyne. It's indisputably nice – it's possible there's never been anything nicer. But, as with the title track, in which Veit's guitars drip like nectarine, it's all a little bit too unspoiled and unspotted. Djong Yun's vocals are beautiful but could scarcely be less disconcerting, borne on the wings of a dove à la King's College choir. A part of you yearns for Conrad Schnitzler to come trundling up in a forklift truck and dump half a ton of rusty chunks of metal into the midst of it all.

There's a problem with the reassuring tonalities of *Hosianna Mantra* – it seems to require a sacrilegious intervention of some sort. Despite the promise in the title of an Eastern/Western coupling, and the ecumenical use of Jewish philosopher Martin Buber's text, there's no real spark of fusion, just a harmless melding that becomes increasingly settled, almost New Age, as the album progresses.

Fricke provides a sort of housing for religious-style or spiritual contemplation – what he calls the 'good rooms'. But if you are required to supply your own religious or spiritual belief, inevitably that leaves a gap if you happen to believe that there is no God to contemplate. Popol Vuh's music can ring hollow with the spurious promise that there is 'some sort of Force out there', which can only be bidden into our thoughts by providing a reverent and spacious receptacle in which it may reveal itself. Religious music is by no means always a problem for the atheist – Bach is a classic example. But then you have the ulterior pleasures of his tirelessly inventive improvisations, his unique, winding musical offering to the Almighty, a staircase to heaven. It provides its own internal force, rather than merely politely signposting the 'out there' one. Popol Vuh's music is highly formal, but as an exercise in formalism, it became increasingly lacking. It also raises the question: could music that declares itself in search of some nebulous, immaterial 'spirituality' often be the most superficial, while that which grapples with materiality and form may be among the most profound?

Fricke was joined by Danny Fichelscher and Renate Knaup, formerly of Amon Düül 2, for later incarnations of Popol Vuh, as he continued, throughout the late seventies, the eighties and beyond to pursue and refine a mode of popular music which took on board and showcased the best features of religious experience – ritual and rapture, but within the controlled setting of well-furnished, ecclesiastical-style arrangements that moved further and further from the group's roving, electronic origins. Ironically, by the nineties, in an effort to keep pace with the times, Fricke took on Guido Hieronymus as a collaborator, and Popol Vuh became a sequencer-driven proposition, as albums like *Shepherd's Symphony* attest, with the old, devotional aspects that had once made them so distinctive now only visible through a gauze of second-hand techno, mere tokenistic Gothic wails. Fricke himself passed away in December 2001, aged just fifty-seven, following a stroke.

All of this would suggest that Popol Vuh's link to the German musical revolution of the sixties and seventies was tenuous and diminished with each passing album. This would be to overlook, however, their most significant contribution, one which has lent them an undying cultural visibility not granted to most of their contemporaries – their soundtrack work for Werner Herzog, which was more than just jobbing day-work but a vital audio-visual collaboration.

Fricke first met Herzog in 1967, during his time as a film critic. He was impressed by his drive, his ability to achieve the improbable, as reflected in the themes and contents of films like *Fitzcarraldo*, and that he himself had been unaffected by his fame, testimony to his singlemindedness and strength of character. They seemed destined to meet – Herzog had further pricked Fricke's interest by using the text of the *Popol Vuh* as the basis for one of the chapters of his 1971 movie *Fata Morgana*, that strange journey across a landscape of documentary African footage which made for a 'Krautrock' experience on celluloid. A natural match, surely.

That they were, but it was a natural match of opposites. Popol Vuh's music is all about ascension to a higher, unsullied place, up into the light. Herzog's films, by contrast, are Conradian in their preoccupation with descent, into the darkness, into the terrible, wilful folly and squalor of the human soul. This was embodied in Klaus Kinski, the man Herzog described as his 'best fiend', an antichrist of sorts who with his unkempt shock of blond hair sometimes resembled Johnny Rotten and certainly more than matched his balefulness. Allegations that have come to light since his death only boost the grave suspicion that, regardless of his force as a screen icon, here was a debased and terrible man. Indeed, it's an uncomfortable possibility that a debased nature was one of the reasons for his onscreen force.

The descent is quite literal in two of the films soundtracked by Fricke and Popol Vuh – *Aguirre, the Wrath of God*, made in 1972, and *Fitzcarraldo*, in 1982. *Aguirre* is set in the sixteenth century, following the annihilation of the Incan empire. It follows the journey of a band of conquistadors, including Kinski as Don Lope de Aguirre, as they set out in search of the mythical El Dorado, the City of Gold, a myth invented by the native South Americans they subjugated. The journey is a hazardous and treacherous one, driven by delusion, greed and conceit, a doomed journey in search of a non-existent place. *Fitzcarraldo* is set in the middle of the jungle around the turn of the last century and tells the story of Brian Sweeney Fitzgerald's preposterous dream of staging an opera bringing together Sarah Bernhardt and Enrico Caruso. To raise the money for this venture, he must reach and exploit a vast area of rubber trees beyond the Ucayali Falls, hauling his steamboat over a mountain with the assistance of the Indian tribes, who are so mesmerised by the gramophone recordings of the great singers that they willingly put themselves at the white man's service.

Everything about these tales runs in precisely the opposite direction to the music of Popol Vuh. ('Too much the darkness,' Fricke once muttered of the travails and disasters that were part and parcel of the making of any Herzog movie.) Fricke's music aspires cleanly heavenward, whereas Fitzcarraldo and Aguirre are on a downward journey, down the slopes of the Andes, through churning mud and the difficult headwaters. Popol Vuh's music actively celebrates and pays homage to other cultures and their equal, relative value to Western Christianity. Aguirre is an imperialist conqueror of native peoples, Fitzcarraldo a man with no qualms about achieving wealth on the backs of the 'savages' he exploits, impressing on them the dominance of his own, 'higher' culture (opera) as he does so. Popol Vuh's music strives for spiritual fulfilment, beyond the bounds of earth; Aguirre and his conquistadors descend deep into its most hellish thickets in search of fool's gold.

Perhaps it's precisely because of its antithetical nature that Popol Vuh's music made for such an appropriate soundtrack to these films. It serves as a counterpoint, an ironic one. Herzog admiringly described as a 'choir-organ' the Mellotron-like device which dominated the soundtrack to *Aguirre*, containing dozens of individual vocal loops which could create an unearthly choral effect, as if the angels themselves were looking down on the proceedings of these dramas with great sadness. Or perhaps it is simply that the music solemnises, bestows a sort of church blessing to Herzog's own artful and arduous efforts to make these movies, his struggles matching those endured by the characters. Certainly, movie critics such as Roger Ebert were moved to remark on the mesmeric qualities of these soundtracks, which might well have been their single acquaintance with Popol Vuh or any German music of that era.

Still more effective was Popol Vuh's soundtrack for *Nosferatu the Vampyre*, released in 1979, in which Kinski this time invites a measure of pathos as a Dracula who keenly feels his loneliness, his lack of love and his exile from the human condition. It's here that the light and shade of Popol Vuh's music really come into their own. Fricke provides pretty, string-soaked background for the pastoral scenes, in the breakfast room for example. However, his high Gothic strains also enhance the more beguilingly terrifying passages of the film – the opening scene, filmed in the Mummies of Guanajuato museum, Mexico, in which the rotten, mummified remains of victims of an 1833 cholera epidemic are frozen forever in expressions of horror at their own mortality, teeth bared, eye sockets voided. Or the electric-blue sequences in which Nosferatu assumes the form of a bat as he makes his attacks, or that of a boat that carries a cargo of coffins downriver for transport to Wismar. As the camera wheels down on that boat, we see Nosferatu has killed the entire crew, the last of them dead and slumped over the ship's wheel to which he has lashed himself.

Each of these scenes is accompanied by a simple but devastating two-note choral leitmotif from Fricke which, once heard, is never forgotten, and which helps engrave the key images from Herzog's movie on the memory. (I recall a lonely walk home through the dark after I first saw the film, which soon broke into a brisk trot.) All of his powers seem to be summoned into this single, magnificently appalling phrase, pointing like a bony finger towards the horror. Although the Herzog soundtracks work admirably as standalone albums in their own right, it's as an enhancement to the difficult, morally mazy but deeply rewarding works of the great auteur of New German Cinema that Popol Vuh achieve their greatest purpose and impact on a wider audience. For those who find the late Fricke's musings on spirituality somewhat conceptually vapid, the marriage of his music and Herzog's content is one made in heaven.

10 astral Travelling: Rolf-Ulrich Kaiser, Ash Ra Tempel and the Cosmic Couriers

Recognising that the word 'Krautrock' is problematic, some resort to the *kosmische* tag. However, for many of the artists who had this hung around their neck, it is equally, if not more, irksome. It's problematic too for those of us who came to Krautrock from a post-punk perspective. 'Cosmic' is a word which resounds to some as if uttered with sardonic wanness by Rodney Trotter, the sceptical younger brother of Del Boy Trotter, who comes from a more sanguine and credulous generation. It has about it the mouldering air of garish, poorly designed album sleeves, the most far-out excesses of seventies escapism. It speaks of astral voyages away from the realities, responsibilities and necessary confrontations of this planet into a never-never lysergic outer zone, where you can float in supine, semi-comatose bliss. It has the air of fraudulence – Tarot cards, magick and quasi-astrological faith in a benign universe in whose recesses are hidden pots of gold just for you, a collection of half-beliefs sometimes bundled neatly in the phrase 'hippie bullshit'. If that's the case, then it's appropriate that the Cosmician-in-Chief was tireless entrepreneur, wordsmith and chancer, in the best and worst senses of the word, Rolf-Ulrich Kaiser.

Kaiser was the founder of the Ohr label and, with the ample assistance of his partner Gille Lettmann, composed the 'Cosmic Music' manifesto, printed in *Eurock* magazine in 1975, which ran under the banner 'Discover the Galaxy Sound of Cosmic Music'. It was intended as a gateway for a new European and American audience for Ohr and its constellation of acts, who included not just the Tarot Band, Wallenstein and Mythos but also Klaus

Schulze, Ash Ra Tempel and Popol Vuh. Before mentioning the roster, however, it began with a clarion call.

> 'Skylab calling Terra. We are living in the new age. TV broadcasts from space. Live. The Saturn Rocket is under way . . . somewhere, far from our earth, the astronauts climb from their spaceship into the galaxy.'

As the paragraphs unfurl, our mind's eye is guided from the 'small blue pea' of our own planet out into the visible universe and its distant galaxies. 'Do other beings live there? Do space vessels chase about at the speed of light?' It then quotes a message from an American scientist who claims to have received a missive from the planet Hoova, of ancient legends from India telling of intergalactic voyagers, before we swing back towards our own solar system, piloted by 'Sternenmädchen' ('Star Maiden') Gille Lettman, who liaises with magicians and zips back and forth across time conferring with Leonardo da Vinci, Beethoven ('everything he can teach you is pure magic') and scientist Wernher von Braun, whose involvement in the creation of the V2 rocket was overlooked by the Americans when they realised his usefulness to their own future rocket-ship ambitions – his role in the space race made him a source of ambivalent pride to some Germans as a true father of the cosmos.

Finally, the roster of artists Kaiser is proud to parade as playing 'Cosmic Music' is announced. 'They tell thrilling stories and sing stellar melodies and dip into the fantastic landscape of Science Fiction.' The more prominent of the artists listed would have protested that they did nothing of the kind, but notwithstanding such objections, the prose sails obliviously on. 'Cosmic Music. Stored in our newly discovered musical frequencies. Transported by electrons, hovering in the flashing of light, in the magic of colours, in the sounds of electrons.'

This isn't quite of the same order as Sun Ra's cosmological/ Egyptological utterances, in which he proclaimed himself to have originated from the planet Saturn, or even Stockhausen's own mental excursions to Sirius, with both these artists appearing to be genuinely in the grip of their creatively fertile delusions. This is the stuff of perhaps Krautrock's most remarkable entrepreneur – visionary, idealist, dreamer and thinker, slippery salesman of cosmic snake oil, ultimately a fallen star.

Rolf-Ulrich Kaiser was born in 1943, in Buckow, near Berlin, later moving to Cologne, where he studied German language and literature, philosophy, sociology and dramatic theory, all of which would feed into his life as a theorist and practical enabler of sixties and seventies German music. He first got a taste for the festival scene in 1964, when he attended the inaugural Festival Chanson Folklore International at Waldeck Castle in south-western Germany, at which an emerging generation, inspired by the folk-protest movement in the USA, were shedding their understandable self-consciousness about singing in the German folk medium and taking up their guitars to write non-Teutonic Deutschvolk songs with a countercultural, anti-Nazi bent.

Four years later, in 1968, it was Kaiser who raised a guarantee of 300,000 marks from the city of Essen to start the international Essener Songtage festival, which, showing a flair for hyperbole, he heralded as 'the biggest thing that ever happened in Europe'. It was certainly the biggest thing that had happened in the rock scene in West Germany up to that date.

'When Kaiser got interested in this new music, or new pop music, whatever you want to call it, he came very much via content and not via music – literature, basically,' says journalist Diedrich Diederichsen. 'So he liked groups like the Fugs, because that was very poetry-based, and from the Fugs he came to the Mothers of Invention. The ideal of the Essener Songtage refers to the kind of singer/songwriter movement that was German in the early sixties, which had nothing to do with rock 'n' roll. It was based on protest songs, which had German traditions and European traditions, but also the American folk-song tradition. But it had never had a moment equivalent to Bob Dylan going electric at the Newport Festival in 1965. Before Essener, music like the Beatles, the Rolling Stones and Cream were seen by the folk-protest people as music for young people, from the charts – only after Essener did these worlds come together.'

Among the artists who performed were Peter Brötzmann, Tangerine Dream, Guru Guru, the City Preachers, Floh de Cologne and an utterly stoned Amon Düül, who all but had to have a shepherd's crook appear from the wings to drag them offstage as they riffed in perpetuity on the same loop. Meanwhile, overseas acts like Julie Driscoll, Brian Auger and the Trinity and Alexis Korner were persuaded to play, alongside Frank Zappa and the Mothers of Invention. Although Zappa's arrival in West Germany was an acknowledged, pivotal event in the development of the emerging rock scene, he himself did not always see eye to eye with the German frontline of countercultural activists, many of whom were sceptical about rock music's role as a medium for social change rather than a hedonistic distraction. At one point, Zappa was overheard to complain, 'Apparently the audience can't decide whether they want to discuss music or listen to music.'

'On the same tour as Essen, the Mothers also played in Berlin at the height of the student demonstrations,' recalls Diederichsen. 'They were attacked for being too politically undecided. Someone destroyed their PA by pouring hummus into their speakers. Some activists stormed the stage, asked him some things, and he was not prepared to show solidarity with them. They expected more after songs like "Trouble Every Day" [from the Mothers of Invention's debut album *Freak Out*, their most earnest, least satirical protest song]. It shows how the political and other countercultural movements were very separated in Germany in 1968.'

Despite its historical importance, and Kaiser's own, extravagant self-praise for the festival which, he had claimed, had 'opened up new ways of experience' for the German people, the first Essener was marred by Kaiser's inexperience, new as he was to the ways of organising a major outdoor event. He made a hash of negotiating the broadcasting rights, resulting in eventual losses of 80,000 marks. Nonetheless, he was emboldened by the enterprise and turned his attention to other media, including books, radio and TV. Although buzzing with the idealism of his day, he was also conscious of the issue of profit and loss and the fact that rock music was a commodity as well as an agency of change. By today's standards he would be considered something of a painful freak for even agonising over this issue. He openly excoriated himself for criticising the rock music 'that ended up being pure profit music; and I identify myself exposedly with a part of this rock music'.

There were others, however, including Nikel Pallat, manager of hard-leftist polemical rockers Ton Steine Scherben, who regarded Kaiser as a typical have-it-both-ways liberal bullshitter. This schism came to a head in a televised debate involving the pair on a WDR talkshow in 1971, whose discussion went under the heading '*Pop & Co – Die "andere" Musik zwischen Protest und Markt*' ('Pop & Co. – The "Other" Music between Protest and Marketplace'), which can be viewed on YouTube. Its period quaintness lies not just in the length of the hair of the participants, the studio smoking or the orangeness of Kaiser's jumper, which merely to look at is to overdose on Vitamin C. It's in the admirably earnest accommodation of those discussing the feasibility and possibility of the overthrow of capitalism through rock music. As Kaiser seeks to dampen this far-left yearning, the debate begins to heat up. Translated, the action runs as follows.

'Societal change will come in an evolutionary process,' says Kaiser. 'That isn't something that'll happen tomorrow, but a development that will take probably a hundred years.' He points out that immediate change was the illusion of the people who marched in the 1960s, important though these protests were.

Pallat angrily dismisses this Fabian talk of slow, evolutionary progress, suggesting that it amounts to support for continued oppression. 'You are working for the oppressor, not against the oppressor. Do you realise that?'

Kaiser defends himself, saying that one has to understand how the media work. 'Who are you working for?' retorts Pallat, sharply. 'You cannot dispute that you are working for the capitalist.'

'Who do you represent here?' comes back Kaiser, with equal sharpness. 'Don't you think the TV isn't also a capitalist organ?' (Here the moderator intervenes to point out that Kaiser isn't speaking on behalf of TV.)

It's all too much for Pallat. 'Here we have TV making this shit-liberal programme we're having an opportunity to go on about anti-materialism – socialism . . . we shouldn't speak about evolution but revolution, yeah? And objectively nothing is changing about oppression. TV is a tool of oppression by general society. And that's why it is completely obvious that if something should still happen, then one has to stand against the oppressor and not be neutral . . . and that's why I am going to destroy this table now.'

Whereupon, true to his word, he produces from his inside jacket pocket an axe and, snarling and swearing, commences to bash the table as the rest of the panellists edge away in consternation. It is not so much the table towards which he bears a grudge but its symbolic role as polite vortex of sedentary, liberal consensus. Once he has completed his attempted assault on the offending piece of furniture, which proves remarkably resistant to his ferocious efforts, he says, 'So, let's continue our discussion.' No one else, however, is inclined to do so. Taking full advantage of the freedom temporarily afforded him by his axe to do as he pleases, he gathers up the microphones abandoned on what's left of the table and stuffs them into his pockets, announcing that he is commandeering them for the oppressed. 'I need the microphones for the young people who are sitting in jail.' The resilience of the table is a metaphor of sorts for the resilience of a certain leftist strain of German tolerance and liberality at that time, whose broadmindedness and reasonableness was capable of withstanding even axe attack.

The very fact that Pallat had an axe about his person in the studio suggests to the cynical an element of premeditation to his outburst. Nonetheless, as insurrectionary television goes, it rather puts the Sex Pistols and Bill Grundy in the shade. Alongside Can and Faust, Einstürzende Neubauten's Blixa Bargeld also listed Ton Steine Scherben as one of the seventies German groups he most admired. On the strength of this performance, it's not hard to see why. It shows also the depth of feeling and revolutionary commitment that had seized the hearts and minds of the more radical young Germans, as well as Kaiser's ability to put people's backs up.

Kaiser said of Ohr, 'In 1970 there were no German record companies interested in German music. We showed the German people that they can trust their own music.' This was not quite true – Germany's major labels moved with surprising alacrity to hoover up groups like Can, Cluster, Kraftwerk and even Faust. However, Kaiser recognised that there was another wave, or tier, of new German groups, divergent in nature but all of whom had the potential to become meaningful propositions and commercial successes.

Kaiser joined forces with one Peter Meisel, who in 1962 had founded Hansa Music Production and had specialised in straightforward Schlager fare. However, he was conscious of the dawning of a new era and had also signed up groups like Tangerine Dream and Xhol Caravan, though somewhat blindly. Meisel knew the music business but not the new music – the altogether hipper Kaiser was the ideal business partner. They set up in business in Berlin, produced a logo of a colourised human ear and the slogan *Macht das Ohr auf* ('Open Up Your Ears'), a clever parody of the despised tabloid *Bild*'s slogan *Macht das Tor auf*, which referred to the Brandenburg Gate, the majestic and inadvertent centrepiece of the Berlin Wall. A slew of albums followed, including Guru Guru's *UFO* and Tangerine Dream's *Electronic Meditation*, which marked the beginning of two great musical journeys – as well as Limbus 4's *Mandalas*, which more or less marked the end of theirs. There were releases too by Embryo and Floh de Cologne, and *Lieder von Vampiren, Nonnen und Toten* by Bernd Witthüser, later of Witthüser and Westrupp. Understandably, there was no sense as yet of a label aesthetic – to an extent, this was a throw of various dice, cast in the hope that at least one or two might land six-side up.

It helped that Kaiser was able to acquire the services of Dieter Dierks, who would go on to help launch the career of the Scorpions but in 1970, like Conny Plank, had a reputation for being able to extract the maximum possible effect from the latest studio technology. Like Faust sound engineer Kurt Graupner, he also had an ability to keep his head in the studio when all around him were off theirs. This, coupled with the design skills of Reinhard Hippen, lent an air of quality and distinction to Ohr. Despite Kaiser's audacity and marketing flair, however, by 1972 the limited pool of Ohr acts was in danger of stagnating. Sales were steady and Kaiser had launched a second label, Pilz, through which to channel quieter, less psychedelic releases, but even a year or so into the early seventies, the late sixties felt like a long time ago. By this point, whatever half-baked revolutionary fervour Kaiser might have harboured had been superseded by his dedication to the joys of hallucinogenic drugs, LSD in particular, which he felt could form the real basis for an alternative society, rather than the eradication of capitalism, which appeared, unnervingly, to involve axes.

In his 1972 book *Rock-Zeit*, he not only extolled the virtue of 'the trip' as integral to the creation and perception of new music but also went to practical lengths to assist readers in hooking up with folk of a like mind. 'He wrote about the scenes in different cities and he actually published the phone numbers of cool people that you could call,' says Diedrich Diederichsen. 'If you look at the issue of this book, there are Berlin phone numbers, some of them people I know now, and I ask, "Was this your phone number in '69?" It was an unbelievable idea, that you could find cool people who had good drugs and stay, maybe, overnight.'

It wasn't just relatively unknown Berlin residents to whose doorsteps Kaiser helpfully directed his readership but also Allen Ginsberg, Nico and the lawyer for the Red Army Faction. However, through his networking Kaiser would eventually forge a very real, if short-lived connection between the Ohr label and the world's most notorious drugs enthusiast, Timothy Leary. Their meeting would make for one of the most forgettable albums and unforgettable stories of the entire Krautrock era.

Timothy Leary had escaped from a low-security prison in the USA, where he had been sentenced to ten years for the possession of two cannabis roaches in 1968, with a further ten added for a previous, similarly heinous offence. Leary bluffed his way through psychological tests, some of which he had written himself during his previous tenure as a Harvard professor of psychology, posing successfully as a mild, cowed fellow resolved to serve out his time. He then carried out a daring plan in which he scaled a tree in the exercise yard, mounted the roof of the prison block and negotiated a telephone wire, evading the attentions of a passing patrol car even as he dropped his glasses into the road. From there, he acquired a fake passport, shaved his head and made his escape to Algeria, thanks to the good offices of the underground revolutionaries the Weathermen, who could not resist gleefully boasting of their involvement in a communiqué which highlighted the esteem in which Leary was held by the counterculture. 'Dr Leary was being held against his will and against the will of millions of kids in this country. He was a political prisoner, captured for the work he did for all of us beginning the task of creating a new culture on the barren wasteland that has been imposed on this country by Democrats, Republicans, Capitalists and creeps. LSD and grass, like the herbs and cactus and mushrooms of the American Indians and countless civilisations that have existed on this planet, will help us make a future world where it will be possible to live in peace.'

Leary would be drawn to Switzerland, the country where Albert Hofmann was born, who first synthesised LSD at the Sandoz laboratories, though it wasn't until five years later, when he accidentally absorbed some of the stuff via his fingertips, that he became aware of the effects – 'a not unpleasant intoxicated-like condition, characterised by an extremely stimulated imagination', as he later recalled. 'In a dreamlike state, with eyes closed, I perceived an uninterrupted stream of fantastic pictures, extraordinary shapes with intense, kaleidoscopic play of colours.' It was Leary's eloquent celebration of these effects and his proposal to the workforce that they 'drop out' rather than continue to endure sober wage slavery that contributed to his being a hunted man in 1973. In Switzerland, Leary was canny, never staying in one place for very long, keeping one step ahead of the forces of extradition as he hopped from canton to canton.

However, although he claimed to be living a high life in Europe among an exotic, alternative aristocracy of mystics, poets and hashishins, Leary was still battling to stave off depression and a hankering for his homeland. To cheer himself up, he hooked up with Brian Barritt, a UK author and self-styled daddy of the psychedelic demi-monde, whom he had met in Algiers. They took a lot of heroin and, in their generally altered state, were readily susceptible to the advances of Hartmut Enke, bass player of Ash Ra Tempel, who sought out Leary and gave him a copy of their latest album, *Schwingungen*. Neither Barritt nor Leary had previously heard the group, but they were taken with *Schwingungen* and instantly, approvingly recognised that it represented a spatial advance on the Anglo-American titans of the late sixties, like Pink Floyd, who, come the 1970s, were beginning to sound bloated and complacent to a more extremist listenership.

Klaus Schulze had the opportunity to record with Leary but was wary. 'I refused to play on this record in any great part because of Leary. His reputation as a "dealer" had already been well established and I had no desire to promote him.' Klaus Mueller, however, now Klaus Schulze's publisher, acted as a roadie for the *Seven Up* sessions. He takes up the story. 'Hartmut travelled to Switzerland and talked to Tim [Leary]. He was thrilled – Tim is inspiring – and a concept for an album was framed. The music should present eight steps of consciousness. In Tim Leary's book *The Politics of Ecstasy*, which was for twenty-five years banned in Germany, it is just seven steps, but meanwhile Tim believes in eight. One: Fear, birth, emotion. Two: Ego. Three: Others, social games, alcohol. Four: Eros, sensuality, blues. Five: Vibrations, harmony. Six: Discovery of outer cosmos. Seven: Discovery of inner cosmos, the DNA code. Eight: White light, rebirth, death . . . something like that.'

Barritt and Leary had sought to travel through these various phases by pharmaceutical means. The further up the staircase they ascended, the more contentious their claims – but the *kosmische* strains of Ash Ra Tempel offered at least a plausible soundtrack to these theoretical states of superconsciousness.

Enke may not have mentioned that Leary was Plan B – the group's initial idea had been to make a recording with Allen Ginsberg, based around his poem 'Howl', which they had referenced on their debut album. Not even the assistance provided by Kaiser's telephone directory could help them track Ginsberg down, however. So Enke and Leary met at a cafe in Berne once frequented by Einstein and signed a contract, which Enke took back to Berlin, and then took it upon himself to recruit new members to supplement the group's line-up. Ash Ra Tempel are often thought of as Manuel Göttsching's baby, but this album was more Enke's initiative. The group ran through some tracks which would provide a basic musical framework for Leary's concept, in which the album would be divided into two modestly ambitious halves – 'Time' and 'Space'.

Since it was out of the question for Leary to travel to West Germany, the group headed for Berne, in an old yellow truck belonging to drummer Dietmar 'Didi' Burmeister which suffered numerous breakdowns. They initially stayed at a large house belonging to one Albert Mindy, a friend of Leary's. This was a convivial time, with Leary making quite an impression on the young musicians, who were as much taken with his affable, sociable nature as with the philosophy he expounded. A matey guru. He put them at ease – however, there was a general unease at the lack of an immediate plan of action, with Kaiser offering little assistance, as Mueller recounts.

'Everything was more or less unclear, vague. Except for the music, which was very clear. We had, for instance, a drum solo planned for the second step, a simple rock beat for number three, and a blues for the fourth step. Part of Ash Ra Tempel's *Schwingungen* was projected for the sixth step, the seventh and eighth should be done "electronically" – also the very first step.' The group tried to rehearse, but a neighbour complained, so that put a stop to that. 'Often we were all on the lawn with Tim, in front of the house. It was very beautiful, the weather, the situation, the friendliness, the whole atmosphere. But nobody knew how the proceedings for the recordings were planned or arranged. Kaiser was not responsive – he was not accessible – and Timothy Leary was asking me how things should be done now. But I was just the roadie and I didn't know a thing. Being the oldest of the Ash Ra Tempel clan, I tried to speak to Kaiser and really had a dispute with him.

'We then discussed the possibility of doing the recording on our own, as an independent project. Now Kaiser got cold feet. He was the official producer [for the Ohr label] and now it seems that he lost control. Finally, the "independent" idea was buried because nobody took the initiative or had the courage for it.' As this tableau of awkward inertia played out, Barritt amused himself by organising an orgy, though none of the Ash Ra Tempel crew participated.

'During these days we met all kinds of people, all friends of Tim,' says Mueller. 'The whole Swiss underground had to do with Tim Leary, so it seemed. There was Sergius Golowin, author and magician. There was Walter Wegmüller, the painter. There was a stranger with a black Stingray car who looked and acted like Keith Richards, and indeed it was whispered that he was from the Rolling Stones' crew, coming over to get some clean dope; of course, this was only rumours, myth.'

Recording started in earnest at the Sinus Studio in Berne, a cramped place below pavement level whose conditions were as stuffy as its name implies. 'This studio in a cellar was weirdly narrow and dreadfully hot,' remembers Mueller. 'Kaiser had also invited his usual German sound engineer Dieter Dierks, in addition to the very nice Swiss engineer. On the first studio day Dierks only fumbled around with the technicals. No music, it was boring for all, we were unhappy.' To enliven proceedings, Leary's son-in-law Dennis DiMartino spiked a bottle of 7-Up with some acid and passed it round the group, without informing them. At least now they had an album title. Leary and Barritt, meanwhile, scribbled ideas for the lyrics, whittling them down from colourful biro abstractions into something acceptably lucid.

'On the second day in the studio, finally, we were ready to rock and roll,' says Mueller. Leary stepped up to the microphone, which, to everyone's surprise, he began to address. 'We played, and Tim was speaking his slogans about the "steps" of consciousness that we were actually playing. At one point we just started to jam and Tim joined the party – this went on for quite some time, it was great fun and no one knew if it was recorded! Later we heard that it was recorded, but neither Kaiser nor his sound engineer liked it, only Tim and the group were more than happy about it. This piece was cut down to twenty minutes and it was planned for the B-side of the album. I play here the tambourine and fumble around a bit. The musicians played in one room; the two singers,

Tim with two friends, Rosie [Manuel Göttsching's girlfriend] and I were in a second room. Tim was running from one room to the other, one time stumbling over a bottle, another time he coughed.' All of this was considered sonic grist for the album.

By day three, the chemically enhanced conviviality of the sessions was beginning to take its toll. 'On the last studio day I was on a horror trip,' says Mueller. 'All the others were just incredibly tired or also on a trip, but the situation was managed, somehow. We recorded enough music for an album. Just three studio days were scheduled, because of the total cost. Kaiser recorded some additional solo voice from Tim, while we wrapped our equipment.'

For all the jollity of these sessions, which at one point could be heard via local radio after Dierks rigged up the studio as a station, it wasn't just the soft drink which had been spiked but any serious possibility of anything really decent emerging from them. There were too many distractions, too many people, and no one with either the experience or the authority to take the project by the scruff of the neck. Kaiser was not considered much of a help, and managed to alienate Leary himself, as well as Mueller. He may also have been practical enough to have realised that what was rolling onto the tapes would need some severe reworking back in the studio. Leary suspected Kaiser would mess with the results, urging Barritt not to let Kaiser 'fuck' with the album back in Cologne, but ultimately he could not complain too much about the outcome. 'The album was released, but only after some rework and re-recordings by Kaiser and Dieter Dierks with studio musicians who had nothing to do with Ash Ra Tempel,' Mueller remembers.

Seven Up, as planned by Leary, consists of two sides – 'Space' and 'Time'. These, however, are further subdivided into individual song segments. The first, 'Downtown', contains the basic track laid down by the Ash Ra Tempel musicians – a surprisingly lethargic bluesy clop that feels antithetical to everything the group had achieved on their albums hitherto. It's as if they've regressed to their days playing together as the pre-Krautrock Steeplechase Blues Band. Was this to assuage Leary's homesickness? Worse, Leary's vocal is absent altogether, having failed to take in the original recording. Dierks was therefore forced to bring in a local session singer, Portia Nkomo, one of the outsiders to whom Mueller refers. Brian Barritt, present at the sessions, attempted to faze her by whispering dirty nothings in her ear, but nothing distracted her from her capable if slightly clockwatching performance, which certainly lacks the epic effervescence of Petula Clark's song of the same name. Out of some sense of psychedelic obligation, Dierks tops and tails the song with washes of abstract, hoovering electronics, as if to compensate for the lo-fi, pedestrian recordings and cover up a general lack of sonic inspiration. These might have worked, in a Pere Ubu style, especially on 'Right Hand Lover', which chugs along like Hendrix in his Chitlin' Circuit days but on which Leary's wayward, faux rock 'n' roll braggadocio vocals – 'got a hinge on my thumb I'll manipulate you baby' – are ruinous, except for their oddity value, especially accompanied by yelping harmonies. The arcing whoosh of the synths drowns out the desperately conventional playing but it's an afterthought, like someone splashing paint on a portrait of a pig's ear to give it a retrospective Pollockesque sheen. What do these perfunctory, slightly undercooked helpings of cod blues have to do with the steps to a higher consciousness?

Whether it's a reflection of the respective dimensions is a matter of debate, but the 'Time' side of *Seven Up* is a significant improvement. This is more the Ash Ra Tempel we know from albums like *Schwingungen* – indeed, it's developed from the climactic segment of that album, with Göttsching's guitars at the forefront, stepping off the edge of planet earth's blues into uncharted, cosmic recesses without any foothold. Over this, weaving around the seahorse shapes that float from Göttsching's fretboard and the milky stretches of organ, phrases emerge intermittently from the infinite darkness, as uttered by Leary: 'Welcome to our time machine.'

Again, the recording feels a little rough, as if the tape stock is cheap or worn, which adds to its grainy charm but doesn't assist clarity. As with 'Space', all the intellectual cogency of the album's supposed conceptual underpinning seems to have dissolved somewhere in the process. 'Free yourself from your body . . .' urges Leary, then mumbles a few near-intelligible words of follow-up. But this could just as easily be the barely sentient trickle of consciousness of a comatose stoner as opposed to the professorial thoughts of the world's leading radical theorist on LSD. Then again, maybe he felt that this was no occasion for the lectern – that an ounce of demonstration was worth a ton of explanation. Words were the mere ladder to heaven; once there, they must be dispensed with.

Seven Up is generally considered to be a bit of a mishap of an album, whose making is far more interesting than its outcome. It's hard to see what it's for, how its musical and theoretical parts were supposed to mesh and how its intentions relate to the result. It's certainly not a tremendous advert for the introduction of LSD at key stages of the creative process. President Nixon, the catastrophic inaugurator of the War on Drugs, described Leary as 'the most dangerous man in America', but if *Seven Up* is testimony to anything, it was to Leary's ineffectiveness in using rock music as a medium by which to take the world by storm. Although Leary himself was said to have been proud of the release, and particularly pleased that, unlike on the other albums with which he was involved, he got a go at the microphone, he passes over it in his autobiographical writings. The US authorities caught up with him not long afterwards. He was arrested in Kabul, returned to America and held on five million dollars' bail. The judge at his remand hearing, who may or may not have heard *Seven Up*, remarked, 'If he is allowed to travel freely, he will speak publicly and spread his ideas.' Leary duped the FBI into thinking he was co-operating with their investigation into the Weathermen, feeding them outdated information, before spending three years of an initially proposed ninety-five-year prison sentence in California. He was released in 1976.

As for Kaiser, the remaining years he had in the music business were as intense and doomed as a supernova. His old colleagues had begun to melt away. Early collaborators Bruno Wendel and Günter Körber had read the writing on the wall, leaving Ohr in 1972 to set up Brain Records, which would be a direct competitor. In May of 1973 Peter Meisel, Ohr's co-founder, also quit. He departed for America, where he would become joint partner of the fast-food chain Wendy's. In their absence, there was no sober counterweight to the ever more extravagant decision-making of Kaiser and Lettmann, who was taking an increasingly influential role in the firm. As for the artists, Klaus Schulze and Tangerine Dream in particular were itching to get out of the onerous contracts to which Kaiser had signed them, whose terms left them mired in near-impossible debt to Ohr. The straight-edged Froese also objected to Kaiser describing Ohr's output, and his own by association, as 'sonic LSD', with all the old labels now bundled under the new banner of Kosmische Kuriere ('Cosmic Couriers'). When Kaiser revealed a plan to farm out management of some of the bands to Brian Barritt and his partner Liz Elliot, Froese wrote sharply to Kaiser, 'From definitive experience we know to which high degree they are addicted to the syringe. It comes along that I cannot comprehend your interpretations of necessary drug use.' Froese would eventually have to fight his way through the courts to win satisfaction from Ohr, not achieving victory until 1978, when it was revealed that the royalties he had been chasing had all been as non-existent as Kaiser's increasingly addled astral projections.

As well as mind expansion, in 1973 Kaiser had envisaged financial expansion, producing a plan that envisaged a turnover increase of more than six hundred per cent, much of which would be reinvested into fresh productions. Full of hope and ambition, the Cosmic Couriers mogul took out massive advertorial spreads in *Rolling Stone*, staging publicity stunts to promote the Ohr product. Kaiser rented a railway car, daubed it in psychedelic colours and packed off some of his more compliant artists in it to visit local newspaper offices all over West Germany. For one press conference, he chartered a bus to take journalists to an unnamed location somewhere deep in a forest, where he had installed a sound system and put up inflatable white plastic chairs. He picked a very public fight with *Sounds* for supposedly having been complicit with the authorities in printing CIA-supplied pictures of Leary in their coverage of the *Seven Up* album release, declaring their intention to boycott the influential magazine. There was an intoxicated, deluded air about Kaiser and Lettmann's behaviour at this time, as if they felt themselves to be bigger than the world. Strangely, however, when *Eurock*'s Archie Patterson went to interview the couple, he found them to be civil and low-key, living in a conservatively furnished, rented Cologne apartment. Perhaps the pair weren't delusional, but rather guilty of a grave miscalculation, for all their grand, expansive schemes were in inverse proportion to reality, which was beginning to contract on Kaiser.

His last great hubristic gesture was a string of releases of albums by the Cosmic Jokers, heralded with typically purple preposterousness in the press release. 'The time ship floats through the galaxy of joy. In the sounds of electronics. In the flashes of light. Here you will discover Science Fiction, the planet of COSMIC JOKERS, the GALACTIC SUPERMARKET and the SCI FI PARTY. That is the new sound. Space. Telepathy. Melodies. Joy.'

To an extent, the albums lived up to their billing. 'Cosmic Joy', from the first album, features the unmoored swirl of an organ as it voyages mazily towards and beyond the stars, its golden, cleansing tones the ideal musical prompting for unlimited exploration of imaginary space. The title track of the second album, *Galactic Supermarket*, is more agitated, as choppy guitars and deep, spacey flute gad about the mix, broken up by piercing synth interventions reminiscent of Sun Ra's 'Cosmic Explorer'. The Cosmic Jokers knew their way around the solar system, for sure. But who were they?

There was the problem. As the story has it, the Cosmic Jokers had no idea that they existed. The albums released in quick succession were gleaned from tapes of impromptu sessions at Dieter Dierks's studio. The participants included Jürgen Dollase and Harald Grosskopf of Wallenstein, as well as Ash Ra Tempel's Manuel Göttsching and, fatefully, Klaus Schulze. These sessions were billed as 'acid parties', in which the jamming musicians were encouraged in their efforts with complimentary drugs. Kaiser took the tapes and edited them down into manageable album-sized chunks, and Gille Lettmann then overdubbed some conspicuously added-on, echo-drenched vocal contributions of her own, as if to pull together and validate the sessions as a conscious piece of finished work.

It is said that Manuel Göttsching only learned that there was such a thing as the Cosmic Jokers when he walked into a record shop in Berlin and, intrigued by the space rock pouring out of the sound system, asked who the record was by. The clerk told him it was by the Cosmic Jokers, and presented Göttsching with a copy of the album sleeve, featuring a photo of the guitarist himself. This story has attained legendary status, but Göttsching would eventually pooh-pooh the notion that he had no idea about the group. 'Of course I knew about the releases, of course I had contracts before, and I received royalties, even in advance. This all was very little money, but that should be no argument to spread around rumours like this. You can say many things about the producer Rolf-Ulrich Kaiser but I have no reason for saying him to have acted incorrectly so far.'

Several of the other musicians involved protested otherwise at the time, however, with Klaus Schulze raising the strongest objection, strong enough to see to it that having burst onto the scene in 1974 with four consecutive albums, the Cosmic Jokers burst just as quickly off it, never to be heard of again. Göttsching probably has a point – listening to these albums, they sound too well thought through, too good, frankly (certainly much better than, say, side one of *Seven Up*), to be regarded as drug-addled party music by a bunch of musicians having a laugh, before being passed off as work intended for wider release. Clearly, however, there was an element of false pretence involved and the wisdom of producing and releasing these albums in the way Kaiser chose to can certainly be questioned.

The Cosmic Jokers fiasco and the court cases that followed it would mark the end for Rolf-Ulrich Kaiser and his seven-year adventure in the music business. Boycotting *Sounds* proved to be unwise – the magazine now rounded on Kaiser and Lettmann, dubbing them the 'Komische Kuriere'. Although their press releases and public statements had doubtless been issued with a P. T. Barnum, over-the-top sense of self-parody, it did their artists no good to be considered a laughing stock.

Manuel Göttsching stuck around the longest with Kaiser but understood that it was the end of the road. 'I had no real problems with him,' he said in 1998. 'I liked him. He had his really strange ideas, and he was really far ahead of his time. What actually happened was that he lost contact with the ground. He became very unpopular with all of the journalists and other people in the music business. They said, "He's just crazy, forget about him." This made him a little angry, and then he reacted like a child and said, "I'm better, I know it." So he always tried to top himself, and, in the end, nobody listened to him any more. It was sad, but I had to leave the company because I had friends who said, "Of course, I will write about your music and I will support you, but not if you are still affiliated with Ohr music." He was sending out promotional material every day, and nobody wanted to read about it any more, because it was just crazy. He said that we are bigger than the

Beatles and that we play on Mars and that this is our century. For a while it was okay, if you can laugh about it or take it as a joke. But after a while, it was just too much.'

In 1975, Cosmic Couriers declared bankruptcy, freeing up artists like Klaus Schulze and Tangerine Dream to sign for other labels and flourish at last. If it were possible to traverse time, today's vinyl collectors, now forced to shell out hundreds of euros for *kosmische* LPs, would be beating a path to their machines and setting the controls for Karstadt, the German department-store chain, where surplus Cosmic Courier stock was being sold off at a price of DM 2.95 a platter, at a time when the price for a new LP was up to nineteen marks. These copies will have traded for not far off a hundred times that amount in the decades since.

There was no comeback for Kaiser and Lettmann. They were forced to give up their Berlin premises and their neatly appointed Cologne apartment, evicted and their goods sold off, another trove for future Krautrock memorabilia bloodhounds with a patience for flea markets and crate-digging. Thereafter, they disappeared off the face of the earth, though not in the astral-travelling sense. Rumours would abound as to their whereabouts. It was said that the pair had been reduced to begging in the streets, that Rolf and Gille had both tuned out to lysergic excess and ended up in a psychiatric hospital, or even that Rolf had died.

The writer Jan Reetze, however, who is probably the strongest authority on Kaiser, his doings and undoings, revealed the truth about Kaiser's quiet, post-Kosmische existence. They moved in with Lettmann's mother outside Cologne and lived there until her death in 1990. They then moved to an apartment in the Sauerland area but, having failed to keep up with the rent, were evicted once more. Eventually, Walter Westrupp (of Witthüser and Westrupp) came to their assistance. In 2007, he found a place for them in an open facility run by the Catholic Church somewhere in the Sauerland area. Kaiser briefly popped his head up from obscurity to lay a claim to monies from the reissue of Ohr and Pilz albums in the late 1980s, only to be reminded that he'd forfeited any rights to these records when he went into bankruptcy. He then relapsed into a silence from which he has never emerged. He has no internet presence, grants no interviews, receives no visitors.

Gille, however, maintained her 'Sternenmädchen' persona. Indeed, that has come to be the only mode of address she will accept, the one that appears on her letterhead. That Cosmic Couriers were laid low by reality has only intensified her retreat from it. Her activities are confined to publishing an 'esoteric magazine' which she sends out to a select group of readers – old friends, politicians, industrialists – though whether they receive the publication at their own request is uncertain.

From all of this, it is strongly tempting to glean a morality tale about *kosmische* and its LSD associations. The more so following the fate of poor Hartmut Enke, who had first so enthusiastically made contact with Timothy Leary and whose constitution proved ultimately unequal to the excesses of his chosen path. As Manuel Göttsching later recalled in an interview with *Mojo* magazine, 'During our last concert in Cologne in February 1973, Hartmut stopped playing bass in the middle of the concert and just sat down on the stage. Klaus and me, we looked at each other, and we continued to play, thinking maybe he wanted a break. And after the concert we asked him, "Hartmut, what happened?" and then he said, "Yeah, the music that you played was just so beautiful I didn't know what to play. I preferred to listen to it."' Enke left the group and never worked in music again. He died in 2005, aged only fifty-three.

Kaiser's story is a strange mixture of idealism and enterprise, of creative opportunism and dodgy dealing. The music world, you feel, needs its Kaisers, maddening and ultimately disaster-prone as they are. Even the artists who successfully sued him had reason at some point in their career to be grateful for his ability to conjure things out of hot air, to provide gateways into the music business. Although he had a strong whiff of the huckster about him, his sheer literary tirelessness alone (in his writer days he was generally at his desk by five in the morning) showed his determination to make a real, working concern out of the good intentions of the sixties German counterculture. His drift from the street-level leftism of the late sixties into the hazy abstractions of the more acid-fried seventies reflected a general shift in the cultural mood as the momentum of 1968 stalled, hampered by the subtly conciliatory air of the Willy Brandt administration, an impatience at mankind's failure to perfect itself overnight and the undertow of violence emerging among the most radical of the movement's voices, of which Nikel Pallat's axe was merely the tip.

What, then, of so-called *kosmische* itself? Tangerine Dream are often saddled with the term, but there was a schism, so far as Edgar Froese was concerned, between his own group and the Ash Ra Tempel axis. 'Ash Ra Tempel live in a dream world,' he told French journalist Jean-Pierre Lantin in 1973. 'They think that everything will turn out okay, that the expansion of consciousness will conquer the world and all the problems will solve themselves. We try and be more realistic: the expansion of consciousness is just one part of reality and misery and horror are another part that you can't ignore.' As reflected in the grim, static expanses of works like *Atem*, Tangerine Dream's view of the universe is gloomily reminiscent of the philosophy of Schopenhauer or Spinoza – vast and indifferent to human concerns, cold and neutral. Although more pessimistic and austere, the Tangerine Dream vision was one that obtained with a larger international audience, enabling them to swap conventional, modified instruments for large banks of state-of-the-art electronic machinery, the sound and spectacle of which further diminished the 'human' element in their *Weltanschauung*.

Klaus Schulze also distanced himself from the *kosmische* label ('it's not very good – all music is cosmic'), stating that he preferred the more precise term *musique planante* 'because I place it above the ground . . . at least ten centimetres off the floor. It allows you to float while it floats around you.'

In truth, only Kaiser and Lettmann were happy to promote the term *kosmische*, for marketing and promotional purposes and also, in Lettmann's case, to surf along in her 'Sternenmädchen' persona. However, within its spurious canon are a handful of works which, at worst, charmingly epitomise the era, daring to open and peer through doors of perception that have long since been slammed shut in our own, more sceptical times. At best, they serve as enduring models of expansion in the twenty-first century, an unhappy post-space age in which rock adventurism has been replaced by a sort of aggressive, conservative cowardice, as if in denial that the future has arrived.

Sergius Golowin was one of those who dropped in on the *Seven Up* sessions. Born in Prague in 1930, the son of a sculptor who continued to pursue his work in Paris while Sergius and his mother emigrated to Switzerland, his day jobs were largely clerical – a library assistant, a local-government office worker and an archivist. However, he had other lives, as a Green Party activist and politician, an expert on folklore and Tarot, an author, a man who counted among his friends, as well as Timothy Leary, men as diverse as Martin 'Tino' Schippert, founder of the Swiss Hell's Angels (there was such a thing), and the brilliant Swiss author and playwright Friedrich Dürrenmatt, whose often macabre and supernatural works go face to face with the horrors of the mid-twentieth century. Golowin was invited by Kaiser to make an album with a selection of musicians in 1972 at Dieter Dierks's studio in Stommeln, including Klaus Schulze and guitarists Bernd Witthüser and Walter Westrupp. The result was *Lord Krishna von Goloka*.

Golowin's guru status had been sealed by the publication of his *Magie der verbotenen Märchen* ('The Magic of the Forbidden

Fairy Tales'), a treatise on herbs, witchcraft and magic mushrooms whose influence spread even to the deep underground community of East German hippies. On the album cover, he sits amid the long grass of an idyllic rural setting, eyes closed, solemnly attuned to nature's aura. On 'Der Reigen', it's as if his backing musicians are a little inhibited by the reverential overtones of the project, falling into a sort of Krishna trance as Golowin delivers his slow, halting incantations. 'Die weisse Alm' ('The White Mountain Pasture') is dominated by the dappled, sunlit finger-picking of Witthüser and Westrupp. Golowin's utterances, often awash with echo and delivered in a thick accent that makes them hard even for native German speakers, drift tantalisingly in and out of the mix. '*Dann fliegt Zeit . . . Stehen sämtliche Ewigkeiten*' ('Then time flies . . . all eternities stand'), he intones, before the more spacious 'Die hoch Zeit' traverses the various *kosmische* styles like solar systems.

It's hard for many nowadays to subscribe to a belief system that holds that some pristine, higher truth can be revealed by casting back to the ragged troubadours of a bygone age, or witchcraft, or through the ingestion and examination of fungi. For those who spell magic with a 'k' or insist there is any such thing as magic at all in the universe, it might be possible, if you stare hard enough at Golowin's laconic utterances, to find enlightenment. However, towed in Golowin's wake are some of the great 'Cosmic Courier' musicians trailing clouds of excellence to which they might not otherwise have been inspired to rise. As an alternative to nothingness, *Lord Krishna* is pleasing indeed.

Witthüser and Westrupp were best known in their own right as purveyors of 'cosmic folk', the best example of which is 1971's *Trips und Träume*. The album doesn't quite match the striking violence of its cover, a clash of mauve and orange, featuring what looks like a hippie who has been brutally eviscerated by a paintbrush. On tracks like 'Trippo Nova', however, there is an astringency and asymmetry to their plucking that is the antithesis of Donovan. It's as if what they are really tripping on is their own strings and chords, as they deliver their almost brusque German lyrics in a manner designed to jolt, rather than induce drowsiness, knocking on their acoustic guitars as if impatiently at the doors of perception.

Walter Wegmüller was another key member of the Cosmic Courier set – like Golowin, he was Swiss-born, a painter who had been working for some years on a set of Tarot cards that reflected his own folkloric interests. Jerry Berkers, Hartmut Enke, Manuel Göttsching, Klaus Schulze, Harald Grosskopf, Walter Westrupp, Bernd Witthüser and Rosi Müller were among the musicians gathered by Kaiser for Wegmüller's double album *Tarot*, which alongside *Seven Up* and *Lord Krishna von Goloka* can be seen as part of a trilogy of spoken-word, guru-led albums. Like Seinfeld episodes, each song title is a single word, preceded by the definite article – 'Der Narr', 'Der Magier', 'Die Hohepriesterin', 'Die Herrscherin', 'Der Herrscher', each representing an individual card. *Tarot* is quite different in feel from the bucolic mysticism of *Lord Krishna* – as 'Die Welt', for example, indicates, it's strikingly funky in places, reminiscent of late Hendrix or fusion-era Miles Davis in its soaring wah-wah and trenchant grooves, intersected by sheet waves of keyboard.

Frankly, such is the groove that they hit that Wegmüller's occasional, prosaic interventions, when they do occur, are about as welcome as that of a janitor appearing from the wings telling them to keep the noise down. Julian Cope described *Tarot* as 'the funkiest record ever played by white boys', which might be a stretch, but it's among the funkiest in the Krautrock canon. Elsewhere, the white noise is of a more acidic nature – on 'Der Magier', for instance – with a generally atypical, maniacal air prevailing across the double album. To what extent this is inspired by tarot philosophy or simply the mood of the sessions is hard to tell. Tarot Rock certainly never really caught on, as a practice. Wegmüller's role on the album is essentially talismanic – no further recordings were made under his name and he concentrated on his career as a visual artist after this.

Finally, let us consider *kosmische*'s most shining and enduring gift to the firmament – Ash Ra Tempel, led by Manuel Göttsching, whose early albums, plus one dazzling electronic return in 1981, both define and exceed *kosmische*.

Göttsching was born in Berlin in 1952 and spent his teenage years steeped in the Anglo-American blues tradition, soaking up the work of Jimi Hendrix, Peter Green and Eric Clapton in his Cream period. Although Göttsching's first group, the Steeplechase Blues Band, formed when he was very young, were clearly imitative, with Göttsching jamming and earning his spurs, he wasn't ultimately interested, as so many of his young German contemporaries were, in simply replicating their licks and thereby sharing in the pretence of being descended from an American-derived pop culture. He paid particular attention to their soloing excursions, the point at which they really took off. He and Ash Ra Tempel would themselves take off where the sixties rockers left off, on the outer edges of rock improvisation – the blues itself would, in the main, be the memory of a launchpad. 'There were a few bands in Germany trying to withstand the Anglo-American invasion,' Göttsching would say in 2000. 'They were creating their own typically German style by turning their backs on common song structures. This was music made from scratch.'

Göttsching was an early player in the Zodiak Free Arts Lab scene, playing briefly in Conrad Schnitzler's Eruption alongside Klaus Schulze. However, like many young Berlin musicians of the time, he took as his mentor Thomas Kessler, the Swiss composer and eventual founder of the Berlin Electronic Beat Studio. Although at this stage he didn't quite understand the 'abstract, mathematical' music made by him, under Kessler Göttsching would take lessons in composition and improvisation, the sort of basic formalist, European grounding which would set him apart from the sixties beat generation.

In 1971, Göttsching, Hartmut Enke and Schulze formed a trio by the name of Ash Ra Tempel. Their name reflects the Eastern-tinged, Age of Aquarius mores of the time: Ra, a reference to the Egyptian sun god; Tempel, the German spelling of temple, indicating that their music would be a contemplative zone. The most significant word was 'Ash', the English word, intended to signify the burnt remains of that which was no more. The group were hereby positioning themselves as 'post-rock', or something which would operate beyond the limits of sixties psychedelic blues-rock. Theirs was the classic power line-up of guitar (Göttsching), bass (Enke) and drums (Schulze). However, whereas in the sixties even the Jimi Hendrix Experience went on a journey of evolution from the relatively compact *Are You Experienced* to the unrivalled expanses of *Electric Ladyland*, with their debut, self-titled 1971 album Ash Ra Tempel had already arrived. Their opening musical statement could just as easily have been their closing one.

Comprising just two lengthy tracks, *Ash Ra Tempel* had an elaborate folding cover involving a pyramid and celestial orbs. However, it is generally free of the sort of period textual cosmic blather or hippie faux-pas trimmings that might deter future generations. Its titles are terse – 'Amboss' ('Anvil') and 'Traummaschine' ('Dream Machine').

On the near twenty-minute 'Amboss', Göttsching's guitar marks out giant crosses in the sky, before going into full ascent mode, borne by Schulze's crests of cymbals, the earth and its blues a distant speck within minutes. Electronic treatments lend the mix an extraterrestrial hue and fabric, as Göttsching moves into full throttle, not so much shredding through space as lighting it up in a blurry series of fretboard explosions, a flat, golden line through a wormhole. This is operating on a celestially higher plane than the virtuoso but earthbound stylings of what was termed 'progressive rock' in the UK, with all its metal and boogie deadweight. The wah-wah chatterings are like a sudden interference of alien radio transmissions, before the guitars pierce a further black velvet layer with a hectic simultaneity as if space has actually collapsed.

'Traummaschine' is longer, at almost twenty-six minutes, and begins in pitch-black ambient mode, after the deluge. Bowed and bent guitar shapes hove in from the distance, drones resound from all registers likes cries from the void. If side one is what happens after rock, then side two is, indeed, what happens after side one – a beatless aftermath, in which the engines have long been jettisoned and all that's left to do is to free-float into the murky infinite. The guitar drones wheel and unfold, but not blissfully – these are fraught, disquieting tones. Distant, percussive thwacks of obscure origin begin to dot the mix, as the ethereal jangle of Göttsching's guitars recedes and Schulze's percussion begins to rumble. Enke's bass is in there somewhere but less easy to discern – on this album, the instrument is not performing its usual function of 'grounding' the sound but, rather, is up and away with it as well. The guitar is now just one of a number of elements engaged in low-level chatter, the odd plunging phrase. Vocal sounds emerge, and with them a reminder of one precedent – Pink Floyd's 'Careful with That Axe, Eugene', which did make forays into space rock but here feels like a distant echo from the past, as Ash Ra kick on way beyond the heart of the sun, towards the fading, amber glow of the piece's remotely beautiful conclusion as once more all the instruments converge on a single point.

Schwingungen followed in 1972, this time with Klaus Schulze having moved on, replaced by Wolfgang Müller on drums, and the mysterious 'John L' on vocals. Side one is split between two relatively short pieces of meditation on the themes of light and darkness. 'Light – Look at Your Sun' represents a curious return to planet blues, reminiscent of Peter Green's playing on Fleetwood

Mac's 'Albatross'. John L continues the Krautrock tradition of interesting failures as a vocalist, his breathy, impassioned assurances that 'we are all one' the sort of embellishment that would have convinced the average passing British rock commentator of the time of the amateurishness of German rock music. Göttsching makes amends with some squealing soloing, but it's unrepresentative and would make a poor and atypical introduction to Ash Ra Tempel for those picking this album out of the rack and laying down the needle on the first track.

'Darkness: Flowers Must Die' is more like it, with the alien chatter of Göttsching's guitar prefaced by some Jew's harp twanging from John L. But then our singing guest returns, hollering waywardly in lamentation at the floral mortality alluded to in the title, flanked by a Matthias Wehler alto saxophone and a chugging, helicopter rhythm reminiscent of Can, exacerbated by some phasing and stereopanning, and fleetingly, the pre-inkling of Cabaret Voltaire in full, manic flow.

Blurry droplets of Wolfgang Müller's vibraphone introduce 'Suche/Liebe', which takes up side two of the album. Göttsching's guitars do an aurora borealis-like shimmering dance against a spectral skyline of keyboards, before a human, hymnal chorus strikes up for the closing 'Liebe' section. It's all quite lovely but, having hurtled so meaningfully and effectively into the beyond with the debut album, it feels regressive and indebted by comparison to the live disc of Pink Floyd's *Ummagumma* in particular, while the wholly original element – the vocals of John L – we could wholly do without.

Following *Seven Up*, 1973's *Join Inn* was recorded and produced by Dieter Dierks during sessions for Walter Wegmüller's *Tarot* and carries over some of the juicy flavours of that album. Klaus Schulze also rejoined the line-up for one last time, and the two engage in some quite aggressively garrulous percussion and guitar banter in the opening passages of 'Freak 'n' Roll'. Schulze also brought along his Synthi A to the sessions, and electronic elements snake through the mix. However, for all the astral ebb and flow of Göttsching's guitars, and the mountainous virtuoso heights scaled by the pair, this feels like a straight instrumental interchange, in which the images conjured are of musicians playing together, as opposed to the cosmic mesh of the debut album.

'Jenseits' ('Beyond'), however, sees Schulze dispense with his drum kit, and what follows is twenty-five minutes of copulating, interweaving guitars and electronics. Singer Rosi Müller, Göttsching's partner at the time, drops spoken-word vocals like petals on a lake, as the glissando effects turn and gleam like the blade of a knife in sunlight and the synths sustain their mechanical, lava undulations. *Join Inn* was released at the same time as Fripp and Eno's *No Pussyfooting* and, although the records have differing emphases, both deserve to be bracketed together as textural experiments in purely musical chemistry (later elaborated on with Fripp and Eno's 'An Index of Metals' on *Evening Star*). Göttsching appears to have arrived at his own discoveries more intuitively, less systematically than Eno.

Having moved on from Ohr, Göttsching achieved some success as a solo artist under the name Ashra before in 1976 releasing *New Age of Earth*, which has rather tarred his output by association since. He looked destined to be another German musician whose early radicalism and experimentalism would give way to a cosier, more commercially friendly turn as his discography developed a middle-aged spread. However, the gentle, grooving pulses of his late-seventies output were, in fact, deceptive stepping stones to the one more piece of major, significant work he had left in his locker. Having attached so many modifying devices to his guitars it was inevitable he would turn to electronic instruments once they became more widely used. In 1981, Göttsching went into his Berlin studio, fired up his array of synthesizers and sequencers and set in train an up-and-down pulsating pattern of such deceptive simplicity that only a man steeped in the less-is-more ethos of Krautrock would have dared go with it – and go with it for just under an hour at that. Undulating between two chords referenced in the title but gently spitting a layered, subtle mass of variations as it does so, *E2–E4* is a minimal electronic masterpiece. If you were being hypercritical, you could say that its florid guitar layerings in the second half gild its lily, but they're by no means superfluous. It prefigures developments in electronica in the 1990s and beyond as effectively, perhaps even more fully than Kraftwerk's *Computer World*, released the same year.

It wasn't until 1984 that *E2–E4* was itself released, with Göttsching 'half-heartedly' offering it to Virgin in 1982, before it eventually saw the light of day on his old friend Klaus Schulze's label Inteam, and eventually gaining retrospective recognition as a precursor of house, techno and trance when it was sampled by the Italian dance outfit Sueño Latino for their hit of the same name.

All of which illustrates the point that the legacy of *kosmische* at its best was structural – in altering the very real, material possibilities for making popular, or even not so popular, music. From Ash Ra Tempel proceeds a whole range of sound manufacture, from dark ambient to bright, arpeggiated Electronic Dance Music (EDM). It is in many ways, as much as Kraftwerk, a mechanical proposition. The music didn't ultimately function solely as a conduit for credulous, mystical, divinatory eyewash, pseudo-biological treatises on nature, Ufology and the revering of other wisdoms for their non-Western origin and ancientness. All of this has been laughed out of the culture along with tie-dye and bellbottoms, you would like to think – except that it hasn't, of course, with New Age remedies of all spurious kinds having taken a continuing, depressing hold on gullible minds as rationalism comes under siege, as documented in such lamentations as Francis Wheen's *How Mumbo Jumbo Conquered the World*. Some would argue that rationalism, synonymous with the great, imposed Western project of industrialisation, has deserved to be brought into question, given the ecological and spiritual havoc it has wrought and the brutal displacement of other peoples, other cultures, and that this would account for the range of belief systems that emerged in the 1960s, from dippy mysticism to post-structuralism. However, although nothing could have been further from the mind of, say, Sergius Golowin, it's indisputable that Naziism drew succour from the same Romantic root as elements of hippiedom – naturism, occultism and so forth. As the countercultural mood shifted from angry political engagement to a flight from reality itself, its verbal pronouncements, if hardly in danger of inadvertently heralding a Fourth Reich, drifted towards the speculative and fatuous.

But then, much as Sun Ra composed some of the greatest music of our time, fusing entire continents of contemporary noise, based on a personal, Egyptological/cosmological philosophy most would find risible, so it was with the *kosmische* sound. It too derived from a similar sense that real life, as it stood, whether it was in the Deep South of the mid-twentieth century, or the Altnazi-presided spiritual ruins of West Germany in the 1960s, was not the place to be. Space, in a very real sense, is the place and the music demonstrates precisely how and why. Which is why *kosmische* need not be regarded solely as a portal to some 'alternative wisdom' but as a thing in itself, whose twists, range and expanses can be regarded with the same non-mystical awe with which an atheist regards a falling meteorite, or the solar system.

11 A New Concrete: Neue Deutsche Welle

As much as in the UK, punk impacted on the German music scene like a cleaver. But although many of the British punk and post-punk generation embraced Krautrock, recognising it as antithetical to the pompous, self-indulgent whimsies of prog rock, in Germany it was a different story. There, the intersection between Krautrock and hippiedom was more keenly felt. It had its trenchant critics. As Diedrich Diederichsen, who wrote for the German music magazine *Sounds* (no relation to the UK version), told me, 'It always felt strange to me that there was this interest in Krautrock during the punk movement from people like Pete Shelley and John Lydon – because for me, growing up in the seventies, at least half of these bands were absolutely horrible – not so much musically, they were musically okay but they were coming from the worst form of hippie culture, believing in the worst, most weird and esoteric hippie bullshit. Much worse than people like the Incredible String Band or T. Rex, who might have believed one or two of these things. This doesn't go for Amon Düül, Can – Kraftwerk I have some problems with, other things about them I like a lot – but all of these India travellers, combined with German romanticism, but no awareness of German cultural history – German romanticism was what led to Naziism. You can't just pick up the thread of German romanticism and mix it with this dreamy hippie shit. And that is what "Krautrock" is for me.'

Where 'Krautrock' was bucolic and wistful, forest-bound and buoyed by warm, instrumental waves of utopian hankering, post-punk German music, later codified under the banner of Neue

Deutsche Welle ('New German Wave'), was, in its earliest incarnations at least, as brutal as a hurled slab of concrete. Where Krautrock was *kosmische*, drifting beatlessly into outer orbit, German post-punk represented a crashing descent to street level, like Bruno Ganz's angel in *Wings of Desire* suddenly mortalised and landing with violent bodily force, face first in the middle of broken Berlin. Where Krautrock dreamed mystical dreams of the Orient, the new German music was a jolting reminder of the reality of the West, riven by cold war. Where Krautrock was warmly immersive, the first wave of shock tacticians of the NDW were like a bucket of cold water in the face. As in the UK, the choice of drugs demarcated the cultural difference. Pot and acid, the stuff of dreams and heavy eyelids, were replaced by more eye-popping stimulants like speed (though heroin was also heavily prevalent). Where Krautrock's players hid behind acres of facial and cranial hair, submerged in their playing and the communal instrumental effort, Neue Deutsche Welle's stars were clean-shaven, spiky, crew-cut, anti-icons hopping madly behind mike stands, demanding eyeball-to-eyeball contact with you, nervy, not laid-back. Whereas Krautrock tended to reduce the role of vocals to a layer among many in their textures of sound, anglicised to ease consumption, the new wavers were singers, screamers *auf Deutsch*, turning all the supposed disadvantages of the German tongue when it came to vocalising to their abrasive advantage.

Despite its feminisation, its rejection of the mores of Anglo-American cock-rock, Krautrock was in many ways riven with the unreconstructed assumptions of its era, in which women at best played nurturing and supportive roles, and at worst were sexual playthings for the horny young men of the communes. As in the UK, NDW saw the beginnings of a new female assertiveness – Nina Hagen was the most conspicuous and popular example, but there was also the brilliant Malaria!, featuring Gudrun Gut, and their broad-ranging, snake-drilling post-punk embraced minimal electronics and liberating squalls of free jazz, building bridges with New York's No Wave scene, Lydia Lunch in particular.

There were also parallels between UK punk/post-punk's social origins and its German counterpart. In Britain, the postwar consensus was beginning to come apart at the seams. The country felt frayed and moribund, stumbling morosely into the brutal, calamitous 'corrective' measure of Thatcherism. In Germany, the height of the Red Army Faction's activities occurred around 1976 and 1977, exposing to a degree the impotence of the prefab construction that was the West German state, whose moral authority was further compromised by the mysterious suicides of key RAF leaders including Ulrike Meinhof, Andreas Baader and Gudrun Ensslin, which some strongly suspected to be state-sponsored assassinations.

West German punks were far more prepared to declare support for the RAF, albeit as a nihilistic sop, than were their more reflective, serious-minded Krautrock predecessors. UK punks would, early on at least, sport swastikas, not out of any fascist sympathy but to annoy their parents' still Germanophobic generation. German punks would wear them too, as a shock tactic but also to cock a snook at the unresolved taboos of a society whose government was even now liver-spotted with Altnazis. But it was the hippies they most detested and their mouldering, shopworn 'counterculture' which, after its radical beginnings, was, as its participants got older and softer, degenerating into the Aquarian blandishments of a mythical New Age.

Berlin would become a key vortex in this Neue Welle. Despite the legend of the Zodiak Free Arts Lab, despite the tag of the 'Berliner School' and despite David Bowie descending on the place and using it as backdrop for his reimagination of himself as a Young European, for practical reasons Berlin tended to be a launching pad for Krautrock careers rather than a permanent home. It had a look of neglect about it, of premature ruin, however, which made it ideal for a musical renaissance. Moreover, with Western governments lurching to the far right, with Thatcher, Reagan and Kohl supplanting Callaghan, Carter and Helmut Schmidt, anxieties about nuclear war, dormant since the early 1960s, were reactivated. Berlin was at the very historical and geographical centre point of what military strategists termed the 'theatre of war'. Its own centre was still a bombsite, architectural testimony to the unresolved geopolitical issues of the Second World War, while the Wall was a daily reminder of the reality of the Iron Curtain. Rather than migrate to the more congenial climes of the Bundesrepublik, however, Berlin punks revelled in their island exile and cultivated a scorn for what they termed *Wessies*, a term used by East Germans of their Western counterparts. On the other side of the Wall, meanwhile, there was a sudden congruence as an East German punk scene erupted, its brave and fatally conspicuous followers treated with a severity by the authorities that far exceeded anything suffered by those on the west side.

In the UK, the first wave of lumpen punks was fairly swiftly superseded, first by the ambitious but equally short-lived *Top of the Pops* entryists of the New Wave (the Motors, the Rezillos), but more long term by post-punk, which occupied the crater space left by punk's detonation. As early as 1981, UK punk was reduced to knots of Doc Martened, Mohicaned reprobates on a bench in the King's Road, posing for tourists, time-lagged power trios from Dumbarton or bus-shelter graffiti insisting with forlorn defiance that 'PUNX NOT DEAD'. In Berlin, around Kreuzberg in particular, the punk scene has proven much more obdurate and long-lasting. Musically, however, the takeover of the Artpunk/Neue Deutsche Welle tendency was swift and, if anything, more formally radical than its UK counterpart, albeit driven by a similar, nervous energy.

The CD and DVD anthology *Berlin Super 80: Music and Film Underground West Berlin 1978–84* showcases how new music and

Super 8 movie-making went hand in hand during the era, particularly in the past and future capital city. These movies are cheap, radical, analogue precursors to the glossy hegemony of the video era. The very scratchiness of the film, the hiss of the reel is key to their textural appeal. They emphasise the importance of the visual dimension in Neue Deutsche Welle, as opposed to Krautrock, which tended to be an eyes-closed, headphones on voyage into inner space by comparison. Popol Vuh find themselves tossed into the mix on Yana Yo's film *Sax*, with Florian Fricke's *Nosferatu* soundtrack played on saxophone by a slow-marching troupe of post-punks, trudging up one of those cracked, broad stairwells redolent of a hundred years of history, familiar to anyone who has lived in or visited a Berlin apartment block. The Berlin Wall itself, the very mention of which is rare in the Krautrock canon but which abounds in Neue Deutsche Welle, features in this collection, splashed with daubs of paint by night. There's a dry despondency at play, as in the oblique, scratchy satire of Die Tödliche Doris's 'Berlin Kitchen Music' – people genuinely assumed that this was the End of Days, that the turbulent history of the twentieth century was about to play itself out in a last, thermonuclear Big Bang. 'No Future' didn't just mean 'poor job prospects' but no future at all. As it turned out, the minimal, prototype electropop captured on the reels of *Berlin Super 80* was a new aesthetic flickering into life.

Berlin was a capsule of new atmospheres, and no one caught this better than Einstürzende Neubauten. For rock fans or commentators slightly detached from German music in general, Einstürzende Neubauten ('Collapsing New Buildings') symbolise the perceived abrasive, destructive difficulty of all things Teutonic. This was exacerbated infamously in January 1984, when they played the ICA in London and presented their *Concerto for Voice and Machinery*, featuring cement mixer, drill and jackhammer. Their onstage pyromaniac tendencies had previously got them into trouble in America and they'd been banned from numerous venues for interfering with the fixtures and fittings with their heavy-duty toolkit. On this occasion, it was their intention to tunnel through the floor to what they believed to be secret underground tunnels leading all the way to Buckingham Palace, all the way down the Mall. Using a combination of petrol-driven chainsaws and pneumatic equipment, they succeeded principally in generating a great deal of noise and smoke, as well as inflaming the audience – discussing the concert many years later, Neubauten's Alexander Hacke suggested that all the group had really done was trigger a disturbingly latent destructive mechanism in the crowd, after which they might well have torn down the building piece by piece themselves had not the plugs been pulled to the ICA's power supply after twenty-one minutes.

Blixa Bargeld, the group's leader, actually played very little part in the *Concerto for Voice and Machinery*, irritably waving the subject away in later interviews ('You should not ask me about this. I was not involved in that'). But his choice of stage name had its roots in outrage for art's sake – it referred back to Johannes Baargeld, the Dadaist painter and poet. 'Blixa' is a female name – his nearest rock relation, in this respect, is Alice Cooper. Real name Christian Emmerich, of all the weeds in human shape that sprang up from the punk rubble, he was one of the starkest. Tall, pale, skinny and goggle-eyed, topped off with an electro-Gothic shock of hair, he physically epitomised the spirit of New German music. He had an ill, messianically consumptive air as if he had personally inhaled for our sins all of the toxic, asbestos-like by-products of the postwar German economic miracle. Whereas Krautrock was an aesthetic upshot of the ruins of the Second World War, Einstürzende Neubauten arose from the notional, impending collapse of the hastily knocked-up, jerrybuilt (so to speak) West German state, whose drably inadequate structures were a conspicuous architectural feature of Berlin. Listening to Neubauten, it is as if they have swept aside in their minds all postwar pop, from rock 'n' roll to prog, even punk, and returned to a theoretical 1946, beginning again with whatever pieces of metal are to hand.

The thing is, Bargeld, although briefly associated with the punk movement, was disdainful of it. For him, it was a continuation of a discredited rock narrative. In 1987, I interviewed Bargeld. Neubauten were in town to promote their latest album, *Fünf auf der nach oben offenen Richterskala* ('Five on the Open-ended Richter Scale'). Stevo of the Some Bizarre Record label, who was handling them at the time, had come up with the scheme of having them play a gig at London's National Club, with seventies UK rock 'n' roll revivalists Showaddywaddy as support. Presumably we were supposed to contrast these two specimens and their place on the rock 'n' roll spectrum, but if this was a joke at the 'has-beens' Showaddywaddy's expense, it backfired – even UK-based Neubauten fans found themselves sticking up for Showaddywaddy and, rather than sneer, cheered along their performance and sympathised with their complaints about their treatment backstage. Neubauten were done no favours – their own set seemed rather precious and theatrical, cast in the mood that had been set on the night.

Bargeld was affable enough before and even after the interview but less so during it. At the time, I thought him deliberately truculent, but there were mitigating factors. I'd been a journalist less than a year and my line of questioning, which I read back now with a grimace, reads as rather clever-clever, provocative and precocious, masking an underlying lack of confidence. Furthermore, throughout the interview I absentmindedly helped myself to the tins of lager he'd brought along presumably for his own consumption, which can't have endeared me to him. Under the circumstances, he was actually quite patient. He brushed aside my enquiry as to whether his physical health was a concern. 'My physical health? No. Not at all. Only my mental health. But the body is important for sensual experience.' When I asked him if Neubauten came out of nowhere, he replied, 'Yes. Out of Kraftwerk.' Who else did he listen to? 'Faust. The blues.' This was honest, since Neubauten, in their introduction of extra-musical equipment onstage and in the sheer, heavy industrial assault of their sound, were preceded by Faust, as evinced on 'Mamie Is Blue' from their album *So Far* in particular.

Bargeld never made any bones about it – for all the contrasts between Neubauten and seventies Krautrock, he was a great fan not only of Faust but also of Can and Kraftwerk, as well as Ton Steine Scherben, whose songs were more overtly lyrical and protest-driven. He had a great deal in common with them, in terms of his ideas of deconstruction/reconstruction as an aesthetic and cultural imperative, despite the punk divide. He was pushing the principle further, however, in different and more desperate times.

One significant difference was in Neubauten's use of the German language. 'There has always been a problem with German music, about singing in our own language,' he told me. 'For countries that did not have this interruption of the Third Reich, such as France and Italy, it is quite natural for bands to sing in French and Italian. I have learned to construct music around the German language, which is not capable of rock 'n' roll inflexions, learned how the music has to be different to accommodate the language.'

This is undoubtedly true. The German language and the modern environment are vital factors in Neubauten's sound topography. They were for a brief while associated with a 'metal bashing' movement, whose adherents included the SPK and the UK's Test Department, but Bargeld, sharing in collective memories of the Nuremberg rallies, was wary of the latter and their regular, inadvertently martial rhythms. Neubauten's beats are always irregular, halting, erupting, never letting the listener settle into line. One of their earliest recordings was in the tiny gap beneath an autobahn flyover. Another took place in a cooling tower. In both, the resonances of the unconsidered architecture were determinants in the music. Fiery woks, smashed breezeblocks, xylophone-like devices wrought from discarded metal sources, power drills and sheet metal all took their place in the Neubauten armoury, alongside remorseless electronic pulses like factory machinery accidentally left on overnight and scathing, abstract broadsides of electric guitar.

Around this, Bargeld coiled himself sensually, postured dramatically, his trademark a 'kettle scream', not so much a mighty, rock 'n' roll roar as something more akin to the death rattle of a horse caught in barbed wire. Although on 'Engel der Vernichtung' ('Annihilating Angel') from 1983's *Zeichnung des Patienten O.T.* he and the music descend like some avenging Passover spirit, and Neubauten's music seems to cackle at apocalypse on tracks like 'Der Tot ist Ein Dandy' ('Death Is a Dandy'), Bargeld epitomises, if anything, a sort of human enervation, a pitiful condition. 'Halber Mensch' ('Half Man'), which achieves all of the trademark Neubauten harshness with recourse only to a large choir, speaks of this inadequacy. Paradoxically, this is Bargeld and Neubauten's great strength, from which they extract a misshapen welter of meaning and material – what Biba Kopf terms the way their great and various noises 'eroticise desanitised and dead zones of contemporary life'.

'Hear with pain', sang Bargeld provocatively; 'ears are wounds', he added. Traditional rock fans would chortlingly concur with this assessment of the Neubauten experience, but it is Bargeld who was absorbing an unacknowledged pain, converting it into an auto-erotic, life-affirming, reinvigorating pleasure. Like Showaddywaddy, Neubauten were 'revivalists' but of a very different sort – of the spirit and weakened flesh fallen victim to an unacknowledged condition. Neubauten never did collapse. They exceeded rock music, rather than fall victim to its fickle, dialectical shifts. They would go on to exceed the introductory outrages of their earliest days, working across media, providing soundtracks for dance and theatre, including works for Heiner Müller and La La Human Steps.

It's one of the great paradoxes of the Berlin scene of the 1980s that it would almost thrive on a fascination with its own decay and its tragic, geopolitical bisection; in reality, it was laying the groundwork for the reunification of the city and its revival as an international cultural force following the collapse of bricks and mortar that actually did occur in 1989 – that of the Berlin Wall, an event universally unanticipated, certainly not by Wim Wenders's melancholic hymn of cinematic praise to the city, *Wings of Desire*, which was released the previous year.

*

Over in Düsseldorf, the West German capital of Neue Rhythmus, previously home to Neu! and Kraftwerk, another new beat was stirring. Deutsch-Amerikanische Freundschaft had already achieved a notoriety of sorts with their first two albums, *Ein Produkt der Deutsch-Amerikanische Freundschaft* (1979) and *Die Kleinen und die Bösen* (1980). The very naming of their 'product' echoed Neu!'s satire of Düsseldorf's industrial and commercial concerns, while their own moniker was more directly pointed about the alliance between West Germany and the USA and all of the empty comforts it had brought after the Second World War. *Produkt* and *Die Kleinen . . .* featured an expanded line-up, midway between scathing punk guitar and raw synthpop, but for a trilogy of albums released on Virgin Records between 1980 and 1982, commencing with *Alles ist Gut*, the group thinned down to absolute basics – vocalist Gabi Delgado-López and Robert Görl on drums and synths. No more guitars.

'We liked the punk energy, but we never understood why they were using the instruments of their fathers, the same old tools and same riffs. So we thought it's good to combine this fresh, new vitality with the new style of music, not with rock and roll,' Delgado-López told *The Quietus* in 2012.

The minimalism echoed Kraftwerk, but Robert Görl professed himself to be disdainful of the Düsseldorf quartet. 'At that time in Europe there were only rich guys with their huge synthesizers, the guys like Kraftwerk or Tangerine Dream. They always used their equipment in a really accurate manner and . . . we really disliked this kind of approach. We wanted to use it in a completely different way, the free way. With no rules, even no rules on how to treat a machine.'

As the son of Spanish immigrants who had settled in the Ruhr belt, Delgado-López felt alienated from the wealthy West German society from which Ralf Hütter and Florian Schneider had emerged with such insouciance. On 'Kebab Träume', D.A.F. highlight and celebrate the Turkish *Gastarbeiter*, and the threat they present to West Germany's cherished, perniciously banal sense of national identity. '*Deutschland, alles ist vorbei!*' chants Delgado-López ('Germany, it's all finished!'), adding, '*Wir sind die Türkeln von Morgen*' ('We are the Turks of tomorrow'). There is no quasi-bourgeois sense of Kraftwerkian ease with the modern world in D.A.F. Their every song feels like a physical tussle. Delgado-López sings in low tones that recall Alan Vega, whose group Suicide were an American precursor to D.A.F., pared down to a two-man combo of vocals and electronics, but Delgado-López sang in German, like Bargeld, exploiting the harshness of the language, his lyrics full of mock-imperatives and sternly debauched injunctions ('Verschwende deine Jugend' – 'Waste Your Youth'). They were bristling with the spirit of the post-punk times. When Nicole won the 1982 Eurovision Song Contest in 1982 for West Germany with 'Ein bisschen Frieden' ('A Little Bit of Peace'), D.A.F. countered on *Für Immer* with the strafing retort, 'Ein bisschen Krieg' ('A Little Bit of War').

Although antithetical to Kraftwerk in many respects, however,

D.A.F. were also taking the principles they had established and boiling them down still further. Where Kraftwerk's dapper four-man set-up exuded a mild perfume of campness, D.A.F.'s two-man set-up, with both men cropped and dressed from head to toe in leather, had distinctly homoerotic overtones, their man–machine relationship as grip-and-grapple as a bout of Graeco-Roman wrestling. Kraftwerk's deadpan and disingenuous stance, in which they placed themselves at a quite precise and consciously calculated distance from mainstream rock and the wider culture, was intensified by D.A.F. with their own highly developed existential and cultural sense of self-placement, as revealed on tracks like 'Der Mussolini' and 'Ich und die Wirklichkeit' ('Me and Reality').

As with Kraftwerk, D.A.F. weren't just revealed through their lyrics, of course, but in the way they wrought the very metal structures of their songs. The rhythms in D.A.F. songs such as 'Goldenes Spielzeug' ('Golden Toy') are like emotional diagrams, or absurdist, Escher-like stairways, or buckled under the heavy weight of irony. In this respect, they were ably assisted by now veteran producer Conny Plank, who used his old methods when working with the group – bonding with them as people, over food and long walks, then helping them realise their visions with maximum force and clarity in the studio. It's Plank's fine-tuning abilities that lend a high shine to 'Der Mussolini', the way it arcs hectically at you in great cubic, synthetic volleys, but tweaked askew here and there, as if to signify human waywardness or the refusal of the machinery to be tamed manually. Like Kraftwerk again, D.A.F. reached a logical creative terminus by the early 1980s – after *Für Immer*, there was little more they could really say and do with their methods. Still, their early albums are both cited as influential and yet stand alone, like hanging mobile sculptures unspoiled by the passing of time or supposed improvements in studio technology – testimonies to the joys of machine art before the greedy humans took over.

Initially, Chrislo Haas had been a member of D.A.F., but as they slimmed down to a twosome, in 1981 he co-founded in Berlin the group Liaisons Dangereuses, with Beate Bartel, formerly of Mania D and Einstürzende Neubauten, and the mysterious Krishna Goineau, who popped all over the mix adding sprightly yelps. Liaisons Dangereuses' debut album was again produced by Conny Plank. Perhaps the most extreme example of their full-blooded riposte to the frigid, measured stylings of Kraftwerkian synthpop is 'Dancibar', a track which featured on an *NME* cassette compilation in 1982. It's like little else before or since: a drum machine spits out an irregular rhythm that's at slight odds with the manic, splattered clusters of synth, punctured by random, angry, zigzagging incursions from other parts of the overheating console, over which a vocalist spills an urgent Hispanic monologue into the mike.

The album is less volatile but, again thanks to Conny Plank, is superbly realised, one of the overlooked masterpieces of electropop, still pristine and surprising. Although not as opulent as Yello, 'Mystère dans le brouillard' is equally cinematic, a perfectly executed monochrome horror short. Other standouts include 'Peut être . . . pas', which makes a hotplate of the dancefloor, and 'Los niños del parque', their best-known track, drawn along a long, thin wire of pulsing bass synth, which along with 'Der Mussolini' was a staple of a weekly Gothic disco I ran in my college days and was later cited as a favourite by the pioneers of the Detroit techno scene. With its insistent, agitating black squiggle, a worm in the machine, it anticipates the 303 squelch of acid house. This precursory role was further reinforced in a series of cassette recordings Liaisons Dangereuses made in 1981, particularly the jackhammer, droning 'Neger brauchen keine Elektronik' ('Black People Don't Need Electronics'). Just a few years later, a derivation of this sound, shorn of its weirder, morbid attachments, would be a staple of the rave scene – but Liaisons Dangereuses had ceased to be by that point, acknowledged in interviews by the likes of Derrick May but unable to capitalise further on the worldwide scene they had, in their small but crucial way, prefigured. Kraftwerk laid down the lines but Liaisons Dangereuses added the black juice, the mutant twist. Chrislo Haas, plagued by problems of alcohol and substance abuse, eventually died aged just forty-seven.

Der Plan had formed in Düsseldorf in 1979 – Kurt Dahlke, aka Pyrolator, had been a member of D.A.F. for a short time. They shared D.A.F.'s interest in mischief and minimalism, and had also made the decision to express their punkishly dissenting, noisy sensibility through the medium of electronics rather than guitars. Songs like 'Adrenalin lässt das Blut kochen' ('Adrenalin Leaves the Blood Boiling'), with its rotorblade rhythms, and 'Gefährliche Clowns' ('Dangerous Clowns') jostle well alongside a contemporary landscape that included the Residents, Throbbing Gristle and Robert Rental and the Normal, at once decadent and highly evolved specimens who reflected both the hopeless decline and the newly laid electric possibilities of their era. However, Der Plan, who would eventually go on to make what they termed 'Elektronische Schlager', brought something uniquely German to the mix – a reconnection with their own cinematic art traditions. Der Plan's *Normalette Surprise* is in many respects a miniaturist rereading of the Robert Wiene-directed 1920 silent horror film *The Cabinet of Dr Caligari*. (In 1982, Der Plan composed the soundtrack for Rainer Kirberg's *Die letzte Rache* ('The Last Revenge'), with the group's Moritz R assisting with the film's set design.)

The electronic treatments leave tripwires and cast long shadows everywhere, the sudden vistas and sudden collapses of perspective truly Caligari-esque in their invention and menace – on tracks like 'Wenn der Sonne ist verblüht' ('When the Sun Has Withered'), with its retreating sound-glimpses of church bells, eerie, wheezing fairground ambience and heavily treated, far from reassuring lullaby vocals, or 'Pausen-Sassa', winding through the dial of a series of MOR German radio stations, juxtaposing a kindergarten song with an extract of pornography. Despite sampling becoming a dull commonplace once samplers became widely commercially available, their use on *Normalette Surprise* suggests a whole gamut of new ways in which a pop song could be assembled, the windows it could throw on the world. On his solo albums, Pyrolator would make great use of Werner Lambertz's invention the Brontologic, a guitar-shaped digital device capable, once all patched up, of producing multiple sequencers running concurrently but in differing cycles. The results can be heard on tracks like 'Happiness' on 1981's *Ausland*, which simulates the orbiting of a satellite around the planet, and whose gleeful, aerial clusters of synthpop melody are way ahead of their time, indeed somewhere out of pop time and space altogether.

Neue Deutsche Welle would eventually become diluted, codified and derided, mocked by Blixa Bargeld as a new Schlager for the 1980s. Its best-known international hit was Nena's '99 Red Balloons', whose medium-paced, drearily slick synthpop tones do, it should be said, belie the fact that it is a song about global annihilation – the song's balloons are released into the air, accidentally triggering World War III. Whether this subject matter impinged on the minds of those who have swayed to the song at a million wedding discos since is another matter. NDW was, however, a source of pride among German music fans, who appreciated and basked reflectively in its triumphs in its own time, rather than decades afterwards.

As for its first wave, however, despite its severe contrasts with Krautrock, there was synthesis and common ground, and the same early take-up of available electronic technology, the same preoccupation with form, with tearing down and beginning anew, the same driving imperative to innovate. Groups like Neubauten, D.A.F. and Der Plan represent not a negation of Krautrock but, rather, a compact postscript.

12 Post-Bowie, Post-Punk, Today and Tomorrow

1977, the year of the so-called 'German Autumn', when the Baader–Meinhof axis flared up in one last burst of terrorist outrage before being effectively eradicated by a wave of suicides, was the year in which Krautrock as a whole was winding down, or settling into mainstream, de-radicalised careers. Neu! had separated into their opposing constituents: Klaus Dinger was pursuing cult glory with La Düsseldorf, and Michael Rother was launching his solo career with guitar- and synth-based albums which flowed just the right side of New Age. The Neu! legend, however, was destined to lie in abeyance for decades. Amon Düül and Popol Vuh ploughed their own individual furrows. Can had actually appeared on *Top of the Pops* the year before but they were beginning to grow weary of one another, dreaming of solo projects and falling back on outside musicians and the modern conveniences of the studio, rather than feeding off the intensity and proximity of one another as in the *Tago Mago* days. Faust slipped off the map entirely following the Munich sessions and would sit out the next decade and a half altogether before raging back as if they'd never been away in the mid-1990s, though sadly minus their key member, the late Rudi Sosna.

Tangerine Dream had gone international, but their anglicised name and their global appeal offset any jarring Teutonic air. Cluster charted a steady course in peripheral, ambient waters, Conrad Schnitzler was still a one-man reminder of the defunct hellraising spirit of the Arts Lab, but overall the energy of the scene that had flourished in the late sixties and early seventies had inevitably dissipated as early middle age approached, and with it the temptation to settle and make a living rather than bash their heads against the immovable wall that lay between avant-garde experimentalism and popularity and prosperity. Most of the key groups had at least laid down their legacy, said and done what they'd be best known for saying and doing. 'Krautrock' had come and gone, and while it had certainly not gone unnoticed, its fate was to remain buried beneath a pile of primarily Anglo-American-generated contemporaneous musical history, from prog rock to glam, from Philly soul to country rock. There was a general, lingering aversion to taking German popular music seriously, or hearing a German accent without breaking into an impromptu comedy goose-step. Europe in general was considered to be good for disco and the odd novelty but was primarily for holidaying in and being amused by.

Running counter to all of this was Kraftwerk. They had long since abandoned their longhair jamming phase. They had fashioned themselves into a human blueprint of an electronic pop revolution to come and, while their contemporaries faded away, they were on the brink of both major international success and producing their most significant and uncompromised body of work. They did, however, carry with them the air of undertaking an unabashedly German project that thrived on rather than wilted under derision. As such, they were the last carriers of the Krautrock virus and, for an upcoming generation, a portal to German music and soundworlds beyond. John Doran, co-founder of the website *The Quietus*, acknowledges as much. 'What was the first, great futuristic movement of the seventies? Krautrock. And what was its flashpoint? "Autobahn". It's to all intents and purposes the first fully electronic pop record – yeah, you had "Popcorn" by Hot Butter or Pierre Henry in the avant-garde realm or whatever, but this was a real game-changer. So, although it's completely arbitrary, it seems to me that "Autobahn" represents the birth of modern music. And then, of course, you have the through-line to Afrika Bambaataa and on to hip hop. If there's not a sonic link there's an aesthetic link – if there's not a formal link there's a philosophical link. Kraftwerk would be our Beatles.'

Dave Ball of Soft Cell felt similarly. 'My first point of contact with electronic music was Kraftwerk, when I heard "Autobahn" in 1975,' he tells me. 'I think between "Autobahn" and hearing the theme to *Doctor Who* got me into the whole idea of electronic music. From there on it was Tangerine Dream – as well as [Isao] Tomita, Wendy/Walter Carlos, *Switched on Bach*, and then our very own Brian Eno, who along with Bowie was dabbling with a lot of the Krautrock ideas anyway. Then Throbbing Gristle, Cabaret Voltaire, who were also taking from that world – the influence of Can was immense.'

'Krautrock' had ended, but 1977, the year of Kraftwerk's *Trans-Europe Express*, was the year Krautrock began – a legend, a posthumous phenomenon. This same year, the UK music paper *Sounds* ran a special issue on what they called the New Musick. Jon Savage in particular was prescient in identifying, in somewhat oblique terms, the energies in the toxified air of the UK in the late 1970s, arising from the crater left by the impact of punk. These included Throbbing Gristle, Cabaret Voltaire and Wire, as well as Kraftwerk, Can and Neu!, whose early 1970s music was now refracted in a whole new context. Siouxsie and the Banshees were also cited, who were developing in their sound an abstract, metallic sheen that would come to characterise post-punk and was best evidenced on their 'Metal Postcard (Mittageisen)', with a lyric based on a photomontage by the German artist and anti-Nazi satirist John Heartfield, 'Hurrah, die Butter ist alle!' ('Hurrah, the Butter Is All Gone!'), in which a family at a dinner table feast on bicycle parts and cans. In their own way, the Banshees were offering up a new mutation of metal for pop consumption. Siouxsie Sioux had been among a number of punks who had worn swastikas in the very early days of the movement, as a thoughtless, reflexive wind-up of their parents' generation living off old war movies and the triumph of the Battle of Britain. This practice was fairly swiftly squashed as more political voices such as Tom Robinson and the Rock Against Racism movement aligned with the forces of punk, in which a love of reggae and a hatred of the National Front became mandatory. Siouxsie herself was among those looking to European culture for more than just shock symbols. In the *Sounds* piece, Siouxsie and the Banshees were dubbed 'coldwave', a term which launched a movement of its own, especially popular in France, and part of a new dialogue between UK (post-) punk and the continent.

The New Musick was the stirring of a new aesthetic, a new pop ice age, drawing on the activities of groups who had been around for a few years, such as Kraftwerk and Can in Germany and Throbbing Gristle and Cabaret Voltaire in the UK. It also prefigured groups who were only just coming into being, such as Joy Division, who were still at that point barely out of their punk nappies, still trading as Warsaw that year.

David Bowie was the precursor of all this. In the mid-seventies, his ascent to stardom also had the effect of plunging his life into chaos, a chaos afforded him by the vast monies of his success and an innate disposition to make himself up as he went along, to live a wholly uncircumscribed existence. He was solo (if not single), thinking and acting without frontiers. As he ran amok, he became frightened of his own shadow, his own unchecked adventures convincing him that he himself was a symptom of a society on the brink of collapse. He also entertained an inflamed Nietzschean foreboding concerning the coming of 'Homo Superior', as he sang on 'Oh! You Pretty Things', none of which exactly enhanced his sense of conventional social obligation. He was inconsiderate of others, callously breaking up the Spiders from Mars and, just when he sensed the glam-rock boat had run its course, abruptly jumping ship and heading for America. There, in keeping with Hollywood and the music business in general, he consumed mountainous quantities of cocaine, his weight dropping to sub-jockey levels of around eighty pounds.

He became paranoid, convinced that every passing light in the sky was a visiting UFO, storing his urine in his fridge, waiving the usual mortal cravings such as the need to eat food regularly, developing an obsessive interest in the occult. He was barely of this world. A sense that he was rooted nowhere, a man without geographical identity, was enhanced by his starring role in Nic Roeg's *The Man Who Fell to Earth*, in which his almost translucent features and penetrating, marble-like eyes made him a thoroughly convincing alien. He felt out of time, too, his appearance both postmodern and futuristic, a singularly striking presence at a time, the mid-1970s, when style was in an utter quandary.

Without his people, his protective PA Corinne 'Coco' Schwab in particular, Bowie could scarcely have functioned at a basic level in this world at this point in his spoiled, deluded, perilous life. However, the mid-seventies were not only his most brilliant period in terms of recorded output but also the time when he was aware, at some deeper motor level, of tectonic shifts in popular culture being in the offing. Messed up as he was, incapable of keeping appointments or the upkeep of his own body, barely able to string a coherent sentence together in TV interviews, Bowie had a hawkeye sense of what was happening, what was going to happen and what should happen. Creatively speaking, he was absorbent, visionary and disciplined.

Bowie arrived in New York in 1974 with the conventional enough ambition, one he shared with groups like Slade, of conquering America. However, on arrival, he immediately became fixated on the real thing that was happening in the States at the time – the soul scene, on the cusp of becoming codified in the nightclubs as disco. New York, Philly, LA, Bowie soaked it all up but not in some abased, 'blackface' manner, adopting soul mannerisms out of a sense of Caucasian inadequacy. He dubbed what he was doing 'plastic soul', a coinage whose frankness recalled Can's 'Ethnological Forgery Series', but in which the word 'plastic' is ambiguous, not just meaning 'phoney' but also referring to the plastic arts. To an extent, as was his wont, he was like a flitting bee sucking nectar from a scene in full flower. However, as *Young Americans* would show, soul music was just one aspect of the canvas he was working on at the time. His overall concerns were rather more morbid.

In 1975, he declared that rock was dead, a 'toothless old woman', and that he was done with it. In 1975, he had a point. His associates at the time were the inebriated likes of Harry Nilsson, Ringo Starr, Keith Moon – and John Lennon, with whom he just about kept it together enough to record the brilliant 'Fame', whose self-excoriating bitterness was like a moment of lucidity amid the raging, hellraising hedonism of the period.

Lennon epitomised the quandary of the dominant rock aristocracy in 1975. Rich but creatively spent, he had neither the need nor the ability to push rock's envelope back any further. He was barely out of his early thirties but his best work was all behind him. What was he still around for, other than to get wrecked? What was the point of ex-Beatles like him, or Starr, or Harrison away with the gurus, or McCartney, touting the conspicuously inferior Wings over America, with his wife in lieu of Lennon? The Rolling Stones, too, struggled artistically in the shadow of the achievements of their recent past, with Richards sinking into heroin addiction and Jagger ascending into the stratospheres of a jetset elite from which street-fighting men were barred by a velvet rope. All they talked about in interviews was the level of income tax they were required to pay in the UK, obliging them to spend their days overseas. Spoiled rich boys.

Led Zeppelin were at a hubristic zenith, for sure, with Robert Plant screaming, 'I'm a golden god!' from the window of his suite at the Hyatt on Sunset Strip in LA, but their creative dip and time of dying was, sadly, just around the corner. Elton John, a talented enough pianist and singer but the sheer scale of whose success in the mid-seventies might well baffle future musicologists, was all-dominant, releasing his hint-hint smash album *Captain Fantastic and the Brown Dirt Cowboy*, but the sheer demand for his services, apparently to fill a gaping superstar void with his outsized glasses and boots, wore him down and he would retire out of sheer exhaustion in 1977.

These spent forces and squandered souls were Bowie's peers. They were going nowhere except down, and Bowie wasn't going to go with them. As he had decamped from UK glam the moment he realised it was done with, he would now decamp to Europe. It was a practical move at one level, to recharge his creative barriers, enjoy a change of scenery, to pick up on burgeoning new influences, and to sober up.

A harbinger of his intentions came on *Station to Station*, released prior to the move, and its opening, ten-minute-plus track in particular, which begins with the stereopanning simulation of a locomotive engine. Kraftwerk hadn't yet released *Trans-Europe Express* at this point – Bowie, who shared Kraftwerk's aversion to planes (one of the technologies they did not celebrate), had undertaken a long railway journey from Japan to Europe in 1973 which afforded him a series of culture shocks as he gazed out of the carriage window. As it builds, it's reminiscent of 'And the Gods Made Love', the feedback-drenched opening of Jimi Hendrix's *Electric Ladyland*, an instrumental prelude that implicitly scours and erases all traces of that which preceded it.

The remainder of the track is segmented, almost rock-operatic as befits Bowie's sense of self-as-theatre and the stations of his creative life. Over a stomping riff that seems to allude to Led Zeppelin's 'When the Levee Breaks', Bowie paraglides away, landing in an imaginary Europe announcing the 'Return of the thin white duke', and working up to the chorus line: 'It's not the side effects of the cocaine . . . The European canon is here.'

In reality, in 1976 Bowie relocated first to Switzerland but found that in that gilded Euro-playground his cocaine habit actually worsened. Once again, at another level his manoeuvrings were disastrous. His comment to a journalist that Britain needed a 'fascist state' in order to acquire some much-needed discipline was one he would rightly have to live down for decades to come. It endangered the credibility of his efforts to reorientate rock minds to a more European way of thinking – that particular historical strand of European thinking which we could well do without. It also came at a time when far-right groups like the National Front were stoking and exploiting public anxieties about the 'problem' of immigration and the higher visibility of ethnic minorities. On the other hand, it clearly wasn't rooted in any serious analysis and research into the condition of British society but in a projection of his own need for some sort of discipline and austerity, a stop to his own bad habits and decay.

Bowie then relocated to Berlin, persuading Iggy Pop to join him. Both would be reconfigured as a result of the move, paring down and purging, reshaping themselves as if undergoing some of the imaginary benefits of the 'fascist' dosage Bowie had recommended. They would meet Kraftwerk and stiffen their sinews. Bowie would work with Eno and benefit from his oblique strategies. The Thin White Duke was still mired in familial strife and mental confusion – but he understood, without quite understanding what it was that he understood, that a move to Europe was imperative, not just for him but for all that he towed in his wake. In transferring from the Young America, and some of the not so young rock 'n' roll company he had kept there, to Berlin, he was anticipating post-punk. The move to Europe was intended as a bleak riposte to its shallow, transatlantic opposite. Here, he would exist among the longer shadows of older cultures, some of whose memory he would help revive, as they in turn revived him artistically. Berlin and its ghosts of the recent past would be the future. This would be the backdrop against which he would pose, to himself and to the world, against which the drama of his songwriting and his changeling persona would play out.

A new Europhilia would have happened with or without Bowie, but his 'Berlin Phase' certainly offered blessing and validation to the movement. Put simply, if Bowie thought Germany was cool, then Germany was cool. His very presence there adjusted the aspect and temperature of the place. Bowie also had a shallow and morbid fascination with Nazi Germany which he shared with some of his fans turned musicians – an undercurrent of flirtation with dubious imagery which would cause tension between some elements of the art-punk/post-punk movement and the Anti-Nazi League. Joy Division, whose name was taken from the concentration-camp brothels, were considered particularly suspicious. The poster accompanying their 1978 debut release, *An Ideal for Living*, featured a member of the Hitler Youth banging a drum and a German soldier pointing a gun at a boy, as well as a photo of Bernard Sumner looking blond and cropped. However, although Ian Curtis had, according to his widow Deborah, an 'obsession with the Nazi uniform', his reading ran to Dostoevsky, Nietzsche, Jean-Paul Sartre and Hermann Hesse, as well as John Heartfield and his photomontages.

As post-punk unfolded, the new Europhilia revealed itself in a host of artists' names, song titles and lyrics: Magazine's Dostoevsky-inspired 'Song from Under the Floorboards', Warsaw, Josef K, Spandau Ballet, Bauhaus, Cabaret Voltaire, Wire's 'Midnight Bahnhof Cafe', the Associates' 'White Car in Germany', Simple Minds' 'Kant-Kino' and 'I Travel', the soundtrack to a new generation of Interrailers, gap-year students doing the Grand Tour on a budget. The impulse was in keeping with punk and, as it happened, with Krautrock – a rejection of the Americanisation of British rock, a reversal of Rod Stewart's *Atlantic Crossing* and all of those painful, caterwauling faux-Stateside accents British superstars felt obliged to adopt in order to maintain their high international profile. In its place, a more cerebral disposition towards European culture, the more serious, radical and futuristic the better.

Moreover, Europhilia was, at this time, tantamount to a political act as well as an aesthetic preference. Ronald Reagan was president elect in 1980, as Heaven 17 warned on their pneumatic, instant electropop classic 'We Don't Need This Fascist Groove Thang'. The special relationship between Margaret Thatcher and Reagan struck many as reducing the UK to the USA's fifty-first state, especially at a time when tensions were rising between the nuclear superpowers, so much so that membership of the Campaign for Nuclear Disarmament went up ninefold following the UK's decision to buy the Trident missile system, the presence of American cruise missiles on UK soil and America's disastrous foreign engagements – in Iran, for example. Europe, caught in the middle and mooted as a future theatre of war, was still experientially etched with the lines and scars of previous terrible conflicts. Better a heightened European consciousness than dreaming increasingly inane American dreams or sharing in the disastrously misplaced optimism of Reagan's 'Morning in America', especially when to many the time felt more like Seven Minutes to Midnight.

Colin Newman, of Wire, was one of those who embraced the idea of Europe as providing a founding identity rather than America. 'It's not that we were selfconsciously anti-American, it's that we were British. If you were from Salford, why would you want to sing about Route 66? But at the same time, singing about the Arndale Centre didn't quite do it,' he says. 'There was something very stifling about Britishness – that hangover from the sixties, that instant nostalgia peddled by groups like the Kinks. Frankly, we were sick to death of Britain. So in 1978, I started a love affair with continental Europe. I wanted to escape a certain British condition, one that started in childhood, with school, when the sort of person you were destined to be was categorised.

Europe meant being the person you wanted to be. That involved going through a certain level of pretension, but that was necessary if you wanted to be something other than an ordinary person.'

Wire once released a live CD of a very early central London performance of theirs in which they played to an absolutely empty room. Although they did attain a following, they were often at odds with their British audiences, who wanted them to stick to playing gobbets of punk like '12XU'. Wire, who had unabashedly arty ambitions, would flaunt them and taunt them. The lukewarm, motorway-service-station churlishness of Britain in the late seventies was, they found, a contrast with the reception awaiting them when they reached Europe.

'In Britain when you played concerts, you were treated like a second-class citizen,' says Newman. 'You might be on the cover of *NME*, but once you got out into the sticks you'd turn up at the venue – there'd be a couple of beers waiting for you, no food, and once you'd finished, everything was shut. We made absolutely no money from gigging. Then we went to Europe. We played the Ratinger Hof in Düsseldorf – the first non-German group they'd put on. It was such a different experience. The people were nicer. They wanted to have conversations with you. The food was good. The bars stayed open late. There was a culture of intelligent, non-American rock music to which we felt really connected.'

It should be said that Wire were greeted as saviours by some sections of the German press, as an example of fine foreign fare that put their own domestic rubbish to shame. However, for Newman, the experience of travelling down Germany's lengthy arterial routes was as symphonic as Kraftwerk had promised. 'I liked Faust, Can, later Neu!, but Kraftwerk most of all. Everything about them was brilliant. The sound, the look, the humour. So po-faced, but also so natural. I could stare at the cover of *Trans-Europe Express* for hours. So fantastically European – the orchestral echoes, the wheels turning infinitely – we related to that from the hours and hours we spent on the autobahns supporting Roxy Music.'

It wasn't just the sheer, existential novelty of European travel that endeared German music to the post-punk generation, or, conversely, its bleak atmospherics. ('Berlin was claustrophobic,' remembers Newman. 'As you made your way from the cafe to the studio you could see the guards along the Wall.') It turned out that most of the new, emergent year-zero groups had spent their formative years listening to Krautrock. While making a point of deriding prog and dinosaur rock of the seventies and its pseudo-classical emphasis on virtuosity rather than communication, Krautrock was something else. Not a pass for all, mind. 'Tangerine Dream I linked to UK bands like Zorch,' says Newman. 'The way they used synthesizers felt very much like prog, as if they were too important things to make pop music with. But names like Can became very hip to drop. The Rich Kids [Midge Ure's interim punk band between Slik and Ultravox] used to say that their favourite bands were Can and Abba.'

Jim Kerr of Simple Minds, who grew up in Glasgow, was another for whom Krautrock was an unlikely teenage epiphany. 'Charlie [Burchill, Simple Minds' guitarist] had an elder brother, Jamie, who was the coolest guy on the housing scheme. He was the first guy to dye his hair, have an earring, buy a guitar and listen to strange music. I lucked out because I was in the next block to Charlie. This was when we were in our mid-teens. My friends had older brothers. Every time you'd go up to their places and they were the ones listening to Faust, Van Der Graaf Generator and Neu!. You'd go to gigs with them at the McLellan Galleries [an exhibition space in Glasgow]. I was only fourteen, seeing people like Cale, Nico – so much of it was over my head, but it was cool to be able to go into school and say you'd seen Nico the night before. But it wasn't just oneupmanship. It was this feeling of, "Thank fuck there's something going on other than these four walls, or whatever's being played on the Tony Blackburn show."'

In Julian Cope's *Krautrocksampler*, he tells the story of how Kerr, in a supposed fit of anti-Kraut pique, threw his Faust albums out of the window of his high tenement building, in what has been cited by some writers as an example of his philistinism. Kerr smilingly corrects the story – he had been so out of it, it transpires, that he threw practically his entire record collection out of the window. Faust were certainly not singled out for defenestration. 'I loved Faust,' he protests. 'I saw Faust in Glasgow, Ian McCulloch [of Echo and the Bunnymen] had been at the Faust gig in Liverpool. We realised how much we had in common, despite the different sounds we came up with.' Ironically, the Simple Minds hit 'The American' was the result of producer Steve Hillage, of seventies group Gong, bringing 'all these Krautrock records, Moebius and Roedelius, Holger Czukay, to the studio. And we got this great track.'

PiL's John Lydon was a lover of Can, with an apocryphal story even floated that he might sing for the group having quit the Sex Pistols. Pete Shelley was a great admirer also, as was Mark E. Smith of the Fall, whose 'I Am Damo Suzuki' tells, in its abstruse, modified and abrasive Smithian way, the story of Suzuki's serendipitous arrival in the group – the meeting in the Cologne Marktplatz, his subsequent defection to the Jehovah's Witnesses. Although Smith did not share Can's anti-leadership ethos, he was clearly influenced by the relationship they struck between singer and band.

Orchestral Manoeuvres in the Dark's Andy McCluskey loved Kraftwerk to a quite scholarly degree; Bill Drummond, who was producer and manager of Echo and the Bunnymen and The Teardrop Explodes in his pre-KLF days, was another early adopter of Krautrock, finding in it an alternative to the baroque prog mores of the early 1970s; Mark Stewart of Bristol's The Pop Group loved Neu! – as well, he says, as some of the more heavy-duty bands sometimes not considered in much depth by German music historians. 'I love Hamburg stuff, German psych-rock and raw freakbeat,' he says. 'Those post-Beatles bands going completely psychedelic in small towns.' Then, of course, there was Julian Cope, who would emerge as a champion of all Krautrock – his early *NME* interviews were dotted with praise for the whole gamut of German music, each reference a little gateway for the sort of ardent reader for whom post-punk was a portal to everything from Stockhausen to Lee 'Scratch' Perry, Charlie Parker to Charlie Feathers.

Although Cope is the most fervent admirer of German music, it's not obviously reflected in The Teardrop Explodes, in the likes of 'Reward' and 'Treason', big, brassy, epic, hearty pop in the grand Liverpudlian manner of the day, as opposed to the more dour Mancunian variety. You can hear it more in the post-industrial pieces of Throbbing Gristle and Cabaret Voltaire, who had been around since 1975 and 1972 respectively. In their use of reconstructed and modified equipment, custom-built modular synths, found sounds as collage, brutal repetition and loops (Throbbing Gristle's 'Discipline', as magnificently inflicted live in Berlin, is a stern example of this), they had much in common with noisenik extremists like Guru Guru and Faust, sharing and emulating many of their methods and their sheer range. In different circumstances and to different ends, however. No Krautrock group would name one of their tracks 'Baader Meinhof', as Sheffield's Cabaret Voltaire did. They captured a prevailing, darkening mood of geopolitical, paranoiac terror in their samples of crazed American preachers, or album titles like *Red Mecca*. Gnarled lines like 'What's going to happen next?', 'Ready to die' and 'Seconds too late' crawl out like survivors from their fractured, dystopian sound scenarios.

Throbbing Gristle's seemingly cruel fixation with toxicity and abjection was similarly rooted in the perniciously dismal experience of 1970s Britain, as opposed to Krautrock's strong inclination towards renewal and reconstruction and utopian dreaming. Yet both Throbbing Gristle and Cabaret Voltaire overlapped with

Krautrock in their rejection of musical tuition, their use of new technology to inflict electric-shock treatment and their insistence that their subject matter and their reason for being required that they tear up the old and, from the rubble, wiring and girders, bend the shape of the new.

For other groups, still working in relatively conventional, four-square formats which bore some resemblance to verse-and-chorus, drums-and-guitar rock and pop, the influence was still palpable. There is in standard post-punk a reconstituted, democratised relationship between the instruments, a sense of space between the players. Stephen Morris's playing with Joy Division is an example of the cyclical, looped approach which harks back to Can's Jaki Liebezeit and which didn't require old-school, Cozy Powell-style octopus skills to execute. Guitars are applied in incisive, abstract painterly strokes (post-punk manages at its best to be both minimal and imagistic), the bass often takes up melodic duties and vocals are delivered with ominous, deadpan solemnity, chin to chest, rather than as an opportunity to emote ostentatiously. Solos are frowned upon, virtuoso wings are clipped and everyone labours for the collective effort. Other influences such as dub and funk were also vital components in loosening the clamp of rock orthodoxy at the time. But Krautrock's artful, necessary resistance to the old way of doing things was a vital model.

Synthpop was clearly of Krautrock ancestry, as Andy McCluskey and Soft Cell's Dave Ball would happily acknowledge. The filmmaker Ben Wheatley, whose black comedy *Sightseers* (2012) uses both eighties synthpop and an underpinning of Krautrock, certainly understands this. 'I'd been getting into Krautrock quite a lot, and I realised I'd been sold this bill of goods when I was a kid that the new wave of punk had been something we invented in the UK,' he told journalist Stephen Dalton. 'But actually if you look at history you realise it was made in Germany. Obviously music's fluid and I'm sure you can trace Krautrock from other places as well – Neu!

being for me the centre of a lot of music, obviously Harmonia came out of Neu!. So I had this idea that there would be two sets of music – this big, brassy synth music that happened in the eighties in the UK, but underneath it was the German music where that had really come from.' Prior to 1980, however, Kraftwerk were considered antithetical to rock countercultural thinking and their benign faith in machinery wilfully naïve in an era when increased automation in the workplace threatened to add to the growing lines of the unemployed. The nuclear-powered future they had appeared to celebrate on 'Radio-Activity', meanwhile, carried with it both the threat of ecological disaster, of which the partial meltdown at a reactor in Three Mile Island in Pennsylvania in 1979 was but a warning, and, at worst, global annihilation. Synthesizers were not the brave new soundworld for all but a cheap, tawdry replacement for organic, human sounds, a present-day blight, the stuff of a coming hegemony of Muzak. Gary Numan's albums, on the covers of which he stared with silicone-faced impassivity, were a grim and unpleasant harbinger to many (though that look was, it turned out, the result of emergency lacquering treatment from the *Top of the Pops* make-up department when he fell foul of a bout of acne prior to his appearance on the show). He personified synthpop for many, and its dystopian prospects, as illustrated in his flangey, heroically despondent songs about sad androids and singing machines.

Daniel Miller, who had recorded the early synthpop single 'Warm Leatherette' in 1978 under the name of the Normal, was an acknowledged fan of German music, much of which he would put out on his Mute label. As he discovered, however, in that politically polarised era, there were those who joined the dots between synthesizer music, its cold, regular rhythmical emphasis and its German origin and drew entirely the wrong conclusions. When he brought Deutsch-Amerikanische Freundschaft, whom he had recently signed, to play in the UK, a number of people in the crowd started pumping along with stiff-armed Nazi salutes. Miller, of Jewish parentage, did not appreciate this irony any more than the (obviously anti-Nazi) D.A.F. Even the innocuous Soft Cell, with their gay lead vocalist and Northern soul cover versions, were not immune from misinterpretation.

'Leeds was so right-wing,' recalls Dave Ball, of the city in which Soft Cell were formed. 'It was such a heavy town for the National Front. I was there between 1977 and 1981. I remember them in their black jackets, skinheads, they were scary. Once a load of them, about sixty, came to one of our gigs at a club called Amnesia. It was us playing and an audience full of New Romantics, and everyone was shitting themselves. I thought, "Oh my God, we're going to get killed." And their leader came over and said, "We really like your music." I think because they'd heard about "Spandau Ballet" and "White Funk", and some of the imagery of New Romantic garb involved things like peaked black caps and jodhpurs or Steve Strange having his photo taken with Helmut Newton, I think they misguidedly thought they'd found some sympathisers. But then, if you look at Kraftwerk, *The Man-Machine*, some of that imagery is slightly dubious – the cropped hair, the uniform. Granted, they're in communist red . . .' But that had not stopped a *Village Voice* reporter, when Malaria! played a concert with Nina Hagen at New York's Studio 54, describing the group, clad in black and red, as 'dressed as Nazis on the day of Yom Kippur!' Such hair-trigger misapprehensions were commonplace even in the left-liberal press.

The eighties grew older, however, and as they did so, the tribalism, apocalyptic anxieties and politically charged atmosphere of the decade's early years gave way to a gradual resignation, a cosy acceptance as the West lurched to the right. Synthesizers became ubiquitous in pop, the world carried on turning as Glasnost beckoned and Kraftwerk, whose man–machine methodology was if anything making them look a little quaint, retired to their studios, ostensibly to convert from analogue to digital, but really, it turned out, because they had nothing more to say to the electric world. 1986's *Electric Cafe* was, to all intents and purposes, their last album. It was also the point at which Krautrock seemed farthest from the rock discourse.

The mid-eighties, when I first joined *Melody Maker*, were a nondescript time for music, in which the overbearing spectacle of Live Aid seemed to suck the life out of everything for a brief time. Stadium megapop appeared to have assumed a permanent global dominance, and the briefly plausible idea of radicalising pop with strategic entries from the left field (ABC, the Associates, Scritti Politti, etc.) felt utterly spent and futile. Indie music was caught in a post-post-punk hiatus, shrivelled into a deliberate smallness, with grey, self-effacing little groups like the Housemartins, the Wedding Present and Bogshed making a virtue of their raggedy second-handness, narrow outlook and lack of sonic ambition.

It was about now that, out of nowhere and on the back of nothing, ReR, formerly Recommended Records, reissued Faust's *Munic and Elsewhere*, their last recordings before their lengthy disappearance. In my review of it, I described the group as 'specks on their own landscape' – their sound, in other words, was much bigger than they were, an inversion of the rock-star norm and the ostentatious histrionics of white soul as personified by Mick Hucknall, Phil Collins, Annie Lennox. It was an idea to fasten to. And then, all of a sudden, like distant explosions on the horizon, a crop of new names began to emerge: in the UK, groups like A. R. Kane, Spacemen 3 and Loop; from Ireland, My Bloody Valentine; from Switzerland, the Young Gods; from the USA, Big Black and a properly emergent Sonic Youth. None of these people were Stones or even Pistols in the making, none of them were making a serious play for the charts, but collectively they played with the impact of a thousand suns. Simon Reynolds declared in a review of Hüsker Dü the 'Return of rock' and, later, the 'raptures of rock', an implied riposte to the early-eighties diktat that guitar music was to be declared 'rockist', too white and male to speak to the *NME*'s new funky and pop-ist creed. At *Melody Maker*, we made an evangelical point of highlighting this new outcrop, making them cover stars, showering them with screeds of adjectival praise in the hope of pushing them towards the wider listenership many of them did indeed ultimately achieve.

All of these groups played guitar, but with a heaviness, a billowing spaciousness that enveloped and immolated their selves. This wasn't cock-rock assertiveness but a dissolution, a neo-psychedelic wipeout. And most of these players had Krautrock in their locker. Kevin Shields of My Bloody Valentine was a massive Krautrock-head, even Steve Albini of Big Black covered Kraftwerk's 'The Model', while Robert Hampson's Loop paid their own homage with a version of Can's 'Mother Sky'.

'Krautrock most definitely had a huge influence on the work of Loop. It was integral to the sound structures and the dynamics as much as the many other influences on Loop,' says Hampson. 'The whole idea of Loop was generated from many facets of music and the ways of trying to merge them to make something new. Of course, Can and Neu! were the biggest influences. Can for the sonic experiments within a song-like structure, and Neu! for the whole *motorik* approach. The use of repetition in Loop was distinctly influenced from two areas – minimalist systems music and Krautrock. From day one, I always knew that Loop would do a version of "Mother Sky" eventually. It started out as simply an encore live, but we quickly decided to devote a whole side of a twelve-inch single to it.

'There's no other period like Krautrock, not even in the UK in the late sixties with bands like Soft Machine or Pink Floyd. Even though those bands influenced the Krautrock bands, along with the Velvets, the Teutonic edge was a million miles away from the more traditional embers of the British psychedelic afterglow. It was far more dangerous, more edgy, more sonically sophisticated. The only real comparison you can make was probably how much hash was being smoked. After that, you simply entered another galaxy.'

The dialectic had shifted. Rock was 'big' again, but only in its physicality. The charts continued to be dominated by tepid neo-soul warblers steeped in palsied reverence to the dead past, jacket sleeves rolled up and mandatory backing gospel singers towed in to affirm the authenticity and soulfulness of their posturing, but that was just so much Schlager. This was a rock whose meaning and implications lay in its overwhelming textures rather than any finger-pointing lyrical stance or on-the-nose, overt politicising. This was a return to form and volume and noise as an imperative, rather than an indulgence – the rediscovery of fire and new ways of being.

In 1989, Can dropped back into the fray with the apposite *Rite Time*, fronted again by Malcolm Mooney, with the press release telling the fishy tale that he had unearthed the return ticket to Europe after his flight from the group in 1969 twenty years earlier and had decided to take advantage of it. I interviewed the group at the offices of Phonogram in west London as the four founder members, minus Mooney, reminisced placidly about the various violent arguments they had had in the studio over the years. If I was awestruck and felt as if in the presence of returning gods, I gave no hint of it in my probing interrogation, asking them, for instance, if it was fair to say that Can were the greatest rock band in the world. Unaffronted, Irmin Schmidt replied to the effect that he could neither confirm nor deny this.

Rite Time isn't the best Can album, but it is superior to most of their post-*Soon Over Babaluma* output, dominated by its lengthiest tracks, such as 'Like a New Child', which is remarkably confluent with Talk Talk's surprisingly radical *Spirit of Eden*, produced around the same time, with its potentially endless, Amazonian slow drift, tropical opulence and occasional strategic sunbursts of noise to break up the reverie, the voyage undertaken with a sort of blissful solemnity. Every now and again, Schmidt replenishes the flow with blue waves of keyboard as if to repel the inevitable dusk. This was Can's belated last stand, a last, elegiac flowering, much as rock itself was entering its supernova phase. Following the acid meltdown of My Bloody Valentine's 'To Here Knows When' and the codification of the 'return of rock' with grunge and Nirvana, its narrative came to an abrupt halt with the suicide of Kurt Cobain. There would be rock after 1994, but only retrograde rock or post-rock. As for Krautrock, it would continue to thrive after death.

The baton continued to be passed from generation to generation of enthusiasts. Geoff Barrow of Portishead had already begun work on *Dummy*, the album that would be foundational to the trip-hop movement of the 1990s, when he happened to switch on the radio and undergo a belated, life-altering experience.

'Mark E. Smith was on Radio 1 being interviewed, in the days when they had interesting guests, about his top ten tracks, one of which was "Vitamin C" by Can. It was on a ghetto blaster in the kitchen, I happened to catch it and said, "What the fuck is this?" I immediately chucked a cassette in the machine – I honestly thought it was a new band. It had a James Brown-style beat and almost a stoner Manc vocal, and the same bassline as something like A Tribe Called Quest. And I thought, "This is mental, this is the best band in the world, someone's done it, someone's lived my dream."

'And then Smith said, that's from 1971 – that was Can. So I legged it down to my local record shop and asked the guy behind the counter, "Have you got this track called 'Can' by this group Vitamin C?" And he's like, "No," very sarcastic, like the *Simpsons* Comic Book Guy. And then he pointed round the corner to the C section, I bought *Ege Bamyası* and I was hooked. It continues to be my favourite record of all time – I never tire of it.'

Following Iggy Pop (and before him Peter Blegvad, the expat who briefly played with Faust), and among the first of the US groups to absorb Krautrock, Can in particular, were Talking Heads. David Byrne had been born in Scotland and was more conscious than most of the post-punk UK scene, impressed by, among others, A Certain Ratio and their mordant, desiccated, Gothic white funk. In tandem with Brian Eno, Byrne would undertake a dialogue between the exploratory but inhibited Caucasian and the dark, ethnic 'Other' on albums like *My Life in the Bush of Ghosts*. He then approached funk and disco in a similar spirit on 1980's brilliant *Remain in Light*, in which he in particular played up the distance between his own neurotic and neurological nerdiness, a hyperconscious brain he couldn't switch off, and the solace he found in the more 'instinctive' rhythms of soul and dance music, in which he could stop making sense, flailing like a lost Livingstone.

The danger of condescension in these relationships was only offset by his self-deprecation and obvious love and grasp of the music. However, it was quite clear that he had been exposed to Can, who had worked out their own relationship between their German selves and their ethnological sources. 'Listening Wind', from *Remain in Light*, is very much a homage to 'Come sta, la luna' on Can's *Soon Over Babaluma*. If Can's influence needed to be remembered in 1980, it was there in the busy presence of Holger Czukay, whose album *Movies* was a huge favourite among the *NME* hipsters and who would work with, among others, Jah Wobble (on the EP *How Much Are They?*) and David Sylvian in his post-Japan days.

Punk's impact in the US was more diffuse than in the UK – it was too sprawling a place to be affected by a single, Sex Pistols-type detonation. Punk came in phases and from different places in the US, from east coast to west coast, in a range of moments, from the Ramones to Black Flag to Sonic Youth to Nirvana. It was with Sonic Youth in particular that US indie rock really opened itself up to a sense of the genre's history and geography. Sonic Youth weren't just players but students, channellers of rock in all its extremes, Krautrock very much included. 'Neu! and Krautrock were important to Sonic Youth,' says Steve Shelley. 'I'd say that Krautrock in general and Can and Neu! specifically were as important to Sonic Youth inspiration-wise as the Velvet Underground, Television, the Stooges and Captain Beefheart were.

'I first heard Kraftwerk on the funk/soul station from Saginaw, Michigan, in the early eighties while living in Midland, MI (and maybe also heard the rare stray copy of *Autobahn* owned by prog-rock fans), I guess around the time of *Computer World* (still my favourite Kraftwerk LP) and soon after in Detroit at the clubs, usually at gay discos – the only clubs that would allow our bands to play at that time.

'I probably heard Neu! when travelling Europe, and specifically Germany, for the first time with Sonic Youth in 1985 and 1986 – we would comb the used-record stores and feverishly grab records by Neu! and Can. Neu! was a big-time fave in the van cassette player – great driving music, obviously. As evident in "Two Cool Rock Chicks Listening to Neu", our minds and imaginations were being blown by two guys [Michael Rother and Klaus Dinger] we never expected to meet – we knew so little of the actual people behind the music that they could only be legends to us.'

Krautrock coursed through the consciousness of alternative late-eighties and nineties rock, cropping up in all kinds of unlikely places – Steve Albini's Big Black covered Kraftwerk's 'The Model', but so too did the late blues-rock guitar picker Chris Whitley. Meanwhile, covering a festival for *Melody Maker* back in 1991, I walked into a concert hall and was astonished to hear a solo guitarist filling the entire room with a staggering volley of echo-drenched chimes which seemed to multiply in mid-air and bounce back off the walls from all angles before crashing and burning. It was, I managed to divine after a few moments, his version of

Kraftwerk's 'Autobahn', his tribute to Germany's reunification. The guitarist was Gary Lucas, who had been a member of Captain Beefheart's Magic Band. I had to go shake his hand – we've been friends ever since.

America remained a heartland of resistance to Euro-music, with its synths and supposed artistic affectation. 'Even in the 1990s, you would meet Americans who still felt that it wasn't real music if it wasn't made with real instruments,' says Colin Newman. However, it found wormholes of underground influence. Early-nineties alt-grunge outfit Pavement's mazy ways and Mercury Rev's slow-exploding, acid-fried guitar excursions both represented the outer limits of the scene from which Nirvana ultimately rose to popularity. Both were touched by Krautrock, Pavement's Stephen Malkmus so much so that in 2012 he went on the road to cover Can's *Ege Bamyası* in its entirety. However, for the strongest, most stratospheric example of Krautrock as a launchpad for wholly new adventures, seek out Boston band Cul de Sac's 'Doldrums', from their 1995 album *I Don't Want to Go to Bed*. Emerging dank and rusty from low in the mix, it works up into an instrumental mantra that summons up the full cyclical force of Can and the blinkered, propulsive thrust of Neu!, as well as the hurricane force of Ash Ra Tempel, Guru Guru and Günter Schickert combined.

In the 1990s there would be Britpop. However, there would also be Stereolab. Co-founded by Laetitia Sadier and Tim Gane, formerly of the indie group McCarthy, Stereolab were a pan-European alliance of a sort. Sadier's deadpan French vocals evoked half-remembered chic chansons of the sixties, as well as hinting at a more submerged left-field Gallic tradition that has never really gained traction outside of France. Tim Gane, meanwhile, looked to channel Krautrock as a means of steering an alternative to the dominance of the formally spent yet suddenly more popular than ever verse–chorus rock tradition, as Britain in the 1990s sought at every level, right down to its national football team, to replicate the swinging euphoria of Britain in the 1960s in every aspect except for its invention.

Prior to forming the relatively straightforward McCarthy, Gane had been a would-be noisenik in the Cabaret Voltaire vein, issuing his music on cassette. He recalls his own Krautrock epiphany. 'It would have been around 1980 – when the first Faust LPs were reissued. There was a review of them by John Gill in [UK] *Sounds* that mentioned all the groups I liked – Throbbing Gristle, Clock DVA, Nurse with Wound, Cabaret Voltaire. *Sounds* was my paper at the time, not *NME* – Sandy Robertson, John Gill, Jon Savage. He made it sound incredibly exciting. And it wasn't that long since it had originally been issued. I was intrigued by the whole soundworld. It struck me as similar to the stuff I liked, the heavy, industrial feedback – but then a brass band wandering through the middle of it. From there, I just naturally progressed on to Can or Neu!. I bought the first Neu! album – that was quite good but I didn't like it as much then as later. I still had that umbilical cord to punk and New Wave. It took me a couple of years to get into other aspects of the sound.'

Although Stereolab's output is dotted with conscious homages to Kraftwerk and Faust, and Gane affirmed his love of Popol Vuh by taking part in a 2012 remix project of their work, it was Neu!, and the Dingerbeat, which would ultimately provide the inspiration for the chassis of the Stereolab sound.

'The way that Klaus Dinger drummed – that straight 4/4. When I did the very first rehearsals with Stereolab I was very strict about getting the rhythm I really wanted – something without rock or indie inflexions, it needed to be neutral, to glide across the surface of the beat. And I had three or four drummers before I found Joe [Dilworth]. None of them could do it. It was so important that you didn't "rockify" it because that took away everything. Once the beat was right, we quite obviously sounded different from whoever was playing at the Camden Falcon or whoever. It was about this sense of space, this rock beat that was somehow unrocklike. Also, I needed something where no great technical ability was required, just an exploratory spirit. At that point, I wasn't aware of anyone else doing that.'

The writer Frances Morgan was part of a scene of groups, including They Came from the Stars (I Saw Them), Now and, as occasional stand-in, Radio 9, who followed a template set down by Stereolab, one involving cheap analogue synths simply played and the endless *motorik* groove. 'It was just continuous music,' she remembers.

'I felt unfortunate being a teenager when Britpop happened. You dislike it if you're intelligent but you do like some of it, because you're young. And in the midst of that you've got Pulp. I credit them very much with getting me into synth music, into Eno, and from there into Krautrock. As for Stereolab, I loved them, quite intensely, quite obsessively and seriously.' So much so that she initially felt 'quite ripped off' when she at last heard Neu!, until the other aspects of the group, including their 'Marxist' lyrics, reasserted themselves. 'Stereolab were more influential as a channelling of Krautrock than some of the original groups themselves,' she says.

For the nineties crowd, however, Krautrock wasn't just cerebral, neo-psychedelic head music but potentially a dance proposition. And while dance music had flourished in the late eighties and nineties, with mass raves tapping into a need, in tribal and fragmentary times, for everyone to gather in a field together, by the mid-nineties this had mutated into a club culture that was every bit as unwieldy and alienating as was the rise of Oasis to many rock fans. 'Clubs were quite horrible at this point,' Morgan recalls. 'This was the era of superclubs, of Ministry of Sound – supermarket clubbing, with all the promise of acid house replaced by this massive dome full of people. It became expensive, homogenous, and DJs were getting paid ridiculous money, which I found really off-putting. I just wanted to go out and have a dance.'

She and fellow writer Mark Pilkington, publisher of Strange Attractor Press, found the more intimate scene they were looking for in the Kosmische Club. Kosmische was founded in 1996, the germ of the idea provided by Julian Cope, whose *Krautrocksampler* had just been printed. Each generation was ready for its own 'Krautrock', and here was the one for the giddy nineties. 'Someone should start a Krautrock club!' Cope suggested, and so they did, with Brian Barritt, erstwhile Timothy Leary compadre, co-hosting its opening night.

'Cherished by the open-minded, loved by the chronically energetic, and only occasionally visited by old men with beards, the Kosmische Club's remit slowly began to include the best danceable, experimental music, non-chin-strokey electronica, and classic underground tracks,' is how Kosmische describes itself on its shamelessly and pertinently self-adoring website. The list of those who have played the club in its various venues, from Islington to Shoreditch to the Elephant and Castle, is awesome in its sprawl, and worth quoting to excess, to convey the sheer mushroom explosion of neo-Krautrock spawned over the past two decades, a boiling, fomenting underground river of activity, from Japan to San Francisco, veteran to teenager, upper case to lower case:

> Add N to (X), Couch (Germany), Damo Suzuki (from Can), Silver Apples, Stereolab DJs, Cul de Sac (USA), Circle (Finland), Chrome Hoof, Jackie-O-Motherfucker, Jean-Hervé Péron (Faust), Delia Gonzalez & Gavin Russom (DFA records USA), Shit & Shine, Ruins Alone (Japan), Brown Sierra, Nem (a krautrock Gamelan), Oh (Germany), V/VM, Cobra Killer (Germany), Charles Hayward (This Heat), Ommm (ADADAAT), Asja Auf Capri, Sunburned Hand of the Man (USA), hush arbors (USA), Sunroof!, Miasmos/Somasim, Steeple Remove (France), Mutarotations (Robert Hampson, ex-Loop, Main), Roedelius (Kluster/Cluster), Appliance,

Tele:Funken, A-Musik, ISAN, Kling Klang, Lithops (Mouse on Mars, Germany), Echoboy, Kreidler (Germany), Murcof (Mexico), Now, Wauvenfold, Rothko, B. Fleischmann, Acid Mothers Temple (Japan), Hunting Lodge, Molotov art terrorists, DJs Barry 7 (Add N to (X)), Sonic Boom (Spacemen 3), Woebot, Sacha Dieu, cylob (rephlex), Jagz Kooner (Primal Scream), Thomas Fehlmann+Alex Patterson (The Orb), Staubgold Records (Germany), Max Tundra, Cluster, Felix Kubin, Turn On (Stereolab), E-Da (Boredoms), Miasma and the Carousel of Headless Horses, Karamasov, Global Goon, Sonic Boom (and Experimental Audio Research), The Vanity Set, Freeform, Radio 9, Prey, Op:l Bastards, Zukanican, Khan with Kid Congo Powers, The Beale, Molotov Organisation, Sonic Catering Band, Shock Headed Peters, Amal Gamal Ensemble, Burning Idiot Noise, Zaum, Hunting Lodge, Duracell, The Early Years.

The Kosmische Club belied its name, in a sense. *Kosmische* the genre was generally beatless, unmoored and astral in character, whereas at Kosmische the club the music was nailed to the floor. Mark Pilkington recalls its regular cast of dervishes and eccentrics. 'You'd never hear Tangerine Dream at Kosmische because you couldn't dance to it. You had groups of people embedded together, flying around, falling over, one guy doing a "dog wiping its bottom" dance.'

'You'd see girls pulling these Egyptian bellydancing moves,' recalls Morgan. 'The way women in particular used to dance at Kosmische was particularly amazing.' Others among the 'communion of misfits' included the Clones, who did contemporary dance in Victorian-style outfits, as well as older gay men, often in their forties and fifties.

Indeed, it was all about latter-day mutation rather than straight nostalgia, says Pilkington. 'People were drawn by the music but also the character of the place – the freaky vibe. But not a hippie vibe. I wonder if anyone who came from mid-seventies Berlin came to Kosmische in the mid-nineties, if they'd recognise what we were doing as being the same as what they were doing.' If, back in the sixties, Krautrock had been a squat-cross-legged-in-a-gallery-space proposition, at the Kosmische Club that simply wasn't an option, says Pilkington. 'There was nowhere to sit – just a space, a stage. There was no option but to dance. I don't think they thought of themselves as making "feet" music, with the exception of Kraftwerk. It was more "head" music – dance music back in the seventies was considered as music that happened in dancing spaces, like discos. There's less separation of that sort today. Kosmische was a disco that played Krautrock. When the mood was right, you could play almost anything if it had a tangible rhythm. It was hard to clear the floor at times.'

Kosmische was ostensibly a live venue, however, and at times this meant showcasing a new breed of bands who were in the sometimes turgid throes of what Simon Reynolds dubbed post-rock, whose slow, eddying instrumental swathes felt like a mourning for the death of guitar music. 'They had to come up with a band every month, so they weren't always great,' remembers Morgan. 'I remember one time there was this Scottish post-rock group, not Mogwai but someone like Mogwai. It was a cerebral, boring post-rock gig, but when it finished, the mood was completely different – lots of crazed people wigging out to Can. German music of that period is taken to be very serious, but these were very hedonistic people – the whole take on Krautrock at this time was very hedonistic. This particular revival was about the connection between Krautrock and dance music.'

Among the favourite staple tracks (mixed in with a large helping of regular dance music of the era) were Faust's 'Giggy Smile', Can's 'Moonshake' and 'I Want More', and 'Hallogallo' by Neu!. Also hugely popular was less on-the-nose fare from Kraftwerk such as

'Ruckzuck', two copies of which the DJ would flip between, from deck to deck, reminiscent of DJ Kool Herc in the earliest days of breakbeat. From here, they would merge into distant relations of the genre, including Yello, Hawkwind, Fela Kuti, Sun Ra, Soft Machine and Spacemen 3.

'It also worked well as trance music. You were pulling people off the ceiling. A lot of people were tripping a lot of the time,' says Pilkington. 'That was the vibe. You look at those great old films of Fassbinder skinning up at Amon Düül gigs – it fits the brief. I'd say that from Add N to (X) through to Stereolab, people were in the thrall of one of the great Krautrock revivals.'

Once again, a Can release marked this revival. *Sacrilege*, released in 1997, was a compilation of remixes of Can tracks by contemporary artists, generations of admirers all still very active in the decade: Brian Eno, Wire's Bruce Gilbert (aka DJ Beekeeper), Steve Hillage, now fronting System 7, who fed upon the glow of idealism of the trance/rave vortex, Pete Shelley, A Guy Called Gerald, U.N.K.L.E., Sonic Youth and Air Liquide. The title of the collection was apt. Can themselves held nothing sacred, as their series of 'Ethnological Forgeries' attested. Everything was in the air for plucking. And now that applied to their own canon, to be played with as a new generation saw fit. The collection showed too how a range of styles and sub-categories flowed off Can like so many distributaries to become rivers of their own – trance, acid, ambient, post-punk.

Kosmische carried on well into the twenty-first century, undertaking world tours and eventually finding a new home in Oslo. During this time, as social and distribution networks improved and media channels expanded, the UK and America's dominance as the inevitable vortices of new music began to loosen. As a reviews editor of *The Wire* during that period, it was quite clear to me that everywhere had its scene, driven often by a handful of enthusiasts, but vital, distinctive and global in their outreach nonetheless – Norway, Finland, Iceland, Japan, Austria, Italy, France, Portugal, China, psych-folk, electronica, neo-post-punk, noise, avant-rock. A narrative thread, a 'history of rock' was quite impossible to sustain at this point, having peeled away into a thousand knotty strands.

If there was still a physical gathering point, as opposed to the virtual, shared space of the internet, it was in Berlin, whose cachet and primacy in Germany had been restored following the collapse of the Wall – it was the cultural as well as the actual capital once more. However, for the time being at least, Berlin still successfully resisted the gentrification and heritage-conscious Blairite makeovers that had pretty much sealed the fate of most UK cities by this point. Rents were cheap, the air was bohemian, the sense of meaningful decrepitude still palpable. Emil Bange is a Berlin-based festival organiser who lives and works out of a grand old apartment whose imperiously shabby front and stairwells have borne witness to it all over the decades. He first became aware that another Krautrock revival was coming up around the year 2007. It became the inspiration for Polyhymnia, the Berlin-based 'neo-Krautrock' festival he continues to organise.

For Bange, 'Krautrock is the missing link between the hippies and the punks. So after the post-punk revival, this feels like the next step. Certainly, when I first listened to *Neu! 75*, I felt it sounded like early demos of the Sex Pistols.'

One of the key groups to emerge from this scene was Camera, who would play alongside Michael Rother and Dieter Moebius and are generally regarded as representing an overdue new German Krautrock-inspired wave. When Rother played in Berlin in 2010 as part of his *Hallogallo* tour with Steve Shelley, the members of Camera were playing outside the venue. They consisted of two men on guitar and one on the *cajón*, a Spanish, box-shaped percussion instrument that resembles a wooden, hollowed-out speaker and originally comes from Peru, on which he was playing a 'pure *motorik* beat', recalls Bange. Already planning the Polyhymnia Festival, he was determined to have them play some role, even it was only to passers-by in the lobby, but they initially demurred, regarding themselves as essentially street musicians rather than a 'proper' group.

Eventually, they agreed to play a warm-up event organised by Bange, but to his disappointment performed on minimal drums rather than *cajón*. Their percussionist apologised, but his playing on the instrument had caused him to bloody his fingers – shades of Michael Rother's first encounter with Klaus Dinger. Bange had them play short, improvised sets in the DJ lounge in between those of the turntablists. 'The lounge was packed absolutely – everyone was fascinated with these guys playing pure Krautrock. They stole the show,' recalls Bange. 'Musically it's Krautrock, but the attitude is DIY and punky and rebellious. They still occasionally busk, on the street, the underground, where they had a lot of run-ins with the authorities. They actually knew very few Krautrock bands – it was more of an instinctive and emotional response to what they had heard.' Krautrock, having infiltrated and altered the whole world, had at last returned home.

Why this interest? 'Maybe on the one hand, when Krautrock first came out, the German youth of the time were quite into politics,' says Bange. 'And maybe now, because of the harsh times we are living in, and capitalism getting more and more heavy, there is a longing for this sort of Utopia – or maybe psychedelia and freaking out is a way of saying, "I want nothing to do with society, I just want to be in the cosmos." These are my two theories . . .'

*

In 1996, Daniel Jonah Goldhagen published *Hitler's Willing Executioners*, in which he asserted that far from having no idea of what was going on in the concentration camps, 'ordinary

Germans' were, in fact, fully aware and cheerfully complicit in the Holocaust, having been uniquely primed as a people for anti-Semitic annihilation. The book's thesis was eventually dismantled by critics but it was a bestseller and did highlight the basic, indisputable fact that it was impossible for German citizens to have been so naïve about the Holocaust. However, Goldhagen did not hold a permanent grudge against Germany – indeed, he went so far as to praise the modern German nation as a 'model state'.

While Germans themselves might well be among the first to scoff at such a description, there is a strong case for stating that, given the enormities of the Third Reich, the terrible, collective moral collapse of the nation and the utter devastation wrought on the country as a result, Germany's eventual material and moral recovery, as well as its reunification, is extraordinary, if not a miracle. A 'model state' might well be an exaggeration, but there is a case to be made that of all the world's major social democracies, it is the least worst state. Unlike the UK, it has retained its manufacturing base and has a relatively healthy dialogue between management and unions, whose workers enjoy a sensible and well-funded work–life balance. Unlike the UK, there is a sane attitude towards housing, with renting the norm and no ridiculous boom-and-bust property market. Its artists enjoy generous cultural endowments, every major city boasts superb galleries and arts facilities, transport networks thrum with functionality, and, *über alles*, the country is a republic, the mark of a nation state's maturity, as opposed to a monarchy, the equivalent of an adult still living with its parents. Bohemians might sneer at this tableau of health and efficiency, but Berlin is now the bohemian capital of Europe.

It's true that Germany's moral recovery lagged significantly behind its economic recovery, that the parents of the Krautrock generation lived in quiet denial about the war, their role and humiliation in it, and that assumptions forged during the Third Reich died hard with some. Yes, old Nazis did still run the towns.

In 1973, the comedian Jonny Buchardt did a televised routine to a mostly middle-aged audience of West Germans. As if to warm them up, he takes them through a speedy series of call-and-response chants. 'Zigger-Zagger, Zigger-Zagger! . . . Hip-hip! (Hooray!)' and then, '*Sieg!*' to which the hall erupts in a worryingly collective '*Heil*', followed by a nervous chuckle from the duped audience. 'A lot of old comrades here tonight,' remarks Buchardt.

Such thoughts and tendencies were a stain on the spirit of that generation, and it was a part of Krautrock's remit to help cleanse it from German culture. However, despite the gnashing, everyday malice of the tabloid *Bild*, and the oppressive moral panic of the 1970s, the idea that West Germany remained a fascist state requiring the violent attentions and overthrow of the Baader–Meinhof gang was a gross overstatement. Moreover, as the Entebbe hijackings showed, if a new strain of anti-Semitism was going to come from anywhere, it was from within some of the more diseased-minded ranks of the Red Army Faction (Jews were separated from non-Jews by the captors and threatened with execution at one point during the crisis). There were many of the older generation who harboured sympathies for the Nazis but, disturbing as this was, it had no great influence on the shape and direction taken by West Germany. Even many of those who did were happy to knuckle down in the peace, prosperity and reconstruction of the postwar years. If they thought Hitler had it right at all, they mostly kept such thoughts to themselves. And year by year, decade by decade, those old men and women died away.

Indeed, Germany's pacifist leanings strike an enlightened contrast to the bellicose British–American alliance. Gerhard Schröder's government refused to have anything to do with the 2003 invasion of Iraq, for which George W. Bush would never forgive the Chancellor. Watching on TV as one of Schröder's ministers publicly berated the visiting US Vice President Dick Cheney about the supposed threat of weapons of mass destruction possessed by Saddam Hussein – 'Where are these weapons? Please, show me where these weapons are' – certainly made me proud to be European and embarrassed to be British. Today, Germany is led by a nominally right-wing administration, but even so, in late 2010, Foreign Minister Guido Westerwelle was calling on the country's NATO allies to remove their stockpiles of nuclear weapons from German soil. In the UK, this has only happened in fiction, in Chris Mullin's novel and TV drama *A Very British Coup*, which imagines what would happen if a radical left-wing leader ever came to power in Britain. To visit Germany can feel like you are visiting broadsheet country; to return to the UK can feel by contrast like you're coming back to Tabloidland. The British have been used to mocking the supposed 'humourlessness' of the Germans but might do well to emulate their seriousness.

Krautrock rejected crude nationalism, representing a process of renewal of identity. Postwar British culture has never been affected by a similar need. Britain itself remains mostly in denial about its own historical crimes, generally against the former colonies, which, while certainly not on the scale of the Holocaust, are severe enough. When in the nineties a movement arose in the UK which combined a sense of national identity with a musical development, the result was Britpop, which in almost every respect, as a concept and a construct, is antithetical to Krautrock. Nostalgic and retrograde, Britpop and the broader sentiments that took a grip on the nation represented a strained and sanguine need to feel pretty good about our country, our selves, our past, our dear old flag. The 'thirty years of hurt' referred to by David Baddiel and Frank Skinner in the England theme song 'Football's Coming Home' were felt more widely than in sport alone. 'Winning the war' meant deferring any deep, purging self-examination at all levels. It is reflected in a more arrested, hidebound culture. Germany remains guilty of all of these things also, for sure, but in other respects, politically, socially and culturally, it is more advanced as a result of having had to make admissions of terrible crimes and to reconcile and rebuild from its foundations.

Krautrock, as we have seen, has been less keenly embraced by German consumers than in Japan, France, the USA and the UK. It would be hard to claim that this was the music that inspired the regeneration of a country, not least because that patently isn't true. However, Krautrock springs from the same energy source, the same great overall traditions of industry, invention and the desire to rebuild as well as the same (potentially hazardous) romanticism that has accounted for the country's recovery and mature pre-eminence. It thrived too in pockets of cultural tolerance that prevailed despite a general, national atmosphere of conservative repression.

Rock often celebrates decay, despondency and implacable rebellion. These are all virtues, some of them shared by, for instance, Einstürzende Neubauten. The plains of Krautrock, however, tend to be fertile – rivers and forests abound, long, straight freeways or railroads lead from city to city. It's ultimately a music of resource and rebirth, of rich ancestry and great vision, as well as an awareness of the enveloping darkness that is the lot of the human condition. From Kraftwerk to Cluster to Kosmische, these are its constituent parts. Traditional rock, from the Doors to Springsteen to Queen, speaks of a desire to 'break free', to 'break on through' to the other side, but Krautrock already is on the other side, truly free, aware of both the expanses and the limitations of 'freedom'.

All of this was done out of a deep-seated cultural necessity that transcends the customary need to give vent to teen spirit. It is rock at its most mature, as opposed to prog, which is rock at its most needlessly overwrought. It is a constructive, healing music – the Coen Brothers' 'nihilist' tag, applied to their fictional Kraftwerk-style group in *The Big Lebowski*, couldn't have been more daft or less apt. It was a serious-as-your-life, solemn and vast undertaking, carried out semi-consciously at times, granted, in a haze of dope, for sure. However, in order to create its collective, overall quilt it drew on multiple traditions, genres and media, of which Anglo-American rock, with its straight line back through the Beatles and the Stones, Elvis and the blues, never even thought to dream until much later.

Krautrock was a product of West Germany, of an extraordinary historical and cultural situation that one hopes could never possibly occur again in our own or any other lifetime. Nowadays, there is no need for modern Germans, or for anyone else for that matter, to contemplate the postwar condition when making music. The Altnazis are long dead; Germany is unified, healed and regenerated and facing up to fresh problems. Krautrock was a product of West Germany, but today it belongs to the world, to the present and, crucially, the future.

For decades now, rock music has felt debilitated by its state of thrall to its increasingly distant yet seemingly inescapable past. Like the huge cliff in Wordsworth's *Prelude*, from which the poet as a young man rows away, only for it to appear to loom larger before him, so it is with rock, whose legendary, arena-filling heroes are perceived to have grown in stature even as they enter their seventies. This veneration is to an extent a sort of optical illusion – the Beatles, Dylans and Stones of this world are great, but not as far-and-away greater than their peers as the inordinate amount of media attention paid to them late in their lives would suggest.

We gaze towards the past out of a sense of inferiority – are the best days behind us? – but also out of a conservative, nostalgic hankering for the big, epic familiar that might well have puzzled the earliest generations of rock 'n' rollers, for whom the freshly minted was where it was at. We also envy the first-generation naïveté of our predecessors, as revealed in their smart yet quaint typefaces, their analogue productions, idealistic lyrics and fresh-faced sentiments from an era when, despite the Bomb and all its attendant anxieties, there was a palpable attachment to the here and now, the today and tomorrow that exuded from every chord, every pore, but whose innocent bloom can only be imitated today. Old genres are revisited and re-mined, pastiched and revered for their wholeness, their authenticity by subsequent generations who feel both fragmented and phoney in their own third-hand simulations. So fragmented are our times that the very use of the words 'we' and 'our' feels presumptuous and in need of qualifying – but retromania, in all its obvious and subtle forms, is certainly commonplace.

For sure, Krautrock belongs to the past. Krautrock is revered for its age and vintage. Its artwork has a residual kitsch quality; its location in the analogue mists of the 1970s lends it a mythical allure. It is the product of a state that no longer exists, which sets it further adrift in the irretrievable realms of yesteryear. Listening to it can evoke the most exquisite, wistful longing for a time when the slate was cleaner and pop culture less supersaturated.

Yet there is something unique about Krautrock compared with other, concurrent 1970s movements – prog, glam, electric soul, all of which have had their 'neo' school of imitators (though prog is rather more neglected than it might well have imagined it would be at the time). For one thing, all of those movements enjoyed significant success and commercial recognition in their own time. They had styles and tropes which would to some degree be their undoing in the long term, but which were a boon for those who later paid homage to them, marks of identifiability. Big hair, big shoes, licks, stomps. This is rather less the case with Krautrock, with the exception of Kraftwerk (who by then were in what many would term their 'post-Krautrock' phase). Krautrock had little visibility of any sort in its own time – there was no distinctive Krautrock mode of dress, no public profile, while the music itself was too abstract to provide easy or obvious footholds. It was music made in the 1970s but, some dubious hairstyles and shirt collars apart, it is relatively free of the perishable signifiers of its era. Its fields of activity have lain relatively unspoiled for subsequent generations. As Frances Morgan puts it, 'It's not time-stamped. It has a mutability.'

Today, there is no place left for music to go but everywhere. And everywhere is waiting in the annals of Krautrock – in the productions of Conny Plank, so bright, colourised, rich and high-definition they feel like they were made next week; in the live performances of Kraftwerk, in which their upgraded, industrial electronic sounds impact with a sheer 3D velocity unavailable in the 1970s. In the organic riffing of Can, in which time is suspended; in the idealism and audacity of Amon Düül, which a generation politicised by increasing adversity, less cosseted and jaded and postmodern than our own, might see fit to take up. It's in the chill stasis of the Berlin School, Tangerine Dream, et al., like some discovered yet barely touched region further down the Milky Way. It's in the linear progress of Neu!, riding away from the cosy verse–chorus–verse anthemic familiarity of rock, the big Glastonbury singalong, into unlit, uncharted realms way past rock's bedtime, its midnight. It's in the brutal, neo-Dadaist juxtapositions between pastoral and concrète of Faust, their instantly soldered mutations and studied atavism, a group particularly crying out for rediscovery by some future, intrepid wave of soundmakers.

For, despite the habit of ageing baby boomers to lament the decreasing quality of new music since their own halcyon days, younger generations do and will continue to exceed their elders in terms of the way they transmit and receive culture. Locality means less, boundaries are dissolved and glided over in cyberspace. Noise and the atonal sonics of everyday life are encroaching on modern music productions where once there was simply empty space between notes. Again, what is still considered 'extremist' by some soft, passéist ears even in the early twenty-first century will seem less so further down the timeline to come.

Krautrock is a well that can and will be returned to again and again – an underground river, a self-renewing, self-purifying resource. It's been visited for inspiration for decades now, and yet it remains untapped, full of potential. Granted, the *motorik* beat has become a slightly familiar borrowing – but Krautrock can't easily be reduced to a set of stylistic motifs or musical tics. It's more about the open-ended, formal, strategic example it offers – how to enter a studio, how to interact in the moment, how to think about making music, what it means to make music in this world, how to create and invent from nothing. These are features that can be emulated but not parodied. We're talking not so much about a mode of playing as a set of values. It's one of the reasons why Krautrock has inspired so many musicians whose own music doesn't on the face of it sound in any way 'Krautrock-ish'. It's also why when the next seventies come around for real, the 2070s, times that might well be more complex and onerous than we can currently imagine, the tools and modifying instruments fashioned in West Germany in the late 1960s and early 1970s will still be as silver and sharp as ever. Krautrock's peace rages on.

Acknowledgements

A book like this is the result of years of cumulative listening, reading and conversing, as well as the research and interviews I undertook once the project was given the go-ahead. Thanks are due to a vast number of people, not least, going way back, my German teacher Mr McGarrigle for igniting a spark of Germanophilia in my mind, even as I struggled abysmally with the language itself. I should also thank my mum and dad for putting up with the fretfulness I caused them as sounds alien even by rock 'n' roll standards boomed disturbingly and repetitively from my teenage bedroom, and my schoolmates, whose ribald mockery of my musical tastes convinced me I was onto something special.

For enabling me to embark on this project at all, I must thank Lee Brackstone at Faber, as well as Kevin Pocklington, my agent. Simon Reynolds, my longstanding compadre, was the first person ever to encourage me to write about music when we were university students together. His constructive suggestions helped create the eventual shape of this text.

I'd also like to thank Dave Watkins at Faber for his encouragement and input, Dan Papps and all of the Faber staff, as well as Ian Bahrami and Eleanor Rees for their diligent and detailed work in helping refine my raw copy.

Günther Simmermacher helped immensely with his insights on the German Schlager pop movement, as well as with the translation of audio material.

Others provided invaluable help along the way, whether by agreeing to share their memories of the era or simply their thoughts on the music and its surrounding culture, despite the misgivings some harboured about the impertinent term 'Krautrock', or by helping with contacts, archive materials and transcription. Very special thanks, therefore, to David Ball, Emil Bange, Geoff Barrow, Chris Bohn, Chris Cutler, Holger Czukay, Geeta Dayal, Diedrich Diederichsen, John Doran, Danny Fichelscher, Tim Gane, Andy Gill, Robert Hampson, Jim Kerr, Felix Kubin, Andrew Lauder, Jaki Liebezeit, Gaby Meierding, Dieter Moebius, Stefan Morawietz, Frances Morgan, Klaus Mueller, Colin Newman, Ash O'Keeffe, Jean-Hervé Péron, Mark Pilkington, Stephan Plank, Jono Podmore, Sandra Podmore, Michael Rother, Roland Rynkowski, Irmin Schmidt, Klaus Schulze, Steve Shelley, Mark Stewart, René Tinner, David Toop, Luke Turner, John Weinzierl, Ben Whalley, Kevin Whitlock, Richard Williams, Sophie Williams, Simon Witter, Keleigh Wolf, Miki Yui (widow of Klaus Dinger) and Rob Young. Sincerest apologies to anyone I might have overlooked. Finally, thanks to Julian Cope for coining the phrase 'a raging peace', which resonated with me throughout the writing of this book.

Bibliography

Bangs, Lester, 'Kraftwerk: The Final Solution to the Music Problem?' (*NME*, September 1975).

Barr, Tim, *Kraftwerk: From Düsseldorf to the Future (with Love)* (Ebury, 1999).

Becker, Jillian, *Hitler's Children: Story of the Baader–Meinhof Terrorist Gang* (HarperCollins, 1978).

Beevor, Antony, *Berlin: The Downfall 1945* (Penguin, 2007).

Behrman, Greg, *The Most Noble Adventure: The Marshall Plan and the Time When America Helped Save Europe* (The Free Press, 2007).

Bell, Max, 'Tangerine Dream: Is This the End of Rock as We Know It?' (*NME*, November 1974).

Buckley, David, *Strange Fascination: David Bowie: The Definitive Story* (Virgin Books, 2005).

Bussy, Pascal, *Kraftwerk: Man, Machine and Music* (SAF, 2004).

Cutler, Chris, sleevenotes, *Faust: The Wümme Years, 1970–73* (ReR, 2000).

Dallas, Karl, 'Faust and Foremost: Faust Profile and Interview' (*Melody Maker*, March 1973).

Dallas, Karl, 'Tangerine Dream: Twilight of the Dream' (*Melody Maker*, December 1976).

Dalton, Stephen, Kraftwerk feature (*The Times*, June 2005).

Dayal, Geeta, Conny Plank feature (*Frieze*, August 2012).

Dedekind, Henning, *Krautrock* (Hannibal Verlag, 2008).

Dellar, Fred, 'Exclusiv Interview mit Tangerine Dream' (*NME*, June 1974).

Diliberto, John, 'Man vs Machine: Conny Plank' (*Electronic Musician*, February 1987).

Doctor Rock, 'Kosmische Polymath Michael Rother: Eno, Bowie & Making Peace with Dinger' (*The Quietus*, November 2009).

Doran, John, 'From Neu! to Kraftwerk: Football, Motorik and the Pulse of Modernity' (*The Quietus*, January 2010).

Gill, Andy, Krautrock retrospective (*Mojo*, April 1997); 'Kraftwerk: Terminal Weirdness à Paris' (*NME*, April 1978).

Goldman, Vivien, 'Can: Tales of the Supernatural' (*Sounds*, December 1975); 'Can Laundered' (*Sounds*, October 1976).

Hesse, Herman, *The Glass Bead Game* (Vintage UK, 1943/2000).

Hewitt, Ben, 'Our Band's Not Electric: Edgar Froese from Tangerine Dream

Interviewed' (*The Quietus*, August 2003).
Higgs, John, 'The Making of Seven-Up' (*Mojo*, April 2003).
Iliffe, Stephen, *Painting with Sound: The Life and Music of Hans-Joachim Roedelius* (Meridian Music Guides, 2003).
Judt, Tony, *Postwar: A History of Europe Since 1945* (Vintage, 2010).
Kaes, Anton, *From Hitler to Heimat: The Return of History as Film* (Harvard University Press, 1992).
Kampmann, Wolf, *Can Box* (book, introduction) (Medium Music, 1998).
Keenan, David, interview with Conrad Schnitzler (*The Wire*, May 2006); interview with Peter Brötzmann (*The Wire*, November 2012).
Kershaw, Ian, *The End: Germany, 1944–45* (Penguin, 2012).
Knight, Julia, *New German Cinema: Images of a Generation* (Wallflower Press, 2004).
Kopf, Biba, Klaus Dinger interview (unedited) (*The Wire*, 2001).
Kotsopoulos, Nikos (editor), *Krautrock: Cosmic Rock and Its Legacy* (Black Dog Publishing, 2010).
Lessour, Théo, *Berlin Sampler: From Cabaret to Techno: 1904–2012, A Century of Berlin Music* (Ollendorff Verlag Berlin, 2012).
MacDonald, Ian, 'Krautrock: Germany Calling' (*NME*, December 1972).
MacDonogh, Giles, *After the Reich: The Brutal History of the Allied Occupation* (Basic Books, 2009).
Miles, 'Krautwerk: This Is What Your Fathers Fought to Save You from' (*NME*, October 1976).
O'Brien, Glenn, 'Kraftwerk: Deutsche Disko' (interview, 1977).
Patterson, Archie, *Eurock: European Rock & The Second Culture* (Eurock Publications, 2002).
Pozo, Carlos M., interview with Conrad Schnitzler (angbase, 1998).
Reynolds, Simon, *Energy Flash: A Journey Through Rave Music and Dance Culture* (Faber & Faber, 2013).
Richter, Hans, *Dada: Art and Anti-Art* (World of Art, 1978).
Sassoon, Donald, *The Culture of the Europeans: 1800 to the Present* (HarperCollins, 2006).
Sebald, W. G., *On the Natural History of Destruction* (Penguin, 2004).
Sereny, Gitta, *The German Trauma: Experiences and Reflections 1938–1999* (Allen Lane History, 2001).
Stockhausen, Karlheinz, *Stockhausen on Music* (Marion Boyars, 1989).
Stump, Paul, *The Music's All That Matters: A History of Progressive Rock* (Quartet, 1998).
Taylor, Frederick, *Exorcising Hitler: The Occupation and Denazification of Germany* (Bloomsbury, 2011).
Taylor-Taylor, Courtney and Rugg, Jim, *One Model Nation* (Titan, 2012).
Toop, David, *Ocean of Sound: Aether Talk, Ambient Sound and Imaginary Worlds* (Serpent's Tail, 1995).

Watson, Peter, *The German Genius: Europe's Third Renaissance, the Second Scientific Revolution and the Twentieth Century* (Simon & Schuster, 2011).

Williams, Charles, *Adenauer: The Father of the New Germany* (Abacus, 2003).

Williams, Richard, *The Can: Monster Movie* review (*Melody Maker*, May 1970).

Wilson, Andy, *Faust: Stretch Out Time 1970–75* (The Faust Pages, 2006).

Witter, Simon, 'Kraftwerk: Ralf Hütter – He's More "Aaaaaah"' (*Dummy*, May 2006); 'Kraftwerk: Paranoid Android' (*Mojo*, September 2005).

Young, Rob (editor), *Undercurrents: The Hidden Wiring of Modern Music* (Continuum, 2002).

Yui, Miki, *Ihr Könnt Mich Mal am Arsch Lecken* (Klaus Dinger archive, Slowboy Gallery, 2012).

INDEX